*Redefining
Social
Problems*

PERSPECTIVES IN SOCIAL PSYCHOLOGY

A Series of Texts and Monographs • Edited by Elliot Aronson

A Continuation Order Plan is available for this series. A continuation order will bring delivery of each new volume immediately upon publication. Volumes are billed only upon actual shipment. For further information please contact the publisher.

Redefining Social Problems

Edited by
Edward Seidman
Bank Street College of Education
New York, New York
University of Illinois at Urbana-Champaign
Champaign, Illinois

and

Julian Rappaport
University of Illinois at Urbana-Champaign
Champaign, Illinois

Published under the auspices of the Society for the Psychological Study
of Social Issues

Plenum Press • New York and London

Library of Congress Cataloging in Publication Data

Main entry under title:

Redefining social problems.
    Includes bibliographies and index.
    1. Social problems—Congresses. 2. United States—Social conditions—Congresses.
3. Social psychology—Congresses. I. Seidman, Edward. II. Rappaport, Julian. III.
Series.
HN65.R43   1986   361.1   85-28217
ISBN 0-306-42052-X

© 1986 Plenum Press, New York
A Division of Plenum Publishing Corporation
233 Spring Street, New York, N.Y. 10013

Printed in the United States of America

To

JEANNE L. SMITH

who, in an introductory course in experimental psychology (circa 1961), instilled in us the excitement of understanding behavior. Moreover, she challenged and taught us to think and question, both logically and creatively. For these invaluable formative experiences we are eternally indebted.

Contributors

CARY CHERNISS
Graduate School of Applied and Professional Psychology
Rutgers University
Piscataway, New Jersey

MICHELLE FINE
Graduate School of Education
University of Pennsylvania
Philadelphia, Pennsylvania

DENISE J. FOISY
Department of Psychology
Simon Fraser University
Burnaby, British Columbia
Canada

LINDA K. GIRDNER
Institute for Child Behavior and Development
University of Illinois at Urbana-Champaign
Urbana, Illinois

NANCY M. HENLEY
Department of Psychology
University of California, Los Angeles
Los Angeles, California

LOUISE H. KIDDER
Department of Psychology
Temple University
Philadelphia, Pennsylvania

DAN A. LEWIS
Center for Urban Affairs and Policy Research
Northwestern University
Evanston, Illinois

JEAN ANN LINNEY
Department of Psychology
University of South Carolina
Columbia, South Carolina

SHARON NELSON-Le GALL
Department of Psychology
University of Pittsburgh
Pittsburgh, Pennsylvania

JULIAN RAPPAPORT
Department of Psychology
University of Illinois at Urbana-Champaign
Champaign, Illinois

TRACEY A. REVENSON
Department of Psychology
Barnard College of Columbia University
New York, New York

STEPHANIE RIGER
Department of Psychology
Lake Forest College
Lake Forest, Illinois

RONALD ROESCH
Department of Psychology
Simon Fraser University
Burnaby, British Columbia
Canada

SEYMOUR B. SARASON
Department of Psychology and Center for Study of Education
Yale University
New Haven, Connecticut

RICHARD R. SCOTT
Quaker Oats Company
Merchandise Mart Plaza
Chicago, Illinois

DIANE SCOTT-JONES
Department of Psychology
North Carolina State University
Raleigh, North Carolina

EDWARD SEIDMAN
Research, Demonstration and Policy Division
Bank Street College
New York, New York

ALTHEA SMITH
Department of Psychology
Boston University
Boston, Massachusetts

STANLEY SUE
Department of Psychology
University of California at Los Angeles
Los Angeles, California

KARL E. WEICK
College of Business Administration
University of Texas
Austin, Texas

NOLAN ZANE
Department of Psychology
University of California at Los Angeles
Los Angeles, California

Foreword

A key element of the American ethos is a constant striving to improve the conditions of life. To achieve this goal requires first identifying problems, then developing an understanding of them, and finally taking steps toward implementing solutions. The actions that are taken typically stem from our understanding of the causes of problems and the conditions that lead to them. It is assumed that solutions derive from correct analysis of causes and consequences. Hence, social scientists expend much time and energy on problem analysis.

Even more fundamental than correct causal understanding, however, is proper identification of the problem itself. In the social sphere, problems are not fixed or given; they are open to interpretation, and problem definition may depend heavily on the viewer's perspective. But the way problems are identified and formulated is crucial—it is the beginning of the chain that leads to social improvement, constraining both our understanding of causes and the potential solutions that are generated. Unfortunately, problem definition receives relatively little attention from either social scientists or policymakers. The present volume, edited by Edward Seidman and Julian Rappaport, attempts to remedy this imbalance by focusing on the importance of getting definitions right.

Seidman and Rappaport have selected as chapter authors both well-established, highly eminent scholars and equally talented younger contributors. Collectively, the authors provide a set of fresh insights that are diverse but complementary. The issues raised in their discussions of redefining social problems are of interest to a broad cross-section of readers.

Problem definition is crucial to academicians, helping professionals, policymakers, and representatives of interest groups. For those concerned with social problems of any kind, the book provides a general analysis of how problem definition and associated social myths can influence the success of attempts to solve these problems. Substantively, the chapters cover a range of issues. Community psychologists and social workers will find the various discussions of social action (especially Chapters 2, 3, 4, 9, and 13) of special interest. For criminologists, there are chapters on crime as stress and on the success of criminal justice system interventions. Developmental psychologists will find that the book encompasses life-span issues from custody determination affecting children to the presumed loneliness of old age. Social psychologists and educators will be particularly interested in the chapters on ethnicity and desegregation. For students and researchers in all the relevant disciplines, the book will provide insights on how and why good intentions have often led to failure, and offer guidance on how better to formulate questions and direct research efforts.

The Society for the Psychological Study of Social Issues (SPSSI) is proud and pleased to sponsor this book. The volume reflects SPSSI's fundamental goals, particularly the application of social science knowledge to the understanding of social issues. But social science knowledge is of value only when it is valid and accessible. Seidman and Rappaport have done a superb job of assembling relevant knowledge that can potentially benefit society as a whole. SPSSI hopes that this publication will contribute to its dissemination to a wide audience of scholars and practitioners interested in social change.

Marilynn B. Brewer

President, 1984–1985
Society for the Psychological Study
of Social Issues

Acknowledgments

This volume grew out of a symposium on which the editors served as chair and discussant, respectively, at the 1982 annual meeting of the American Psychological Association. The symposium was sponsored by the Society for the Psychological Study of Social Issues (SPSSI) under the banner of the 1982 annual theme, "Redefining Social Problems." As a result of the wide array of interesting symposia presented at the convention under this theme and the importance and timeliness of the topic, we began to think about the need for an integrated volume for students and scholars of social issues.

After discussing the idea with Dan Perlman, SPSSI co-publications chair, we were encouraged and decided to move forward. We solicited selected contributions from participants at the APA annual convention, for the most part from symposia sponsored by SPSSI, and from a few additional scholars who, we thought, had something important to offer in such a volume. This volume consists of the sixteen best contributions, and an integrative overview, woven around the theme of redefining social problems.

We are deeply appreciative of the confidence, support, and encouragement Dan Perlman provided us throughout the entire process, and we are also thankful to five anonymous SPSSI reviewers, whose thoughtful comments helped us rethink the volume's organization in important ways, and the last minute editorial and/or typing assistance of Sharon Medlock and Judith Rapp.

Contents

8

Debunking the Myth of Loneliness in Late Life.......................... 115

Tracey A. Revenson

9

In Praise of Paradox: A Social Policy of Empowerment over
    Prevention.. 141

Julian Rappaport

10

Child Custody Determination: Ideological Dimensions of a Social
    Problem 165

Linda K. Girdner

11

Crime as Stress: On the Internalization of a Social Problem 185

Dan A. Lewis and Stephanie Riger

15

Jean Ann Linney

16

Richard R. Scott

17

Nolan Zane and Stanley Sue

CHAPTER 1

Framing The Issues

EDWARD SEIDMAN and JULIAN RAPPAPORT

A major thesis of this volume is that the definition of a social problem is time, place, and context bound.[1] It is not difficult to cite examples from the disciplines of law, psychiatry, sociology, and psychology. In the not very distant past the question of children's rights was a rather simple matter; children's rights were entrusted to the hands of their parents or parental substitutes (e.g., school officials) and required little legal scrutiny. Yet today it is not unusual to hear calls for a children's liberation movement. There is now more than enough debate to justify entire legal casebooks devoted to problems on children and the law that refer to much psychological knowledge (eg., Mnookin, 1978). In the 19th century, certain problems of the rights of blacks could be defined away by the United State Supreme Court's assumption that blacks were property rather than citizens *(Dred Scott v. Sanford)*. Similarly, when homosexuality was no longer thought of as a disease by the American Psychiatric Association, it both reflected and changed the nature of the relationship between the larger society and a subset of its members. When intelligence is seen as genetically determined and stable, we are posed with different questions and social problems than when we see it as environmentally determined and malleable (Gould, 1981; Hunt, 1961). If women are assumed to belong more in the home than in the work place, then child-rearing practices may present a different set of problems than when day care

[1] For the purpose of introducing this volume, we make no attempt to delimit what may be considered to be a social problem, other than to assert that each of the issues addressed by the current authors qualifies. Discussion of what constitutes a social problem may be found in several chapters included in this volume and in related references found at the end of each chapter.

EDWARD SEIDMAN · Research, Demonstration and Policy Division, Bank Street College, New York, New York 10025.   JULIAN RAPPAPORT · Department of Psychology, University of Illinois at Urbana-Champaign, Champaign, Illinois 61820.

is seen as an essential service contributing to family life. Our social values with regard to "crimes without victims" influence our solutions to social problems as diverse as delinquency, prostitution, gambling, and mental illness (Shur, 1973; Szasz, 1970). The list could go on; and it is the time, place, and context-bound nature of such social problem definitions that this book is about. The volume suggests new ways to think about social problems and different ways to see people, do things, and ask research questions.

To assume that social problems are time, place, and context bound is to recognize that problem definitions represent a particular social construction of reality that becomes widely shared and institutionalized as part of the "collective stock of knowledge" (Berger & Luckmann, 1966). Although socially generated, such knowledge, in the form of expert opinion, takes on an appearance of objective reality. That appearance, in turn, heavily influences both the perception of social problems and ideas about how to deal with such problems. In short, what we call a problem and how we describe the problem is to some extent a function of the implicit assumptions of our culture, which both limit potential solutions and predetermine who and what are seen as problems (Seidman, 1983b).

Because we are locked in a particular culture and political-social zeitgeist, we all share a common social construction of reality and similar social problem definitions. As a result, social problems are rarely seen by either the scientific community or the public as dual or multisided; a social problem is most often seen as simply "the" problem. This volume will intentionally and repeatedly bear witness to the "other sidedness" of social problems.

The intimate relationship between preconception, problem definition, and proposed solution is not one from which social scientists are immune. Because they are a part of the culture and the society they study, they are also influenced by the opinion leaders of that society. Nevertheless, in the public mind social scientists are experts, and the solutions they propose have a kind of institutionalized legitimacy that, ironically, may reify the original, culturally determined problem definition. This necessitates acceptance by social scientists of a special responsibility to question the conventional wisdom of inherited problem definitions (Rappaport, 1977).

Levine and Levine (1970) have noted that in politically conservative times psychological theory and practice tend to view individuals as the source of their own mental health problems, whereas during more politically liberal eras the environment is more often seen to be at fault. The solutions follow logically from the definition. In a different, but somewhat similar vein, others have described human services as alternately focusing on either the "needs" or the "rights" of dependent and neglected individuals (Rappaport, 1981, Chapter 9 this volume; Rothman, 1980) as a function of the political-social zeitgeist of the day. Finally, recall that during the administration of Franklin Delano Roosevelt, a variety of welfare and employment programs were initiated. Yet the problem was not laid at the doorstep of poor and unemployed individuals. More recently, the Reagan administration's formulation of similar problems was quite different. Perhaps not coincidently, we have seen a resurgence of intrapsychic explanations for social problems, ranging from the biological to the cognitive.

Although it would be foolhardy to propose that such political swings directly cause theoretical emphases, and in turn applied solutions, it may be wise to ask if the social climate does not influence the preconceptions of those who define social problems for a living. For the sake of argument, let us assume that the particular constellation of time, place, and context determine the definiton of the social problem accepted by the majority of the social scientific community, and, for the most part, the eventual solution proposed (Seidman, 1978, Chapter 14, this volume; 1983b). What happens when that assumption is taken seriously and we attempt to reframe the problems? Is this a useful exercise? Does it make a difference? When we propose problem definitions other than the currently acceptable ones do we see people differently? Do we think of different solutions and research questions? Before turning to the specific substantive areas in which the authors of the chapters in this volume attempt to answer these questions affimatively, this chapter provides an overview of some of the implicit communalities that we believe underlie most popular social problem definitions. In making the implicit explicit, we hope to set the stage for redefinitions that to some extent, challenge those communalities.

SOME UNEXAMINED PREMISES OF SOCIAL PROBLEM DEFINITION

As an orienting framework we turn to an analysis of the unexamined premises, assumptions, and processes characterizing the dominant contemporary North American social construction of reality. These premises underpin, usually implicitlly, most current definitions of a social problem. Seidman (1983b, 1984) has explicated several of these premises and processes: individualism, a single standard, pragmatism and rationality, generalization from extreme examples, problemizing and overextension, and uniform solutions. Collectively, these premises and processes implicitly help form both the definiton of any social problem and its eventual solution. Let us examine the manner in which each "quietly" predetermines the particular way a social problem is conceptualized and defined.

Individualism

The notion of *individual motivation and responsibility* has always been a cherished, dominant, and pervasive value in American society. It is at the root of our legal and constitutional structures. It has led to what Caplan and

Nelson (1973) and Ryan (1971), *inter alia*, have referred to as a person-centered, causal attribution, bias, or "victim-blaming" ideology. This refers to the tendency to find individuals responsible for their own problems, despite the antecedent and contextual economic, social, and political factors. The premise that the individual is not only the culprit but also the proper focus of social intervention is characteristic of problem solving in Western culture.

A Single Standard

Victim blaming is part of a larger set of social processes in which our institutions work toward the socialization of almost everyone to a "single standard"; those who fail to behave in conformity with the norm are labeled *deviant* (Rappaport, 1977; Ryan, 1971). Consequently, diverse standards of success, competence, or living are eschewed.

Pragmatism and Rationality

The dominant cultural groups in Western society hold pragmatism and rationality in high esteem with regard to personal, organizational, and institutional functioning. This is accomplished by a quantitative supply-and-demand orientation with a tendency to convert cultural, social, and psychological considerations into monetary or tangible values.

Generalization from Extreme Examples

Another characteristic mode of thinking in our society is the conceptualization of a large class of often loosely related problems and solutions based on extreme deviant and atypical examples. For example, much of our thinking about the causes of, and solutions to, the "delinquency problem" stems from our images of the rare youth who repeatedly commits the most heinous crimes. This social construction is reified by the mass media, which give such events extensive and sensationalistic coverage. All of us, including juvenile justice system personnel and legislators, come to view these extreme examples as characteristic of youth who are labeled *delinquent*. We come to believe that if they have not yet performed such acts, they eventually will.

Problemizing and Overextension

Watzlawick, Weakland, and Fisch (1974) and Rappaport and Seidman (1983), among others, have discussed a process of transforming difficulties into problems. Rosenheim (1976) has referred to a similar process in human service as *problemization:* "the activity of individuals and agencies in organizing and applying their particular apparatus of classification and cure" (p.

52). This process compounds the problems created by the former process of generalizing from the extreme. Given this mind set, low-level deviance comes to be viewed as a problem in need of intervention. The result is ever-expanding boundaries of the identified social problem and an overextension of services by professionals and experts, further reifying the problem definition.

Uniform Solutions

The previously noted premises and processes combine with other societal values to enhance the premium placed on uniform solutions to social problems. Deviants are identified on a basis of victim blaming and a single standard. These so-called deviants (who undoubtedly exist, though in very small numbers) serve as exemplars for the generation of social policy solutions. Thus, from the atypical members of a designated group, a solution is developed. The resulting solution is then inappropriately and unfortunately applied to large numbers with a particular deviant label. Rationality and pragmatism enter in the form demanded by the social policy process for rapid simple answers that are easily implementable. Consequently, uniform solutions are often mandated for a wide variety of particularistic and heterogeneous problems.

We see this process play itself out in contemporary society when violent crime is accounted for by only 4 to 12% of juvenile arrests (Strasburg, 1978); yet it results in social policies to "get tough" with all juveniles, no matter how trivial or insignificant the offense. We also see it when the rare released mental patient commits a violent act that leads to calls for a change in involuntary commitment laws. Paraphrasing Monahan (1972, p.21), "How many innocent people are we willing to confine in order to control a small number of potential dangerous individuals?" The answer to that question is to be found in part in how we define social problems.

SHOULD SOCIAL PROBLEMS BE REDEFINED? IF SO, HOW, AND FOR WHAT PURPOSE?

Our answer to the question of whether social problems should be redefined should be quite apparent by now both from the volume's title and the preceding discussion; it is an unequivocal "yes." The reasons should be equally apparent. The often unexamined and implicit premises and processes undergirding our culture's construction of social problems create simple, stereotyped problem definitions leading to similarly narrow and constrained solutions. Several other difficulties result as is evidenced most clearly from an analysis of the proposed solutions and their efficacy. First, these solutions are often ineffective (see Seidman, 1983a, for an extensive review of a wide array of social interventions). Second, these solutions often perpetuate the problems they were designed to solve; in other words, "the more things seem to change, the more they stay the same," or they simply provide the appearance of change while maintaining the status quo (Rappaport, 1977; Seidman, 1983b). Third, these solutions are often iatrogenic, in that they cause more problems than they solve (Illich, 1976; Morgan, 1983).

The concept of *iatrogenesis* has received only scant attention in the field of social relations. The term, which refers to a negative effect of a treatment, is most well developed in the field of clinical medicine. Its most familiar form is in discussions of the "side effects" of medication and surgery. As is well know, it is not uncommon for a treatment to cause an adverse reaction that is worse than the original malady. However, Illich (1976) has extended the concept to include what he calls *"social and cultural iatrogenesis."* He views the social iatrogenic effects of medicine as those that are created by a medical bureaucracy that increases stress and dependence while reducing individual choice and self-care. It is, in his view, the medical monopoly itself that has a negative impact on individuals—quite independent of any positive or negative clinical effects of a given treatment—by depriving people of control over their own bodies. Cultural iatrogenesis is more subtle; in the context of medicine it refers to a society that is robbed of the will to understand its own pain, sickness, suffering, and dying. An essentially moral enterprise has been turned over to a technocracy rather than retained by everyman.

In a book bringing together contributions from psychologists, physicians, sociologists, economists, philosophers, and journalists, Robert F. Morgan suggests that:

> If we enlarge the word iatrogenic to include any disorders caused by members of the *helping* professions in the process of helping, then we may hold accountable a more comprehensive range of disciplines and services actually affecting the consumer. (1983, p. vi)

In an amazingly wide range of examples, his book does exactly that. Here we suggest that *clinical, social,* and *cultural iatrogenesis* are concepts that may be enlarged beyond the helping professions. They apply equally to those who would analyze as well as those who would help. Indeed, the very problem definitions which provide sanction for "helping" may be at the root of iatrogenic effects of every variety because how we see the problem will determine how we try to solve it.

What do we gain from redefining social problems? We expand the possible "universe of alternatives" (Sarason, 1972) for understanding the nature of a social problem and constructing potential resolutions. However, this is not a guarantee of defining the problem "correctly" or designing the "right solution." It simply makes us aware of the options and encourages a more thoughtful analysis. It is to be hoped that this should increase the probability of designing successful solutions and minimize the likelihood of negative outcomes, intended and unintended, because it will increase the competitive comparison of the outcomes resulting from differing viewpoints. It will not solve the problems for all time. As Mitroff (1983, p.165) has asserted, "problems have to be defined and solved anew for every generation." If that assertion is correct, then the task of redefining social problems is one that is of paramount importance for every generation, including our own.

What are the costs of redefining social problems? The costs are considerable because as citizens, human service professionals, and social scientists we must confront, question, and challenge our most cherished values and premises. This task will be neither pleasant nor easy. In essence, both individually and collectively, we need to step outside of our socialization histories and question our fundamental assumptions about our thinking patterns, society, human service, and scientific methods.

How can we address this challenge to redefine social problems, solutions, and scientific methods? In order to make progress, it is necessary to reframe the very way in which we state the problem to ourselves (Watzlawick, Weakland, & Fisch, 1974). Rather than accepting the problem definition with which we are presented, reframing explicitly calls for a different way of thinking about the problelm before one even looks for a solution. This becomes a critical mind-set. Beyond this mind-set, mechanisms are necessary to explicitly facilitate the likelihood of reframing. Many of the chapters that follow address these processes in considerable detail, both in general and in specific substantive contexts.

ORGANIZATION OF THE VOLUME

The themes of this volume concern (1) the way in which our social constructions constrain our problem definitions, solutions, and related research questions and designs; (2) the time, place, and context boundedness of our definitions and solutions; (3) the ways in which problem definitions have hindered the development of more novel and constructive solutions, in both the arenas of action and of research; (4) the fact that these definitions have perpetuated misleading and inaccurate information as well as suggestions for alternative frameworks for thinking about social problems, action, and research. The volume is organized into four major sections: frameworks for redefining social issues, rethinking demographic deviance, rethinking systems for action, and alternative research agendas. Although different sections have different emphases, the aforementioned themes occur in all four of these sections.

REFERENCES

Berger, P. & Luckmann, T. (1966). *The social construction of reality.* Garden City, NY: Doubleday.

Caplan, N. & Nelson, D. (1973). On being useful: The nature and consequences of psychological research on social problems. *American Psychologist 28,* 199–211.

Dred Scott v. Sandford, 19 How. 393 (1857).

Gould, S. J. (1981). *The mismeasure of man.* New York: W. W. Norton.

Hunt, J. McV. (1961). *Intelligence and experience.* New York: Ronald Press.

Illich, I. (1976). *Medical nemesis: The expropriation of health.* New York: Panthenon.

Levine, M. & Levine, A. (1970). *A social history of the helping professions, clinic, court, school and community.* New York: Appleton-Century-Crofts.

Mitroff, I. I. (1983). Beyond experimentation: New methods for a new age. In E. Seidman, (Ed.), *Handbook of social intervention.* Beverly Hills, CA: Sage Publications.

Mnookin, R. H. (1978). *Child, family and state: Cases and material on children and the law.* Boston: Little, Brown.

Monahan, J. (1976). The prevention of violence. In J. Monahan (Ed.), *Community mental health and the criminal justice system.* New York: Pergamon Press.

Morgan, R. F. (Ed.). (1983). *The iatrogenics handbook.* IPI Publishing: Toronto.

Rappaport, J. (1977). *Community psychology: Values, research, and action.* New York: Holt, Rinehart & Winston.

Rappaport, J. (1981). In praise of paradox: A social policy of empowerment over prevention. *American Journal of Community Psychology, 9,* 1–25.

Rappaport, J. & Seidman, E. (1983). Social and community intervention. In C. E. Walker (Ed.), *Handbook of clinical psychology.* Homewood, IL: Dow Jones-Irwin.

Rosenheim, M. K. (1976). Notes on helping juvenile nuisances. In M. K. Rosenheim (Ed.), *Pursuing justice for the child.* Chicago: University of Chicago Press.

Rothman, D. J. (1980). *Conscience and convenience: The asylum and its alternatives in progressive America.* Boston: Little, Brown.

Ryan, W. (1971). *Blaming the victim.* New York: Random House.

Sarason, S. (1972). *The creation of settings and the future societies.* Jossey-Bass: San Francisco.

Seidman, E. (1978). Justice, values and social science: Unexamined premises. In R. J. Simon (Ed.), *Research in law and sociology* (Vol. 1). Greenwich, CT: JAI Press.

Seidman, E. (1983a). *Handbook of social intervention.* Beverly Hills, CA: Sage Publications.

Seidman, E. (1983b). Unexamined premises of social problem-solving. In E. Seidman (Ed.), *Handbook of social intervention.* Beverly Hills, CA: Sage Publications.

Seidman, E. (1984). The adolescent passage and entry into the juvenile justice system. In N. D. Reppucci, L. A. Weithorn, E. P. Mulvey, & J. A. Monahan (Eds.), *Children, mental health and the law.* Beverly Hills, CA: Sage Publications.

Shur, E. M. (1973). *Radical non-intervention: Rethinking the delinquency problem.* Englewood Cliffs, NJ: Prentice-Hall.

Strasburg, P. A. (1978). *Violent delinquents: A report to the Ford Foundation from the Vera Institute of Justice.* New York: Sovereign.

Szasz, T. S. (1970). *The manufacture of madness: A comparative study of the inquisition and the mental health movement.* New York: Harper & Row.

Watzlawick, P., Weakland, J. H. & Fisch, R. (1974). *Change: Principles of problem formulation and problem resolution.* New York: W. W. Norton.

PART 1

Frameworks for Redefining Social Problems

The four chapters in this part provide both a critique of our past and constructive alternatives for our future. Although they emphasize different weaknesses in our traditional views, these authors are frank and consistent in conveying the sense that our habitual way of constructing social problems requires redefinition.

Seymour B. Sarason suggests that scientists have had little sense of social history, and that psychologists are no exception to the rule. His thesis is that because social scientists have tended to identify with the assumptions of the physical sciences, wherein problems once solved are considered obsolete, history is, at best, of intellectual interest.

The nature of social problems is such that they need to be solved continuously, and in different ways each time. One of the realities of the social world is the salience of values. To make positive use of the intractable nature of social problems and of historical perspective, one must understand that social action is always informed by contemporary values. As we have suggested in our introductory chapter, many social values are time, place, and context bound. To remain unaware of our values and our history, while applying the methods of science, is to ignore one of our most helpful tools for problem solving.

Karl E. Weick suggests that to view social problems on a massive scale is to preclude constructive action. His proposal to redefine social issues as small problems allows a series of small wins to build to a pattern of success. He draws creatively on a set of psychological principles to make his case that optimism breeds success. Although at first glance Weick and Sarason seem to disagree, we think that their positions are compatible. One way to reduce social problems to a manageable size is to place them in historical and contemporary context and to search for solutions that are effective in the present rather than those that assume the necessity of a single universal solution that will end the need for further solutions as social contexts change.

The third chapter in this part, by Louise H. Kidder and Michelle Fine, explicates the assumptions of the two most prevalent ideologies at the root of our explanations for social problems—conflicts of interest and missed opportunities. They describe the implications of these ideologies for level of analysis, source of support, and strategies of change. In their view, the obligation of social scientists is to explain to the public that there is always more than one way to construe a social issue. They suggest that when multiple diagnoses of the causes of social injustice exist, it is useful to ask, "Whose interest is being served by the diagnosis offered?" They further suggest a role for the researcher as one who helps give voice to the victims by telling the victims' stories rather than by presuming to speak for them. If social scientists can serve as a kind of amplifier for the small voice of the powerless they may, on the one hand, help the powerless themselves to discover the possibility of collective action, and, on the other hand, offer to the larger society an alternative conception of the causes and consequences of current social structures. In the process we may learn much about the value of redefining social problems.

The final chapter in this part, by Nancy M. Henley, bridges this part and the next. She discusses several ways in which the process of problem definition may be studied and the role of the psychologist in such study. Her connection between the study of the sociology of "claims making" and the psychological processes of perception, attitude formation, persuasion, psycholinguistics, and conflict resolution provides an agenda for the social psychology of social issues.

Henley demonstrates her thesis using themes that emerge when women, by virtue of their being members of a group visible on the basis of demography, are seen as a social problem. She introduces us to a trap that seems to captivate much of our thinking: persons are often seen as problematic when the larger society see them as members of a class. In this way social processes by which we categorize people simultaneously lead us to blame them for belonging to the category. The category of woman has traditionally led to the assumption of certain, albeit changing, social problems. But the thrust of Henley's chapter is broader. She suggests that we engage the question "What is the natural history of a social problem?" as a means to understand the processes of definition and redefinition. Her analysis leads us to a consideration of how, by doing research, we necessarily take sides, and she raises the issue of social responsibility beyond the publication of our empirical studies and conceptual analyses in scientific journals.

CHAPTER 2

The Nature of Social Problem Solving in Social Action

SEYMOUR B. SARASON

You cannot understand a past era unless it leaves some kind of record or evidence of what people said or did. We look back from a vantage point that allows us to scan for myriad evidence, a scanning impossible for anyone in that past era. We like to believe that our vantage point is high enough, that our vision is unclouded by all of those factors that put blinders on those who lived in that past era, and that we have the accrued knowledge, skill and wisdom to explain not only what happened, or how forces were related to each other, but also the why of it all. And the why of it all almost always has to do with ways of thinking that give order and direction to daily living. What lends fascination to historical constructions and reconstructions is the process of deducing or intuiting what people in that era took for granted. But if the process is fascinating, it is inherently problematic. For one thing, there are many vantage points—so many, in fact, that it is literally impossible for one person or group to achieve them all. No less serious for those who have to believe that they are on the road to truth, and that the road has an end, is that reconstructions of the past always reflect what we from our present vantage points take for granted. Can you deduce what people in a far-off era took for granted without having what you take for granted affecting your conclusions in ways that you cannot know but that people in future

This article was originally presented as an invited address at the meeting of the Eastern Psychological Association, Boston, April 14, 1977. It appeared in the *American Psychologist*, *33*, 370–380, 1978. Copyright 1978 by the American Psychological Association. Reprinted by permission.

SEYMOUR B. SARASON • Department of Psychology and Center for Study of Education, Yale University, New Haven, Connecticut 06520.

eras will think they know? The process of historical reconstruction inevitably says as much about the present as it does about the past. If history strikes so many people as uninteresting and irrelevant, it is, in part, because they do not understand that what we call history is literally manufactured by the present. When Henry Ford, that self-made sage, said "history is bunk," he was saying a good deal about himself and many others in our society, far more than he was saying about the past. That was obviously less true, but still true, in the case of Gibbon's *Decline and Fall of the Roman Empire.*

The social-historical stance has not been a dominant feature of American psychology. An amusing but illuminating example—back in the late 40s the American Psychological Association began to accredit graduate programs in clinical psychology. An APA committee came for a site visit to Yale, and part of their time was spent talking with our graduate students. At the end of the visit I talked with one of the committee members, who expressed satisfaction with our program with one exception. He had asked one of our graduate students if he had read Köhler's (1925) *The Mentality of Apes,* and the reply was: "No one reads that any more. That's old hat." We both laughed, very uneasily. Both of us were pre-World-War-II-trained psychologists and very much aware that as a result of the war, the face of psychology was being changed. For both of us, the Henry Ford type of statement by the graduate student presaged something disquietingly new in psychology, but it was hard to put into words. The downgrading of the historical stance was not new, but if what this student said was at all representative of his generation of psychologists, the small place held by history in the field of psychology would shrink to near invisibility. If I had to say what bothered me, it would be that I placed a lot of weight in living on the sense of continuity, a belief not created or particularly reinforced by my training in psychology. Beyond that personal need, my unease had little conceptual substance. But something told me that what the student said was very important, and I have been trying ever since to make sense of it. The first conclusion I came to was that there was really nothing new in what the student said. By virtue (among other things) of psychology's divorce from philosophy and its marriage to science, history in psychology became a lot of narrow histories depending on the particular problem that interested you. That is, if you were interested in reaction time to a type of stimulus, you had the obligation to know what others in the past had done and found. This obligation served several purposes: to deepen your knowledge of the particular problem to avoid repeating what others had done, and to increase the chances that what you were going to do would shed new light on the problem. This might be called the rational justification of the use of history. But, as is always the case, there were nonrational factors at work. In fact, justifying the use of history only on rational grounds, or describing it as a completely rational process, should have been warning enough that these justifications were incomplete and misleading. Behind these justifications were some beliefs and hopes. One of them was that you were going to add something new to an understanding of the problem precisely because you were building on knowledge provided by others from the past.

In the scientific tradition, knowledge is cumulative: You either add a new brick to the edifice of knowledge so that it looks different or, better yet, you destroy the edifice and present your colleagues with a foundation for a new and better structure. One part of this tradition says that knowledge is cumulative; the other part says that your contribution is proportionate to how must past knowledge you have rendered obsolete. You use history, so to speak, with the hope of destroying its usefulness. This kind of attitude or hope is subtly but potently absorbed by young people entering scientific fields, and I believe it has been particularly strong in psychology, less because of psychology's youth as a scientific endeavor and more because of its self-conscious desire to identify with that endeavor. This has tended to produce still another belief: If a study was done 10 years ago, it is unlikely that you will learn much from it; if it was done 20 years ago, the chances are even smaller; and if it was done before World War II, do not forget it but be prepared quickly to do so. Put in another way, it would go like this:

> We have come a long, long way in a relatively short period of time and there is not much from the past that is usable to us now. What is more worrisome than whether we are overlooking anything from the past is whether someone in the present is rendering what I am doing as wrong or obsolete.

Köhler studied apes during World War I. Obviously, the odds are small that he has anything to say that is important to the here and now of psychology! Yes, he probably belongs in the Museum of Greats, but you only go to museums when you are not working.

My purpose is neither to discuss nor question the implicit and explicit uses of history in scientific research. What I wish to suggest is that these uses (and, therefore, perceptions and conceptions of the past) have been very influential in shaping people's attitudes toward the significance of history in general. That is, among all those who think of themselves as scientists, there has been a noticeable tendency to view the social world as having been born a few days ago. This should not be surprising when one considers the status and functions society has given to science. Within the confines of its own traditions, science long has been on an onward-upward trajectory in the course of which it has displayed a seemingly boundless capacity to solve its problems. This did not go unnoticed by society as it saw that in solving its problems science could also contribute to the welfare of society. Scientists and the public came to agree that the deliberately impractical goals of science (knowledge for knowledge's sake) had very practical implications. No one ever said it, and perhaps no one ever thought it, but the agreement between science and society contained a "message": Society had problems *now* and science could be helpful in solving them *now* or *in the foreseeable future*. There was no disposition to recognize that the relatively ahistorical stance of science might be mischievously inappropriate to social problems. Put in another way, the pride that science took in rendering past scientific knowledge obsolete, the view of its past as more interesting than it was usable, the concentration on now and the future—these stances fatefully determined the degree to which, and the ways in which, society's problems would be placed in a historical context. This type of influence seemed proper and productive as long as the findings of science had two types of consequences: one was of the technological, thing-building or thing-creating variety, and the other was of the illness-prevention or the illness-curative variety. It may be more correct to say that the nature of the influence went unnoticed as long as there was near-universal social acceptance of what science seemed to be able to do. As long as society posed essentially nonhistorical questions for science, science came up smelling technological roses. Agriculture, industry, medicine, the military—they asked the kinds of here-and-now questions to which the finding of science could be applied.

It is hard to overestimate how total identification with science eroded whatever significance social history had for psychology. For one thing, it seriously limited the capacity of the field to examine its past in order to illuminate its present, that is, to try to fathom how its view of the past (and its projections into the future) might be a function of the myth-making present. For another thing, it blinded psychology to the obvious fact that any field of human endeavor is shaped by forces beyond its boundaries and that its structure and contents can never be wholly explained by that endeavor's narrow history. For example, can one understand the history of behaviorism or psychoanalysis by restricting oneself to what behaviorists and psychoanalysts did and said? Boring did his best to sensitize psychologists to zeitgeist, but his efforts have been honored far more in the breach than in the practice. "The spirit of the times" is such an apt metaphor because it warns us that what we think and do, what we think we are, what we say the world will be—all of these in part reflect influences that are time bound and hard to recognize. The word spirit (an uncongenial one in psychology), like the concept of the unconscious, reminds us that as individuals or fields we are affected by forces near and far, known and unknown, inside and outside.

At its best, social history serves the purpose of reminding us that we, like those of past eras, are very biased, time-bound organisms. We differ in all kinds of ways from those of past eras, but one thing we clearly have in common: we breathe the spirit of our times. If we use social history for the same purpose that we do a table of random numbers, we stand a little better chance of avoiding the worst features of uncontrolled bias. At the very least, sensitivity to social history makes it hard to ignore several things. First, despite all the diversity among human societies, past and present, each dealt with three problems: how to dilute the individual's sense of aloneness in the world, how to engender and maintain a sense of community, and how to justify living even though one will die. Second, each society defines and copes differently with these problems, and as a society changes, as it inevitably does, the nature of the definitions and copings changes. Third, these changes, more often than not, are not recognized until people see a difference between past and present definitions and copings. Fourth, the three problems are always here and there in the life of the individual and the society, but not in the sense that inanimate matter is here and there. Fifth, these are not problems that people have created, and they can never be eliminated or ignored. Sixth, any planned effort to effect a social change (as in the case of scientists who seek to apply their knowledge and skills for purposes of social change) that does not recognize and understand the history and the dynamics of these three problems will likely exacerbate rather than dilute the force of these problems.

Applying scientific and technological knowledge and skills in social action is not like applying paint on a wall, except as both applications literally obscure what one may not like to look at. Scientists who enter the world of social action like to think themselves possessed of the basic knowledge and problem-solving skills of their science, and they often have a feeling of virtue because they are applying these to practical social issues. What they fail to see is that because science does not start with the three problems, because it in no explicit way recognizes or is controlled by them, science qua science has no special expertise to deal with them. Everyone knows the old joke about the graduate student who had learned about Latin-square design and was looking for a problem that fitted it. There is a way of looking at science and seeing some similarity between it and this student. Science has learned a lot about problem solving, but when it looks beyond its confines to the arena of social porblems, it has tended not to ask what the "basic" problems are there but rather to seek problems that fit its problem-solving style: clear problems that have unambiguously correct solutions. The separation of science from disciplines concerned with social history will always obscure from science that not all basic problems in nature can be molded to its problem-solving models.

SCIENCE AND SOLUTIONS

Before World War II, academic psychology never quite made up its mind whether it was a social or biological science. The image of the laboratory was very attractive. After all, look at what had been discovered in laboratories and was not society grateful? If psychology was to earn society's gratitude, and also be accepted by the older sciences, what was needed, among other things, was a certain kind of place where problems could be analyzed, dissected, and studied. A laboratory was a place where one solved problems. One could study problems outside of a laboratory but that meant that one had drastically reduced the chances of finding solutions to basic problems. In a laboratory one could manipulate variables, and, obviously, one could not arrive at rigorous solutions without experimental manipulation of variables. The image of the laboratory contained several features: physical isolation, clearly stated problems, experimentation, hard work, solutions. It was such an attractive image that few psychologists seriously questioned its appropriateness for their new field. There were psychologists for whom the laboratory was not an appropriate place to study problems, but they did not question the other features of the image. Their task, they would say, was the same but harder because experimental manipulation outside the laboratory was so difficult. They felt inferior, and were made to feel inferior, because it was so unlikely they could "really" solve any problem. The "real" general laws of human behavior were going to be found by studies done in certain ways and places. Science could not tolerate sloppiness of method and uncertainty of solution.

Take, for example, pre-World-War-II psychology's view of psychotherapy. My guess is that psychologists would not have been in favor of making the practice of psychotherapy illegal. They would have agreed that if people had personal problems there should be trained individuals to try to help them. But, they would have added, psychotherapy is an art, and a pretty poor one at that, and do not confuse it with science or technology derived from science. So, they could have been asked, what are you doing about it? The answer would have been that psychological science is seeking the basic laws of human behavior and not until the basic questions are clarified, studied, and solved in the most rigorous ways can a foundation be provided for truly effective psychotherapeutic practice. It's like building bridges: basic science had to solve a lot of basic problems before engineers could build bigger and better bridges. It is, they said, going to take us time, and one of the worst things we could do would be to start studying an applied problem like psychotherapy to the neglect of more basic psychological issues. Let us not kill the goose that lays the golden eggs, as an eminent psychologist once said.

Now, if one knew something about social history and had the courage, one could have asked: Is it possible that these problems are of a human and social nature and are not solvable by science? Is it not obvious that in the chasm between your scientific findings and solutions, on the one hand, and the realm of human affairs, on the other hand, there is a mine field of values for the traversing of which your science provides no guide? If we can build magnificent bridges, or develop life-extending vaccines, is it only because of basic problem-solving research or is it also because society wanted those fruits from the tree of science? Just as technology depends on basic science, do not both depend on or reflect the wishes of the larger society? What will happen if and when the social world changes and the relation between society and psychology is altered so that psychology is asked and willingly attempts to solve social problems it never encountered, and never could encounter, either in the laboratory or through employment of any of its research strategies? Will psychology be found inherently wanting?

These were questions that could not be raised in psychology before World War II. Some of these questions were explicitly raised by one psychologist, J. F. Brown, in his 1936 *Psychology and the Social Order*, but no one paid him much mind. In the midst of a social catastrophe, the Great Depression, Brown saw the crisis in psychology. He was able to because social history in its Marxist version had become part of his conceptual framework. His was not a parochial mind—witness his attempt to bring together Marx, Lewin, and Freud. Robert S. Lynd, a sociologist, raised similar questions in his 1939 book *Knowledge for What?* Having studied Middletown before and after the Great Depression, Lynd, like Brown, questioned the traditional directions of the social sciences and asserted their conceptual and moral bankruptcy.

In one crucial respect, Brown and Lynd were in basic agreement with an underlying assumption of science: All problems of society, like those in the rest of nature, had solutions. The problems might be of a different order, the way of studying and controlling them might require new theories and methodologies and their solutions might be a long way off, but they were solvable. Who would deny that the creativity and ingenuity that had unraveled the mysteries of the atom, exemplified in the work of Rutherford and Bohr, or that allowed Einstein to supercede Newton, would falter when faced with the problems of social living? But what if these problems were not solvable in the sense to which science was accustomed?

The concept of solution in science is by no means a clear one, and it is beyond my purposes to examine the different and overlapping meanings that concept has been given. In one respect, however, the lay and scientific understanding of a solution is very similar: A problem has been "solved" (a) when it does not have to be solved again because the operations that lead to the solution can be demonstrated to be independent of who performs them; (b) when the solution is an answer to a question or set of related questions; and (c) when there is no longer any doubt that the answer is the correct one. If there are competing answers, the problem has not yet been solved. So, when geneticists around the world were trying to "solve" the genetic code, they could agree on only one thing: someone would find the answer. And the answer would be of the order of "4 divided by 2 is 2." There is or will be only one correct solution. There are times, of course, when the solution about which there is consensus is proved wrong, and then everybody is off and running to find the "really" correct solution. The correct solution always raises new questions, but at least the earlier question does not have to be solved again. The question was asked, the solution was found, and now for the next question.

Problem solving is a venerable and sprawling field in psychology. I wish to note two of its characteristics. The first is that almost without exception the human subject is presented with a problem that is solvable, although the correct answer may be arrived at in different ways. Indeed, how an individual arrives at a correct solution has been considered no less important than the fact that he or she got a right solution. One of the major influences of the Gestaltists (Wertheimer, Koffka, Köhler, Lewin) on research in problem solving was in their emphasis on the psychological factors and processes (e.g., set, insight, perceptual reorganization) that preceded solution. The graduate student's opinion notwithstanding. Köhler's (1925) studies of problem solving in apes are still instructive reading, as is Wertheimer's (1959) classic *Productive Thinking*. The fact remains, however, that the distinctive emphasis of the Gestaltists had meaning in the context of solvable problems. It is not fortuitous that Wertheimer illustrates his ideas by a description of how Einstein solved problems with which physicists of the time had been grappling.

A second characteristic of the problem-solving literature is that the types of problems used in research almost defy categorization. It is an exaggeration to say that each researcher develops his or her own stimulus problem, but it is not a gross exaggeration. It would be understandable if someone concluded that when researchers used the words *problem solving*, they were far more interested in *solving* then they were in *problems*. Let me illustrate the significance of these two characteristics of the problem-solving literature by asking this question: Why, for all practical purposes, is there nothing in this literature on how artists solve their problems? For example, what was the problem or problems Cézanne was trying to solve? This question has nothing to do with his personality, although it does with his times. What was the cognitive substance of the problem, how was he trying to solve it in a visual form, what made for such a long struggle, and did he solve the problem? Several answers could be given to these questions. One would be that we cannot be sure what the problem was, and even if he were alive we could not accept his version of the problem. How do you justify studying problems whose clarity and formulation you know ahead of time must be of dubious status and when there are no known ways of determining what the "real" problem is? If you are fuzzy about the nature of the problem, how can you ever state criteria by which to judge successful outcomes? And what would we do if Cézanne had said: "In this painting I solved the problem, in that one I did not." Do we accept his judgments, and what have we learned by doing that? And what do we learn from fellow artists who are awed by Cézanne's accomplishments? Their judgments permit no firm conclusions about the relationship between problem and solution. Besides, not every artist, then or now, agrees either about the substance of Cézanne's artistic problems or artistic solutions. A final answer might be: Cézanne is a great artist, but his problem-solving accomplishments cannot be understood and judged in the way the works of great scientists can be. In short, they would say Freud was right: before the artist you throw up your hands. These are problems that are not science's cup of tea. There is problem solving that does not fit the researcher's requirements of a clear, manipulable problem and unambiguous criteria for the correct solution. So, science has always left that problem alone, albeit from a stance of superiority. The problems of social living were also left alone until the emergence of the social sciences, led by economics. Just as the natural sciences had developed laws about the nonhuman world, the social sciences would seek the laws of human society, not only for the purposes of explaining the workings of society but for controlling it. They would be the embodiment of Plato's philosopher-kings. Apparently they were not impressed with the fact that Plato saw the problems of social living as so difficult to understand and cope with, requiring of philosopher-kings such a fantastic depth of learning and wisdom, that one could not entrust social responsibility to them until they were well along in years. And to my knowledge, Socrates infrequently answered a question and never solved a problem. He was too impressed with man's capacity for self-justification and self-deceit. Neither Plato nor Socrates ever assumed that the accomplishments of Greek scientists reflected a model of question asking and problem solving that was appropriate to the development of the good society. In the millenia that followed, there were many people who took a similar position. Science never really came to grips with them, least of all social science.

SOCIAL ACTION

Let us now turn to a moment in history when the workings of impractical science led to a most pratical product, one that our scientists and society desperately wanted. It was a moment that simultaneously illustrated the fruitfulness of scientific problem solving and exposed its inappropriateness for solving social problems. I refer, of course, to the successful solution of all the problems, theoretical and technical, leading to the harnessing of atomic energy for military purposes. As soon as it became evident that a successful atom bomb was in the offing, some scientists began to ask themselves questions: Should it be used, how should it be used, and how could the seemingly endless uses of atomic energy be exploited for human welfare? They saw a problem, many problems, and as in the case of Cézanne, the substance of the problem was by no means clear. The end result of a successful solution seemed clear: A world in which the destructive uses of atomic energy were rendered impossible or nearly so and in which it uses for human welfare were maximized.

But how do you go from here to there? What was the bearing of the scientific tradition on that problem?

As best as I can determine, none of the scientists thought they were dealing with a scientific problem. They recognized that they had been catapulted into a social world that was fantastically complicated, constantly changing, and seemingly uncontrollable. It was not even a maze, because that image conjures up entry points, stable pathways, and some kind of end point. The social world was not a maze. It was not even a cloud chamber, because that is a device rationally constructed to record and measure predictable events. It may be a world of facts and events, but it is ruled by passions. It is ironic in the extreme that at the same time that the world saw these scientists as at the apogee of human achievement, the scientists saw themselves as angry, bewildered, impotent people. They became like most other people: passionate, committed, partisan, rhetorical, and irrational. Those are not characteristics foreign to scientific controversy and investigation, but the morality of science and the critical eyes of the scientific community are effective controls against the undue influence of these characteristics. If you suspect a fellow scientist of lying and cheating, or of just being a damn fool, you have ways of finding out and spreading the word. But that means there is consensus about the rules of the game. The social world is not the scientific world. As a physicist friend once said to me, "What the hell kind of world is it?" He used exactly the same tone of petulance/anger that Professor Henry Higgins used in *My Fair Lady* when he asks why women cannot be like men. My friend also went on to say (paraphrased),

> I can't deal with a world where everybody has his own definition of the problem, where facts are an intrusive annoyance and of tertiary importance, where who you are is more important than what you know, and where the need to act is more decisive than feeling secure about what the consequences will be.

And he concluded with this: "I will stick to my world where there are answers, and if I don't find them, someone else will." When the atomic scientists entered the world of social action, that world could not be molded to fit the problem-solving strategies to which they were accustomed. But, many social scientists thought, those were atomic scientists and one should not be surprised that when they left the world of minute matter and entered the world of human matters, they faltered. After all, they were not social scientists whose stock in trade was human matters. The fact is that up until World War II, the social sciences had contributed to our understanding of the social world, but, with one noteworthy exception, these contributions were mainly descriptive, or analytic or historical. They were not contributions stemming from the social scientist's effort to participate in and solve social problems. Like the natural scientists, the social scientists were the dispassionate observers, and deliberately so, who sought to formulate clear questions to which clear answers could be obtained. They saw their task as understanding the social world, not changing it. The one exception was economics, which for decades had an intimate tie with the practical world of government, business, industry, and finance. Early on, economists not only described the world as they saw it, but they drew conclusions about what should or should not be done. They were listened to, and they took responsible positions in the social arena. Heilbroner (1961) has aptly called them the *"worldly philsophers."* They lived so to speak in two worlds: the scientific problem-solving world, and the world of social action.

It was the Great Depression that really made the world of social action accessible to increasing numbers of economists. The underlying assumption, of course, was that economists had knowledge and skills that could inform public policy and action. If, during the 30s, the atomic scientists had developed firm friendships with their university colleagues in economics (unlikely events in the community of scholars), they would have learned much earlier than they did that scientific knowledge as power in the social arena is of a different order than it is in the research community; that in the social arena one is always dealing with competing statements of a problem and there is no time or intention to experiment in implementation with one or another of the formulations; that the choice of formulation has less to do with data than with the traditions, value, world outlooks, and the spirit of the times; that the goal of social action is not once-and-for-all solutions in the scientific sense but to stir the waters of change, hoping and sometimes praying that more good than harm will follow; that the very process of formulating a problem, setting goals, and starting to act not only begins to change *your* perception of problems, goals, and actions but, no less fateful, the perception of *others* related to or affected by the process in some way. *In the phenomenology of social action, problem changing rather than problem solving is figure, and you know what that does to solutions regardless of how you define them!*

World War II opened up many opportunities for social scientists to be in social action or policy-related roles. It was truly the first global war bringing us into contact with scores of different cultures and peoples. So, as never before, anthropologists became socially important people. And sociologists and psychologists were even in short supply. World War II forever changed the social sciences. They were exposed to new problems, and much that they thought they knew was proved either irrelevant or wrong. More important, they tasted the heady wine of influence and action, and they liked it. Government needs us, they said, and government seemed to agree. At least one noted psychologist (Doob, 1947) had his doubts and wrote a brief paper beautifully describing the naive scientist in the world of social action. Doob's paper is noteworthy in two other respects. First, his recognition that in social action, the scientist qua scientist is like a fish out of water—dead.

Where social science data are inadequate or where social science itself can provide only principles or a way of approach to a problem, the social scientist must hurl himself into the debate, participate on an equal or unequal footing with men and women who are not social scientists, toss some of his scientific scruples to the winds, and fight for what seems to him to be valid or even good. A strict adherence to the scientific *credo* in such circumstances leaves the social scientist impotent and sterile as far as policy is concerned. (Doob, 1947, p. 78)

Second, the fact that Doob early on learned that if he responded seriously to his and others' needs for mutuality and community, even if some of those others were opponents, social action could be rewarding despite the fact that one never knew whether one was having an intended programmatic effect, that is, whether one was solving a problem. In the aftermath of World War II, the government become both patron and employer of social science. After all, the argument ran, if the government respected and supported social science research, as it did research in the biological and natural sciences, the social atom might be split and its energies harnessed for the greatest good of the greatest number. For 20 years after World War II, the social sciences became, and with a vengeance, vigorous, quantitative, theoretical, and entrepreneurial. If you wanted to solve in a basic and once-and-for-all way the puzzles of individual and social behavior, you needed resources of the wall-to-wall variety. True, it would take time to learn to ask the right questions, to develop the appropriate methodologies, before you could come up with the right answers. What we were after were those bedrock laws of social behavior and process that would allow a society "really" rationally to diagnose and solve its problems. Give us time (and money) and you will not regret it. In the meantime, if you think we can be helpful to you with your current problems, please call on us. And call they did, and go they went. The results have been discouraging and shattering, discouraging because of the lack of intended outcomes, and shattering because they call into question the appropriateness of the scientific-rational model of problem definition and solution in social action. Nelson (1977), a noted economist, has summed it up well in his book *The Moon and the Ghetto.* (I am sorry he did not retain the original subtitle: *A Study of the Current Malaise of Rational Analysis of Social Problems.* The malaise is real and, to my knowledge, Nelson is one of the few who has dared to articulate what others only think about.)

The search for "the Great Society" entailed highly publicized efforts at turning the policy steering wheel. Broad new mandates were articulated—the war on poverty—and specific policies were designed to deal with various aspects of the problem. The histories of these departures clearly identify the key roles often played by research reports, social science theory, formal analytical procedures. More recent years have seen an increasing flow of proposals for organization reform: vouchers for schools, health maintenance organizations, greater independence for the post office, a national corporation to run the passenger railroads, pollution fees, revenue sharing. It is easy to trace the intellectual roots of many of these ideas. The technoscience orientation has come later, and never has had the thrust of the others. Nonetheless the intellectual rhetoric has been strong, and has generated at least token efforts to launch the aerospace companies on problems of garbage collection, education and crime control, and programs with evocative titles like "Research Applied to National Needs."

The last several years have seen a sharp decline in faith, within the scientific community as well as outside, regarding our ability to solve our problems through scientific and rational means. Those who want to get on with solving the problems obviously are upset about the loss of momentum. It is apparent that many of the more optimistic believers in the power of rational analysis overestimated that power. There are strong interests blocking certain kinds of changes. Certain problems are innately intractable or at least very hard. But the proposition here is that a good portion of the reason why rational analysis of social problems hasn't gotten us very far lies in the nature of the analyses that have been done. John Maynard Keynes expressed the faith, and the arrogance, of the social scientist when he said, "The ideas of economists and political philosophers, both when they are right and when they are wrong, are more powerful than is commonly understood. . . .I am sure that the power of vested interests is vastly exaggerated compared with the gradual encroachment of ideas." But surely Abe Lincoln was right when he made his remark about not being able to fool all of the people all of the time. In addition to their clumsy treatment of value and knowledge (a problem that seems to infect analysts generally), analysts within each of the traditions have had a tendency to combine tunnel vision with intellectual imperialism . . . . Members of the different traditions have had a tendency to be lulled by their imperialistic rhetoric. This has often led them to provide interpretations and prescriptions that the public and the political apparatus, rightly have scoffed at. Failure to recognize the limitations of one's own perspective has made analysis of problems that require an integration of various perspectives very difficult. Indeed a kind of internecine warfare obtains among the traditions over the turf that lies between them. (Nelson, 1977, pp. 16, 17, 19)

Nelson illustrates his position using day care, breeder reactor programs, and the SST. Nelson argues that there are inherent limitations to the scientific problem-solving model as the basis for social action, and he also suggests that there are problems that are inherently intractable. The very word *intractable* is foreign to the scientific tradition. In science, problems may be extraordinarily difficult, but they can never be viewed as intractable, and if some fool says a problem is intractable it is because he or she is not posing the problem correctly or does not have the brain power to work through to the solution. In science, fools are people who say problems are intractable. In the realm of social action, fools are people who say all problems are tractable.

THE CHALLENGE OF INTRACTABILITY

Why is it so difficult for people, particularly scientists, to entertain, let alone accept, the possibility that many problems in social living are intractable, not solvable in the once-and-for-all-you-don't-have-to-solve-it-again fashion. I have already given one part of the answer: science has been such a success in solving so many of the problems in nature that people became persuaded that the dilemmas and puzzles of the human social world would likewise become explicable and controllable. In fact, people in Western society were so persuaded that it became an article of unquestioned faith. And when religion's hold on people's minds began to disappear and the scientific outlook and enterprise took its place, it tended to go unnoticed that one article of faith (the world is divinely ordered) had been supplanted by another (the world, animate and inanimate, is ordered, knowable, and controllable). And the tendency of science to be ahistorical in general, particularly in regard to social history, effectively obscured for people that the rise of modern science not only coincided with the Age of Enlightenment but was its major beneficiary. And few things characterized that age as did the belief in the perfectibility of man and society. As Becker (1932) so well described, the heavenly city of St. Augustine would be built on earth, not through divine inspiration but through human reason. Science could not recognize the possibility of intractable problems, and like the religions it supplanted, it purported to give clear direction and meaning to living.

What would happen if one accepted intractability, which is no less than to accept the imperfectibility of man and society? What would keep us going? How would we justify our individual strivings and our commitment to social action? What happens to the idea of progress? What will permit us to look forward to tomorrow? Do we seek, as some people do, new religious experiences and tell us we are not alone in this vast world, that there are solutions to the problems of living, and that mortality can open the door to immortality? And that last question, I submit, contains the substance of the real challenge of intractability to science in that it says that humans need to deal with three facts: they are inevitably alone within themselves, they need others, and they will die. These are facts that create problems, but they are not the kinds of problems that fit into science's problem-solving mode. Leaving religion aside (although it is true for many believers), the problems created by these facts need to be solved again, and again, and again. At different times in our lives, the same problem has a different answer.

It has not gone unnoticed that the wonders of science and technology have had little or no effect on society's capacity to help its members feel less alone in the world, to enjoy a sense of community, and to help them cope with anxiety about death. Some would argue that the failure of science to start with and to be governed by these facts of human existence has exacerbated the pain associated with them. And when value-free science entered the realm of human affairs, it exposed its naivete, its ignorance of social history, its hubris, and its blindness to man's need to deal with his aloneness, to feel part of and needed by a larger group, and to recognize and not deny his mortality. This is what the atomic scientists learned, or should have learned.

There is a malaise in all the sciences. For the first time in modern science, as well as in modern Western society, people are questioning whether the fact that science and technology can accomplish a particular feat is reason enough to do it. In psychology we have been brought up short by the fact that as adherents of science we do not have license to conduct research in any way we want. We are accountable, and that means that we should feel and nurture the bonds of similarity and communality between ourselves and the people we study. It is the difference between *knowing* that you are studying people, like yourself, and not "subjects." Society does not exist for the purposes of scientists. It is arrogance in the extreme to look at society from a noblesse oblige stance, expecting that the gifts you give it will be responded to with gratitude, not questions or hesitations. Today, both among scientists and the public, there is the attitude that one should look a gift horse in the mouth.

What bearing does this have on social action? Well, let us talk about Norway. As you know, several years ago they found a lot of oil under the Norwegian Sea. Far from this being greeted with hosannas and visions of a bountiful future, Norwegian leaders reacted with a kind of fear. What could happen to their society if they plunged into the development of the oil fields and began to collect the billions of dollars from the sale of oil? What would be the consequences for Norwegian culture, for their sense of continuity with their past, for their sense of community? A decision was made to go as slowly as possible, to give priority to what they regarded as the important issue in living! The Norwegians know that they live in a world they cannot control, that they will be subject to pressures within and without their society to develop the oil fields quickly and fully, that they may be unable to act in ways consistent with their needs and values. They may not be able to have it their way. Indeed, we can assume they will fall short of their mark. What will keep them going is what is wrapped in what a poet said: "Life takes its final meaning in chosen death." That may sound melodramatic but only to those who cannot understand that the fact of death informs the experience of living. We live each day as if we were immortal, although our rationality tells us how silly a basis for living that is. If our own rationality does not tell us, we can count on all sorts of events and experiences to shock us, not into the recognition of the fact that we will die, but into confronting how we justify why we have lived and how we planned to live (Becker, 1973; Sarason, 1977). And when scientists confront those questions and each one does at one time or another, they frequently find that there was a lot they took for granted that they wish they had not. But that is the fate of everyone. At each vantage point in our lives we see our history differently.

As for the scientists who enter the arena of social action (and that may be in different roles), they would do well to be guided by the values they attach to the facts of living in much the same way that the amazing Norwegians are trying to do. This will present scientists with a type of problem (and transform their concepts of solution) for which their scientific models are inappropriate and may even be interfering. They will find themselves dealing in persuasion, not only facts; the problems will change before and within them; they will not be concerned with replicability because that will be impossible; there will be no final solutions, only a constantly upsetting imbalance between values and action; the internal conflict will be not in the form of "Do I have the right answer?" but rather "Am I being consistent with what I believe?"; satisfaction will come not from colleagues' consensus that their procedures, facts, and conclusions are independent of their feelings and values, but from their own convictions that they tried to be true to their values; they will fight to win not in order to establish the superiority of their procedures or the validity of their scientific facts, concepts, and theories, but because they want to live with themselves and others in certain ways.

Most scientists who entered the arena of social action have left it bloodied, disillusioned, and cynical. They came with data and solutions, but even when they had neither, they assumed that their training and capacity for rational thinking and their ability to pose clear problems and find appropriate methods leading to solutions would establish their credibility as well as their right to an important role in rational social change. Most of them did not realize, if only for their lack of knowledge or respect for social history, that they were fully agreeing with Karl Marx, who had said that it was not enough to try to understand the world. You had to change it and in a scientific way! Marx considered himself a scientist, and the arrogance of scientism permeated his writings and actions. He had his theory, he stated the problems, collected his data, developed procedures, and had no doubt about the correct solution. And what scorn he had for his unscientific opponents! But Marx did not fool himself about what was behind his science, indeed prior to it. He saw man pathetically alone, separated from others, afraid of living and dying. Unfortunately, his dependence on his science led him to give priority to methods dictated by that science and not to what those methods meant *at that time* to man's plight. The solution to that plight was put off to the distant future. In the meantime, trust Marx's scientific theory and procedures. Look what it explained and promised!

The scientist is committed to seeking and saying his or her truths and must not be concerned with whose ox is being gored, an imperative that science has never questioned because to do so would be to destroy the enterprise at its foundation, which is, of course, moral in the sense of describing how scientists should live with each other. To the extent that they live together on the basis of that imperative, scientific problems can be solved. In the social arena, whose ox is being gored cannot be ignored. It can, of course, be ignored, but history contains countless examples of how bloody the consequences can be. And yet, there are times when one takes a position and acts, knowing that the oxen of other individuals and groups will be gored. But somewhere along the way one should be aware that as important as the desire to prevail over your opponents is, the need on both sides is to feel some bond of mutuality. Winning no less than losing can increase one's sense of loneliness and decrease the sense of belonging. In science, how you did something is no less important than what you say you found. Some would say that how is more important. There are hows in social action, but of a very different cast, so different that it becomes understandable why so many scientists who entered the arena of social actin faltered. They could not unlearn fast enough to start learning that the nature of problem solving in the kitchen of social action bore no resemblance to what they had been accustomed to. It is not a kitchen for everyone. But as my favorite president liked to say: "If it's too hot in the kitchen, get the hell out."

Even if you can get out, you will still be dealing with the same issues in your personal life and social circle. But even as a scientist, a new problem has arisen. I refer, of course, to the growing sentiment, already reflected in certain legislation, that what science studies, and the ways it conducts its studies, will be determined by the larger society. And one of the diverse factors behind that determination is the feeling that despite our dazzling capacity to gain new knowledge and skills, to open new vistas for human experience, perhaps even to create new forms of life, we still feel alone, socially unconnected, unhappy in living and fearful of dying. It is a very hot kitchen, not one that the wonders of science and technology have been or will be able to air condition.

What I have said is no excuse for inaction or pessimism, or any other attitude that only deepens the sense of aloneness, accentuates the lack of community, or makes facing the end an intolerable burden. Nor have I in any way intended to denigrate science or intellectual endeavor. There is a difference between science and scientism, between modesty and arrogance, between recognizing limitations and seeing the whole world from one perspective.

Social action takes on a very different quality when it is based on or controlled by certain facts and values. In a book, some colleagues and I (Sarason, Carroll, Maton, Cohen, & Lorentz, 1977) describe an effort over a 3½-year period to develop and sustain a barter economy network of relationships, the purposes of which were to deal more effectively with the fact that resources are always limited and people have a need for a sense of community. I should emphasize that it was an effort not only to increase people's access to needed resources but to do it in a way that also widened and deepened their sense of belonging. The members of this network range from high school students to researchers from different colleges and universities. It is an ever-expanding network of human relationships that makes it a little easier and sometimes a lot easier, to cope with personal and intellectual needs. Central to the story we tell is a remarkable woman we call Mrs. Dewar, whose distinctive characteristic is the ability to scan her world to see and create opportunities whereby people unknown to each other are brought together because each has something the other person needs. There is resource but no money exchange, and people stay together and have call on each other.

The problem-solving literature is not helpful in trying to understand a Mrs. Dewar or several others like her that we describe. None of these individuals has dealt with solvable problems defined in the traditional scientific sense, but they have transformed their worlds. How they did it is no less important than why they did it, but their distinctiveness in social action lies in the way they put the whys and hows together. In these days when social scientists, suffering from the burnt-child reaction, are either retreating from the world of social action or scaling down their claims to credibility, they would be well advised to pay attention to people like Mrs. Dewar who are not burdened by the concept of "problems" but whose thinking and actions are explicit powered by the concepts of "opportunities" and "matching," concepts in the service of a clear vision of what makes learning and living worthwhile.

REFERENCES

Becker, C. L. (1932). *The heavenly city of the eighteenth century philsophers.* New Haven: Yale University Press.

Becker, E. (1973). *The denial of death.* New York: Free Press (Macmillan).

Brown, J. F. (1936). *Psychology and the social order.* New York: McGraw-Hill.

Doob, L. W. (1947). The utilization of social scientists in the overseas branch of the office of war information. *American Political Science Review, 41(4)* 649–677.

Heilbroner, R. L. (1961). *The worldly philosophers.* New York: Simon & Schuster.

Köhler, W. (1925). *The mentality of apes.* New York: Harcourt, Brace.

Lynd, R. S. (1939). *Knowledge for what? The place of social science in American culture.* Princeton, NJ: Princeton University Press.

Nelson, R. (1977). *The moon and the ghetto.* New York: W. W. Norton.

Sarason, S. B. (1977). *Work, aging, and social change. Professionals and the one-life-one-career imperative.* New York: Free Press (Macmillan).

Sarason, S. B., Carrol, C., Maton, K., Cohen, S., & Lorentz, E. (1977). *Human services and resource networks.* San Francisco: Jossey-Bass.

Wertheimer, M. (1959). *Productive thinking* (enlarged ed.). New York: Harper.

CHAPTER 3

Small Wins

REDEFINING THE SCALE OF SOCIAL ISSUES

KARL WEICK

There is widespread agreement that social science research has done relatively little to solve social problems (Berger, 1976; Cook, 1979; Kohn, 1976). Common to these assessments is the assumption that social science is best suited to generate solutions, when in fact it may be better equipped to address how problems get defined in the first place.

A shift of attention away from outcomes toward inputs is not trivial, because the content of appropriate solutions is often implied by the definition of what needs to be solved. To focus on the process of problem definition is to incorporate a more substantial portion of psychology, specifically, its understanding of processes of appraisal, social construction of reality, problem finding, and definition of the situation.

Whether social problems are perceived as phenomena that have a serious negative impact on sizable segments of society (Kohn, 1976, p.94), as substantial discrepancies between widely shared social standards and actual conditions of life (Merton, 1971), or as assertions of grievances or claims with respect to alleged conditions (Spector & Kitsuse, 1977, p. 75), there is agreement that they are big problems. And that is the problem.

The massive scale on which social problems are conceived often precludes

This chapter appeared in the *American Psychologist, 39*, 1984. Copyright 1984 by the American Psychological Association. Reprinted by permission.

KARL E. WEICK · College of Business Administration, University of Texas, Austin, Texas 78712.

innovative action because the limits of bounded rationality are exceeded and arousal is raised to dysfunctionally high levels. People often define social problems in ways that overwhelm their ability to do anything about them.

To understand this phenomenon, consider the following descriptions of the problems of hunger, crime, heart disease, traffic congestion, and pollution.

To reduce domestic hunger we grow more food, which requires greater use of energy for farm equipment, fertilizers, and transportation, adding to the price of energy, which raises the cost of food, putting it out of the price range of the needy.

To solve the problem of soaring crime rates, cities expand the enforcement establishment, which draws funds away from other services such as schools, welfare, and job training, which leads to more poverty, addiction, prostitution, and more crime.

To ward off coronary heart disease, people who live in cities spend more time jogging and cycling, which exposes their lungs to more air pollution than normal, increasing the risk of coronary illness. To ease traffic congestion, multilane highways are built, which draws people away from mass transit so that the new road soon becomes as overcrowded as the old road.

To reduce energy use and pollution, cities invest in mass transit, which raises municipal debt, leading to a reduction in frequency and quality of service and an increase in fares, which reduces ridership, which further raises the municipal debt (Sale, 1980).

When social problems are described this way, efforts to convey their gravity disable the very resources of thought and action necessary to change them. When the magnitude of problems is scaled upward in the interest of mobilizing action, the quality of thought and action declines, because processes such as frustration, arousal, and helplessness are activated.

Ironically, people often cannot solve problems unless they think they are not problems. If heightened arousal interferes with diagnosis and action, then attacking a less arousing "mere problem" should allow attention to be broader and action to be more complex. Responses that are more complex, more recently learned, and more responsive to more stimuli in changing situations usually have a better chance of producing a lasting change in dynamic problems.

To recast larger problems into smaller, less arousing problems, people can identify a series of controllable opportunities of modest size that produce visible results and that can be gathered into synoptic solutions. This strategy of small wins addresses social problems by working directly on their construction and indirectly on their resolution. Problems are constructed to stabilize arousal at moderate intensities where its contribution to performance of complex tasks is most beneficial.

AROUSAL AND SOCIAL PROBLEMS

The following analysis of small wins[1] assumes that arousal varies among people concerned with social problems but tends to be relatively high, which affects the quality of performance directed at these problems. Arousal is treated as a generic concept under which is assembled a variety of findings that cohere because of their mutual relevance to the Yerkes–Dodson Law (Broadhurst, 1959). Although arousal mechanisms are neither simple nor uni-dimensional, they do seem to be localized in at least two physiological sites (reticular formation, limbic system), are visible under conditions of sensory deprivation, produce differences in the quality of learning and performance, and have observable physiological effects. The specific effects of arousal on performance associated with the Yerkes–Dobson Law are that (a) there is an inverted-U relationship between arousal and the efficiency of performance with increasing levels of arousal, first improving and then impairing perfor-mance, and (b) the optimal level of arousal for performance varies inversely with task difficulty. Even though these coarse propositions have been amended, tuned more finely, and differentiated, they remain basic principles in which an analysis of social problem solving can be anchored.

Key assertions for the present analysis culled from previous investigations of arousal and performance include the following:

1. Arousal coincides with variation in degrees of activation and varies along at least two dimensions, energy/sleep and tension/placidity (Eysenck, 1982; Thayer, 1978a,b).
2. As arousal increases, attention to cues becomes more selective, and this editing is especially detrimental to performance of difficult tasks (Easterbrook, 1959, although this generalization has received mixed support. See Baddeley, 1972; Pearson & Lane, 1983; Weltman, Smith, & Egstrom, 1971, for representative work).
3. At relatively high levels of arousal, coping responses become more primitive in at least three ways (Staw, Sandelands, & Dutton, 1981): (a) people who try to cope with problems often revert to more dom-inant, first learned actions; (b) patterns of responding that have been learned recently are the first ones to disappear, which means that those responses are most finely tuned to the current environment are

[1] Tom Peter's (1977) original description of small wins was a crucial point of departure for this formulation. Subsequent discussions with Peters, as well as with Linda Pike, Richard Thaler, Joseph McGrath, Sharon McCarthy, David Anderson, Marianne LaFrance, and students and faculty of the Psychology Department at Rice University contributed to my understanding of the phenomenon. I am grateful to all of them for their help.

the first ones to go; and (c) people treat novel stimuli as if they are more similar to older stimuli than in fact they are, so that clues indicating change are missed.

To invert this list, highly aroused people find it difficult to learn a novel response, to brainstorm, to concentrate, to resist old categories, to perform complex responses, to delegate, and to resist information that supports positions they have taken (Holsti, 1978).

When these findings are focused on problem solving, they suggest that to call a problem serious is to raise arousal, which is appropriate if people know what to do and have a well-developed response to deal with the problem. This is analogous to the situation of a simple task, the performance of which improves over a considerable range of activation because selective attention does not delete the few cues that are essential for performance. High arousal can improve performance if it occurs after a person has decided what to do and after she or he have overlearned how to do it.

To call a problem minor rather than serious is to lower arousal, which is also appropriate if people do not know what to do or are unable to do it. If we assume that most people overlook the fine-grain detail of problems, think only in terms of force as a response (Nettler, 1980), and overlook minor leverage points from which the problem might be attacked, then it is clear they have neither the diagnoses nor the responses to cope. This means that people need lower arousal to keep diagnostic interference at a minimum and to allow for the practice of relatively complex skills. To keep problem-related arousal at modest intensities, people need to work for small wins.

Sometimes problem solving suffers from too little arousal. When people think too much or feel too powerless, issues become depersonalized. This lowers arousal, leading to inactivity or apathetic performance. The prospect of a small win has an immediacy, tangibility, and controllability that could reverse these effects. Alinsky (1972, pp. 114–115) persuaded a demoralized neighborhood group to picket for reinstatement of Infant Medical Care, which he knew would be granted if they merely asked. Organizing for the protest, making the demand, and then receiving what they asked for energized people who had basically given up.

EXAMPLES OF SMALL WINS

Small wins have been designed and implemented in a variety of settings. For example, the Pittsburgh Steelers in the National Football League have won 88 games and lost 27 under their coach Chuck Noll (as of February 4, 1980). Those statistics become more interesting if they are partitioned on the basis of whether the Steelers were playing against teams with winning records or teams with losing records ("Superbowls," 1980). Against opponents who won more than half of their games, the Steelers won 29 and lost 26, or slightly more than half of these games (53%). However, against opponents with winning percentages below .500, the Steelers' record was 59–1, meaning they won 98% of these games.

Thus a professional team renowned for its power got that way by consistently and frequently doing the easy stuff. The Steelers did not become great by winning the big one. Against tough opponents, they did no better than anyone else. These data suggest that winning teams distinguish themselves by more consistent behavior in games in which their skill advantage should make a difference, a condition that is part of the prototype for a small win. Thus, the best indication of good coaching may be the ability to induce consistent high performance against weak opponents (Peter, 1977, p. 286).

The successful effort by the Task Force on Gay Liberation to change the way in which the Library of Congress classified books on the gay liberation movement is another example of a small win. Prior to 1972, books on this topic were assigned numbers reserved for books on abnormal sexual relations, sexual crimes and sexual perversions (HQ 71-471). After 1972, the classifications were changed so that homosexuality was no longer a subcategory of abnormal relations, and all entries formerly described as "abnormal sex relations" were now described as varieties of sexual life (Spector & Kitsuse, 1977, pp. 13–14). Labels and technical classifications, the mundane work of catalogers, have become the turf on which claims are staked, wins are frequent, and seemingly small changes attract attention, recruit allies, and give opponents second thoughts.

The feminist campaign against sexism has been more successful with the smaller win of desexing English than with the larger win of desexing legislation (ERA). The success of attempts to make people more self-conscious about words implying sex bias is somewhat surprising, because it represents an imposition of taboos at a time when taboos in general are being removed. "For even as books, periodicals and dictionaries (not all, to be sure) are liberally opening their pages to obscenities and vulgarisms, they are unliberally leaning over backward to ostracize all usage deemed offensive to the sexes" (Steinmetz, 1982, p. 8). This hypocrisy notwithstanding, the reforms have been adopted with little objection, due in part to their size, specificity, visibility, and completeness. As one commentator on Steinmetz's essay put it, "winning equality in the language was necessary; and while the winning shouldn't be overestimated, it will work—the drops of water on the rock—to change consciousness, and in time, unconsciousness" (Williams, 1982, p. 46).

When William Ruckelshaus became the first administrator of the U. S. Environmental Protection Agency in the early 1970s, he laid aside his mandate to clean up all aspects of the environment and went instead for a small win.

> He discovered some obscure 80-year old legislation that permitted him to go after some cities on water pollution. He took advantage of the legislation, effectively narrowing his practical agenda for the first year or two to "getting started on water pollution." On day one of the agency's formal existence, Ruckelshaus announced five major lawsuits against major American cities. The impact was electrifying. The homework had been meticulously done. Noticeable progress was made quickly. It formed the beachhead for a long series of successes and distinguished EPA from most of its sister agencies. (Peters, 1979, p. 5)

Ruckelshaus did not tackle everything, nor did he even tackle the most visible source of pollution, which is air pollution. Ruckelshaus identified quick, opportunistic, tangible first steps only modestly related to a final outcome. The first steps were driven less by logical decision trees, grand strategy, or noble rhetoric than by action that could be built upon, action that signaled intent as well as competence.

Alcoholics Anonymous has been successful in helping alcoholics, partly because it does not insist that they become totally abstinent for the rest of their lives. Although this is the goal of the program, alcoholics are told to stay sober one day at a time, or one hour at a time if temptation is severe. The impossibility of lifetime abstinence is scaled down to the more workable task of not taking a drink for the next 24 hours, drastically reducing the size of a win necessary to maintain sobriety. Actually gaining that small win is then aided by several other small measures such as phone calls, one-hour meetings, slogans, pamphlets and meditations which themselves are easy to acquire and implement.

Several studies of microinnovation are also compatible with the idea of small wins. For example, Hollander's (1965) closely documented microeconomic study of decreases in production costs of viscose rayon yarn manufacturing at five DuPont plants between 1929 and 1960 demonstrates that minor technical changes—rather than major changes—accounted for over two thirds of the reductions. A technical change is a change "in the technique of production of given commodities by specific plants, designed to reduce unit production costs" (p. 23). Major technical changes (e.g., introduction of compensation spinning) differ from minor changes (e.g., introduction of forklift trucks) in time, skill, effort, and expense required to produce them.

Analyses showed that the cost reductions were substantial (e.g., from 53.51 to 17.55 cents per pound of rayon from 1929 to 1951 at the Old Hickory plant). Technical changes, as opposed to changes in quality of pulp input, management practices, quality of labor, and plant size accounted for approximately 75% of the reductions, and most of these technical changes were minor (specific percentage of reduction attributable to minor changes in the five plants was 83%, 80%, 79%, 100%, and 46%, the last being a new plant making a new product, tire cord yarn).

The minor technical changes were small improvement inventions, rather than major inventions, made by people familiar with current operations (p. 205). Experience with the process was crucial because the very acts of production that created the problems in the first place were also the sources of the minor improvements that could solve the problem. People learned by doing.

Left for further research is the interesting possibility in this study that minor innovations were dependent on preceding major innovations. Ten to 15 years after a major change, the number of minor changes that were improvements was close to zero (pp. 205–206). Small alterations in technique can improve productivity for some time after a major change, but these improvements may not go on indefinitely.

Implied in Hollander's analysis is the possibility that older plants can produce almost as efficiently as newly built plants if technical changes are identified and funds are invested in them. Thus, contemporary fascination with quality circles may be appropriate if it aids in identifying needed minor technical changes.

The point to be drawn from Hollander's analysis is summarized by Machlup (1962):

> A technological invention is a big step forward in the useful arts. Small steps forward are not given this designation; they are just "minor improvements" in technology. But a succession of many minor improvements add up to a big advance in technology. It is natural that we hail the big, single step forward, while leaving the many small steps all but unnoticed. It is understandable, therefore, that we eulogize the great inventor, while overlooking the small improvers. Looking backward, however, it is by no means certain that the increase in productivity over a longer period of time is chiefly due to the great inventors and their inventions. It may well be true that the sum total of all minor improvements, each too small to be called an invention, has contributed to the increase in productivity more than the great inventions have. (p. 164)

CHARACTERISTICS OF SMALL WINS

A small win is a concrete, complete, implemented outcome of moderate importance. By itself, one small win may seem unimportant. A series of wins at small but significant tasks, however, reveals a pattern that may attract allies, deter opponents, and lower resistance to subsequent proposals. Small wins are controllable opportunities that produce visible results.

The size of wins can be arranged along a continuum from small to large. Lindblom's (1979) example of monetary control makes this point. Raising or lowering the discount rate is a smaller win than is the decision to use the discount rate as a method of monetary control. Both of those actions are smaller than introducing the Federal Reserve system, which is smaller than a change that eliminates the use of money entirely. Lindblom summarizes the example by drawing the generalization that a small change is either a change in a relatively unimportant variable (people tend to agree on what is an important change) or a relatively unimportant change in an important variable (Braybrooke & Lindblom, 1963, p. 64).

Small wins often originate as solutions that single out and define as problems those specific, limited conditions for which they can serve as the complete remedy. I emphasize the importance of *limits* for both the solution and the problem to distinguish the solutions of small wins from the larger, more open-ended solutions that define problems more diffusely (e.g., "burn the system down").

Once a small win has been accomplished, forces are set in motion that favor another small win. When a solution is put in place, the next solvable problem often becomes more visible. This occurs because new allies bring new solutions with them and old opponents change their habits. Additional resources also flow toward winners, which means that slightly larger wins can be attempted.

It is important to realize that the next solvable problem seldom coincides with the next "logical" step as judged by a detached observer. Small wins do not combine in a neat, linear, serial form, with each step being a demonstrable step closer to some pre-determined goal. More common is the circumstance where small wins are scattered and cohere only in the sense that they move in the same general direction or all move away from some deplorable condition. Ideals, broad abstract ends, and lasting ambitions are less influential in defining a means–ends structure for a series of small wins than they are in articulating the specific trade-offs that occur when each win improves something at the expense of something else (Lindblom, 1979, p. 519).

A series of small wins can be gathered into a retrospective summary that imputes a consistent line of development, but this post hoc construction should not be mistaken for orderly implementation. Small wins have a fragmentary character driven by opportunism and dynamically changing situations. Small wins stir up settings, which means that each subsequent attempt at another win occurs in a different context. Careful plotting of a series of wins to achieve a major change is impossible because conditions do not remain constant. Much of the artfulness in working with small wins lies in identifying, gathering, and labeling several small changes that are present but unnoticed (e.g., the

Aquarian conspiracy, megatrends, back to basics), changes that in actuality could be gathered under a variety of labels.

Small wins provide information that facilitates learning and adaptation. Small wins are like miniature experiments that test implicit theories about resistance and opportunity and uncover both resources and barriers that were invisible before the situation was stirred up. Attempts to induce self-consciousness about sex references in speech revealed that language was more susceptible to change than had been thought earlier (e.g., Basic English never took hold); that opponents to language change were more dispersed, more stuffy, and less formidable than anticipated; that sex-biased language was more pervasive and therefore a stronger leverage point than people realized; and that language reform could be incorporated into a wide variety of agendas (e.g., APA *Publication Manual* revision). Language experiments uncovered entrenched sexism that had been invisible and created a more differentiated picture of allies, opponents, bystanders, and issues.

A series of small wins is also more structurally sound than a large win because small wins are stable building blocks. This characteristic is implicit in Simon's (1962) analysis of nearly decomposable systems and is illustrated by a fable (Kuhn & Beam, 1982):

> Your task is to count out a thousand sheets of paper, while you are subject to periodic interruptions. Each interruption causes you to lose tract of the count and forces you to start over. If you count the thousand as a single sequence, then an interruption could cause you, at worst, to lose a count of as many as 999. If the sheets are put into stacks of 100, however, and each stack remains undisturbed by interruptions, then the worst possible count loss from interruption is 108. That number represents the recounting of the nine stacks of 100 each plus the 99 single sheets. Further, if sheets are first put into stacks of ten, which are then joined into stacks of 100, the worst possible loss from interruption would be 27. That number represents nine stacks of ten plus nine single sheets. Not only is far less recounting time lost by putting the paper into "subsystems" of tens and hundreds, but the chances of completing the count are vastly higher. (pp. 249–250)

Small wins are like short stacks. They preserve gains, they cannot unravel, each one requires less coordination to execute, interruptions such as might occur when there is a change in political administration have limited effects, and subparts can be assembled into different configurations. To execute a large win such as ratification of the Equal Rights Amendment required much greater coordination because interdependencies are more dense, timing is more crucial, and defections are a greater threat. If one crucial piece is missing, the attempted solution fails and has to be restarted.

Parts of Saul Alinsky's (1972) model for building community organization parallel the notion of small wins. Alinsky's three criteria for working goals are that the goals be highly specific, realizable, and immediate (Peabody, 1971, p. 525). If people work for something concrete, if people have an opportunity for visible success from which they draw confidence, and if people can translate their excitement and optimism into immediate action, then a small win is probable, as is their heightened interest in attempting a second win.

As an example of how these goals might be directed toward solving the problem of pollution. Alinsky suggests that people try to influence polluters by influencing the polluters' bankers. To do this, the normal time-consuming process of opening and closing a savings account is turned to advantage by having 1000 people enter the bank, each with $5, to open a savings account. Although this volume of business may paralyze the bank, it is not illegal and no bank is eager to be known as an institution that forcibly ejects depositors. Once the deposits have been made, the people come back a day later, close their accounts—again a time-consuming activity—and the process continues until this secondary target, being punished for someone else's sins, brings pressure to bear on the offender. Making mass changes in savings accounts is a specific, realizable, immediate, small, and controllable opportunity. It is just like defeating a second-rate team, changing the card catalog, finding a chairperson, suing five cities, staying sober for an hour, or introducing a forklift into a work procedure.

THE PSYCHOLOGY OF SMALL WINS

From a psychological perspective, small wins make good sense. This is evident if we review what is known about cognitive limitations, affective limitations, stress, and the enactment of environments.

Cognitive Limitations

Given the reality of bounded rationality (March, 1978; Perrow, 1981), small wins may be effective as much because they are "small" as because they are "wins." The growing documentation of ways in which people take cognitive shortcuts on larger problems (e.g., Kahneman, Slovic, & Tversky, 1982; Kiesler & Sproull, 1982; Miller & Cantor, 1982) suggests that smaller wins may suffer less distortion from these heuristics. People with limited rationality have sufficient variety to visualize, manage, and monitor the smaller amount of variety present in scaled-down problem environments. When people initiate small-scale projects there is less play between cause and effect; local regularities can be created, observed, and trusted; and feedback is immediate and can be used to revise theories. Events cohere and can be observed in their entirety when their scale is reduced.

An example of scaling down problems to more manageable size is an incident that occurred during the Apollo 13 mission when the astronauts staged what some regard as the first strike in space on December 27, 1973. Mission control had been sending more and more directions, corrections, and orders to the astronauts until finally Commander Gerald Carr said, "You have given us too much to do. We're not going to do a thing until you get your act in better order." He then shut off communications for 12 hours, and the astronauts spent their day catching up and looking out the windows. They regained control over their circumstance. They did so partly by complicating themselves—an astronaut who both disobeys and obeys mission control is a more complicated individual than one who merely obeys—and partly by simplifying their system—they cut off one whole set of demands and reduced their problems simply to dealing with their own preferences. Their system became simpler because they had fewer demands to accommodate and simpler schedules to follow.

To gain some control over interdependent problems, people can disconnect the parts so they do not affect each other. Problems escalate only because they are tied together in a circular fashion and become vicious circles. A system with fewer interdependent events is a simpler system. It is easier to comprehend, easier to control, easier to improve.

Small wins disconnect incomprehensible systems such as the Library of Congress, a DuPont factory, EPA, or NASA. Once the system is disconnected, people then focus their attention on specific events that have been stripped out of their context, specific events such as the HQ portion of the Library classification system or a sequence of space experiments. What is common in instances such as these is that the "mere problem" that people finally end up with becomes manageable, understandable, and controllable by fallible individuals and stays that way until the larger system is reconnected. Arousal is reduced because control and predictability increase. The mere problem is also seen more clearly, which improves the chances that a small, specific solution that fits it will be invented. The resulting small win becomes a visible change in a highly inertial world. The change was made possible because the bounds of rationality were not exceeded. The change also becomes more visible to other people because its size is compatible with their own bounded rationality.

Affective Limitations

Repeatedly, psychologists have demonstrated that small changes are preferred to large changes. The small scale of small wins is important affectively as well as cognitively. Examples are plentiful.

Successive small requests are more likely to produce compliance (Freedman & Fraser, 1966). Changes in the level of aspiration are most satisfying when they occur in small increments. Positions advocated within the latitude of acceptance modify opinions more often than does advocacy that exceeds these limits. Orders within the zone of indifference are followed more quickly and reliably. The central measure of perception is the *just noticeable* difference. Theories are judged interesting when they disconfirm assumptions held with moderate intensity (Davis, 1971). People whose positions are close to one's own are the targets of intensive persuasion, whereas those whose positions are farther away are dismissed, isolated, or derogated. Social comparison is more stable the more similar the comparison other is. Small discrepancies from an adaptation level are experienced as more pleasurable than are larger discrepancies. Brief therapy is most successful when the client is persuaded to do just one thing differently that interdicts the pattern of attempted solutions up to that point. Extremely easy or extremely difficult goals are less compelling than are goals set closer to perceived capabilities. Learning tends to occur in small increments rather than in an all-or-none fashion (this generalization is highly sensitive to the size of the building blocks that are postulated in all-or-none positions such as stimulus sampling theory). Programmed learning works best when there is a gradual progression to complex repertoires and a gradual fading out of stimulus prompts for answers. Retention is better when people are in the same emotional state in which they learned the original material (Bower, Monteiro, Gilligan, 1978). Numerous other examples could be given. The point is that incremental phenomena such as small wins have a basic compatibility with human preferences for learning, perception, and motivation.

Small wins are not only easier to comprehend but more pleasurable to experience. Although no one would deny that winning big is a thrill, big wins can also be disorienting and can lead to unexpected negative consequences. The disruptiveness of big wins is evident in the high stress scores associated with positive changes in Life Events Scales (e.g., Dohrenwend, Krasnoff, Askenasy, & Dohrenwend, 1978). Big wins evoke big countermeasures and altered expectations, both of which make it more difficult to gain the next win (e.g., attention paid to Nobel prize winners often makes it impossible for them to do any further significant work).

Stress

Because arousal is a central construct in stress research, the soundness of small wins should be evident when stress formulations are examined. Recent work by McGrath (1976) and Kobasa (1979) reveals just such a fit. McGrath argued that there is a potential for stress when people perceive that demands exceed capabilities under conditions where it would be extremely costly to ignore the issue (p. 1352). The severity of perceived stress becomes stronger as uncertainty about the outcome increases. Uncertainty intensifies the closer the perceived demand is to the perceived ability. Large demand–capability discrepancies in either direction virtually assure successful or unsuccessful outcomes compared with situations of smaller discrepancy in which the outcome could go either way.

When people scale up to gravity of social problems, they raise at least the importance of the issue and the magnitude of the demand. The crucial question then becomes: What happens to the third variable of perceived capability to cope with demands?

Although numerous assumptions about perceived ability are possible, it would seem that the generic statement, "this problem affects you, and you can make a difference" reduces the perceived discrepancy between demands and abilities. If people respond to "you can make a difference" with the retort, "that's nonsense," then larger discrepancies will be created and stress will be minimal. If, however, people respond with a different reaction such as "that might just be true," then the demand–capability discrepancy is narrowed, which makes the outcome more uncertain and the stress more intense. As stress increases, the disruptive effects of arousal on problem solving increase. Just when people feel most encouraged to do something about a problem, they become least capable of translating that growing optimism into detailed diagnoses and complex responses. They become disabled by their own optimism, because it intensifies the perceived uncertainty of outcomes.

Once the gap between ability and demand begins to narrow, it becomes crucial that people see how their abilities can unequivocally *exceed* demands in order to remove some uncertainty. This assurance of success is precisely what people begin to feel when they define their situation as one of working for a small win. When a large problem is broken down into a series of small wins, three things happen. First, the importance of any single win is reduced in the sense that the costs of failure are small and the rewards of success considerable. Second, the size of the demand itself is reduced (e.g., all we need to do is get one city to discipline local polluters). And third, existing skills are perceived as sufficient to deal with the modest demands that will be confronted.

A small win reduces importance ("this is no big deal"), reduces demand ("that's all that needs to be done"), and raises perceived skill levels ("I can do at least that"). When reappraisals of problems take this form, arousal becomes less of a deterrent to solving them.

The potential attractiveness of a small win is that it operates simultaneously on importance, demands, and resources and defines situations away from the "close calls" where higher uncertainty and higher stress reduce problem-solving performance. Small wins induce a degree of certainty that allows greater access to the very resources that can insure more positive outcomes.

Additional researach on resistance to stress, especially Kobasa's work with hardiness (Kobasa, 1979, 1982; Kobasa, Maddi & Kahn, 1982), suggest the psychological soundness of the strategy of small wins. Although Kobasa has interpreted hardiness as a personality disposition, pursuit of a small wins strategy could induce more generally the perceptions associated with this disposition.

Hardiness is composed of commitment, control, and challenge. *Commitment* refers to involvement and a generalized sense of purpose that allows people to impose meaning on things, events, and persons. *Control* is the tendency to act and feel as if one can have a definite influence (not *the* influence) on situations through the exercise of imagination, knowledge, skill and choice. People with a sense of control tend to experience events as natural outgrowths of their actions rather than as foreign, overwhelming events. *Challenge* is the belief that change is an incentive to grow rather than a threat to security. Thus, incongruent events are opportunities rather than disasters.

Deliberate cultivation of a strategy of small wins infuses situations with comprehensible and specific meaning (commitment), reinforces the perception that people can exert some influence over what happens to them (control), and produces changes of manageable size that serve as incentives to expand the repertory of skills (challenge). Continued pursuit of small wins could build increasing resistance to stress in people not originally predisposed toward hardiness.

Enactment of Environments

Small wins build order into unpredictable environments, which should reduce agitation and improve performance. Most "reality" surrounding social problems is disorganized, fragmented, piecemeal. When people confront situations that contain gaps and uncertainties, they first think their way across these gaps. Having tied the elements together cognitively, they then actually tie partial events together when they act toward them and impose contingencies. This sequence is similar to sequences associated with self-fulfilling prophecies (Snyder, Tanke, & Berscheid, 1977).

A crucial element in thoughtful action consists of "presumptions of logic" (Weick, 1979, p. 138) about situations that will be confronted. These presumptions draw people into situations in anticipation that the situations will make sense. This anticipation sets the stage for the second half of the process where, finding themselves in a presumably sensible situation, people take action. In doing so, they create patterns and consolidate scattered elements, both of which create the sensible situation that was anticipated.

This sequence of events is especially probable in the case of small wins. A small win is a bounded, comprehensible, plausible scenario that coheres sufficiently that people presume in advance that a forthcoming situation will be orderly. Having imposed the logic of small wins on a situation cognitively, the person then wades into the situation and acts with persistence, confidence, and forcefulness (Moscovici, 1980). Such decisive action is appropriate for an ostensibly orderly situation which, of course, has actually become more orderly precisely because forceful action consolidated it. Forceful action monopolizes the attention of other actors and becomes a causal variable in their construction of the situation. As a result, their actions become more interdependent and more orderly than they were before the intervention occurred.

Even though the actions associated with small wins are brief, specific, and localized, they can have a deterministic effect on many problem situations, because those situations are often even less coherent than the actions directed at them. The situations are loosely coupled, subject to multiple interpretations, and monitored regularly by only a handful of people. The confidence that flows from a pursuit of small wins frequently enacts environments in which the original problem becomes less severe and the next improvement more clear.

THE POLITICS OF SMALL WINS

Small wins can penetrate the main occupational hazard in Washington—information overload. The pace of work in Washington is fast, incessant, and unavoidable. The Obey Commission in 1977 found that in an average 11-hour day, a House member has only 11 minutes for discretionary reading (O'Donnell, 1981). That is where small wins have power. Small wins are compact, tangible, upbeat, noncontroversial, and relatively rare. They catch the attention of people with short time perspectives who have only 11 minutes to read.

Small wins also attract the attention of the opposition, though this is not inevitable. Opponents often assume that big effects require big causes, which means that they discount the importance of small wins. Opponents also often assume that attempted solutions cluster. Because small wins are dispersed, they are harder to find and attack than is one big win that is noticed by everyone who wants to win big somewhere else and who defines the world as a zero-sum game.

Because someone's small win is someone else's small loss, the stakes are reduced, which encourages the losers to bear their loss without disrupting the social system. A vague consensus is preserved by small wins because basic values are not challenged. People can accept a specific outcome even if they disagree on the values that drive it or the goals toward which it is instrumental.

The fact that small wins attract attention is not their only political virtue. In the world of policy, there are seldom clear decisions or clear problems (Weiss, 1980). Outcomes are built from bits and pieces of action, policy, and advice that are lying about. Because small wins are of a size that lets them supplement rather than dominate policy, they are more likely to be incorporated than are other more conspicuous solutions (McNaugher, 1980; Redman, 1973).

Despite their apparent political advantages, however, small wins may sound hopelessly naive, because they rely heavily on resources such as hope, faith, prophecies, presumptions, optimism, and positive reappraisals. Authors of many of the policy articles that have appeared in the *American Psychologist* have criticized psychologists for being naive and knowing relatively little about playing "hardball" with constituencies that have serious resources and know the game (e.g., Bazelon, 1982; Dörken, 1981; Hager, 1982; Sarason, 1978). Psychologists have responded by deprecating the game (e.g., March, 1979), making efforts to learn hardball (e.g., DeLeon, O'Keefe, VandenBos, & Kraut, 1982), or by defining new games (e.g., Fishman & Neigher, 1982). The thrust of the present analysis, however, is that we need to be less apologetic for our apparent naivete than we have been.

First, being naive simply means that we reject received wisdom that something *is* a problem. Being naive means nothing more than that. We are always naive relative to some definition of the situation, and if we try to become less so, we may accept a definition that confines the definition of small wins to narrower issues than is necessary.

Second, being naive probably does have a grain of denial embedded in it. But denial can lower arousal to more optimal levels, so that more complex actions can be developed and more detailed analyses can be made.

Third, to be naive is to start with fewer preconceptions. Since it is usually true that believing is seeing, strong *a priori* beliefs narrow what is noticed (e.g., concern with sexism leads people to ignore threats that could annihilate both sexes). People with naive preconceptions will see a different set of features and are less likely to become fixated on specific features.

Fourth, naive beliefs favor optimism. Many of the central action mechanisms for small wins, such as self-fulfilling prophecies, affirmation, self-confirming faith that life is worth living (as first described by William James), the presumption of logic, trust, the belief in personal control, and positive self-statements, all gain their energy from the initial belief that people can make a difference. That belief is not naive when the world is tied together loosely. Firm actions couple events. And firm actions are more likely to occur when belief is strongly positive than when it is hesitant, doubtful, or cynical.

Optimism is also not naive if we can deny the relevance of hopelessness for the spirit of optimism. We justify what we do, not by belief in its efficacy but by an acceptance of its necessity. That is the basis on which Don Quixote survives.

> Don Quixote embraces the foolishness of obligatory action. Justification for knight-errantry lies not in anticipation of effectiveness but in an enthusiasm for the pointless heroics of a good life. The celebration of life lies in the pleasures of pursuing the demands of duty. (March, 1975, p. 14)

One can argue that it is our duty as psychologists to be optimistic. To view optimism as a duty rather than as something tied to unsteady expectations of success is to position oneself in a sufficient variety of places with sufficient confidence that events may be set in motion that provide substance for that hope. Small wins may amount to little, but they are after all wins, and wins encourage us to put the most favorable construction on actions and events.

Naivete can be a problem when optimistic expectations are disconfirmed (small flops), for although it increases the likelihood that good things will happen, it does not guarantee they will. Disconfirmation often leads people to abandon their expectations and adopt skepticism and inaction as inoculation against future setbacks. The important tactic for dealing with the flops implicit in trying for small wins is to localize the disconfirmation of expectations. Cognitive theories of depression (e.g., Beck, Rush, Shaw, & Emery, 1979) suggest that people often generalize disconfirmed expectations far beyond the incident in which they originated. The faith that makes life worth living can suffer setbacks, but these setbacks are specific and, in the case of small flops, limited. Highly aroused people who have flopped attempting a large win cannot see those specifics, so they abandon all faith and all possible scenarios for how life might unfold. That is the generalizing that needs to be contained and often is contained by trying for smaller wins, with smaller stakes.

CONCLUSION

The preceding analysis leaves several questions unanswered. For example, is the concept of arousal really necessary to understand why attempts to cope with large problems are self-defeating? Cognitive explanations (e.g., "I simply can't cure cancer so I'll work to make terminally ill patients more comfortable") may make it unnecessary to resort to motivational explanations. I favor motivational explanations under the assumption that social problems are emotional issues argued under emotionally charged conditions.

What is the natural distribution of arousal around social problems? The preceding analyses assume that most people feel intensely about social problems most of the time, or at least at those crucial times when they try to diagnose what is wrong and rehearse what to do about it. That assumption is a simplification, because it is clear that participation is uneven, unpredictable, and easily distracted (Weiner, 1976). Furthermore, interest in a given issue soon diminishes, and bored people wander off to other problems (Koestler, 1970). Nevertheless, there are problem elites, opinion leaders, and hubs in networks. These people are central because they feel strongly about issues. Those strong feelings can affect their thought and action directly, and others who model this thought and action indirectly.

What role do individual differences in arousability or sensation seeking (Zuckerman, 1979) play in strategies to cope with social problems? Implicit in the preceding argument is a rule of thumb: If you can tolerate high levels of arousal, go for big wins; if you cannot, go for small wins.

Questions such as this notwithstanding, it seems useful to consider the possibility that social problems seldom get solved, because people define these problems in ways that overwhelm their ability to do anything about them. Changing the scale of a problem can change the quality of resources that are directed at it. Calling a situation a mere problem that necessitates a small win moderates arousal, improves diagnosis, preserves gains, and encourages innovation. Calling a situation a serious problem that necessitates a larger win may be when the problem starts.

REFERENCES

Alinsky, S. D. (1972). *Rules for radicals.* New York: Vintage Books.

Baddeley, A. D. (1972). Selective attention and performance in dangerous environments. *British Journal of Psychology, 63,* 537–546.

Bazelon, D. L. (1982). Veils, values, and social responsibility. *American Psychologist, 37,* 115–121.

Beck, A. T., Rush, A. J., Shaw, B. F., & Emery, G. (1979). *Cognitive theory of depression.* New York: Guilford.

Berger, B. M. (1976). Comments on Mel Kohn's paper. *Social Problems, 24,* 115–120.

Bower, G. H., Monteiro, K. P., & Gilligan, S. G. (1978). Emotional mood as a context for learning and recall. *Journal of Verbal Learning and Verbal Behavior, 17,* 573–585.

Braybrooke, D., & Lindblom, C. E. (1963). *A strategy of decision.* Glencoe, IL: Free Press.

Broadhurst, P. L. (1959). The interaction of task difficulty and motivation: The Yerkes–Dodson Law revived. *Acta Psychologica, 16,* 321–338.

Cook, S. W. (1979). Social science and school desegregation: Did we mislead the Supreme Court? *Personality and Social Psychology Bulletin, 5,* 420–437.

Davis, M. S. (1971). That's interesting: Towards a phenomenology of sociology and a sociology of phenomenology. *Philosophy of Social Science, 1,* 309–344.

DeLeon, P. H., O'Keefe, A. M., VandenBos, G. R., & Kraut, A. G. (1982). How to influence public policy: A blueprint for activism. *American Psychologist, 37,* 476–485.

Dohrenwend, B. S., Krasnoff, L., Askenasy, A. R., & Dohrenwend, B. P. (1978). Exemplification of a method for scaling life events: The PERI Life Events Scale. *Journal of Health and Social Behavior, 19,* 205–229.

Dörken, H. (1981). Coming of age legislatively: In 21 steps. *American Psychologist, 36,* 165–173.

Easterbrook, J. A. (1959). The effect of emotion on cue utilization and the organization of behavior. *Psychological Review, 66,* 183–201.

Eysenck, M. W. (1982). *Attention and arousal: Cognition and performance.* New York: Springer.

Fishman, D. B., & Neigher, W. (1982). American psychology in the eighties: Who will buy? *American Psychologist, 37,* 533–546.

Freedman, J. L., & Fraser, S. C. (1966). Compliance without pressure: The foot-in-the-door technique. *Journal of Personality and Social Psychology, 4,* 195–202.

Hager, M.G. (1982). The myth of objectivity. *American Psychologist, 37,* 576–579.

Hollander, S.(1965). *The sources of increased efficiency: A study of DuPont rayon plants.* Cambridge, MA: MIT Press.

Holsti, O. R. (1978). Limitations of cognitive abilities in the face of crisis. In C. F. Smart & W. T. Stanbury (Eds.), *Studies on crisis management* (pp. 35–55). Toronto: Butterworth.

Kahneman, D., Slovic, P., & Tversky, A. (Eds.).(1982).*Judgement under uncertainty: Heuristics and biases.* Cambridge, England: Cambridge University Press.

Kiesler, S., & Sproull, L. (1982). Managerial response to changing environments: Perspectives on problem sensing from social cognition. *Administrative Science Quarterly, 27,* 548–570.

Kobasa, S. C. (1979). Stressful life events, personality, and health: An inquiry into hardiness. *Journal of Personality and Social Psychology, 37,* 1–11.

Kobasa, S. C. (1982). Commitment and coping in stress resistance among lawyers. *Journal of Personality and Social Psychology, 42,* 707–717.

Kobasa, S. C., Maddi, S. R., & Kahn, S. (1982). Hardiness and health: A prospective study. *Journal of Personality and Social Psychology, 42,* 168–177.

Koestler, A. (1970). Literature and the law of diminishing returns. *Encounter, 34,* 39–45.

Kohn, M.L. (1976). Looking back – A 25-year review and appraisal of social problems research. *Social Problems, 24,* 94–112.

Kuhn, A. & Beam, R. D. (1982). *The logic of organizations.* San Francisco: Jossey-Bass.

Lindblom, C.E. (1979). Still muddling, not yet through. *Public Administration Review, 39,* 517–526.

Machlup, F. (1962). *The production and distribution of knowledge in the United States.* Princeton, NJ: Princeton University Press.

March, J.G. (1975). Education and the pursuit of optimism. *Texas Tech Journal of Education, 2,* 5–17.

March, J.G. (1978). Bounded rationality, ambiguity, and the engineering of choice. *The Bell Journal of Economics, 9,* 587–608.

March, J.G. (1979). Science, politics, and Mrs. Gruenberg. In the *National Research Council in 1979* (pp. 27–36). Washington, DC: National Academy of Sciences.

McGrath, J.E. (1976). Stress and behavior in organizations. In M.D. Dunnette (Ed.), *Handbook of industrial and organizational psychology* (pp. 1351–1395). Chicago: Rand McNally.

McNaugher, T.L. (1980). Marksmanship, McNamara, and the M16 rifle: Innovation in military organizations. *Public Policy, 28,* 1–37.

Merton, R.K. (1971). Epilogue: Social problems and sociological theory. In R. Merton & R. Nisbet (Eds.), *Contemporary social problems* (pp. 793–846). New York: Harcourt Brace Jovanovich.

Miller, G.A., & Cantor, N. (1982). Book review of Nisbett and Ross, "Human Inference." *Social Cognition, 1,* 83–93.

Moscovici, S. (1980). Toward a theory of conversion behavior. In L. Berkowitz (Ed.), *Advances in experimental social psychology* (Vol. 13, pp. 209–239). New York: Academic Press.

Nettler, G. (1980). Notes on society; sociologist as advocate. *Canadian Journal of Sociology, 5,* 31–53.

O'Donnell, T.J. (1981). Controlling legislative time. In J. Cooper & G. C. Mackenzie (Eds.), *The house at work* (pp. 127–150). Austin: University of Texas Press.

Peabody, G. L. (1971). Power, Alinsky, and other thoughts. In H.A. Hornstein, B.B. Bunker, W.W. Burke, M. Gindes, & R.J. Lewicki (Eds.), *Social intervention: A behavioral science approach* (pp. 521–532). New York: Free Press.

Pearson, D. A., & Lane, D.M. (1983). *The effect of arousal on attention.* Unpublished manuscript, Rice University.

Perrow, C. (1981). Disintegrating social sciences. *New York University Educational Quarterly, 12,*2–9.

Peters, T.J.(1977). *Patterns of winning and losing: Effects on approach and avoidance by friends and enemies.* Unpublished doctoral dissertation, Stanford University.

Peters, T.J. (1979). *Designing and executing "real" tasks.* Unpublished manuscript, Stanford University.

Redman, E. (1973). *The dance of legislation.* New York: Simon & Schuster.

Sale, K. (1980). *Human scale.* New York: Putnam.

Sarason, S.B. (1978). The nature of problem solving in social action. *American Psychologist, 33,* 370–380.

Simon, H.A. (1962). The architecture of complexity. *Proceedings of the American Philosophical Society, 106,* 467–482.

Snyder, M., Tanke, E.D., & Berscheid,E. (1977). Social perception and interpersonal behavior: On the self-fulfilling nature of social stereotypes. *Journal of Personality and Social Psychology, 35,* 656–666.

Spector, M., & Kitsuse, J.I.(1977). *Constructing social problems.* Menlo Park, CA: Cummings.

Staw, B.M., Sandelands, L.E., & Dutton, J.E. (1981). Threat-rigidity effects in organizational behavior: A multi-level analysis. *Administrative Science Quarterly, 26,* 501–524.

Steinmetz, S.(1982, August 1). The desexing of English. *The New York Times Magazine,* pp. 6, 8.

Superbowls super coach. (1980, February 4). *Time Magazine,* p.58.

Thayer, R.E. (1978a). Factor analytic and reliability studies on the activation-deactivation adjective check list. *Psychological Reports, 42,* 747–756.

Thayer, R.E. (1978b). Toward a psychological theory of multidimensional activation (arousal) *Motivation and Emotion, 2,* 1–34.

Weick, K.W. (1979). *The social psychology of organizing* (2nd ed.). Reading, MA: Addison-Wesley.

Weiner, S.S.(1976). Participation, deadlines, and choice. In J.G. March & J.P. Olsen (Eds), *Ambiguity and choice in organizations* (pp.225–250). Bergen, Norway: Universitesforlaget.

Weiss, C.H. (1980). Knowledge creep and decision accretion. *Knowledge: Creation, Diffusion, Utilization, 1,* 381–404.

Weltman, G., Smith, J.E., & Egstrom,, G.H. (1971). Perceptual narrowing during simulated pressure-chamber exposure. *Human Factors, 13,* 99–107.

Williams, C.T. (1982, September 5). Letter to the editor about "Desexing the English language." *The New York Times Magazine,* p.46.

Zuckerman, M. (1979). *Sensation seeking: Beyond the optimal level of arousal.* Hillsdale, NJ: Erlbaum.

CHAPTER 4

Making Sense of Injustice

SOCIAL EXPLANATIONS, SOCIAL ACTION, AND THE ROLE OF THE SOCIAL SCIENTIST

LOUISE H. KIDDER and MICHELLE FINE

A psychologist interested in casual attributions asks, "What do people *think* are the causes of injustice?" not "What are the real causes of injustice?" A practical realist may reply, "What does it matter what people think, if it bears no relation to reality?" The thesis of this chapter is that what people think about the causes of injustice affects how they feel about any particular injustice and informs their actions. In this chapter we examine how social scientists can help to legitimate alternative views of injustice and social change strategies. We argue that by generating alternative views, social scientists exercise a significant social responsibility (Buss, 1979; Fine, 1983, 1983–84; Wexler, 1982). Taking our lead from the work of Philip Brickman and colleagues (1982), we see this as a two-phase process: helping people to locate the sources of social problems in economic and social structures and conceptualizing collective strategies for change.

LOCATING THE PROBLEM

There are two "pure" perspectives on the causes on injustice. One emphasizes societal conflicts of interests. The other focuses on individual missed opportunities. These viewpoints differ in where they locate the source of injustice and how they conceptualize responses to the injustice. In the first

LOUISE H. KIDDER · Department of Psychology, Temple University, Philadelphia, Pennsylvania 19122.   MICHELLE FINE · Graduate School of Education, University of Pennsylvania, Philadelphia, Pennsylvania 19104.

instance, injustice is recognized as endemic to societal *conflicts of interests.* As in trade unions, the interests of workers and those of management are assumed to be in conflict. Management's privilege over workers is viewed as illegitimate and leads workers to unite to demand their rights.

People who endorse a conflict-of-interest perspective locate the cause of injustice in competitive structures rather than individual flaws and defend their analysis with evidence of material conflict, hegemony, and power differentials (Apfelbaum, 1979; Giroux, 1984; Rappaport, 1981; Riegel, 1976). Reformist social programs are viewed skeptically from this perspective because they deny the fact that existing social arrangements insure unequal opportunities and outcomes (cf. Bowles & Gintis, 1976; Ryan, 1981).

The second belief system, as embodied in many social programs, locates the root of injustice in *individual deficits* and *missed opportunities.* Job skills programs, for example, organized around the assumption that "if only this individual had the appropriate job skills, she would find employment" promote the ideology that unemployment problems derive from individual inadequacies.

A focus on missed opportunities characterized the "Progressive" period of the 1900s through the 1920s and emerged again in the 1960s. Attentive to the needs of "disadvantaged" groups, Progressives believed that once remedial programs compensated for missed opportunities, disadvantaged people could compete fairly for social and economic outcomes (Rothman, 1978), Committed to equal opportunities but not to equal outcomes (Ryan, 1981), Progressives presupposed no permanent opposition between social classes in U.S. society.

What concerns us in this chapter is how social scientists' framing of injustice—in terms of conflict of interests or missed opportunities—affects public perceptions of social injustice and the politics of social action.

DEFINING SOLUTIONS

These two perspectives, or diagnoses of social injustice, imply distinct solutions. From the conflict-of-interests view, in order to create social change, individuals must collectively wage a fight. A *group* questions the legitimacy of power differentials, acknowledges adversarial relationships and mobilizes toward collective social change. The system of suppport is lateral and reciprocal, not top to bottom. Trained professionals or experts have a limited role in waging this struggle.

From the missed opportunities view, "clients" must receive help from "experts" who have more power and legitimate authority. Trained professionals define the needs of their clients and often determine how these needs will be met. Unquestioned are the structural arrrangements that sustain power differentials between helpers and recipients.

We contrast the conflict-of-interests and missed opportunities perspectives in terms of level of analysis, systems of supports available, and prescribed strategies for change.

Level of Analysis: Collective versus Individual

Compensatory social programs exemplify the model of missed opportunities because the unit of analysis is the individual. A person considered "truly needy" or "deserving" receives assistance and once rehabilitated is expected to function autonomously. Underlying these programs is the assumption that the problem is individualistic and anomalous; helping the individual will resolve the problem (Piven & Cloward, 1982).

Consider as an example, the problems experienced by battered women. Many social programs promote individual or couple-based explanations for violence, for example, mental illness and prescribe individual or couple-based counseling. Many abused women have internalized this analysis, often thinking of themselves as guilty rather than wronged. They privatize and individualize what they (and others) consider a personal condition.

But women frequently leave available shelters after a short, subsidized stay and return to their men—because they cannot establish economic, social, and psychological well-being in 14 to 30 days. These women often blame themselves for violence they were incapable of avoiding (Frieze, 1979; Walker, 1979). Individual-level interventions may tend to further the idea that abuse is a personal rather than a social problem because solutions offered are aimed at the person experiencing the difficulty.

In contrast to a missed opportunities perspective, activist Susan Schechter (1982) presents a conflict-of-interests perspective to explain male violence against women. She argues that domestic violence against women reflects and reinforces patriarchal social structures and that social interventions must redress those economic and social arrangements that keep women dependent on men. Social programs that reflect such a perspective aim to undo self-blame and focus on structural and psychological conditions that maintain male violence against women. These programs help battered women recognize the social roots of domestic violence and facilitate their connections with other battered women. What was once considered a secret and personal problem of an individual woman becomes reframed in terms of gender and class-based power relations (Schechter, 1982).

More consistent with this analysis than most U. S.-based social programs are the collective actions initiated by the Igbo women of Nigeria to defend an abused woman. Igbo women form associations (*mitkin*) of farmers and sell their produce at market. Collectively, they defend their members against unruly behavior of boys in the market place and unkind or abusive behavior of husbands at home. A group of women "make war" on any man who abuses his wife. They gather outside his house and sing scurrilous songs to shame him. Group demonstrations remove the burden of blame from the individual woman and offer collective, public solutions (cf. Kidder, Fagan, & Cohn, 1981).

Grass roots political groups, including disabled veterans, lesbian mothers, neighborhood associations, and labor unions focus on conflicts of interests and use collective action to find solutions. The groups identify social structures that deny them their rights and fulfillment of their needs. They seek a reallocation of resources to make the system more equitable and to suit the needs of all involved. The assumption is that individuals' needs reflect a faulty system—not a flawed individual.

But merely belonging to an oppressed group does not insure individual consciousness of inequity or a willingness to fight (Crosby, 1982). In most contemporary Western societies, children and adults develop beliefs in a meritocracy (Ryan, 1981). In schools and beyond, people are taught that individual outcomes derive from personal efforts. Social inequities, we learn, stem from inadequate motivation or ability. It is no surprise that in contemporary American culture most individuals see victims as responsible for their own misfortune (Lerner, 1970). And victims often see themselves as alone in their misery, if not responsible. Victim-blaming ideologies make it difficult to generate collective consciousness.

So what role do social scientists play in promoting one or another perspective? Historically, psychologists have nurtured the missed opportunities analysis of social problems, generating explanations that deemphasize the social and focus on individual dimensions of problems. Much of psychological research has torn human behavior from historical and social contexts through individualistic explanations, for example, women's "masochism" (Caplan, 1984), black children's "slowness" (Mercer, 1973), working class children's "inability to delay gratification" (Bowles & Gintis, 1976), and low-power individuals' "external locus of control" (Caplan & Nelson, 1973; Furby, 1979). Social problems appear individual in origin, advancing the belief that change must occur in individuals rather than in the social arrangements that shape the relations between people. We will argue later that social scientific analyses that illuminate the relationship of structural and social arrangements to individual experiences must neither deny the agency of the individual nor tear human experience from its social context.

System of Supports: Self-Help versus Reliance on Trained Professionals

In the conflict-of-interests analysis, peers define the problems and generate the solutions. Affected individuals turn to each other for support and action, although they may identify experts or organizers to deliver particular aspects of help. Collectively responsible for diagnosing their problems, they identify their own needs and solutions, enlisting experts as provocateurs, celebrities, technicians, resources and media draws.

To illustrate, organizers from the Metropolitan Council on Housing in New York City have as their policy a committment to training tenants in the skills of maintaining the building, collecting rents, and placing them in escrow until landlords produce adequate building renovations or tenants take over ownership of the building themselves. The organizers have a clear and finite role—to transfer skills to tenants, to offer necessary resources, and to leave once expertise has been transferred but to remain available for technical assistance (Surrey, 1984).

Self-help, as advanced by the conflict-of-interests view, need not reject all outside assistance and need not always involve a local reference group. The collective may exist only in the actor's consciousness. Analyzing injustice as a collective problem enables people to fight for outcomes they will control rather than to ask for help controlled by authorities. What Rappaport calls *empowerment* (1981) occurs when a worker who uses a wheelchair perceives that her building lacks ramps or elevators and that she deserves access. The situation is defined as a denial of rights, not a personal deficit. She initiates a fight for access rather than a request for an attendant to carry her upstairs. She fights on behalf of a group, including future disabled workers, even if she takes up the fight alone (see also Vanderslice, Cherry, Cochran, & Dean, 1984).

In contrast, receiving help that is defined, controlled, and delivered by trained professionals conforms to the view that injustice derives from a missed opportunity. To make up for presumably missed opportunities, educators, therapists, and other trained professionals attempt to condense the missing lessons, resources, or opportunities into the necessary hours, week, or years to place their client on a par with peers. Given the individualism of psychological research and theorizing, and given the jobs guaranteed for psychologists when missed opportunities perspectives are operational, psychologists' committment to a missed opportunities perspective is sometimes an admission of self-interest.

Action: Waging a Fight or Requesting Help?

The conflict-of-interests perspective advocates a structural analysis, collective action, and a "fight," whereas missed opportunities theorists encourage individuals to seek help toward improving themselves. We have deliberately chosen the term *fight* because it sharply distinguishes the two diagnoses. In a chapter entitled "A Word about Words," Alinsky (1972) wrote:

> The question may legitimately be raised, why not use other words — words that mean the same but are peaceful and do not result in such negative emotional reactions. There are a number of . . . reasons for rejecting such substitution. First . . . we begin to dilute the meaning . . .we dissolve the bitterness. (p. 49)

Actors who acknowledge that they are engaged in a fight must identify the oppposition or the enemy. A willingness to question the legitmacy of existing power differentials, to identify enemies, and to fight is the sine qua non of a diagnosis of conflict of interests (Gurin, Gurin, Lao, & Beattie, 1969).

On the other hand, to receive help or compensation for missed opportunities requires that one seek assistance or resources from those in power. The task is not to identify enemies, to confront them, or to generate collective consciousness. One need not think of oneself as having been wronged, but rather passed by or neglected. And one need not identify with other victims, many of whom seem worse off than oneself.

In dichotomizing fighting and receiving help, perhaps we overstate these as exclusive strategies. Some of the most important struggles against social injustice have involved dialectical analyses that demand *help* through a *fight*— ramps for disabled employees, paid child care leave for workers, or food stamp benefits for the unemployed. Individuals and groups can fight to have their human needs recognized as legitimate and not neglected. *Fighting* to get *help* should not be viewed as an inherent contradiction (Petchesky, 1984).

Yet fighting and asking for help represent fundamentally different postures toward social change. Unlike requests for help that are often experienced as passive (Wills, 1982), fights are undeniably active, acknowledging conflict. Receiving help involves acknowledging helpers, not necessarily mistreatment. Receiving help requires being protected by those in power. Fighters do not expect to be protected by those in power.

Again we ask, how have social scientists promoted one action or the other? Social scientists who study individualistic help-seeking strategies and cooperative conflict resolution rarely acknowledge the material bases of conflict or the need for a fight (see Apfelbaum, 1979). Often miscommunication or lack of assertiveness is offered to explain problematic social interactions. But others have begun to study the conditions under which collective consciousness is activated and fights initiated (see Crosby, 1982; Fine, 1979, 1983, 1983–84; Gurr, 1971; Kidder, Fagan, & Cohn, 1981; Moore, 1978). This line of research has produced a complex story of consciousness raising and coalition formation.

The decision to wage a fight against injustice is not simply a function of a collective consciousness, the ability to recognize an enemy, analyze structural injustice, or the willingness to engage in self-help. In her study of working women in Newton, Massachusetts, Crosby (1982) found that many women believed that women in general were underpaid at work but did not see themselves as underpaid.

What distinguished women who felt justly paid from those who felt underpaid as women in general? Women who felt underpaid had lower salaries than those who felt adequately paid. Further, these women perceived their bosses as having "let me down," "sometimes" or "fairly often." Women who identified themselves as victims of injustice named their bosses as the opposition.

How one responds to injustice depends on one's access to resources, power, and politics. Each strategy carries with it material and psychological consequences. A fight instigated by a relatively high-prestige manager may be viewed as evidence of initiative and risk taking; the same fight instigated by a relatively low-prestige secretary may be recorded as an event of insubordination. The life conditions of individuals who most need to wage fights against social injustice are often so complex as to impede collective action. Yet many such collective actions have been mobilized (Piven & Cloward, 1982; Schechter, 1982).

It is important to understand the process by which conflict-of-interests perspectives have been activated. Alinsky proposed that community organizers identify personal enemies by name. Naming an enemy, or at least someone who has "let me down" makes it easier to identify injustice and to specify the parameters of the fight. A Chicago neighborhood called *Back of the Yards* was entitled to services from the Infant Welfare Society but was in receipt of none. A representative from the neighborhood was supposed to call the office for services. Rather than ask for help, Alinsky used this opportunity to stage a "cinch fight." With an emergency committee of residents, he entered the offices of the agency and began a tirade. He allowed the woman at the desk to say only "yes" or "no" to the group's demand for medical services.

She said "yes." Alinsky gave her no chance to explain that the group would only have had to ask for the services to have them provided. He wanted the group members to feel they had won. As they left the office, members were overheard saying "If we could get this with just the few people that we have in the organization now, just imagine what we can get when we have a big organization" (Alinsky, 1972, p. 115). Alinsky set the group on a course of action, giving them a sense that they could fight and win, even if the cinch fight was a sham victory.

Waging a fight may produce radical change but the process carries material risks for many. Adopting a missed opportunities perspective, in contrast, may produce more modest change but paradoxically help individuals cope psychologically with daily life. In a study of disabled adults, Sweidel and Fine (1983) found that the closer an individual disabled man or woman is to the nondisabled mainstream of educational and economic life, the more likely they are to endorse individualistic, meritocratic beliefs and oppose collective action. Disabled adults nearer the mainstream, although fully aware of unwanted attention, stares, patronizing attitudes, and discrimination, believed "if I try hard I will be accepted." This missed opportunities explanation may enable people who are systematically excluded from the mainstream to psychologically resist that exclusion. Launching a collective campaign against discriminatory policies may be too risky for some disabled adults — particularly given their enormous isolation from other disabled adults (Bogdan & Taylor, 1976). But relying on a missed opportunities perspective to "get through" may mean denying antidisability policies and practices that do exist.

WHOSE DIAGNOSIS PREVAILS?

Although multiple diagnoses of injustice are possible, they are not randomly advocated. People with relative power tend to promote diagnoses that hold those who are least advantaged responsible for their own circumstances (Fine, 1979, 1983–84; Rothman, 1979; Ryan, 1981). People with political power and resources are more likely to advocate missed opportunities diagnoses than are "victims" themselves, and are more likely to have the resources to propogate this perspective as "truth." Individuals who are treated most unfairly are more likely than perpetrators or beneficiaries of injustice to ascribe to a conflict of interests perspective (e.g., Deutsch, 1974; Fine, 1979, 1983).

The power differential between people who benefit from injustice and those who suffer makes it obvious why missed opportunity diagnoses prevail as most valid and objective. So, again we ask, "What is the role of social scientists in advancing conflict-of-interests perspectives on social injustice?" Social scientists have a responsibility to explain that multiple diagnoses of injustice coexist and that individuals within a system of injustice are often vested in promoting self-serving diagnoses. Social scientists must further explain how those with authority and power create the hegemonic circumstances under which their diagnoses are disseminated as most legitimate (see Lifton, 1961; Moore, 1978; Seidman, 1978). By unearthing these contradictions, social scientists can promote redefinitions of social problems and provoke social change.

Social Scientists Must Deprivatize and Deindividualize Social Injustice

Social injustices are kept private for a number of reasons. First, evidence of injustice contradicts the alleged benevolence of prevailing economic social arrangements. High unemployment rates, domestic violence, and the extreme percentages of minority adolescents who drop out of high school, to name a random set of social injustices, betray prevailing ideologies that a capitalist economy, the nuclear family, and contemporary educational institutions are inherently good for all people. Once we learn that what some call *progress* others call *oppression*, the benevolence and necessity of these structures grow more vulnerable to public criticism.

Although those who benefit from social injustice may be motivated to keep injustice private, we also find that those who have been victimized often contribute to the privatization. Perhaps embarrassed or made to feel responsible for losing a job, being abused, or failing in school, individuals most oppressed frequently collude in privatizing social injustice.

What can social scientists do about this? We would argue that social scientists have the tools to connect what seem to be idiosyncratic and "personal" stories to other presumably personal stories so that workers laid off, women abused, and students who are turned off begin to see commonalities in their experiences, recognize that they are not unique in their experience, that their problems are neither an embarrassment nor a reflection of personal inadequacy. The methods of social research can help isolated individuals connect to others and link their experiences to social and economic structures.

Understanding the relationship of "my plant closing" to an engorgement of the military budget (U.S. Bureau of Labor Statistics, 1984); recognizing that an individual man who abuses an individual woman is reenacting broader power relationships between men and women (Schechter, 1982); or acknowledging that many minority students who drop out of high school are intellectually and politically astute as well as most critical of hidden curricula in schools (Fine & Rosenberg, 1983) may force individuals and policymakers to shift their analysis of structures and arrangements as they affect individuals and groups. Although we do not wish to encourage mechanistic structural analyses that obfuscate the ways in which individuals transform social injustices, we do wish to encourage social scientists to broaden their conceptual scope to investigate the relationships of personal experiences and structural arrangements.

Social scientists have the tools and the responsibility to unearth inequities that are systematically exempted from public discourse, to give voice to individuals who are excluded from the public mainstream, and to illuminate those conflicts of interests obscured by prevailing ideologies. When previously "private" problems become visible, social scientists and activists must expose ideologies such as "they like to be treated that way" or "they must have asked for it" that justify inequitable social arrangements.

Social Scientists Can Examine Competing Perspectives on Injustice and the Differential Power Bases of Involved Advocates

As an illustration, let us note that three Haitian women, all undocumented workers, were referred to their trade union mental health service. The foreman placed each on probation for behaviors decribed as *paranoid*. Unaware of the circumstances of the other two women, each woman revealed that the foreman made sexual advances toward her, creating unbearable working conditions. The foreman's charges of paranoia located the problems within the individual women. He argued that these women needed mental health services. But union social workers argued that a conflict of interests existed and that the foreman should be sanctioned by the union. They tried to get a sexual harassment policy instituted. The union was unwilling to side with the women. Mental health services were provided. No policy on sexual harassment was instituted.

In this situation *multiple diagnoses of injustice* coexisted. The foreman promoted a missed opportunities model: if only these women received some psychological counseling they would not feel harrassed on the job. The women, joined by the social workers, accused the foreman of abusing his position of power and of misrepresenting the problem to appear as if it were wholly psychological. A conflict-of-interests diagnosis threatened to disrupt the solidarity necessary for union politics. The union representatives appropriated a missed opportunities perspective to obscure a structural injustice.

It is important to recognize that multiple perspectives coexisted in this situation, but they did not carry equal weight. Individuals with relatively more power (the union leadership and the foreman) promoted a missed opportunities perspective, whereas those with less power (the three women and the social workers) advanced a conflict-of-interests perspective. It is perhaps paradoxical that within a progressive trade union, designed to promote conflict-of-interests arguments, a very conservative diagnosis of injustice prevailed in an internal dispute.

This case signals questions about whose diagnoses prevail and when mental health practitioners are invited in to justify missed opportunities analyses. Mental health researchers and practitioners are frequently called upon to make psychological diagnoses of problems that are structural in origin. Attributing injustice to a missed opportunity required that specific services be provided to the presumed "victims." These services could be offered in isolation with few repercussions for those in charge. Compensating for missed opportunities allows people who are not victims to appear benevolent, supportive, and still retain a relative advantage. We are not saying that these women did not need counseling—they did, especially by the time they reached the social work office; we are saying that the provision of counseling should not be used to obfuscate a structural injustice.

It is important for mental health researchers and practitioners to reveal the multiple diagnoses of injustice by listening to voices of the "accused" or "referred" and acknowledging their legitimacy. If they do not, mental health workers and researchers may function as pawns in promoting victim-blaming ideologies that maintain inequitable power structures and convince dissenters that they are angry or crazy, fragile or overly sensitive.

In this situation, as in other contexts of injustice, trying to figure out who is the "victim" and who is the "victimizer" is a process focused on individuals, again deflecting away from structural arrangements. Even the terms victim and victimizer are individualistic. In this case, the women were victimized; the foreman was the "victimizer." But this foreman, although responsible for incidents of abuse and deserving to be punished, was not behaving in aberrant fashion. A sexually stratified workplace constitutes a structure that perpetuates sexual harassment of women (MacKinnon, 1979). It is as unreasonable to limit blame to this foreman as it would be to blame the women for their own victimization.

Social scientists have the tools to conduct structural analyses of injustice—without removing, in this case, responsibility from the sexually harassing foreman involved. We can document the incidence of a particular type of injustice, trace patterns of who victimizes, who is victimized, and under what conditions victimization does not occur. Social scientists can investigate when victimized individuals complain and when they silence complaints of injustice. By extracting stories from individuals directly victimized by injustice, we can generate bottom-up views of social systems (cf. Sarason, 1978).

But it would be naive to expect persons with power to welcome such conflict-of-interests analyses. Miller (1976) describes how "dominants" ignore structural conflicts, believe they represent a consensus view and focus on how well their systems work. In an overly simplified dichotomy, she maintains that "subordinates" are expected to collude in denying conflicts and act as if satisfied.

Social scientists, as "outsiders" imbued with objectivity, have a responsibility to voice social criticism, seek contradictions between the perspectives of those in power and those victimized by oppressive structures, and validate the voices of those unheard.

Social Scientists Can Transform Prevailing Diagnoses of Injustice and Encourage Social Action

The first half of the 1980s has witnessed enormous welfare and social service cutbacks, government deregulation, and an engorgement of the military budget. Individuals who may have been considered "deserving" of social services in the 1960s and 1970s have been removed from the eligibility rolls. Aid to Families with Dependent Children has been cut dramatically; CETA job-training programs have been withdrawn reducing both the numbers of jobs available to low-income persons as well as the availability of social services such as battered women's shelters, rape crisis centers, job-training programs (Stallard, Ehrenreich, & Sklar, 1983). With the present budget cuts, militarization of federal priorities, and tax shelters for the rich, 1983 witnessed a cumulative loss of $5.8 billion in household income for households earning less than $10,000 annually and a cumulative gain of $14.4 billion for households earning more than $80,000 (Stallard, 1983).

The missed opportunities programs of the 1960s were supposed to "fix" these individuals. Yet they remain poor, hungry, and undereducated. Today we hear they are no longer among the "truly needy," despite a recent government report that found that the percentage of poor people increased from 11.7% in 1979 to 15% in 1982 (Pear, 1984). Even the missed opportunities perspective slipped into a total denial of injustice within the Reagan Administration:

> What we have found . . . is one problem that we've had even in the best of times and that is the people who are sleeping on the grates, the homeless who are homeless, you might say, by choice. (President Ronald Reagan quoted by Sydney Schanberg, 1984)

How can social scientists analyze prevailing political contexts in ways that expose rather than obsure social injustices? We have already described a number of roles social scientists may assume in this struggle. Emerging as activists should be coterminus with our work. Social research can demonstrate contradictions in social experience, discrepancies between public ideologies and social practices, and the gaps in experience reported by those in high- and low-power positions. Social scientists can document and legitimate the voices of those most intimately affected by social injustice.

Let us elaborate, drawing on the writings of Foucault (1972) and, more recently, Frank (1981), a methodology by which social scientists can enrich these voices and experiences toward the development of an empowering social science. Social scientists must stop speaking for people low in social power but instead draw on phenomenology and life history to present their stories, analyses, and views on injustice. Social scientists must validate differences and plurality and abandon artificially created hierarchies and statistical models of "better" or "worse." Social theories must not be parsimonious but instead seek the complexity, contradiction, and inconsistencies that characterize social injustice (Wexler, 1982).

Social research aimed at empowerment of low-power persons respects their voices and their views (Fine, 1983–1984). Unless "victims'" diagnoses of injustice are explored, their coping strategies articulated, and their skepticism of available social programs and research appreciated, social science research on injustice will be a tool for obscuring social inequity.

Social scientists can investigate the contradictory chorus of perspectives present in any context of injustice. Psychological concepts such as *resistance* or *defenses* need to be understood from the perspective of the individual who appears to be resisting or defending (see Fine, 1983, 1983–1984). Not only must these multiple perspectives be represented, but we would further recommend that informants be asked to comment on our raw data and our manuscripts and that these comments be incorporated as data (Kidder, 1982). In this way, "making sense of injustice" through social research can involve a dialectical conversation rather than the imposition of some abstracted conception of *truth* onto the lives of others.

This strategy for validating divergent perspectives and democratizing research may, however, introduce a number of methodological and ethical problems. As Miller has indicated (1976), frequently individuals with power are disinterested in the "self-motivated" viewpoints of "victims" of injustice. Put more bluntly, getting federal money from those in power, in order to question their power, seems to be an inherent contradiction.

A further, even more knotty ethical concern may emerge with an empowering social science. As human subjects committees grow more diligent in their work, a number of research projects are being monitored such that previously exploited "victims" including battered women, incest victims, mentally retarded adults, and others are now "protected" and inaccessible to researchers. In one attempt to study mentally retarded adults' views of their social treatment, the human subjects committee required a student to survey counselors and assistants but *not the retarded adults themselves* about social stigma. Another student interested in a dissertation on victims' stories of incest has been warned that she can interview the nurses, physicians, police, social workers, and auxiliary staff involved—but not the girls. Procedures designed to minimize harassment of informants may paradoxically annul their voices. Explanations of injustice are being provided by individuals who are either peripheral to the injustice and/or invested in maintaining the prevailing explanations for the injustice. In the name of protection, the voices of "victims" are once more silenced.

For those of us who have tried to write about these voices, ethical questions continue to loom large (see Fine, 1983–1984, author's note). Having reproduced the words and perspectives of a rape survivor in a hospital emergency room, the author remains uneasy about having published this article. Was she "liberating" a voice that did not ask to be liberated.

If we are to establish research strategies that facilitate social change we must expect ethical and methodological contradictions to emerge. Numerous such contradictions exist under the prevailing conditions in which social science more often than not obscures the social and structural nature of injustice. Structural, relational, and psychological components of injustice must serve as the focus of social science research and action. Neither social scientists nor practitioners can continue to collude in obscuring the context, riddled with conflicts of interests, from which social injustices derive.

REFERENCES

Alinsky, S.D. (1972). *Rules for radicals.* New York: Random House, Vintage Books.

Apfelbaum, E. (1979). Relations of domination and movements for liberation: An analysis of power between groups. In W. Austin & S. Worchel (Eds.), *The social psychology of intergroup relations.* Monterey, CA: Brooks/Cole.

Bogdan, R. & Taylor, S. (1976, January). The judged, not the judges. *American Psychologist, 1,* 47–52.

Bowles, S. & Gintis, H. (1976). *Schooling in capitalist America.* New York: Basic Books.

Brickman, P., Rabinowitz, V., Karuza, V., Coates, D., Cohn, E., & Kidder, L. (1982). Models of helping and coping. *American Psychologist, 37,* 368–384.

Buss, A. (Ed.). (1979). *Psychology in social contest.* New York: Irvington.

Caplan, N. & Nelson, S. (1973). On being useful: The nature and consequence of psychological research on social problems. *American Psychologist, 28,* 199–211.

Caplan, P. (1984). The myth of women's masochism. *American Psychologist, 39* (*2*), 130–139.

Crosby, F. (1982). *Relative deprivation and working women.* New York: Oxford University Press.

Deutsch, M. (1974). Awakening the sense of injustice. In M. Ross & M. Lerner (Eds.), *The Quest for Justice.* Toronto: Holt, Rinehart & Winston.

Fine, M. (1979). Options to injustice: Seeing other lights. *Representative Research in Social Psychology, 10* (*3,4*), 61–76.

Fine, M. (1983). Perspectives on inequity: Voices from urban schools. In L. Bickman (Ed.), *Applied social psychology annual,* (IV). Beverly Hills, CA: Sage Publications.

Fine, M. (1983–1984). Coping with rape: Critical perspectives on consciousness. *Imagination, cognition and personality: The scientific study of consciousness, 3,* 249–267.

Fine, M. & Rosenberg, P. (1983, Summer). Dropping out of high school. The ideology of schooling and work. *Journal of Education, 165* (*3*), 257–272.

Fine, M., Surrey, D., Vanderslice, V., & Barr, D. (1983, July). *Perceptions of injustice: The paradox of options.* Paper presented at the International Society for Political Psychology in Oxford, England.

Foucault, M. (1972). Intellectuals and power. *TELOS, 16,* 103–109.

Frank, G. (1981). *Venus on wheels: The life history of a congenital amputee.* Unpublished doctoral dissertation, University of California at Los Angeles.

Frieze, I. (1979). Perceptions of battered wives. In I. Frieze, D. Bar-Tal, & J. Carroll (Eds.), *New approaches to social problems: Applications of attribution theory.* San Francisco: Jossey-Bass.

Furby, L. (1979). Individualistic bias in studies of locus of control. In A. Buss (Ed.), *Psychology in social contest.* New York: Irvington.

Giroux, H. (1984). *Theory and resistance in education.* South Hadley, MA: Bergin & Garvey Press.

Gurin, P., Gurin, G., Lao, R. & Beattie, M. (1969). Internal-external control in the motivation dynamics of Negro youth. *Journal of Social Issues, 25,* 29–53.

Gurr, T. (1971). *Why men rebel.* Princeton: Princeton University Press.

Kidder, L. (1982). Face validity from multiple perspectives. In D. Brinberg & L. Kidder (Eds.), *Forms of validity in research.* San Francisco: Jossey-Bass.

Kidder, L., Fagan, M. & Cohn, (1981). Giving and receiving: Social justice in close relationships. In M. Lerner & S. Lerner (Eds.), *The justice motive in social behavior.* New York: Plenum Press.

Lerner, M.(1970). The desire for justice and reactions to victims. In J. Macaulay & L. Berkowitz (Eds.), *Altruism and helping behavior.* New York: Academic Press.

Lifton, R. J. (1961). *Thought reform and the psychology of totalism.* New York: W.W. Norton.

MacKinon, C. (1979). *Sexual harassment of working women.* New Haven: Yale University Press.

Mercer, J. (1973). *Labeling the mentally retarded.* Berkeley, CA: University of California Press.

Miller, J. B. (1976). *Toward a new psychology of women.* Boston: Beacon Press.

Moore, B. (1978). *Injustice: The social bases of obedience and revolt.* New York: M. E. Sharpe.

Pear, R. (1984, February 23). Rise in poverty from '79 to '82 is found in U.S. *The New York Times,* p. Al.

Petchesky, R. P. (1984). *Abortion and women's choice.* New York: Longmans.

Piven, F. & Cloward, R. (1982). *The new class war.* New York: Pantheon.

Rappaport, J. (1981). In praise of paradox: A social policy of empowerment over prevention. *American Journal of Community Psychology, 9* (*1*), 1–25.

Riegel, K. (1976). The dialectics of human development. *American Psychologist, 31* (*10*), 689–700.

Rothman, D. (1978). The state as parent: Social policy in the Progressive Era. In W. Gaylin, I. Glassler, S. Marcus, & D. Rothman (Eds.), *Doing good: The limits of social benevolence.* New York: Pantheon.

Ryan, W. (1981). *Equality.* New York: Pantheon.

Sarason, S. (1978). The nature of problem solving in social action. *American Psychologist, 33,* 370–380.

Schanberg, S. (1984, February 4). Reagan's homeless. *The New York Times,* p. 23.

Schechter, S. (1982). *Women and male violence.* Boston: South End Press.

Seidman, E. (1978). Justice, values and social science: Unexamined premises. In R. Simon (Ed.), *Research in law and sociology* (I). Greenwich, CT: JAI Press.

Stallard, K., Ehrenreich, B. & Sklar, H. (1983). *Poverty in the American dream: Women and children first.* Boston: South End Press.

Surrey, D. (1984). Communities take control: Rent strikers and squatters' rights. Paper presented at the Society for Applied Anthropology, Toronto.

Sweidel, G. & Fine, M. (1983). *Disability, discrimination and politics: Coping along the mainstream.* Unpublished manuscript, University of Pennsylvania Graduate School of Education.

Vanderslice, V., with Cherry, F., Cochran, M. & Dean, C. (1984). *Communication for empowerment: A facilitator's manual of empowering teaching techniques.* (Family Matters Project). Ithaca: Cornell University.

Walker, L. (1979). *The battered woman.* New York: Harper & Row.

Wexler, P. (1982). *Critical social psychology.* Boston: Routledge & Kegan Paul.

Wills, T. (Ed.). (1982). *Basic processes in helping.* New York: Academic Press.

CHAPTER 5

Women as a Social Problem
CONCEPTUAL AND PRACTICAL ISSUES IN DEFINING SOCIAL PROBLEMS

NANCY M. HENLEY

In recent years women have become increasingly visible in social issues recognized by our society. These years have seen the successive parade of the issues of sex roles, woman battering, rape, employment discrimination, sexual harassment, incest, pornography, the aged, and homeless ("shopping bag") women, followed by a succession of attempted remedies. As social scientists, we may wonder why these particular issues have been targeted for action as social problems; how particular responses to them are carried out; and why the intended solutions may not be lasting. In this chapter I wish to examine the definition and redefinition of social issues, with special attention to women's relation to them, and to women as social problems themselves. (In this discussion, although I may use the term *social problems* more often than *social issues*, I will use the terms almost interchangeably.[1])

Women have long been social problems. Like men, they have been social problems when they have deviated from society's norms, for example, as homeless women or as prostitutes. Prostitution is a prime example of deviant women as a social problem: prostitutes have been seen, in the traditional analysis, as women who deviate from societal laws and threaten the social organization, in particular that calm and smooth-functioning cog in the machine, the family. The classic response to a social problem has been made to prostitution: labeling it as such, having governmental and social science in-

---

[1] Donnelly (1981) has made a distinction between these terms, defining *social problems* as "harmful conditions rooted in the social structure" and *social issues* as conditions "real or imagined, over which there is a great deal of controversy because of the purported harm" they do.

NANCY M. HENLEY • Department of Psychology, University of California at Los Angeles, Los Angeles, California 90024.

vestigations of it, setting policy concerned with it, and implementing the
policy, typically in the form of legal restrictions and arrests. This classic
treatment has been so successful that it has been used repeatedly in the case
of prostitution: there are raids on prostitutes every few months in most large
cities.

Women are social problems not only as deviates; they have also been a
social problem, or part of one, when they adhere rather strictly to societal
norms. For example, in recent years women following traditional sex roles
have themselves been seen as a social problem, with the identification of
"housewife's syndrome" and "the problem without a name" (Friedan, 1963).

Women have been seen as social problems when they do not contribute
to the economy, that is, in exchange-value rather than in use-value production
— for example, as welfare mothers. On the other hand, when women have
entered the workforce to become part of this economy they have constituted
a social problem as "working mothers" who neglect their children.[2] As wom-
en's entry into the workplace has received renewed attention in recent years,
their role in the economy as well as the sexual discrimination and sexual
harrassment to be found in the workplace have become social issues.

Women are often connected to social problems as victims: of battering,
of rape, of incest, of sterilization abuse. Yet even as victims they are, in the
manner made so clear by Ryan (1971), blamed for the social problem: they
are said pathologically to seek out batterers or refuse to leave them, or to
incite battering; they provoke or, in the idiom of a newer generation of social
scientist blamemongers, "precipitate" rape, even as children;[3] they invite sterilization by having more babies than the state thinks they can care for, or
having them while not in a state-sanctioned relationship with a male. Thus,
when women are linked to social problems as victims, they may be defined
to be social problems as deviates. Furthermore, Fine writes,

> Often definitions of social problems, e.g., by social agencies, are not only indivi-
> dualized, but deproblematized and desocialized. The problem and solution are
> seen as inherent in the individual women and unrelated to power structures, social
> class, gender, etc. (M. Fine, personal communication, November 22, 1983)

Women are part of social problems even when not overtly identified or
recognized as such — problems of the poor and the elderly, for example, are
problems of women, who predominate in the ranks of the poor and the aged.
And women are, of course, half of racial and ethnic minorities and half the
working class, on all of whom many social burdens fall. But particularly,

---

[2] Bernard had to argue in 1957 for women (somewhat defensively): "It is not a generation of
willful, headstrong, egocentric ambitious women who have changed the family and, more
specifically, the quality of mothering which women give, but a style of living which has made
19th century mothering impossible" (p. 377).

[3] A Wisconsin judge in 1982 gave a 24-year-old rapist of a 5-year-old girl a 90-day sentence in
a work-release program, describing the victim as an "unusually sexually promiscuous young
lady" ("Judge Faces Recall," 1983).

women bear the brunt of many problems that do not fall solely or directly on them, and in so doing become themselves solutions to social problems. An Italian activist, Giuliana Pompei (1978), has written compellingly of the effects of economic distress on traditional women:

> Prices rise and women face the first consequences: sick people are inadequately cared for and women work to make up for the shortage of medical facilities. Neighborhoods turn into unlivable ghettos and only women's work can make them bearable. Only women can absorb the lack of schools, shops, green spaces and services in general without rebelling. Only they can mediate between society and members of the family to see that the men don't dismantle the factories and burn up the neighborhoods, to see that the old just grumble and don't go mad, that children don't end up institutionalized and that starvation wages go on feeding the family. (pp. 196–197)

In this passage, Pompei suggests another dimension of women's relation to social problems: they cool them out, serving as buffer so that real social problems are not addressed, enabling an exploitative social organization to continue just that much longer. No matter what women have done, they have been, it seems, social problems.

The other side to this function of women helping the society "run" smoothly is their involvement in social problems as activists: women have been notorious reformers and humanitarians, in the fights against child exploitation, for Negro suffrage and black civil rights, for temperance, for social welfare, in the settlement house movement, for woman suffrage and women's liberation, and so on.

Women have been intimately tied to social problems, probably to a greater extent than men—as perpetrators and as elicitors, as victims and as copers, as activists. Yet they have not been largely involved as social scientists, at least from the printed evidence; they are underrepresented as authors of books and articles on social issues.[4]

[4] Of 699 card catalog entries on the topic of "Social Problem" in UCLA's Research Library, only 6% were written by women: few of the entries on "Social Problems" in *Sociological Abstracts* are authored by women; in a sample of articles printed by the *Journal of Social Issues* (JSI) in its 36-year history to 1980 (McGrath & Karr, 1980a) only 16% were by women; and only 15% of issue editors in those years (McGrath & Karr, 1980b) were women.

From the card catalog count, 108 entries were excluded as having authors whose sex could not be determined. Figures for authorship and editorship in JSI were obtained from McGrath and Karr (1980a): a full count was made of editors, but for authors a sample was taken of 362 names, all those from every fifth page of the 105 1/2-page index.

For editors, all editors (including those of "Selected Articles" issues) were counted when there was multiple editorship; supplements were counted. There was a total of 228 issue editors over the 36 years, of whom 8 were of undetermined sex; 32 were women, 188 were men. Half of the women editors appeared in the last 10 years, half in the preceding 26.

For authors, all authors of multiple-author articles were counted, with no differentiation between first and subsequent authors. Issue introductions were counted as articles. The article was the unit of analysis, so that authors who had more than one article were counted each time they appeared in the index. Of 337 entries for which author sex was determined (it could not be for 25), 54, or 16.0%, were women.

But women social scientists have, in fact, worked with women's groups to open rape hotlines, battered women's shelters, and women's health clinics; it is largely they who have written a new literature on woman battering, sexual harassment, rape, and incest. But it does seem they have worked more on specific issues than with the abstraction social issues, and may have contributed more direct care than "primary prevention" of social problems, that is, prevention through systemic analysis. Feminist theory may be seen as systemic analysis, but it is seldom cited as part of the social problems literature. Thus, despite women's intimate connection to social problems, they remain visble mainly as problems themselves, not as students of problems.

DEFINING SOCIAL PROBLEMS

Following the parade of "women's issues" cited at the beginning of this chapter have been such remedies as governmental commissions on the status of women, shelters for battered women, rape hotlines and crisis centers, educative measures to combat discrimination and sexual harassment through legal means, public education and increased attention by social workers and legal authorities to incest, governmental commissions and grass roots education around pornography, and as-yet-evolving remedies to problems of aging and homeless women. Each issue is treated as an independent issue, as funds drain from one area into the next year's hot topic—greatly shaping the nature of research, even shaping careers.

The rapid succession of problems has been remarked upon. A social problem has its own life cycle: its birth is attended by investigative bodies —grass roots, professional, governmental; its childhood is marked by research grants and task forces; its maturity by implementation grants, special issues of journals and books, the founding of agencies, hotlines, clinics, sometimes even federal departments and cabinet-level posts. Its aging is accompanied, or precipitated, by the drying up of vital juices—of funds and official interest, of publication outlets; its death, like so many, is generally unnoticed. But is this death a natural death? Why the short life of a social problem? Does it go away when we stop thinking about it? What is, so to speak, the half-life of a social problem?

Why do some problems get major attention and others not? Unassertiveness among women is an example of an issue that has received grass roots, but not official, attention as a social problem: this attention has produced articles and books on assertiveness, training groups and workshops sponsored by activist and professional groups, but no official commissions or agencies. Issues of reproductive freedom—sterilization abuse, the right to abortion— have also received clear definition as a social problem by informal bodies and legislative and judicial attention but not official "social problem" recognition by governmental agencies. Who defines what is and what is not a social problem? How does a social problem get recognized?

It is clear that agencies of federal, state, and local government have the power to label or create social problems, and so do the media, to an extent, mostly by creating the necessity for a governmental response. Social scientists, too, name social problems when they study them and write about them. But how much do we get to name the problems, and how much do we simply accept the problems others have defined (see Seidman, Chapter 14, this volume)? How is it, for example, that we come to write of women selling sexual services as the problem of prostitution rather than as a problem of women's employment (L. Kidder, personal communication, October 1983)?

Within psychology, the Society for the Psychological Study of Social Issues (SPSSI) has been the center for discussion of this question. A SPSSI task force co-chaired by Clara Mayo and Harry Triandis was formed in 1979 on the topic *What Is a Social Issue?* Questions that arose in that task force were (a) what social processes transform a "topic" into an "issue" and (b) how do changes in social issues manifest themselves both within the larger society and within SPSSI? There is also the perennial question of the social scientist's relation to social issues: should study or advocacy be the stance? Ought SPSSI's involvement to be proactive or reactive?

One way to examine how a "topic" becomes a "social issue" is to find out what topics have been identified as such. Joseph McGrath's (1980b) paper "What are the Social Issues?" in the *Journal of Social Issues* is a good source for this purpose. McGrath identified the "three P's"—prejudice, poverty, and peace (broadly interpreted)—as the main themes of the journal over its 36 years of publishing up to 1980. Certainly, recognition by being a theme of a JSI issue is one indicator of being a social issue.

We could examine other places where recognition is conferred for similar a-social-problem-is-whatever-gets-treated-like-a-social-problem definitions; what issues engender task forces of professional associations, for example, or what issues create new professional association divisions or boards. Breaking outside of psychology, we could look at topics of other publications or of such television programs as "60 Minutes," at documentary films, governmental commissions and boards, and so on.

But, apart from which issues we recognize and how we recognize them, what is a social issue or social problem? Books on social problems typically state that no adequate definition of social problems exists (Hastings, 1979, p. 150; Spector & Kitsuse, 1977, p.1) But there are at least several aspects of a social problem that can be identified:

1. It affects some large number of people, that is, it is not an individual problem.
2. Some objective condition exists that can be pointed to.

3. Some people are aware of the objective condition and are concerned about it.

When does a condition reach that point at which it must be recognized as a social problem? There are several common approaches to this question.

Functional

The functional approach identifies conditions that upset the presumed equilibrium of society. By this view, all activities and behaviors within a social system have a purpose in maintaining the functioning of that system, whether the actors and behavers realize it or not; when there is dysfunction in the system, it is felt by the members, and the cause of the dysfunction is identified and remedies are sought.

A functionalist analysis requires, among other things, a belief in a society theoretically in equilibrium. This is a widespread implicit assumption in much of our thinking on social problems, and it is a questionable assumption at best. Has there ever really been the smooth-functioning social order this model posits, or is this not a dangerous fiction (Fuller, 1938)? Is the traditional family the haven of calm and cornerstone of societal equilibrium it is made out to be, or is it perhaps always challenged and in flux? Is prostitution a threat to the family and to society, or is it just another part of the same unified system? As Richard Fuller said in 1938, "when and where do we sociologists find this nice equilibrium of forces [social organization] from which we are supposed to be slipping into a morass of confusion [social disorganization]?" (pp. 433–434)

Normative

The normative approach, contrasted with the functionalist, emphasizes not the disorganization or dysfunction of society as the criterion for recognition of a social problem, but deviation from cherished social norms held by large numbers of people. The normative analysis must identify those people whose norms are violated and show their upset with this violation. But because social scientists' own definitions of social problems may agree or be at odds with those of the members of a group, the norm keepers and their perceptions are not always readily identifiable. Spector and Kitsuse (1977) wryly suggest that sociologists' definitions unwittingly reflect this perceptual agreement or conflict: when there is agreement the situation may be identified as the "normal" social condition (no problem) or as a "manifest" social problem (problem); when there is disagreement the situation may be labeled a *spurious* social problem (sociologists think there is no problem; members think there is) or a "latent" social problem (sociologists think there is a problem; members do not). This possibility of conflict in perceptions points to the objective and subjective sides of social problems—what has been referred to as the problem's ability to either harm or worry a large number of people. These two aspects account for two distinct and prominent definitions and approaches to the study of social problems.

Objective

The objective analysis is older and more traditional than the subjective. According to this analysis, a social problem is defined when the objective conditions just cannot be ignored — when the number of rapes or batterings, or of prostitutes or of welfare mothers, simply thrusts itself in our faces. It assumes that the number at time A was not so great as to justify recognition as a social problem, but that at time B it was (and, of course, assumes that such numbers are obtainable and "true").

Subjective

The more recent perspective has been the addition of the subjective perception of the problem to the definition process, with the observation that by any objective criteria social problems exist; yet without subjective perception of them as such they do not "become" social problems, with the concomitant public response. The subjective analysis is of particular interest to psychology because it involves our realm of interest — how people perceive social issues, how they think about them, rather than the citing of numbers and their history that document the problem.[5]

By the subjective analysis, it is the shifting of definitions, for example, of what constitutes rape, that creates recognition of the social problem as well as shifting perceptions of the causes of rape: not so much provocative behavior by females as the socialization of males to violence; a climate of violence, the allocation of certain spaces within the community and certain times of day to males, with the right to defend them violently; and ideology of females as possessions and objects of struggle between males. And there are perceptions of what the problem is — not just the act of rape, but the treatment by police, the courts, the laws, by society, of the victim of rape.

Another example of this perceptual shifting, occurring within psychiatry, and by extension, or contagion, within psychology, is the rescinding of the definition of *homosexuality* as a category of mental illness and redefining it as one possible, but not mandatory, source of "disturbance," announced by the American Psychiatric Association in 1972.

---

[5] Spector & Kitsuse (1977) state that the subjective approach also "logically provides the subject matter for a sociology of social problems" (p.5).

These two examples show redefinition at two different levels, informal (or grassroots) and formal. When we consider the lives of all the gay men and lesbians who suffered because of that older formal definition (not to suggest that we are totally free of that definition today), and the difference in psychiatric care that people might receive — for example, involuntary institutionalization or not — on the basis of this shift in formal definition, we have some idea of the life chances that hang on definitional whim.

Value Conflict

A more recent perspective on defining social problems has been the value–conflict approach. Value-conflict theorists have focused on the definitions of social problems made by members of a society and on the distinction between objective conditions and those definitions:

> Social problems are definitions constructed by members of a society, and . . . these constructions are expressions of value judgments. . . . The causes of the condition, or variations in the condition, are entirely different from the causes of the definition or variations in the definition. (Spector & Kitsuse, 1977, p.43)

Thus, conditions may remain the same but be labeled at one time as, for example, the presence of women disrupting the workplace, and at another time, as sexual harassment.

According to the value conflict position, different groups that are in contact hold different cherished values or interests and engage in activities that defend or enhance these values, such as labeling groups with different values from their own as social problems (Hastings, 1979, pp. 134–139).

McGrath (1980a) took a value conflict approach when he wrote of the emerging form of social issues as a basic opposition of two or more "valid" principles (e.g., equality vs. equity; opportunity vs. entitlement; privilege vs. right). I am not sure the opposing principles always have equally valid claims, however; and I am not sure the opposition is basic. I would ask what puts the principles in opposition: why is it that we face now, for example, in the issue of pornography versus censorship, an agonizing confrontation of the principles of free speech, on the other hand, and freedom from defamation, degradation, and exploitation, on the other? [6] Are these principles naturally in opposition, or is it that the confrontation is artificially constructed and exploited?

I can imagine a society in which my freedom of speech was seen to be part and parcel of my freedom from defamation, and in which the debate was not around some supposed opposition of rights but around how rights entail responsibilities; not about how we will only keep our freedom of speech

---

[6] My definition of the principles in conflict here differs from that of McGrath, who wrote of freedom of speech versus protection from exposure to noxious stimulation.

by allowing others to lie in ways that may lead to harm but about how we will only keep our freedom of speech if we recognize and meet the responsibilities that come with those rights.[7]

The introduction of values into the discussion of social problems makes explicit, too, the values that are inherent in describing so-called "objective conditions." Much of critical psychology of recent years has been devoted to exposing these values — for example, the values underlying judgments of mental illness in women who do not conform to societal stereotypes, or the values of white society imposed on black families with different values in the area of family. This approach exposes the naming of social problems as a result of intergroup conflict. Because the definition of a social problem is an important determinant of governmental actions, it is no wonder that intergroup conflict takes place over such definition.

Claims-Making

We have moved from objective to subjective to value-conflict approaches to the definition of social problems, rounding up these beasts, social problems, ever deeper and deeper into psychology's corral. There is one more approach I wish to describe, put forward by Spector and Kitsuse, sociologists, in their book *Constructing Social Problems* (1977). This approach may, I think, finally harness the animals.

According to Spector and Kitsuse, the thrust of attempts to reformulate the sociology of social problems in the past 50 years has been to shift the focus of analysis from the causes of presumed objective social conditions to the processes by which members of a society define certain conditions as social problems.

These authors propose a definition of social problems not as conditions, or definitions of conditions, but as activities, *claims-making* activities: "*the activities of individuals or groups making assertions of grievances and claims with respect to some putative conditions*" (p. 75). According to this definition, values are not to be studied as "causes" of social problems, but are simply one of the resources that members use in their efforts to define conditions as social problems; they are part of the phenomena to be described and explained, along with such concepts as motives and interests. According to this definition, objective conditions do not help explain the subjective elements of social problems, that is, definitions of them; rather than look at changes in objective

---

[7] This is, in fact, a small side argument one hears in reference to freedom of speech, that it does not extend to include freedom to yell "Fire!" in a crowded theater, but rather that it entails the responsibility to use speech so as not to harm others in that way. Why the same concern is not shown for harm to people that may come from verbal and visual incitement to such harm must be laid, I suggest, at the door of a society's choice of how to address social issues— and is a fine example of this question of subjective definition.

conditions to explain the identification of something as a social problem, we should look at the claims-making activities of people and groups, and examine the origins of the claims-making activities.

THE NATURAL HISTORY OF A SOCIAL PROBLEM

These activities take place over time; I raised the question, at the outset, of the history, or life cycle, of a social problem. Spector and Kitsuse (1977) review the natural history approach to the study of social problems, an approach that gets at the questions not only of who defines a social problem, but of who redefines it, of what happens once a problem is defined, of how a social problem gets undefined. They present the first developed model of the stages of a social problem, put forward in 1941 by Fuller and Myers to account for the activities around the "social problem" of trailer camps in Detroit in the years from 1920 to about 1939. The stages those authors identified are three: awareness, policy determination, and reform.

The model was elaborated by Bossard (1941) into 12 stages, with people working on the problem moving back and forth between Fuller and Myers's three stages; with some attention to changes within and among those who are addressing the problem.

More recently, Blumer (1971) presented a five-stage model that borrows from stages identified in collective behavior but introduces the concept of *contingencies,* that is, certain events may or may not occur that propel the social problem to a subsequent stage. Thus, there may be fixation and the "life cycle" may not be played out. Blumer's (1971, p. 301) stages are:

1. The emergence of a social problem
2. The legitimation of the problem
3. The mobilization of action with regard to the problem
4. The formation of an official plan of action
5. The transformation of the official plan in its empirical implementation

Finally, Spector and Kitsuse offer their own reformulation, building on and incorporating many of the ideas from the previous natural history formulations, but going beyond the final step of the other analyses. In their model, the first stage is *claims-making*—creating an issue by asserting its existence. The next stage is *official response*—recognition of the legitimacy of the claims-making groups, investigation and/or steps toward reform. Going beyond implementation, where other formulations typically end, Spector and Kitsuse see a third stage in which the complainants (or others) express dissatisfaction with the official response and reassert claims. Finally in Stage 4 the complainant group rejects the official agency and develops alternative, parallel, or counterinstitutions—the women's health centers and shelters, hotlines, and safe houses. In this dialectical model, then, each stage is both an outgrowth of and an opposition to the previous stage.

FURTHER ISSUES IN DEFINITION AND NATURAL HISTORY

Both Bossard's model and that of Spector and Kitsuse are admirably complex and recognize that things do not go calmly and smoothly. Spector and Kitsuse's claims-making dialectic as well as their stage dialectic makes intuitive sense: defining a social problem is a matter of negotiation.

However, these authors did not put their conceptualization forward as a finished product. Women's experience with social problem claims activities raises other questions about social problem definition that can refine and perhaps expand that model. For example:

1. It is clear that for many of the women's issues to emerge in recent years, the process is one of *redefinition* as much as, or more than, definition. Does a redefined social problem go through the same processes as a newly defined one? The claims-making activities must differ somewhat: rather than assertion of claims that a social problem does or does not exist (and to what extent, and affecting whom, etc.), there are assertions of how to name and view a problem, what the "real" problem is, what is wrong with the old definition, and so on. Revising a definition or perception of a social problem may be more difficult than identifying one in the first place. Might this affect the contingencies, and consequently the later stages?

2. Spector and Kitsuse point out that the first steps in asserting the existence of a problem (Stage 1) need not be taken only by grass roots groups, but may be taken by official groups.[8] We would certainly want to know what differences may result in the life of a problem based on that contingency. A branching stage model, which incorporates contingencies as Blumer's (1971) does, but goes beyond his and specifies alternative paths through stages depending on contingencies, may better describe such relationships.

3. Definitional drift ought to be accounted for somehow. It may occur as an effect of official response; the restraints on availability of funds, for example, manage to squeeze many causes into conceptual Procrustean beds. Definitional drift may preclude Spector and Kitsuse's third and fourth stages. Is definitional drift an inevitability?

4. We especially need to focus on the death as much as the birth of social problems. What activities occur to make math anxiety, for example, a passé issue or, in the polite euphemisms reserved for the dead, "no longer

---

[8] Another aspect of who initiates the definition of a social problem is that of "insiders" (e.g., victims) versus "outsiders." Wharton (1982) has written a paper examining the implications of a social movement—against woman battering—consisting largely of outsiders, women who have not themselves been battered.

fundable"? Does a social issue die or get killed, and if the latter, how and by whom? What happens after Stage 4 when the shelters cannot stay open? Death must surely be the final stage in any natural history.

5. However, we can examine *resuscitation* efforts — what claims activities determine whether a social issue gets "born again" or not? How does resuscitation differ from redefinition?

The claims-asserting model is especially relevant for psychology because it focuses on definition as the primary activity to study with regard to social problems, and definition is very much a psychological activity. Adding a psychological dimension to traditional sociological approaches has tremendous potential to add understanding of how individuals perceive issues, how definitions change, and under what circumstances they do. The study of the definitional process in social problems can benefit from much already accumulated psychological knowledge, but especially from that in perception, in attitudes and persuasion, in intergroup conflict, even in psycholinguistics, which would include study of definitional shift (semantic change).

THE ROLE OF THE SOCIAL SCIENTIST

I cast my vote, then, for psychology's examining social problems from this subjective, quite psychological, claims-making perspective, as a way to understand how social problems get defined and redefined, created, and dismantled. Because how a problem is defined is a prime determinant of the actions taken to resolve it, studying a definition can be a direct road to affecting action and social change. It remains to address the question, raised again and again over the years by social psychologists, of what the role of the social scientist ought to be vis-à-vis social problems.

McGrath (1980a), writing on the relation of social science to social action, saw three distinct periods in the 36 years of JSI publication:

1. Pessimism (about the world) and Pollyanna (about social science)
2. Rising doubts (about social science and about the social scientist)
3. Bitter disillusionment (about social science and about the scientist)

Not a few have seen those who study social problems as a social problem themselves (Beckman, 1972; Coon & Gagan, 1978; Wardell, Gillespie, & Leffler, 1980), and the "bitter disillusionment" McGrath writes of shows that the criticism is not only from outside social psychology (paraphrased):

> Is the study of social problems by social scientists futile or even harmful? Ought we to be advocates or objective researchers? These questions create a false dichotomy: the way we carry out our research—the problems we study, the questions we ask, the way we word our questions, the measures we use, our interpretation of results—these become a form of advocacy, whether we mean them as such or whether they are seen as such or not. If to do research is to take sides, then the question of advocacy or none melts into the old question, "which side are you on?"

Is study itself helpful? I will not offend those who are tired of hearing Lewin quoted on the practicality of theory. But study and development of theory are useful; application is not a universal, unqualified good; premature application may be no good at all. Not all issues defined as social problems should be acted on in ways their accepted definition prescribes. For example, assertiveness training was developed and broadly applied to remedy women's nonparticipation in leadership and political structures, their subordination in relationships, and so on. But as it has developed in practice, it often carries basic assumptions about defects and weaknesses in women, and has become in many ways a program to resocialize American women (Henley, 1979). Study to understand the ramifications of such a program might have been better than the massive action brought to bear, with questionable consequences (Henley, 1981).

To accept the claims-asserting definition of social problems is to believe that social problems are a matter of ideology and, essentially, manifestations of political conflict. We do not absent ourselves from usefulness when we attempt to understand these processes. As Kirscht (1976) and others have said, what social psychologists can best contribute to the study of social problems is our skill in analyzing, creating perspectives, and interpreting information. Is this ineffectual? Only if we assume publishing is the end and the only end to our efforts, if we assume that the only application of our research is through official means. We have the means to get social psychological knowledge out. For example, we can do the following.

1. For every publication in a scholarly source, we can also publish or present in a popular forum such as to grass roots groups, in the local newspaper, or to a PTA (Mayo, 1982).
2. We can write jargon-free abstracts of current social issues articles for the newsletter of a local community organization.
3. We can begin theme issues of social issues journals with an examination of the definition(s) of the social problem(s) addressed, with particular attention to the implications of different definitions.
4. We can apply social psychological ideas in innovative, outrageous, and constructive ways, as Aronson and his colleagues (Aronson, Blaney, Stephan, Sikes, & Snapp, 1978) did with the "jigsaw classroom."
5. We can involve the lay public in researching social issues, in the way that amateurs are involved in the scientific enterprise in archaeology, ornithology, and astronomy.

We have seen ways in which the study of social problems is important for the psychology of women and of gender, and that women are involved as social scientists in social problems affecting women at the local level. They can contribute much by extending their study to include the abstract level, making and testing theory based on changing understandings of these, and other, social problems. Not only women, of course, but men and women both can carry on this study.

We can study the fractionation of problems — how a single large problem with complex manifestations is broken down into seemingly unrelated issues that come on stage and are hooked off after a year of glory; the death of social problems, and under what circumstances they are kept alive; definitional drift, and how original definitions may be retained; the resuscitation of a social problem, to be studied even as it occurs. With this study we may bring some unique psychological knowledge to bear on the core activities of social problems; and more, we may apply ourselves as both active citizens and concerned psychologists to change our world into one more closely meeting the needs of the women and men who inhabit it.

ACKNOWLEDGMENTS

Conversations with (in alphabetical order) Dair Gillespie, Jacqueline Goodchilds, Marianne LaFrance, Ann Leffler, Jeffrey Rubin, and Barrie Thorne aided me immeasurably in developing these ideas. In addition, I wish to thank Jeff Rubin for invaluable suggestions for revision at a crucial point, and Michelle Fine, Louise Kidder, and the editors of this volume for thoughtful ideas for revision later. Finally, Lynda J. Fuerstnau and Mary M. Smith were most helpful in assisting with background research.

REFERENCES

Beckman, L. (1972). Psychology as a social problem; an investigation into the Society for the Psychological Study of Social Issues (SPSSI). *Rough Times 2*, (6), 10–11.

Bernard, J. (1957). *Social problems at midcentury: Role, status, and stress in a context of abundance.* New York: Dryden Press.

Blumer, H. (1971). Social problems as collective behavior. *Social Problems, 18,* 298–306.

Bossard, J. H. S. (1941). Comment. *American Sociological Review, 6,* 320–329.

Coon, M., & Gagan, R. J. (1978, September). *Social structure and personal consciousness.* Paper presented at meeting of society for the Study of Social Problems, San Francisco.

Deutscher, I. (1973). *What we say/what we do: Sentiments and acts.* Glencoe, Ill: Scott, Foresman.

Donnelly, P. G. (1981, August). *Social problems versus social issues: Towards a clarification and synthesis.* Paper presented at meeting of Society for the Study of Social Problems, Toronto.

Friedan, B. (1963). *The feminine mystique.* New York: W.W. Norton.

Fuller, R. (1938). The problem of teaching social problems. *American Journal of Sociology, 44,* 415–435.

Fuller, R., & Myers, R. (1941). The natural history of a social problem. *American Sociological Review, 6,* 320–328.

Hastings, W. M. (1979). *How to think about social problems. A primer for citizens.* New York: Oxford University Press.

Henley, N. M. (1979, August). *Assertiveness training: Making the political personal.* Paper presented at meeting of the Society for the Study of Social Problems, Boston.

Henley, N. M. (1981, December). *Women's nonverbal behavior: Underlying assumptions in the admonition to change.* Paper presented at the First International Interdisciplinary Congress on Women, Haifa, Israel.

Judge faces recall. (1983). In L. Richardson, & V. Taylor (Eds.), *Feminist frontiers: Rethinking sex, gender and society.* Reading, MA: Addison-Wesley.

Kirscht, J. P. (1976). Has SPSSI had an effect? *American Psychologist, 31,* 97–98.

McGrath, J. E. (1980a). Social Science, social action, and the *Journal of Social Issues. Journal of Social Issues, 36 (4),* 109–124.

McGrath, J. E. (1980b). What are the social issues? Timeliness and treatment of topics in the *Journal of Social Issues. Journal of Social Issues, 36 (4),* 98–108.

McGrath, J. E. & Karr, K. A. (1980a). Author and article index of the *Journal of Social Issues* Volumes 1–36 (1945–1980). *Journal of Social Issues, 36 (4),* 127–232.

McGrath, J. E. & Karr, K. A. (1980b). Issue index of the *Journal of Social Issues* Volumes 1–36 (1945–1980). *Journal of Social Issues, 36 (4),* 235–242.

Pompei, G. (1978). Wages for housework (trans. by Joan Hall). In A. M. Jaggar & P. R. Struhl, *Feminist frameworks.* New York: McGraw-Hill.

Ryan, W. (1971). *Blaming the victim.* New York: Random House.

Spector, M., & Kitsuse, J. I. (1977). *Constructing social problems.* Menlo Park, CA: Cummings Publishing.

Wardell, L., Gilespie, D. L., & Leffler, A. (1983). Science and violence against wives. In D. Finkelhor, R. J. Gelles, G. T. Hotaling, & M. A. Straus (Eds.), *The dark side of families: Current family violence research* (pp.69–84). Beverly Hills: Sage Publications.

Wharton C. (1982). *Claims-making activities of the battered women's movement: The role of outsiders.* Manuscript available from author, Department of Sociology, University of Richmond, Richmond, VA.

PART 2

Rethinking Demographic Deviance

In this part the usefulness of reevaluating our preconceptions becomes more concrete in the form of specific social problems that have been traditionally defined on the basis of demographics. Here the authors take a fresh look at black families, black women, and the elderly. Although these are but three of the categories of people who are often viewed in negative terms as a function of our demographic characteristics, like Henley's discussion of women as a social problem in the preceding part, the issues raised may be exemplary of an attitude that challenges preconceptions and can be applied to other groups who are traditionally expected to show only the negative consequences of a devalued social status. Here the overarching orientation is to ask, "What do we see if we challenge the assumption that certain demographic characteristics are necessarily related to negative outcomes, and if instead we look for positive consequences of group membership?"

Each chapter finds that certain assumptions about the negative consequences of group membership may be as much a function of stereotype and superficial analysis, or the unquestioning acceptance of conventional wisdom, as of the reality of the lives of the people under consideration. A common theme in these chapters is the observation that some of the weaknesses attributed to individuals on the basis of group membership may be both inaccurate and a mask that covers many of the strengths and positive qualities of identified "problem groups." A second theme is the suggestion to look outside as well as inside the group in order to understand and redefine the nature of the problem.

The first chapter in this section, by Diane Scott-Jones and Sharon Nelson-Le Gall, provides a reassessment of the nature of black families in the United States. They discuss the structure and the functioning of black families with regard to frequently noted differences from white families, and examine the extent, origin, and meaning of the differences. By applying a cultural-ecological model that requires consideration of family configurations and interaction patterns in context, rather than in simple comparison to a presumed standard, they demonstrate how the way in which our research is approached can change the data we find as well as the interpretation of that data, including issues of causal direction of relationships often left implicit. Indeed, the very language used in discussions of black families reveals much about our assumptions, and simply reading the language of this chapter helps to redefine social problems. This chapter refers to a wide variety of informative empirical data, historical information, and cultural interpretations that are striking in their logical contradiction of standard definitions of the black family as a social problem. Their reframed analysis has powerful implications for understanding what we already know as well as for shaping our future research questions and our future social policies.

Althea Smith's chapter suggests that the concept of *marginality* as it has been traditionally understood is one sided in its expectation of negative consequences. She examines the structural, functional, social, and psychological meaning of marginality and argues that being in a marginal social status may create as much of a potential for positive as for negative consequences. Although her approach is to use the experiences of exceptional black women, that analysis is simply a means to highlight the positives. By examining the views of successful individuals who hold marginal status, rather than limiting our analysis to the views of observers, we may be able to provide a vehicle for encouragement of others in similar social positions and are more likely to have a realistic grasp of the potential value and experienced reality of those who are traditionally assumed to be simply problematic.

The final chapter in this section, by Tracey A. Revenson, critically examines the common belief held to a substantial degree by people of all ages that the elderly are more lonely than their younger counterparts. She presents data from her own study, collected from three different geographical areas as well as a wide array of other studies to support the observation that loneliness as a necessary condition of late life is more myth than reality. Revenson goes on to suggest a variety of reasons why the myth is maintained in the face of contradictory evidence and the implications of her analysis for research and policy. Her chapter points to a variety of social processes and paradigmatic assumptions inherent in the way in which we think about aging. Her observations include: the tendency to confuse being alone with being lonely, to view aging as disease and decline, to narrowly define what is acceptable as successful adjustment in late life, to ignore social forces in favor of individual person blame, and the tendency to generalize from extremely deviant and negative examples to all members of a class. These tendencies, as noted in the introduction to this volume, are of the sort we believe to be common among those who study and seek solutions to other social problems as well.

CHAPTER 6

Defining Black Families
PAST AND PRESENT

DIANE SCOTT-JONES and SHARON NELSON-Le GALL

Many changes are occurring in the families of our society. The rates of divorce and of single parenthood have increased dramatically in recent years. Roles within families are changing as the number of women in the workforce has increased. These changes in families have occurred as our society experienced great economic difficulty. As the attention of psychologists is given to new and evolving family forms and functions, it is important to reexamine black families, which have frequently been viewed as problematic. The purpose of this chapter is to discuss the ways in which black families have been defined and conceptualized in the past and present and to suggest alternative conceptualizations.

Discussions of black families generally involve the assessment of differences between black and white families (Staples, 1978). Three basic issues arise, all of which involve disagreement and misconceptions. First is the issue of the extent of differences. Because researchers typically assess central tendencies and emphasize mean differences between groups, the overlap between groups and variability within groups tend to be ignored. The conclusion is drawn that black families are totally different from white families and are identical to one another. The notion of variability is especially important as a preface to a discussion of black families. Although they often are presented as a monolithic group, black families are characterized by diversity (H.

DIANE SCOTT-JONES • Department of Psychology, North Carolina State University, Raleigh, North Carolina 27695.   SHARON NELSON-Le GALL • Department of Psychology, University of Pittsburgh, Pittsburgh, Pennsylvania 15260.   This chapter was completed while the first author was supported by a grant from the Rockefeller Foundation.

McAdoo, 1981; Staples, 1978). The diversity among black families should be considered before generalizations are made.

A second issue is the origin of differences between black and white families. Researchers disagree on whether African culture, slavery, poverty, or some combination of the three account for the structures and functioning of black families. A third issue is the meaning of differences. Some researchers, assuming that no differences should exist between black and white families, have interpreted differences to mean that black families are deficient. Deviant family forms and functions have been blamed for many problems experienced by blacks. Conceptions of black families as deviant, however, have come under recent scrutiny.

Existing volumes (e.g., H. McAdoo, 1981) have addressed the many misconceptions about black families held by researchers, policymakers, and helping professionals. These misconceptions persist, however, and are not easily dismantled. In this chapter, we shall critically examine the myths and misinterpretations regarding black families' structure, that is the configuration of family members, and functioning, that is the patterns of interactions among family members. At the same time we will note the beneficial attributes inherent in black family structures and functions. We will argue that a cultural-ecological model (Ogbu, 1981b) is most useful in studying black families. According to this model, it is necessary to study and understand black families in context, rather than to make comparisons using white families as a standard. Finally, we look at the implications of this analysis for future research and policy regarding black families.

FAMILY STRUCTURES

Extent of Differences

A commonly accepted stereotype is that black children grow up in fatherless female-dominated homes that are pathological (Frazier, 1939; Moynihan, 1965; Sciara, 1975). Single-parent families are now increasing among blacks, but this increase reflects a current social trend occurring among majority families as well. From 1970 to 1979, the number of families maintained by females increased by 51%, whereas the total number of families increased by only 12% (Rawlings, 1980). In 1982, 46.5% of black families and 15% of white families were headed by women (Cummings, 1983). An examination of census data since 1950 indicates that single-parent families have increased at about the same rate for both blacks and whites, from 8.3% and 2.8%, respectively, in 1950, to the 1982 rates. If the current rate of increase continues, by 1990, only one-third of black children will live with both natural parents (Glick, 1979).

Although the increased divorce rate accounts for some of the households maintained by women, the 1978 divorce rates were not dramatically different for black (8.2%) and white (5.8%) women (Mills & Palumbo, 1980). More black (9.6%) than white (1.9%) women were separated without being divorced (Mills & Palumbo, 1980). These rates may appear somewhat low because they include all women over 14 years in each of the racial groups. Also contributing to the current higher percentage of single-parent families among blacks is the relatively high percentage of unmarried black teenagers who give birth. In 1980, the out-of-wedlock birth rate was 80 per 1,000 for unmarried black women, age 15 to 19 years, and 20 per 1,000 for their white counterparts (Cummings, 1983). The birth rate for unmarried black teens, although still high, has declined since 1970 and has increased for unmarried white teens during that same period of time. In addition, white teens who conceive out of wedlock are more likely than black teens to have abortions; in 1979, 41% of pregnant white teens had abortions, compared to 26% of pregnant black teens (Cummings, 1983). Although separate data for teens are not available, data from the National Center for Health Statistics indicate that 49.5% of white women who conceive out of wedlock marry before the birth of the child, compared to 11.75% of black women. Out-of-wedlock conception is more likely to result in out-of-wedlock birth for blacks than for whites.

The statistics cited previously indicate that single-parent families comprise a higher percentage of black families than of white families. The single-parent–two-parent distinction, however, does not provide an adequate framework for understanding family structure. Families often are defined as being comprised of a husband, wife, and their dependent children, that is, a nuclear family. Many families, majority and black, do not fit this model. Family structures extending beyond the nuclear family often exist in black communities (Stack, 1974). A black child may not live with his or her biological father, yet the father role may be filled by a grandfather, uncle, or other male. In addition, a black child may be a member of more than one household, living most of the time with the mother and father but also spending several nights a week or having meals with a nearby relative. Grandmothers may contribute to child rearing, especially if the mother is a teenager or is single (Stevens, 1984; Wilson, 1984). The family might be defined more appropriately as the "smallest, organized, durable network of kin and non-kin who interact daily, providing for domestic needs of children and assuring their survival" (Stack, 1974, p. 31). Defined in this manner, a family that does not fit the nuclear form is not necessarily pathological, but may in fact provide the child with a rich network of family relations.

The notion that the nuclear family is the optimal form of family organization is debatable. The extended family has been the model family structure throughout the world, both presently and historically. Extended family forms appear to be adaptive, especially in economic hard times and in dual-career families. Extended families allow for meaningful roles for elderly adult family members, who are often made to feel useless in American society. Rather than ask why black families are not nuclear, one might ask why white families are not extended.

The nuclear family arose in American society as industrialization resulted in more mobile families, in fewer family members living in the same household, and in the loss of some traditional family functions, such as education and job training (Uzoka,1979). Because it was predominant in industrial societies, the nuclear family came to be considered the optimal form. Uzoka (1979), however, argues that the degree to which families in general became functionally "nuclear" has been greatly exaggerated. Although the nuclear family unit may live in a separate household, be economically independent, and even be geographically distant from the larger family group, a functional extended family may exist because of close psychological relationships among family members from different households. Studies cited in Uzoka (1979) demonstrate regular, frequent, and voluntary interaction among extended kin, such as visits and recreational activities, telephone contacts, assistance to the elderly, care for young children, support during family celebrations such as weddings, support during family crises such as deaths or accidents, and mutual financial aid. When these close psychological relationships are considered, the nuclear family, from which the black family is judged to be deviant, may not be the prevalent functional form in the majority group.

Origin of Differences

The extent of differences between black and white families has been exaggerated; however, there remain some differences in the percentage of single-parent families, extended families, and single-parent families embedded in extended families. The origin of differences has been addressed mainly from the view of black families as fatherless, matriarchal structures. The pathology of the black family is said to stem from experiences in slavery (Frazier, 1939), when family members could be sold separately at the whim of the slavemaster. The effect of these experiences, supposedly, was to destroy the black family.

Although the enslavement of blacks is a well-known historical fact, the impact of this institution on black families may not be well understood. As Gutman (1976) has documented, even in slavery, blacks made extraordinary efforts to preserve their family ties. In spite of harsh measures used to control them, slave families often managed to maintain contact with separated family members. During slavery, the black family typically was composed of the husband, wife, their children, and some combination of grandchildren, other relatives, and nonkin (Sudarkasa, 1981). An approximately equal sex ratio among slaves permitted the development of monogamous, two-parent families (Blassingame, 1979). Female-headed households were rare in slavery, occurring in one of two situations: when the husband died or was sold, or when the woman who had children out of wedlock, often for the slavemaster, had her own cabin built (Sudarkasa, 1981). Slavemasters sold husbands and wives separately in 32.4% of slave marriages; the most important single factor in marital disruption was the high death rate (Blassingame, 1979). The slavemasters' authority, particularly regarding the sexual and physical abuse of slave women and the sale of family members, undermined the stability of slave families. Slavemasters, however, sometimes encouraged strong family ties because of religious beliefs or more often, in order to facilitate discipline (Blassingame, 1979). As suggested earlier, a distinction can be made between "family" and "household" (Mbiti, 1969; Stack, 1974; Sudarkasa, 1981; Uzoka, 1979). The slave family did not make its own decisions about its residence, and the composition of the household may have been limited by the size of the slave cabin (Sudarkasa, 1981). Because not all family members lived in the same residence, "transresidential cooperation" occurred (Sudarkasa, 1981). Visits took place among kin having different owners, with and without owners' permission (Gutman, 1976). Some men were allowed to visit their families on weekend passes, taking their clothes to be washed as well as special treats for their families.

Gutman (1976) also studied northeastern urban and southern rural black families after emancipation, up to 1925. At no point during this time were black families predominantly headed by women. Census data for Southern counties in 1870, 1880, and 1900 indicate that the percentage of black households with both spouses present was almost the same as that of white households in each year, ranging from 80% to 88% (Jones, 1985). Thus, the notion of the pathological mother-headed black family arising from slavery has largely been discredited.

Because blacks' experiences in slavery do not adequately account for their contemporary family structures, some researchers have looked to African cultures for precursors of black family structures. Few American blacks are able to trace their ancestry directly to a specific African country. Most blacks came from West Africa, however, and although cultural diversity existed there, similar cultural features among the tribes provided a common heritage for blacks who came to the United States (Nobles, 1978). In West Africa, kinship groups were strong. Extended families were the norm, with great respect shown for elderly family members (Mbiti, 1969). Many activities were communal; individuals developed strong loyalties to their tribes and an intense sense of belonging. Parents provided firm guidance for their children as the children became adults; children, however, "belonged" to the large corporate body of kinspeople (Mbiti, 1969). The household—the "family at night" (Mbiti, 1969, p. 140)—was the smallest unit of the family.

Although many features of contemporary black families are not directly traceable to West African family forms, one salient feature may be attributed to West African roots (Sudarkasa, 1981). In West African societies, consanguinal structures—family groupings based on adult siblings with their mates and offspring—were more important than conjugality—the organization of the family around the husband and wife (Mbiti, 1969). Consanguinity, according to Sudarkasa, is especially important among low-income and rural southern black families. In these family structures, marital instability is not necessarily family instability because family ties based on consanguinity remain intact. Stack (1974) provides descriptions of low-income black families, without explicitly labeling them, that fit the consanguinal structures discussed by Sudarkasa. The exchange of goods and services occurred among adult siblings and kin. Obligations to kin and to a spouse or potential spouse sometimes created conflict, with the kin relationships usually remaining more durable. Middle- and upper-class blacks, however, are more likely to have extended families that are conjugally related (Sudarkasa, 1981).

Economic conditions, both historically and presently, also play a major role in the family structures of black people. The relationship between poverty and family structure is a complicated one. Some researchers assume that black family structures cause poverty (e.g. Moynihan, 1965). The accurate causal direction, however, may be that poverty leads to some of the family forms that exist among blacks. Poverty creates stress that exacerbates the ordinary tensions in marital and family relations. Black families have exhibited resilience and flexibility in coping with impoverished conditions. Black family forms, rather than being pathological, may be partly an adaptation to, or a reflection of, conditions of poverty.

Because blacks first came to the United States involuntarily as slaves and generally were not allowed to work for their own economic advancement, their beginnings in this country were radically different from those of other immigrant groups. Vestiges of blacks' initial status in American society remain; after slavery was abolished, blacks remained in a castelike position that exists today, despite many efforts to change this situation. Lieberson (1980), comparing blacks and white immigrants since 1880, found that blacks faced more severe barriers, such as discrimination in labor unions and lowest preference for all jobs, even those requiring minimal skills. Pleck (1979) found that racial discrimination in employment prevented black migrants to Boston, in the period 1865 to 1900, from experiencing the economic advancement enjoyed by Irish immigrants. Black unemployed husbands in Boston in 1880 were more likely to leave their wives than were employed black husbands;

black husbands in menial jobs were twice as likely to leave their wives as were black husbands in more lucrative occupations. Furstenberg, Hershberg, and Modell (1978) view blacks' urban experience after slavery, characterized by economic discrimination, poverty, and disease, as a contributing factor to family structures. In their review of Philadelphia census data from 1850 to 1880, they found that most black families, like those of other ethnic groups, were headed by two parents. Female-headed households among blacks were caused mainly by the extremely high death rate for black men (life expectancy for black males in 1880, reported in Lieberson, 1980, was 22.04 years) and the difficulty widowed black women with children faced in remarrying.

Currently, disproportionate numbers of black families live in poverty; approximately 34% of black families live below the poverty level, compared to approximately 9% of white families (Cummings, 1983). For female-headed households, both black and white, the poverty rates are much higher; 57% of black and 28% of white female-headed households live below the poverty level. These statistics might suggest that a two-parent household would be most advantageous for black females; however, black two-parent families live below the poverty level at three times the rate of white two-parent families (Edelman, 1980).

A major difficulty is the extremely high unemployment rate for black males, coupled with their lower incomes when they are employed (Cummings, 1983). In 1982, only 55% of black men were employed. Because not all black men are included in these data, the percentage of employed black men is probably even lower. The median income for white men, $15,964, is approximately 1½ times that of black men, which is $10,510. Barriers to employment still exist, and are not simply the result of a lack of education. The rate of unemployment for a black high school graduate is greater than that for a white grade school dropout; the rate of unemployment for a black college graduate is twice that of whites with no college attendance (Edelman, 1980). Although the argument has been made that black unemployment and underemployment ultimately can be traced back to the family, which does not prepare children adequately for school and the world of work, the facts cited previously suggest that the high proportion of poverty among black families can be traced at least partly to discrimination—in hiring and promotion as well as earlier in the educational system. Thus, the economic difficulties of black families are interrelated with the discrimination they face. Black families experience the "consequences of the double stratification of class and racial caste" (Ogbu, 1981a, p. 144).

The relatively high rate of employment outside the home for black women may have contributed somewhat to the rate of separation, divorce, and single-parent families among blacks. Black women traditionally have worked, in spite of their being limited to low-paying service jobs and, until the 1960s, barred from even the secretarial and sales work to which white women were confined (Jones, 1985). Because they worked, black women could support themselves and their children, at least as well as men who were not employed or earned very little money. Among blacks in Boston from 1870 to 1900, wives were more likely than husbands to disrupt marriages; working wives were twice as likely as nonworking wives to leave their husbands (Pleck, 1979). During World War II, black wives' employment was thought to be associated with marital disruption (Jones, 1985). The contrasts between black and white wives' labor force participation rates in the last century are striking. In 1890, 23% of black but only 2% of white wives worked. At that time, however, comparable differences between blacks and whites in the proportions of female-headed households did not occur. Labor force participation increased, especially for whites, so that by 1970, 51% of black and 39% of white wives worked (Weiner, 1985). Currently, 60% of black and 48% of white wives work (Jones, 1985).

Financial independence, however limited it may be, may contribute to the present high divorce rate. Median incomes are approximately equal for black women ($7,802) and white women ($7,640) (Cummings, 1983). The nearly equal median incomes mask the discrimination black women experience vis-à-vis white women. Black women have more work experience, more seniority on their jobs, and work longer hours than do white women (Wallace, 1980), which should lead to higher incomes. Although women's median income is only half that of white men (Cummings, 1983; Jones, 1985), it is two-thirds that of black men. White women derive more economic benefit from marriage than do black women. Some single mothers may receive payments from welfare programs such as Aid to Families with Dependent Children. Male absence as an eligibility requirement for such programs has been related to the disproportionate rise of black female-headed households (Jones, 1985); however, the majority of black single mothers work, mainly in low-paying jobs (Wallace, 1980).

Middle-income black families also have extended forms, which may help to provide child care and financial aid as well as emotional or cultural support (H. McAdoo, 1978, 1981). McAdoo states that the economic security of middle-income blacks is tenuous because it is dependent upon the employment of wage earners. Because there is rarely wealth to be passed from one generation to the next, the cycle of upward mobility must be recreated in each generation. Support from an extended family network thus may be needed in a middle-income black family. In H. McAdoo's (1981) study of middle-income black families, the majority were the first generation of their families to have attained middle-class status. In addition, it appeared that middle-class status achieved in one generation was not necessarily maintained at the same level in succeeding generations. The middle-class families reported that reciprocal obligations to kin outside the nuclear family were not an excessive burden. This perception is in contrast to Stack's (1974) conclusion that kin obligations among low-income blacks prevented the family's economic advancement.

Economic necessity, and a long-standing tradition of extended family contact, shape the family forms among blacks. The resulting forms are adaptive and are not indicative of a pathological inability to maintain a nuclear household. Currently, difficult economic conditions plague not only black families but majority families as well. As a result, majority families are returning to housing arrangements involving extended families. According to Thornton (1981, p. 56), economists have stated that "a prolonged period of low housing starts will bring the extended family back into being." It is important to note that the extended family forms now appearing among majority families are perceived to result from economic conditions, whereas extended family forms among blacks have been taken as evidence of internal pathology.

Meaning of Differences

The meaning attached to differences said to exist between black and white families typically has been that black families are deficient. The lack of assimilation of blacks into American society has then been attributed, not to institutional barriers, but to deviant family structures (Moynihan, 1965). To understand the relationship between black family structures and the lack of assimilation of blacks, however, it must be acknowledged that American society has not been a "melting pot." The blending of diverse cultures into a new, distinctly American entity has not occurred. Rather, groups that have assimilated were required to fit into the dominant Anglo-Saxon cultural pattern. Some immigrant groups changed their names, religious beliefs, cultural traditions, and language usage in order to be accepted as "Americans" (Lieberson, 1980). Black Americans were barred from the process of assimilation. Many mechanisms that fostered successful assimilation were effectively closed to blacks: voter registration, participation in trade unions, access to adequate housing and schools, and the use of public facilities were among the many civil rights systematically denied. Blacks are unique among the ethnic groups in American society in that many of the barriers facing them were institutional—racial segregation was once the law of the land. Even when laws were changed in positive ways, implementation of laws and changes in attitudes of the majority were not immediate outcomes.

Much attention has been given in the recent past to understanding the relationships among racial and ethnic groups in our society. The distinctive characteristics of black families have been variously described as "culturally deficient" or "culturally different." Notions of cultural deficiencies have been largely discounted; at least lip service is given to the idea that families can be different without necessarily being deficient. In practice, however, the distinction between "deficit" and "difference" models fades (Valentine, 1971). The labeling of a group as *different* is not necessarily a neutral act; it may entail either a positive or negative evaluation. Thus, cultural differences, when they are not appreciated, may have the effect of precluding positive interactions with mainstream institutions and individuals, so that the end result is the same as that predicted by the cultural deficit model.

Rather than being described as culturally *deficient* or *different,* blacks might be viewed more appropriately as *bicultural* (Valentine, 1971). Black family members are socialized into a black culture but at an early age are also exposed to the mainstream culture. The "black culture" in which black families live has variation; one would expect to find differences according to socioeconomic status, geographic area, and rural or urban community setting. Ogbu (1981b) describes a cultural-ecological model for studying and interpreting child rearing in black families in relation to their own culture, rather than in relation to the standards of other cultures. Understanding blacks in their own culture is viewed as a necessary first step to the understanding of blacks vis-à-vis other cultural groups. In Ogbu's model, it is not family structures that lead to family socialization practices. The adult cultural tasks, especially that of earning a living, and the opportunity structure available to adults determine the manner in which characteristic family processes develop.

FAMILY FUNCTIONS

Extent of Differences

Black family structures developed as adaptive responses to economic, social, and psychological demands. Black families have been similarly innovative in performing family functions. Most notable is the development of a greater degree of egalitarianism in black than in white families. The most common authority pattern among contemporary black families, both middle- and low-income blacks, is egalitarianism (Billingsley, 1968; McAdoo, 1978; Willie, 1981). Scanzoni (1977) found that equality in conflict resolution occurred more frequently for black than for white husbands and wives. Both black husbands and wives ascribed more power to the wife in their marital relationships than did whites.

Although past assessments of black families judged the mother's role too strong and the father's role too weak (e.g., Moynihan, 1965), majority families now aim for the similarity and flexibility of roles that have long existed between black spouses. Underlying past assessments of the black family was the idea that men should be dominant. This point of view is expressed clearly in Moynihan's (1965, p. 29) analysis of black families:

There is, presumably, no special reason why a society in which males are dominant in family relationships is to be preferred to a matriarchal arrangement. However, it is clearly a disadvantage for a minority group to be operating on one principle, while the great majority of the population, and the one with the most advantages to begin with, is operating on another. This is the present situation of the Negro. Ours is a society which presumes male leadership in private and public affairs. The arrangements of society facilitate such leadership and reward it. A subculture, such as that of the Negro American, in which this is not the pattern, is placed at a distinct disadvantage.

Because of the white women's movement, egalitarian modes of family functioning once judged to be pathological in blacks are now recognized as highly desirable strategies for coping with present social and economic conditions. Black families are not egalitarian in an absolute sense; a discordant counterpoint to the theme of egalitarianism is the existence of sexist attitudes and behaviors in black men (see Hull, Scott, & Smith, 1982; Smith & Stewart, 1983). Some black families have imitated the role distinctions of whites (Jones, 1985) but their relative egalitarianism is particularly salient, considering the subordinate role white women generally have played in relation to white men in their families. Scanzoni (1977, p. 339) states that because of female economic aspirations, "the long-term trend for whites is likely to be convergence with the gender-role egalitarianism of blacks."

Past research has ignored the role of the black father in family functioning and has focused more on the effects of father absence. The role of fathers, black or white, has only recently begun to receive serious attention (Lamb, 1981). White fathers, however, have been omitted from research in the past because of assumptions about the primacy of mother–child interactions. Black fathers, on the other hand, have been omitted because they were assumed to be absent or ineffectual (Harrison, 1981). Past conceptualizations of the father's role, based on white middle- and upper-class families, emphasized the instrumental or provider role, with the expressive role viewed as the province of the mother (Parsons & Bales, 1955).

This division of roles has not been as strong among blacks. Scanzoni (1977) found that both black husbands and wives perceived themselves as more task oriented or instrumental than white husbands and wives perceived themselves and, simultaneously, as more person oriented or expressive than whites perceived themselves. Work outside the home has long been a part of the female role for most black women (Jones, 1985). Both single and married black mothers report that they always expected to work and prefer working to staying at home; almost all these mothers were themselves reared by working mothers (Malson, 1983). In a study of middle-income black fathers, J. McAdoo (1979, 1981) found the predominant pattern of interaction with children to be nurturance, a part of the expressive role, which was equally evident in interactions with boys and with girls. In contrast to the finding that black fathers behave similarly toward their girls and boys, Margolin and

Patterson (1975) found that white fathers gave twice as many positive responses to boys as to girls. A complicating factor is that the father's role in
American families is changing, as is the inclination of researchers to study
fathers. White fathers have been described as nurturant in interactions with
their preschool children, with middle-class fathers being more nurturant than
lower-class fathers (Jordan, Radin, & Epstein, 1975). Paternal nurturance
was positively associated with intelligence test scores for middle-class boys
only and not for girls or lower-class boys.

Few differences in child-rearing attitudes are found between black mothers and fathers, and few differences are found in parents' attitudes toward
girls and boys (Bartz & Levine, 1978). Bartz and Levine found that black
parents encourage the child's independence, especially regarding self-help
skills; encourage the wise use of time, emphasize respect for children's ideas,
and support children's right to have input into family decisions. Black parents
believe in strict discipline, including physical punishment, but this discipline
occurs in the context of strong emotional support. Although the discipline
techniques employed by black parents have been judged to be inferior to the
love-withdrawal approaches documented in white families, Peters (1981) argues that blacks' discipline techniques serve the parents' goal of instilling
obedience in their young children.

As would be expected, given egalitarian patterns of family functions,
black parents do not inculcate rigid sex-role standards in their children (Lewis,
1975). Sex-role socialization tends to be characterized by a remarkable degree
of overlap between the male and female roles, with more emphasis on competence and age than on gender (Peters, 1981). Many behaviors seen by the
dominant American culture as appropriate for only one sex are considered
equally appropriate for both sexes, or equally inappropriate for both sexes.
In the dominant American culture, assertiveness, independence, and self-
confidence have traditionally been viewed as more appropriate characteristics
of males than of females. In her study of child rearing among black Americans,
Young (1970) found that these characteristics are valued in females as well
as in males. In addition, both males and females share in child care functions,
displaying similar styles, and both are nurturant and interact physically with
children. As black children grow up, they may be subjected to pressures to
conform to sex-role stereotypes prevalent in the wider society. Early socialization stresses achievement, independence, self-confidence, and value for interpersonal relations in both sexes. In later socialization, black families, out
of sheer necessity in the struggle for survival, may prepare their offspring to
adapt their sex-role expectations to the existing economic, social, and educational opportunities.

In addition to the development of egalitarianism, black family functioning
differs from that of white families in that family members must acquire ways
of coping with their castelike status in American society. The child-rearing

task of black families is a difficult one: they must socialize their children into their own way of life and also socialize their children into the mainstream culture, in which blacks hold a decidedly subordinate position. The dilemma posed by this task can hardly be exaggerated. Black families must teach their children to value themselves and their culture but also to live in the larger society. Black mothers and fathers report that racism affects parenting strategies and that they attempt, directly and indirectly, to prepare their children to cope with racism (Peters, 1981). Banks' (1984a,b) studies of middle-class black families living in predominantly white suburban communities suggest that some parents are successful in rearing bicultural children, who have a strong positive sense of their identity as blacks and who also are comfortable in predominantly white settings.

Origin of Differences

In most traditional West African societies, women were subordinate to men (Blassingame, 1979). During slavery, a harsh and cruel form of equality occurred; slavemasters ignored gender in assigning arduous field labor and administering severe beatings to both male and female slaves. Slave women who worked in households usually worked in the fields also and generally did not have a lighter workload (Jones, 1985). Although some sexual division of labor occurred in slave quarters, black men and women were "equal in the sense that neither sex wielded economic power over the other" (Jones, 1985, p. 14). The "transformation of African familial roles led to the creation of America's first democratic family in the [slave] quarters, where men and women shared authority and responsibility" (Blassingame, 1979, p. 178).

Egalitarianism in black family functioning continued after slavery. Adverse economic conditions required that wives and sometimes children work in order to provide for the basic needs of the family. Even when basic needs could be provided by the father, upwardly mobile families worked toward middle-class status by augmenting the father's income with that provided by the mother's employment. Black working wives contribute a greater proportion of total household income than do white working wives (Jones, 1985; Wallace, 1980). In H. McAdoo's (1981) study of middle-class black families, the point of attainment of middle-class status was clearly related to the employment of the mother. Employment of the mother led to shared child rearing, shared household tasks, and shared decision making among all family members. Scanzoni (1977) states that male authority based on resources provided by the husband is accepted as legitimate by both black and white men and women. Because the earnings gap between men and women has not been as great for blacks as it has been for whites, blacks have not experienced as strong an economic basis for the subordination of women, either in marital roles or in the preparation of girls for schooling, jobs, and careers.

The economic conditions and the racism experienced by blacks are intimately intertwined. Ogbu (1978) conceptualizes a "job ceiling" as an overriding feature of blacks' perceptions of economic opportunity for themselves and their children. Because of social structural limits on job opportunities for even well-educated blacks, black parents may have some difficulty in maintaining and effectively communicating to their children high aspirations and expectations for education and career achievement. The socialization and education of black children thus occur in the context of struggling against rather than fitting into the existing structure of social and economic roles for black and white men and women. Precursors of this mode of socialization occurred during slavery, when black parents taught their children obedience but not unconditional submission to the social order (Blassingame, 1979).

Meaning of Differences

As is true for differences in family structures, differences in family functions have been interpreted as deficiencies in black families and have been used to explain many of the problems experienced by blacks, such as the low school achievement of black children and the disproportionate occurrence of poverty among black adults. Deficit interpretations of family functioning as well as of family structures have been challenged and have to some extent been replaced with "difference" explanations. The most appropriate view of differences, however, is, as stated earlier, that blacks are bicultural.

A careful consideration of the relationship between child-rearing strategies and the adult roles in a society is necessary for understanding black families (Ogbu, 1981b). Most research on the child-rearing strategies of black parents assumes that child-rearing strategies cause adult behavior. An alternative perspective is Ogbu's cultural-ecological model, which assumes that the roles allowed for individuals in a society will determine the child-rearing goals and strategies a family adopts. The goals and strategies are adaptive for the culture in which the family lives. The cultural-ecological model is in contrast to the prevailing universal model that assumes that white middle-class standards are the goal of child rearing for all families, that child-rearing differences are the result of differences in parental skills, and that differences in child-rearing strategies represent deficiencies in parental skills. The assumption that there are universal principles of child-rearing that lead reliably to universally desired outcomes in children is unwarranted (Kagan, 1979; Ogbu, 1981b). The cultural-ecological model involves the interpretation of child-rearing strategies and goals in terms of the adult roles and cultural tasks of the group being studied. It also requires that comparisons of the adequacy of child rearing in different cultural groups not be made unless the cultures share the same environment and the same cultural tasks.

DIRECTIONS FOR RESEARCH AND POLICY

Research on black families has involved misconceptions and misinterpretations. Often, however, black families have simply been ignored in research. Johnson (1981), reviewing the contents of five sociology, five social work, and three black journals from 1965 to 1968, found that empirical articles on black families comprised only 1% of all articles and only 3% of all empirical articles. Of the empirical articles on black families, 38% appeared in the black journals and in a special issue on black families of the *Journal of Marriage and the Family*. Similarly, Super (1982) found that, except for a period during the 1960s when some studies included participants of diverse socioeconomic and racial backgrounds, most research published in *Child Development* from 1930 to 1979 was on middle-class whites. A major problem is the lack of empirical research on various kinds of black families.

The deficit model, with its assumptions about the value of white middle-class behavior patterns, has been recently replaced in some instances by more neutral or more positive views of black families. Ogbu's (1981b) cultural-ecological model provides an appropriate framework for studying families. In this model, families would be studied in context rather than compared inappropriately with other groups. A second and related problem has been the means of analyzing and interpreting data. Central tendencies and mean differences between groups have been emphasized more than the variability within groups and the overlap between groups. A third problem has been the confounding of race with social class. Even studies that equate groups for social class have problems in that assessing social class in black populations is difficult. A fourth problem is that studies sometimes focus on structural variables to the exclusion of functional or process variables. Family structures are important because the composition of a family may affect the interactional processes within families. Ultimately, attention must be given to family processes and their relationship to the healthy development of family members (Scott-Jones, 1984).

The cultural-ecological model might be interpreted to mean that appropriate studies of black families should include only blacks in the samples. The issue, however, is not that simple. McLoyd and Randolph (1984), in their content analysis of empirical articles on black children in major journals from 1973 to 1975, found that studies comparing black children with other groups were not more likely than studies including only black children to espouse an explicit deficit model. The authors conclude that race-homogeneous studies may implicitly involve race comparisons and that race-comparative studies often appear to be atheoretical, reporting race differences of little informative value.

The use of a cultural-ecological model to study black families has implications for policy as well as for research. If it is assumed that child-rearing strategies cause adult behaviors, the appropriate policy is to intervene in families. If it is assumed that the roles allowed for individuals in a society determine the strategies parents use, the appropriate policy is to make changes in the structure and institutions of the society. Unlike the universal model, the cultural-ecological model would require changes in the society rather than in families. Although black families should be studied and may benefit from interventions based on research, the ultimate goal is to remove the societal barriers that limit black people.

SUMMARY AND CONCLUSIONS

Some of the family forms and functions that characterize blacks are found increasingly in majority families. In majority families, however, these forms and functions are attributed to current economic conditions and to social movements such as the women's movement rather than to family pathology. Single-parent families, extended families, and egalitarianism in the family are viewed more positively, now that they are not seen as being characteristic of black families alone.

In conclusion, the perspective needed in research with black families is one that acknowledges the broad social context in which families live. In research with all families, care must be taken to accurately identify important features of family life and to avoid misconceptions and negative value judgments that ignore the social context in which the family is embedded. If family structures and functions that are adaptive to social and economic conditions are defined as social problems, the policies and practices based on those inappropriate definitions may be the real social problem.

ACKNOWLEDGMENTS

The authors wish to acknowledge the helpful comments of James D. Anderson, Herbert Exum, and Wilma Peebles.

REFERENCES

Banks, J. A. (1984a). *An exploratory study of assimilation, pluralism, and marginality: Black families in predominantly white suburbs.* Paper presented at the annual meeting of the American Educational Research Association, New Orleans.

Banks, J. A. (1984b). Black youth in predominantly white suburbs: An exploratory study of their attitudes and self-concepts. *Journal of Negro Education, 53,* 3–17.

Bartz, K., & Levine, E. (1978). Child-rearing by black parents. *Journal of Marriage and the Family, 40,* 709–719.

Billingsley, A. (1968). *Black families in white America.* Englewood Cliffs, NJ: Prentice-Hall.

Blassingame, J. W. (1979). *The slave community: Plantation life in the antebellum south* (2nd ed.). New York: Oxford University Press.

Cummings, J. (1983, November 20). Breakup of black family emperils gains of decades. *The New York Times,* pp. 35–36.

Edelman, M. W. (1980). *Portrait of inequality: Black and white children in America.* Washington, DC: Children's Defense Fund.

Frazier, E. F. (1939). *The Negro family in the United States.* Chicago: University of Chicago Press.

Furstenberg, F. F., Hershberg, T., & Modell, J. (1978). The origins of the female-headed black family: The impact of the urban experience. In R. Staples (Ed.), *The black family: Essays and studies* (2nd ed.). Belmont, CA: Wadsworth.

Glick, P. C. (1979). Children of divorced parents in demographic perspective. *Journal of Social Issues, 35,* 170–182.

Gutman, H. (1976). *The black family in slavery and freedom, 1750–1925.* New York: Random House.

Harrison, A. (1981). Attitudes toward procreation among black adults. In H. P. McAdoo (Ed.), *Black families.* Beverly Hills, CA: Sage Publications.

Hull, G. T., Scott, P. B., & Smith, B. (1982). *All the women are white, all the blacks are men, but some of us are brave: Black women's studies.* Old Westbury, NY: Feminist Press.

Johnson, L. B. (1981). Perspectives on Black family empirical research: 1965–1978. In H. P. McAdoo (Ed.), *Black families.* Beverly Hills, CA: Sage Publications.

Jones, J. (1985). *Labor of love, labor of sorrow: Black women, work, and the family from slavery to the present.* New York: Basic Books.

Jordan, B. E., Radin, N., & Epstein, A. (1975). Paternal behavior and intellectual functioning in preschool boys and girls. *Developmental Psychology, 11,* 407–408.

Kagan, J. (1979). Family experience and the child's development. *American Psychologist, 34,* 886–891.

Lamb, M. E. (1981). Fathers and child development: An integrative overview. In M. E. Lamb (Ed.), *The role of the father in child development.* New York: Wiley.

Lewis, D. K. (1978). The black family: Socialization and sex roles. In R. Staples (Ed.), *The black family: Essays and studies* (2nd ed.). Belmont, CA: Wadsworth.

Lieberson, S. (1980). *A piece of the pie: Blacks and white immigrants since 1880.* Berkeley: University of California Press.

Malson, M. R. (1983). Black women's sex roles: The social context for a new ideology. *Journal of Social Issues, 39,* 101–114.

Margolin, G., & Patterson, G. R. (1975). Differential consequences provided by mothers and fathers for their sons and daughters. *Developmental Psychology, 11,* 537–538.

Mbiti, J. S. (1969). *African religions and philosophy.* New York: Praeger.

McAdoo, H. P. (1978). Factors related to stability in upwardly mobile black families. *Journal of Marriage and the Family, 40,* 761–766.

McAdoo, H. P. (1981). Patterns of upward mobility in black families. In H. P. McAdoo (Ed.), *Black families.* Beverly Hills, CA: Sage Publications.

McAdoo, J. (1979). A study of father–child interaction patterns and self-esteem in black preschool children. *Young Children, 34,* 46–53.

McAdoo, J. (1981). Involvement of fathers in the socialization of black children. In H. P. McAdoo (Ed.), *Black families.* Beverly Hills, CA: Sage Publications.

McLoyd, V. C., & Randolph, S. M. (1984). The conduct and publication of research on Afro-American children: A content anaylsis. *Human Development, 27,* 65–75.

Mills, K. M., & Palumbo, T. J. (1980). *A statistical portrait of women in the United States: 1978* (Current Population Reports, Special Studies Series P-23, No. 100). Washington, DC: Bureau of the Census.

Moynihan, D. P. (1965). *The Negro family: The case for national action.* Washington, DC: U. S. Government Printing Office, Department of Labor.

Nobles, W. (1978). Africanity: Its role in black families. In R. Staples (Ed.), *The black family: Essays and studies.* Belmont, CA: Wadsworth.

Ogbu, J. U. (1978). *Minority education and caste.* New York: Academic Press.

Ogbu, J. U. (1981a). Black education: A cultural-ecological perspective. In H. P. McAdoo (Ed.), *Black families.* Beverly Hills, CA: Sage Publications.

Ogbu, J. U. (1981b). Origins of human competence: A cultural-ecological perspective. *Child Development, 52,* 413–429.

Parsons, T., & Bales, R. F. (1955). *Family, socialization and interaction process.* Glencoe, IL: Free Press.

Peters, M. F. (1981). Parenting in black families with young children: A historical perspective. In H. P. McAdoo (Ed.), *Black families.* Beverly Hills, CA: Sage Publications.

Pleck, E. H. (1979). *Black migration and poverty: Boston 1865-1900.* New York: Academic Press.

Rawlings, S. W. (1980). *Families maintained by female householders 1970–1979* (Current Population Reports, Special Studies Series P-23, No. 107). Washington, DC: Bureau of the Census.

Scanzoni, J. H. (1977). *The Black family in modern society: Patterns of stability and security.* Chicago: University of Chicago Press.

Sciara, F. J. (1975). Effects of father absence on the educational achievement of urban black children. *Child Study Journal, 5,* 45–55.

Scott-Jones, D. (1984). Family influences on cognitive development and school achievement. *Review of Research in Education, 11,* 259–304.

Smith, A., & Stewart, A. J. (1983). Approaches to studying racism and sexism in black women's lives. *Journal of Social Issues, 39,* 1–16.

Stack, C. B. (1974). *All our kin.* New York: Harper & Row.

Staples, R. (1978). The black family revisited. In R. Staples (Ed.), *The black family: Essays and studies* (2nd ed.). Belmont, CA: Wadsworth.

Stevens, J. H. (1984). Black grandmothers' and black adolescent mothers' knowledge about parenting. *Developmental Psychology, 20,* 1017–1025.

Sudarkasa, N. (1981). Interpreting the African heritage in Afro-American family organization. In H. P. McAdoo (Ed.), *Black families.* Beverly Hills, CA: Sage Publications.

Super, C. M. (1982, Spring). Secular trends in *Child Development* and the institutionalization of professional disciplines. *Newsletter of the Society for Research in Child Development,* pp. 10–11.

Thornton, J. (1981, March 9). Why so many families are doubling up. *U.S. News and World Report,* pp. 52–54.

Uzoka, A. (1979). The myth of the nuclear family. *American Psychologist, 34,* 1095–1106.

Valentine, C. (1971). Deficit, difference, and bicultural models of Afro-American behavior. *Harvard Educational Review, 41,* 137–157.

Wallace, P. A. (1980). *Black women in the labor force.* Cambridge, MA: MIT Press.

Weiner, L. Y. (1985). *From working girl to working mother: The female labor force in the United States, 1820-1980.* Chapel Hill, NC: University of North Carolina Press.

Willie, C. (1971). Dominance in the family: The black and white experience. *Journal of Black Psychology, 7,* 91–97.

Wilson, M. N. (1984). Mothers' and grandmothers' perceptions of parental behavior in three-generational black families. *Child Development, 55,* 1333–1339.

Young, V. H. (1970). Family and childhood in a southern negro community. *American Anthropologist, 57,* 269–288.

CHAPTER 7

Positive Marginality

THE EXPERIENCE OF BLACK WOMEN LEADERS

ALTHEA SMITH

The concept of *marginality* has a long history of investigation in the socio-logical literature. For example, Stonequist (1937, p. xv) introduced the concept of the *marginal man* as "one whom fate has condemned to live in two societies and in two not merely different but antagonistic cultures." Classical sources of marginality in America have included race (e.g., Afro-American), religion (e.g., American Jews), age (e.g., adolescence), and ethnic origin (e.g., Italian-Americans) (Park, 1950; Stonequist, 1936). More contemporary definitions include those persons on the border of two groups or systems (e.g., Wright & Wright, 1972). Marginality has been and still is characterized as producing negative psychological effects for the person caught between two reference groups because of the differing values, goals, and norms. In general, it has been assumed that marginality leads to tension, conflict, and ambivalence, thereby causing the marginal person to feel anxious, confused, and alienated.

Another less documented side of marginality, acknowledged by Stone-quist in his original work, is its positive possibilities. For instance, there is the potential of marginal people to become social critics and to bring creative perspectives to social situations. Goldberg (1941) questions the assumption that everyone from a marginal culture always suffers from tension, ambiva-lence, and alienation thought to accompany a marginal status. These re-searchers raise the possibility that there are certain benefits, or advantages to marginality, for both the person and the situations in which he or she is involved. For the most part, however, the definitions and consequences of

ALTHEA SMITH • Department of Psychology, Boston University, Boston, Massachusetts 02215.

marginality have been associated with conflict, turmoil, ambivalence, and general ineffectiveness, negating the equally likely strengths and benefits.

North American black women in leadership roles provide an excellent opportunity to examine the concept of marginality and its duality. Black women have long been leaders in a variety of fields, but we do not understand much about the costs and benefits of their experiences. Because they are black in a predominantly white context and female in a traditionally male role, black women leaders are uniquely marginal. This unique status requires special attention from researchers and theoreticians who are interested in black people or women as serious topics of inquiry. Unfortunately, black women have generally been ignored or cast in a negative role by social science researchers (Hull, Bell-Scott, & Smith, 1982; Moynihan, 1967). Much of the research on black people has emphasized race differences without regard to differences between black men and women. Similarly, research on women does not distinguish between the effects of being black or white. In order to understand black women leaders we need to explore their distinctive quality as blacks and their unique status as women. Greater efforts must be made to unravel the unique structural, social, and psychological situation of black women who hold positions of advocacy.

The purpose of this chapter is twofold: first, to examine the concept of marginality, and second to use this concept to better understand black women's leadership experience.

One would expect black women in leadership positions to be victims of negative marginality because they are marginal in so many ways. The most obvious marginality is demographic because they are black in a world dominated by whites and female in a world dominated by males (Beale, 1970). As black women, they do not identify exclusively with blacks because of issues that affect them as women, such as sexual oppression, nor do they identify exclusively with women because of the issues that affect them as blacks, such as class oppression (Hull, Bell-Scott, & Smith, 1982; Smith & Stewart, 1983).

Another aspect of their marginality is in their role as leaders who traditionally have championed the causes of weak and powerless groups, such as blacks, women, the poor, and children (Dumas-Graves, 1980). Their neither-fish-nor-fowl status does not afford them the protection of belonging exclusively to one social group. It is no surprise that the general tendency has been to view the experiences of black women in leadership positions as generally negative. Dumas-Graves (1980), for example, describes other ways that black women's leadership experiences reflect negative marginality. Black women are often caught in the stuggles between the boss and subordinates, blacks and whites, men and women, between units in the organization, and between the organization and the community in which it is located. Dumas-Graves further argues that because of her blackness the black women is expected to curb the aggression of black males and temper the forcefulness of other black women. Due to this tension, stress, and strain from their marginality, Dumas-Graves sees black female leaders as particularly vulnerable to "burn out."

PERSPECTIVES ON MARGINALITY

When we start to think about marginality, we need to be careful to distinguish the reactions of others to the person in the marginal position and the individual's own response to that position. The previous formulations emphasizing the negative aspects of marginality have primarily been from the view of a third party—the reaction of others to seeing the person in a borderline position. How others perceive and respond is an important part of the experience of marginal people and has contributed in a major way to our negative impression of marginality.

But there is another perspective that has been ignored: that of marginal persons perceptions and reactions to their own position. There is no reason to assume that they would necessarily perceive their own condition in the same way as an outsider. In this chapter, I emphasize the concept of marginality from the perspective of individuals who are in such positions. But, first, I begin by questioning the underlying assumptions of the traditional view of marginality and then propose alternative formulations.

Traditional Assumptions of Marginality

There are two preconditions that are assumed to form the core of a marginal position: (a) a presumed lack of an identifiable reference point or sense of direction; and (b) a lack of stable, enduring bonds or connections to a group (Brown, Cotton, & Golembiewski, 1977). In the first instance, marginal persons are thought to be "fuzzy" headed and unclear about their mission and goals. They are thought to be uncommitted or confused about their convictions because they are thought to have no allegiance to either of the two groups they border. The marginal person is considered to be a free spirit, independent, with no sense of loyalty to any one group. This contributes to the image of the marginal person as objective and impartial but also supports an image of a social isolate.

Researchers have also assumed that those in a marginal position are psychologically unbiased and ideologically uncommitted (Ziller, 1973; Ziller, Start, & Pruden, 1969). Because their position is borderline, they are expected not to show favoritism or loyalty to either group. Marginal persons are not supposed to be egocentric or ethnocentric in their attitudes, judgments, or behaviors (Ziller, 1973). It has been assumed that marginality requires the individual to have no specified reference group or attachment to a group. Without a clear reference point or a strong attachment to a group it is easy to see how images of conflict and ambiguity lead to social isolation and alienation.

A second implicit assumption is that the structural qualities of marginality dictate only one function for the role. That is, a marginal position is structually on the edge of two groups, and therefore the function of this role is to bring the two groups closer together or to bridge a gap between the two. The location of the position is assumed to be the same as the purpose of the role, that is, a bridge. As such, thinking about the functional roles of marginality has been limited to that of interpreter, coordinator, or arbitrator (Ziller *et al.,* 1969). These roles assume only one form of compatibility or match between the position and function of the marginal person.

It should be noted that, in part, the assumptions that underlie marginality come from the perspective of past researchers. Early research on marginality was conducted primarily by sociologists who were interested in large social groups, cultures, and societies. They tended to view marginality as an undesirable, isolated position, somewhere on the fringe of two or more groups or systems. They were more interested in the structural aspects of marginality and less in the individual's social and psychological responses to his or her marginality.

Alternative Assumptions of Marginality

Recently, psychologists have begun to explore the concept of marginality and to question its sociological assumptions. Some have suggested alternate perspectives for thinking about the concept (Mayo, 1982; Ziller, 1973). Ziller proposed a social psychological analysis that conceptually separates the marginal person from a marginal position. His argument is that being in a marginal position does not necessarily lead to negative consequences for the person. Other factors should be taken into account, such as the individual's psychological reaction to the position, which could be either unfavorable or favorable. An unfavorable reaction could be ambiguity of purpose, a sense of powerlessness, or helplessness. A favorable reaction could be clarity of purpose, determination, and a sense of conviction.

Mayo (1982) has argued that the marginal person may necessarily be biased, supportive of one group, and even expected to speak in behalf of his or her group to another. The marginal person may be required to be psychologically and socially invested in an ideology or a group's welfare and act as a spokesperson or advocate for that cause. This formulation contradicts the assumptions that the structural qualities of marginality dictate neutral and unbiased social and psychological responses by the marginal person. Marginal positions such as ombudsmen, activist, and change agent are good examples.

This formulation assumes that the functional aspects of marginality operate independently of its structural dimensions. Although the position is structurally boundary spanning, the role could require the person to assess both the merits and faults of both systems (Mayo, 1982). That is, the functional role could be that of social critic, advocate, or activist.

Another assumption of marginality made in earlier work is the lack of social support available to the marginal person. Negative social support situations would include no role models, no supportive reference group, or group affiliation. Positive situations could include supportive family ties and friendships, strong racial/ethnic group or community bonds, and an identifiable reference group. Any formulation of marginality should include the individual's social situation and an analysis of available supportive resources.

Given the previously mentioned limitations, a broader, more useful formulation of marginality should incorporate several dimensions, not only structural and functional, but also social and psychological, that lead to either positive or negative marginality. In comparing positive and negative conceptualizations of marginality, the structural definition remains the same: it is the border or boundary position between two or more groups or systems. In negative marginality, the functional role is conceived as intermediary with limited resources, whereby both groups ignore and even ostracize the person in that position. Socially, the marginal person is isolated and alienated under the guise of being "independent." Psychologically, that person may feel powerless and lack a sense of control.

Although in the same structural position, the concept of positive marginality views the position as advantageous. Functionally, this marginal role is one of a spokesperson or advocate for one of the groups they bridge or connect. Socially, these marginal people accept their roles as advocates and respond as critical evaluators or agents of change. They assess the groups they span and advocate change in support of a better quality of life. Psychologically, the marginal person may be seen as confident and egocentric, nonconformist, and rebellious. Positive marginality stems from a match between a positive orientation of the individual and the position held. Positive marginality highlights the advantages of being both on the inside and the outside of a group or system.

POSITIVE MARGINALITY AND BLACK WOMEN LEADERS

The positive dimensions of marginality offer a useful conceptual framework for understanding black women in leadership roles. By using both positive and negative marginality, we can consider the functional, social, and psychological consequences to both the individual and the groups served. By conceptually separating the marginal woman from the marginal position, we

can identify personal and interpersonal supports (and barriers) that contribute
to successful marginality. Marginality then acts as a useful focal concept for
analyzing both the positive and negative psychosocial dimensions of black
women's leadership experience.

Ida B. Wells, Shirley Chisholm, and Angela Davis are three black female
political leaders who are marginal in their roles in the black or white community. They were chosen because they describe in their own words, through
autobiographies, the conditions and consequences of their marginality. Ida
Barnett Wells was born in Holly Springs, Mississippi, in 1862. She left her
position, teaching black children, to protest the poor treatment of blacks in
the South. As a journalist, she began to write for black and white newspapers,
including her own, about the lack of educational resources, unfair treatment
of blacks in the criminal justice system, Jim Crow, and the politics of lynching.

Shirley Chisholm was born in Brooklyn, New York, in 1924. She was
trained as an educator but later turned to politics as a strategy to help blacks
and the urban poor. She was the first black women to be elected as a
Democratic member of the U.S. House of Representatives. She served as the
congresswoman from the Bedford-Stuyvesant section of New York from 1969
to 1983.

Angela Davis, born in Birmingham, Alabama, in 1944, is a political
activist and educator. She was accused (later acquitted) of conspiracy in an
attempted courtroom escape by prisoners from Soledad prison in which four
persons were killed. She is an active member of the Communist party and
was their vice-presidential candidate in 1980.

These women are obviously socially marginal in the demographic sense,
but they have been successful leaders and are excellent examples of positive
marginality. Drawing on examples from their personal histories, one can see
certain factors as instrumental in their success. Each mentions moderating
variables, such as role models, social supports, and strong identifications with
their black communities, which enhanced their success as leaders and helped
them to form a positive orientation. Next, I consider the structural, functional,
and psychological dimensions of positive marginality as reflected in the leadership experiences of these women.

Structural

Each of these women had positions that allowed a closer look at the
strengths as well as the weaknesses of both the black and white communities.
Their positions gave them the opportunity to be both an insider and an
outsider. Shirley Chisholm (Chisholm, 1970) decided that she was unhappy
with the operation of the political machinery in her neighborhood, and she
put herself in a position to change it. She began working on campaigns, fund
raisers, and through community organizations to get the opinion of poor

people, while at the same time attending political meetings to better understand how the leadership of the political system functioned.

In a similar way, Ida B. Wells (Duster, 1970) decided early in her teaching career that she could best voice her concerns about social injustice through editorial writing. She established her own newspaper, *Free Speech,* to do so. Both Chisholm and Wells were outside the white community by membership, but their commitment to the black community often took them inside the white community as advocates. Much of their work was *outside* the black community, as activists and liaisons, but *inside* by virtue of membership. Both women had meager resources, limited influence, and were thought by many of their contemporaries to be "sassy" troublemakers. They used the freedom of being outside to develop broad-based support, diverse coalitions, and followers who might not have been willing to help had they been exclusively part of either a black or a white community. A major structural asset for both of these women is reflected in Shirley Chisholm's campaign slogan and the title of her autobiography, *Unbought and Unbossed.* Being marginal to her means being independent of the two groups she bridges. Marginality frees her from blind allegiance and loyalty. Her obligations are to herself and the role she fills. She sees herself as not owned by any one group and her actions cannot be dictated by any one group.

Functional

A functional dimension of positive marginality is that of a critical evaluator. Because their positions border systems, both Chisholm and Wells were able to combine the knowledge of an insider with the critical attitude of an outsider to critique both systems (Stonequist, 1937).

In her autobiography, Chisholm (1970) described her experiences as a spokesperson for the poor and minority constituency in the Bedford-Stuyvesant section of New York. In an address to Congress she spoke out against the Vietnam War and advocated for a redirection of resources to fight America's lack of investment in ending poverty and racism:

> I am deeply disappointed at the clear evidence that the number one priority of the new Administration is to buy more and more and more weapons of war, to return to the Cold War and ignore the war we must fight here, the war that is not optional. There is only one way, I believe, to turn these policies around. The Congress must respond to the mandate that the American people have expressed. They have said: End this war. Stop the waste. Stop the killing. Do something for your own people first. (p.111)

In speaking to militant groups in the black community, she criticized the effectiveness of their strategies for change. She wrote:

> What is the sense of shooting, burning, killing? What will it bring? All they have to do is press a button in Washington and every black neighborhood will be

> surrounded with troops and bayonets. What are you going to do against the
> massive forces of government? . . . When you get through burning, won't you still
> have to go to the Man and ask for an apartment? (Chisholm, 1970, p. 144)

Chisholm again portrayed this initial evaluator role in her reactions to
committee spending. Early in 1970, she voted against a trip to Asia for the
Education and Labor Committee, describing it as a "little pleasure jaunt to
while away a recess." She said, "to consider the money spent on hearings,
committees, commissions, studies and trips and think what else it would be
used for is depressing" (Chisholm, p. 105). In her marginal role of representing
the poor and minority groups, Chisholm acted both as a critic of governmental
policies that affected her constituents and as a critic of her constituents
themselves.

Ida B. Wells was also a critic attacking Southerners' accusations that
black men were raping white women. In her role as a marginal leader she
wrote about the black experience in both black and white newspapers and
magazines. In her own newspaper in 1892, she wrote [sic]:

> Eight negroes linched since last issue of the *Free Speech,* three for killing a white
> man, and five on the same old racket, the alarm about raping white women. The
> same program for hanging, then shooting bullets into the lifeless bodies.
>
>   Nobody in this section of the country believes the old threadbare lie that
> negro men rape white women. If Southern men are not careful, they will over
> reach themselves and public sentiment will have a reaction. A conclusion will then
> be reached which will be very damaging to the moral reputation of their women.
> (Sterling, 1979, p. 82)

Wells takes on the dangerous position of arguing that white men have
been using white women as an excuse to justify their own fears and racism
toward black men. Using critical journalism and public speaking, she took
the opportunity to function as a critic and raise issues that others within the
system could not see or would not challenge.

Marginal persons may also use their position to support their values and
world views. Ziller (1973) proposed that marginality, as a world view, should
be associated with neutrality and objectivity. In contrast, Mayo (1982) argues
that positive marginality can also involve advocacy for better relations and
positive social change. She suggests that the marginal person should take
seriously the responsibility to speak, write, and act in support of an ideology,
individual, or group. Neutrality, in her model, had no relevant virtue, whereas
advocacy represents an important positive orientation and viewpoint toward
society or a group.

Positive marginality can provide an opportunity to advocate for social change, humanitarianism, fairness, and equality. Marginal people can be socially aware of problems and advocate changes and improvements. In her autobiography, Wells provides a good example of this advocacy orientation. In a pamphlet called *Southern Horrors,* she writes about the humanity of blacks:

> Somebody must show that the Afro-American race is more sinned against then sinning, and it seems to have fallen upon me to do so. The awful death-role that Judge Lynch is calling every week is appalling, not only because of the lives it takes, the cruelty and outrage to the victims, but because of the prejudice it fosters. The Afro-American is not a bestial race. If this work can contribute in any way towards proving this, and at the same time arouse the conscience of the American people to a demand for justice to every citizen, I shall feel I have done a service. (Sterling, 1979, p. 85)

Psychological

The psychological dimension of positive marginality must consider the personal qualities of the individual that holds that position. Some socially marginal people will possess the endurance, drive, determination, rebelliousness, and the ability to tolerate the pressures that come from criticizing the system and fighting for unpopular causes. A person may be required to have these qualities to be selected for such a leadership position and to be successful. It is also reasonable to assume that changes occur in an individual by virtue of growing up in a marginal position. This experience can lead to the development of these positive qualities and to a conscious survival strategy. Although it is not so clear that marginality necessarily leads to the development of these positive psychological qualities, it is reasonable to assume that they are needed for survival, especially among leaders.

Each of the political leaders I have been discussing shows some version of these traits. Angela Davis, for instance, describes how painful and agonized her life was after of the death of George Jackson. But she was determined to act, to continue to fight against the oppression of poor, black political prisoners. George Jackson was a militant Black Panther accused with two others, known as the *Soledad Brothers,* of killing a guard at Soledad prison. Angela Davis was an active member of the Soledad Brothers Defense Committee. She became particularly involved with George Jackson and his family. He was killed while still in prison by the San Quentin guards. She writes:

> George's death was like a lodestone, a disc of steel deep inside me, magnetically drawing toward it the elements I need to stay strong and fight all the harder. It would refine my hatred of jailers, position my contempt for the penal system and cement my bonds with other prisoners. (Davis, 1974, p. 319)

We see a similar determination and independence by Wells as she filed suit against the Chesapeake, Ohio, and Southwestern Railroad in 1884 because it put her in a segregated railroad car reserved for smokers and blacks. When the conductor tried to physically remove her from her seat, she bit him on the hand. It took three men to pry her out of her seat. The psychological dimension of positive marginality suggests a personal resilience coupled with courage and drive.

The dimensions of positive marginality discussed so far are related to the orientation to the role and the effective use of the position. The question that arises is what helps to develop and maintain the positive functional, social, and psychological dimensions of marginality. The autobiographies of Chisholm, Davis, and Wells show consistencies in the importance of three major resources in enhancing success: positive role models, supportive kin and nonkin social networks, and strong identification with their respective communities.

IMPLICATIONS OF MARGINALITY FOR MAJORITY AND MINORITY GROUPS

This analysis proposes a more complex view of the concept of marginality and the importance of at least two perspectives when discussing the concept. One perspective is of the person who holds the marginal position, and the other is that of those who view the marginal person. Most of the work on marginality in the past focused on the views of the observer, majority group, or nonmarginal toward the marginal person. In contrast, I have emphasized the views of the marginal actor. Now I turn my attention to the observer and the implications for change.

The negative assumption about marginality by observers is in part based on the premise that the marginal person was refused entry into the majority group and was on the outside but wanted to be on the inside (Park, 1950; Stonequist, 1937). Expectedly then, a majority or nonmarginal person assumes that there is necessarily stress and tension among minority groups and marginal people and tends to stereotype them as experiencing only negative consequences.

Even supposedly positive qualities are seen as having negative consequences for the marginal person. Stereotypes of black women, for example, as strong, powerful, superwomen cause them to be treated in certain ways. Dumas-Graves (1980), for instance, argues that these stereotypes lead majority group members to expect black women to be all things to all groups, to calm the anger of black men, and to speak in behalf of all women. This stereotype and expectation negates her uniqueness, putting her in the position of choosing between her blackness and womanhood. Such stereotyping can be overcome by realistic portrayal of the positive use of marginality and a stress on the importance of positive role models, supportive kin and nonkin social networks, and strong community ties.

It must be recognized that black women have their own issues they want addressed, collectively and individually. Black women in general and black women leaders in particular need to be free to pursue their own issues and not be pigeon holed in a way that obscures their individuality as both black and female. Social scientists can help in reducing the stereotyping and expectations of the black superwoman by not perpetuating the myth in books, articles, and research reports. Researchers and writers must not continue to lump black women together with all blacks or women in their discussion of research findings, social problems, and social issues. The tendency to combine all blacks together (regardless of gender) and to combine all women together (regardless of race) ignores the singular experience of black women. Any discussion of gender or race should always include race differences within gender, and sex differences within race, and, of course, any discussion of either race or gender must include individual differences and personalities.

One consequence of the stereotype of the powerful black superwoman is the expectation that she can represent the view of the black community. Policymakers, administrators, and community workers must become aware of the fact that there are diverse perspectives in the opinions found in any community—black or otherwise. No one person or group can speak to all community issues and concerns. It should also be remembered that the marginal woman may not endorse the popular views of her community. The insider–outsider role allows or even forces the marginal person to have differing opinions and perspectives on problems and solutions. Shirley Chisholm's integrationist stance was in direct opposition to the separatist ideology of the Black Panthers in New York during the 1970s and is but one example of differing views in black communities. Majority group members should keep in mind that marginal people may, by definition, be at odds with the views of their minority communities and not expect them to represent or speak in behalf of the larger black community. Expecting one person or type of person to speak for all blacks adds to the burden of being marginal. To be treated as the only voice in the black community is a large responsibility for anybody to live up to.

The experiences of black women leaders that I have noted in this chapter provide tangible evidence that the concept of marginality is not a necessarily negative experience. There are many less well-known black women for whom marginality may be a positive rather than a negative experience or both positive and negative. Future research using the concept should incorporate aspects of both the positive and negative dimensions and the dynamic qualities of the concept. An effort should be made to include the opinions of both the actors and the observers, because in this case they are often quite different.

We can learn much from the lives and achievements of black women leaders, past and present, about the personal and professional costs as well as the benefits of being demographically marginal and holding a marginal status position. The use of personal documents by and about black women is a source of untapped knowledge and information. Greater efforts should be directed at using this information to tell the story of minority group members as actors in marginal positions. This is especially critical in light of the fact that many more minorities have traditionally been excluded. The strategies that have proven to be effective in the past, understood through the direct experience of black women leaders, can be used to benefit individuals who are currently in marginal positions.

By identifying the functional, social, and psychological aspects of the marginal position or person, we can better understand how and why it is necessary to shift from a negative to a more positive approach. By examining the strategies of previous marginal leaders, future marginal persons may be able to capitalize on the experiences of others in buffering their psychological sense of self, and reaffirm their commitment to self and community. Realizing that other leaders have experienced similar frustrations and joys may strengthen marginal leaders to continue toward their goals and dreams.

REFERENCES

Beale, F. (1970). Double jeopardy: To be black and female. In T. Cade (Ed.), *The black woman.* New York: New American Library.

Brown, P.J., Cotton, C.C., & Golembiewski, R.T. (1977). Marginality and the OD practitioner. *Journal of Applied Behavior Sciences, 13,* 493–506.

Chisholm, S. (1970). *Unbought and unbossed.* Boston: Houghton Mifflin.

Davis, A. (1974). *Angela Davis: An autobiography.* New York: Random House.

Dumas-Graves, R. (1980). Dilemmas of black female leadership. In L. Rodgers-Rose (Ed.), *The black women.* Beverly Hills, CA: Sage Publications.

Duster, A. (Ed.). (1970). *Crusade for justice: The autobiography of Ida B. Wells.* Chicago: University of Chicago Press.

Goldberg, M. (1941). A qualification of the marginal man theory. *American Sociological Review, 4,* 52–58.

Hull, G.T., Bell-Scott, P., & Smith, B. (Eds.). (1982). *All the women are white, all the blacks are men, but some of us are brave.* New York: Feminist Press.

Mayo, C. (1982). Training for positive marginality. In L. Bickman (Ed.), *Applied social psychology annual* (Vol. 3). Beverly Hills, CA: Sage Publications.

Moynihan, D.P. (1967). *The Negro family: The case for national action.* Washington, DC: U.S. Government Printing Office.

Park, R.E. (1950). *Race and culture.* New York: The Free Press.

Smith, A., & Stewart, A. (1983). Approaches to studying racism and sexism in black women's lives. In A. Smith & A. Stewart (Eds.), Racism and sexism in black women's lives. *Journal of Social Issues, 39 (3),* 1–15.

Sterling, D. (1979). *Black foremothers: Three lives.* New York: Feminist Press.

Stonequist, E.B. (1937). *The marginal man.* New York: Scribner's.

Wright, R.D., & Wright, S.N. (1972). A plea for further refinement of the marginal man theory. *Phylon, 33,* 359–368.

Ziller, R.C. (1973). *The social self.* Elmsford, NY: Pergamon Press.

Ziller, R.C., Start, B.J., & Pruden, H.O. (1969). Marginality and integrative management positions. *Academy of Management Journal, 12,* 487–495.

CHAPTER 8

Debunking the Myth of Loneliness in Late Life

Tracey A. Revenson

Older people have demonstrated their ability to cope and survive. Nevertheless, many have been discarded in this technological age and alienated from themselves and society at large....We are against agism (sic) that forces any group to live roles that are defined purely on the basis of age.
—The Gray Panthers, *Statement of Principles*

The perception of aging and more specifically, loneliness, as social problems has emerged in tandem with what is colloquially known as the *graying of America*. In response to a changing demographic composition of our population in which people are living longer and are in greater need of medical and social services, a perception of the American aged as an economic and social burden has developed. One could argue that aging was recognized "officially" as a social problem when Congress passed the Older Americans Act in 1965 and established the Administration on Aging to provide health care services, adequate housing, (supplemental) income, and the opportunity for employment without discrimination for the elderly. However, social problems become social problems largely by their definition as such by the dominant forces in a society (Estes, 1979; Levin & Levin, 1980). As Estes writes,

> The major problems faced by the elderly in the United States are, in large measure, ones that are socially constructed as a result of our conceptions of aging and the aged. What is done for and about the elderly, as well as what we know about them, including knowledge gained from research, are products of our conceptions of aging. In an important sense, then, the major problems faced by the elderly are the ones we create for them. (1979, p. 1)

TRACEY A. REVENSON • Department of Psychology, Barnard College of Columbia University, New York, New York 10027.

This chapter raises and addresses a number of issues related to research and theory involving aged populations. As Kuhn (1962) suggests, we tend to develop scientific paradigms for studying phenomena that become widely accepted long before empirical support for the paradigm is conclusive. These paradigms take on *mythlike* qualitites. From a social psychological vantage point, this has happened to a large degree in the field of social gerontology. Although this chapter focuses on one particular social myth of aging—loneliness—the issues raised are more general and can be applied to other "social problems of aging," such as housing, political power, economic assistance, and nursing homes.

AGEISM

Age stereotypes and intolerance of old age have existed in America for a long time, even though the term *ageism* was coined as recently as 1969 (Butler, 1969). Jane Austen wrote in *Emma* (1816,1976), "The older a person grows, the more important it is that their manners should not be bad; the more glaring and disgusting any loudness, coarseness or awkwardness becomes. What is passable in youth is detestable in old age" (p.24). More recently, B.F. Skinner came to a similar conclusion:

> At issue is how behavior changes as one grows older....*Aging* should be the right word for this process, but it does not mean developing. In accepted usage, *to develop* is not simply to grow older but to unfold a latent structure, to realize an inner potential, to become more effective. *Aging* on the other hand usually means growing less effective....The aged are old people. Aging is growing not merely older but old. (1983, p. 239)

Both anecdotes reflect one of the primary components of ageism: prejudicial *attitudes* toward the aged, old age, one's own aging, and the aging process. Old people are thought to be (among other things) conservative, inflexible, withdrawn, passive, dependent, religious, ugly, and suffering from a variety of physical and mental ailments (Butler, 1975). Ageism is also defined by discriminatory practices against the elderly (*individual behavior*) and by institutional practices and *policies* that perpetuate stereotypic beliefs or stereotypes (see Butler, 1980). These three components—attitudes, individual behavior, and policy—are distinguishable yet interlocking. Although current attitudes about old age are perhaps less negative than they were in the past, due in large measure to the efforts of groups such as the American Association of Retired Persons and the Gray Panthers, the persistence of *compassionate stereotypes* (Binstock, 1983) or what Kalish (1979) has dubbed the *new ageism* is pervasive.

The new ageism involves concern and advocacy for the elderly, but in terms of their infirmities, helplessness, and generally miserable situation (in contrast to old-ageist views of aversion and oversight). The new ageism has emerged as a compassionate response to the "old" ageism but has unintentionally drawn attention to those elderly with overwhelming needs for economic and medical assistance. Unfortunately, the end result is overgeneralization from this smaller segment of the older population that reinforces the old myths and stereotypes.

Many discriminatory public attitudes and policies have been predicated on social myth—myths which may have no basis in fact. For example, the assumption that retirement has an adverse effect on physical and mental health was refuted by evidence suggesting that although individuals differ, retirement often has only a minimal impact on health (Sheppard, 1976).

Social myths are, by definition, false beliefs. The fact that they are beliefs implies that they can be verified and debunked. *Is* loneliness to be expected in old age? After reviewing the research literature on loneliness across the life span, I will examine some of the reasons the myth of predictable loneliness in old age (and others like it) has persisted despite research evidence to the contrary. Finally, I will offer suggestions as to future research directions as well as individual and policy level interventions.

THE CONCERN ABOUT LATE LIFE LONELINESS

Unsuccessful aging is defined by, among other things, loneliness. The emphasis on loneliness stems in part from culturally based assumptions that social integration is necessary for both the maintenance of the social structure (Durkheim, 1951) and the emotional well-being of individuals (Larson, 1978; Palmore & Luikart, 1972). Indeed, a wealth of recent research has touted the stress-buffering qualities of social relationships in relation to a variety of life crises (Gottlieb, 1981). Social relationships perceived as satisfying have been shown to act as a protective cushion against the role losses attributed to the aging process (e.g., Lowenthal & Haven, 1968). Consequently, loneliness has been a central theme in research pertaining to well-being in later life (Nydegger, 1977). Beyond the inherent discomfort of loneliness and its impact on mental health, it has been linked to physical health problems and somatic complaints (e.g., Kivett, 1979; Lynch, 1977).

For a long time, loneliness has been viewed as a major problem of old age. More recently, concern has increased because of the rising proportion of the population that is over 65 and the growing number of older people living alone. The print and entertainment media often portray the elderly as socially isolated and overwhelmingly lonely, especially widows, who having outlived both their husbands and their industrial value, supposedly pine away in isolation until they die (Gordon, 1976). Clinicians, too, have written of the inevitability and sorrow of loneliness in old age (e.g., Buhler, 1969; Burnside, 1971; Moustakas, 1961).

Both elderly and nonelderly people apparently agree with this image. In a 1981 national survey conducted for the National Council on Aging that sampled a representative group of nearly 3,500 American adults, 65% of the respondents aged 18 to 64 felt that loneliness was a very serious problem for most people over 65. More suprisingly, 45% of the respondents over 65 agreed that it was a very serious problem for the elderly, though only 13% said that they were personally affected seriously by loneliness (Harris & Associates, 1981).

Apparently, age is not a discriminating factor in vulnerability to believing popular negative stereotypes. There is evidence that both young *and* old people hold negative attitudes toward older people and old age (Brubaker & Powers, 1976). As elders see others perceive them in a negative way, negative attitudes toward themselves may develop or may be reinforced (Hess, 1976). For some, these attitudes may have a deleterious influence on self-concept and self-esteem, as loneliness is a sign of social failure in our culture (Gordon, 1976), stigmatizing those whom it touches.

By comparison with the young and middle aged, the old *are* more vulnerable to isolation and being alone. There is a greater likelihood of becoming widowed or chronically ill or of suffering from minor yet physically limiting health problems. Retirement and relocation, too, often bring with them changes in social interaction. These are somewhat expectable "on-time" events in the normal adult life cycle (Neugarten, 1977). Such age-linked events may affect the size of and satisfaction with one's social network, and more noticeably, intimate attachments, but the degree to which they engender social losses and loneliness varies considerably from person to person.

THE EXPERIENCE OF LONELINESS

Loneliness is almost always described as an aversive and painful experience, although several emotional and motivational states have been identified with it. Affective manifestations include sadness, anxiety, restlessness, boredom, anger, alienation, desperation, helplessness, isolation, and an empty feeling (cf. Rubenstein & Shaver, 1982). Motivational correlates have been described in terms of arousal (e.g., Sullivan, 1953) and contrarily, decreased motivation and paralyzing hopelessness. From a cognitive perspective, Perlman and Peplau (1982) define *loneliness* as the perception of a discrepancy between one's desired and achieved levels of social contact. Although it is difficult to organize these affective, motivational, and cognitive components into a coherent picture of the experience of loneliness, two broad dimensions emerge. This distinction is supported by empirical descriptions of the phenomenological experience of loneliness. *Loneliness due to emotional isolation* results from absence of a close personal attachment and is accompanied by feelings of anxiety, restlessness, and emptiness. *Loneliness due to social isolation* results from the absence of meaningful friendships or a sense of community and is characterized by feelings of boredom or alienation (Weiss, 1973). Older people tend to report feeling both types of loneliness (e.g., Blythe, 1979; Weiss, 1973). When people label themselves as *lonely*, the feelings they mention most often are depression, self-deprecation, desperation, boredom, and restlessness (cf. Rubenstein & Shaver, 1982).

LONELINESS ACROSS THE LIFE SPAN

To examine whether the contemporary popular conception of predictable loneliness in old age is congruent with research evidence, I will begin with a recent study of loneliness across the adult life span conducted with my colleague Jeffrey Johnson (J. Johnson, 1981; Johnson & Revenson, 1981; Revenson & Johnson, 1984). Data were obtained from an extensive survey questionnaire published in the Sunday magazine section of three North American daily newspapers during the first half of 1980 (the *Anchorage Daily News*, the *Rochester* [New York] *Democrat Chronicle*, and the *Winnipeg Tribune*). Readers were informed of the link between loneliness and health, and that the researchers were interested in learning more about who is lonely and who is not and what loneliness feels like. Over 2,000 adults returned questionnaires. A broad age range (18–89) was represented, with somewhat of an undersampling of those over age 65 (6% compared to the national average of 11.2%). The sample was largely female (76.3%), as is often the case with magazine and newspaper questionnaires (Shaver & Rubenstein, 1983), and better educated than the national norm (about 45% are college graduates compared to a national average of 12%). The higher than national percentage of divorced respondents (23% vs. 3%) is most likely due to the divorced person's greater interest in, and susceptibility to, loneliness. (Complete demographic data are presented in J. Johnson, 1981.)

Reflecting national demographic trends, respondents over 65 tended to be widowed, retired, and living alone. Seventy percent have children, although only 4% live with their children. Half had at least some college education, and slightly more than half had an annual income of $10,000 or more.

In this study, as in most others, *loneliness* refers to a self-reported, self-labeled affective state. The measure used, the NYU Loneliness Scale, directly addresses the intensity of current loneliness, self-labeling as a lonely person (in the past, present, and future), and comparisons with one's age peers as well as frequency of experience. The scale has been found to have high face validity, internal consistency, and proven applicability in survey research (J. Johnson, 1981; Revenson, 1981; Rubenstein & Shaver, 1982).

Perhaps the most striking finding was that older respondents were much less lonely than younger or middle-aged respondents. An analysis of variance comparing levels of loneliness for seven age groups showed that, with one exception (those aged 45 to 54 were more lonely than those aged 35 to 44), there was a linear decrease in loneliness with age (see Figure 1). This decrease remained stable and statistically significant when men and women were analyzed separately and when those living alone versus those living with others were analyzed separately.

The survey method was chosen for its advantage in reaching a large number of elderly people, although there are clearly problems with generalizability. To compensate for this, the three newspaper samples were initially analyzed separately. Identical results were obtained in each sample, and the samples were combined for this chapter to simplify presentation. Although not strictly a solution to the problem of sample bias, successful replication of results across the three samples partially offsets the possibility of idiosyncratic geographic effects in any individual nonprobability sample. The data base is large enough to yield information from lonely and nonlonely people of different ages and diverse social characteristics. And, as will be demonstrated, these data are consistent with studies using more representative sampling methods, which are less vulnerable to self-selection biases (e.g., Harris & Associates, 1976, 1981; Lowenthal, Thurner, & Chiriboga, 1975; Shanas, Townsend, Wedderburn, Friis, Milhoj, & Stehouwer, 1968).

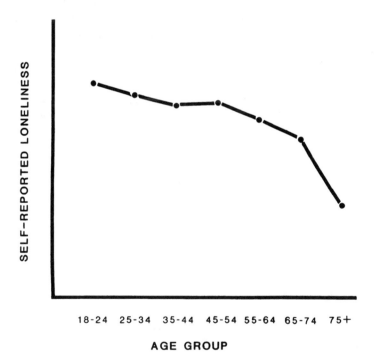

Figure 1. Self-reported loneliness by age group.

EVERYTHING OLD IS NEW AGAIN

The experience of severe loneliness in old age as neither a predictable nor prevalent phenomenon is not a new finding, but it is a well-hidden one. Over 20 years ago, a study of social integration in retirement housing revealed that only a minority of old people were lonely (Rosow, 1962). An extensive cross-cultural study of old people in Denmark, Great Britain, and the United States also reached the conclusion that the vulnerability of old people to loneliness had been exaggerated (Shanas *et al.*, 1968). In the U.S. sample, 70% of those over 65 reported they "never" or "rarely" felt lonely, 21% were "sometimes" lonely, whereas only 9% responded that they "often" felt lonely. A study of rural elderly (Kivett, 1979) yielded similar results: 42.6% reported never feeling lonely, 41.8% were sometimes lonely, and 15.5% were often lonely. A study of the very old Swedish aged (over 70 years old) found loneliness to be a problem for only 27.7% of the sample (70.1% "never"; 11.2% "rarely"; 12.2% "sometimes"; and 6.5% "often," in Berg, Mellstrom, Persson, & Svanborg, 1981).

Two studies that have compared loneliness prevalence rates for different age groups have produced findings congruent with ours. Although excluding individuals over 65, an investigation of the stages of adult life revealed that the youngest subjects (high school graduates) were the loneliest (Lowenthal *et al.*, 1975). Here, too, there was a decrease in reported loneliness through preretirement age. Another newspaper survey (Rubenstein, 1979) also reported a linear decrease in reported loneliness with age in five U.S. cities.

Although there have been a number of studies addressing age-linked differences in loneliness, this topic is often woven into studies with other primary focuses (e.g., Rosow's, 1962, larger study of social integration). The empirical evidence needed to debunk the loneliness myth essentially has been hidden, and it has taken the rising concern over the growth of the elderly population to bring it to the fore. As the studies cited previously confirm, the relatively low prevalence of reported loneliness in old age and its age-linked decline have been replicated a number of times. Only recently, however, have these studies been integrated as a body of research (Peplau, Bikson, Rook, & Goodchilds, 1982) and even then, not in the gerontological literature.

Overall, the quality of information available for documenting the prevalence of loneliness among the aged has been poor. Many of the earlier conclusions describing a predictable loneliness in old age were drawn from clinical observations of patients seeking psychological help, or of institutionalized populations of very old people (Buhler, 1969; Burnside, 1971; Moustakas, 1961). Samples were often small and biased toward the very old, frail elderly. And studies often used a single-item measure indexing how often the respondent was lonely. Further, loneliness was often equated with social isolation, so that loneliness was operationalized as elders who lived alone or had no family.

In sum, research does not confirm the popular set of beliefs linking old age with predictable loneliness. I will now turn to an examination of factors that may account for the development and persistence of the loneliness myth.

THEMES AND ISSUES IN THE STUDY OF AGING THAT CONTRIBUTE TO THE LONELINESS MYTH

Aging and Decline

The perspective of old age as a stage of life entailing change, challenge, and opportunities for personal growth is relatively new. For example, studies of attachment and intimacy have focused for the most part on the early stages of the life cycle, particularly infancy. Only recently has a life-span theory of attachment been proposed, emphasizing that intimacy and the need for reciprocity in relationships continue through very old age (see, for example, Antonucci & Beals, 1980; Kalish & Knudtson, 1976; Lerner & Ryff, 1978; Lowenthal & Robinson, 1976).

Although attitudes toward older people became more positive over the past century, over time a less idealized picture of old age developed as decline and deterioration became the focal characteristics (Achenbaum, 1978). As new information on senescence and the physiology of aging emerged, a medical or disease model became the underlying framework for understanding the aging process. Inherent in this model is the belief that old age is a disease that deprives us of immortality (A. Caplan, 1984; Korenchevsky, 1950, cited in Levin & Levin, 1980). This medical perspective is fostered today by the fact that physicians and social service providers see mainly ill or impoverished old people, biasing their conceptions of aging in that direction. Although the association between the onset of chronological old age and the increased incidence of chronic or disabling illness is strong, it is by no means perfect. Unfortunately, many social gerontologists and geropsychologists have adopted a disease and decline model in their work on the nonmedical, social-psychological aspects of aging, and loneliness has not been immune. For example, disengagement theory (Cumming & Henry, 1961) proposed that the aging process consisted of "an inevitable mutual withdrawal or disengagement" between old people and their social environments. As people aged, they withdrew from society and their social roles; at the same time their social environment contracted (due to, for example, retirement or death of friends). Thus, according to disengagement theory, loneliness would be an inevitable and universal part of growing old. Yet many older people appear to develop and maintain satisfactory relationships (e.g., Lowenthal & Robinson, 1976).

Successful Aging

Research on the problems of the aged has disproportionately addressed the individual's ability to adjust—or rather, failure to adjust—to environmental demands and social stressors; the relationship between aging and successful adaptation may be the oldest, most investigated issue in social gerontology. But how does one define success in aging? To give but one example, relevant to this discussion of loneliness: studies utilizing activity theory (Havighurst, Neugarten, & Tobin, 1968; Lemon, Bengston, & Peterson, 1972) have demonstrated that continued social interaction from middle to late life is related to increased morale and life satisfaction in old age. According to this theory, physically and/or social isolated elderly cannot successfully adapt to old age. Yet other studies have shown some lifelong social isolates to exhibit high levels of morale and life satisfaction; they demonstrate a different adaptational pattern, one of aloneness. It is erroneous, then, to equate loneliness with unsuccessful aging. Adjustment is multidimensional (Lawton, 1982) with different paths leading to it.

Age as a Social Characteristic

Chronological age is only a gross reflection of the aging processes, de-emphasizing the vivid differences across sex, ethnic, and class boundaries within the same age group. Reviewing a large number of studies covering many aspects of the aging process, Atchley concluded that "the older a group of adults born at the same time gets, the more *dissimilar* the individuals in the group become"(1978, p. 6). As a result, their behavior is less well predicted by a small and finite set of factors. Studies examining the prevalence of loneliness in old age may produce widely varying results depending on the populations studied, the questions framed, and the respondents' life circumstances. To obtain a more accurate description of the phenomenon, relationships between age (or life stage) and loneliness should be examined in light of demographic, cultural, and economic factors. Loneliness in old age may be more derivative of particular old age experiences, such as frail health. Thus, theories that draw broad conclusions fail to capture the variety of life experiences of older people.

Social Victimization

In addition to the concept of decline integral to these paradigms of successful normal aging, there is hidden another much more dangerous one: blaming the victim (Ryan, 1971). From this perspective, aging is viewed as something that happens to individuals. Problems of the aged are often attributed to the characteristics of aged people and not to the social forces that may create or magnify those problems. We may convince ourselves that lonely old people deserve to be so, because they are selfish, rigid, and overly demanding on their families. But these convictions serve only as a cognitive charade. According to Lerner (personal communication), derogation or blaming of the elderly is necessary in order to maintain a belief in a just world, and to protect us from feeling vulnerable to the same undesirable fate.

Demographic Shifts in Population Composition

The emergence (and persistence) of the myth of predictable loneliness in old age is rooted in the technological and medical advances of the past half century. Life expectancy has increased dramatically, and with it, the proportion of older people in the population. Census data indicate that there were approximately 25.5 million people over 65 in 1980, comprising 11.2% of the total population. (This represents a 50% increase over the 16.7 million elders in 1960.) It is estimated that by the year 2000 there will be a 35% rise in the number of people over 65, from 26 million to 31.8 million, and by 2030 there will be 55 millions persons 65 or older, or 18 to 22% of the population. Among the elderly, the cohort aged 85 and older will increase most rapidly, followed by the 75-to 84-year-old cohort, and then the 65-to 75-year-old cohort (U.S Bureau of the Census, 1983).

Other demographic changes, as well, have served to perpetuate the myth of loneliness in late life. Later first marriages, fewer children, children becoming independent at an earlier age, and increased rates of family breakdown and divorce all combine to suggest that the ties between older people and their families have weakened. Empirical evidence, however, casts doubt on the notion that old people, as a group, are severely isolated from family and friends (e.g., Lowenthal & Robinson, 1976; Shanas, 1979; Shanas et al., 1968). Shanas (1979) found that most elders lived in close proximity to at least one of their children or other relatives, and had seen at least one of these people within the past two days. Fisher and Phillips (1982), too, found only 8% of older men and 15% of older women to be severely isolated from their families. Thus, research indicates that most older people do have regular family contact.

Being Alone versus Lonely

Although older people are more likely to live alone, there is little empirical support for the claim that living alone in old age is related to increased loneliness. According to the definition of *successful aging* as described in the disengagement or activity theories, it is assumed that the amount of time spent with others, the number of social activities one participates in, and the number of social roles one fills are reflections of the degree to which an older person is not lonely. However, research demonstrates that being alone and loneliness are two distinct phenomena. For example, Heltsley and Powers (1975) found that some older people who had substantial amounts of contact with others still experienced feelings of loneliness, whereas others with minimal contact did not feel lonely at all.

Although single older persons are more objectively isolated than married ones, they have not been shown to be more lonely (Gubrium, 1975; Townsend, 1968; Tunstall, 1966). Forty percent of the most isolated people in Townsend's study of British elderly reported feeling lonely. On a similar note, Lowenthal (1964) provides evidence that those who have maintained a lifelong pattern of social isolation are less lonely in late life than individuals who were strongly integrated into their social environment. Perlman, Gerson, and Spinner (1978) found that single old people who lived with relatives were lonelier than those who lived alone. Thus, as Rubenstein and Shaver (1982) suggest, the link between living alone and loneliness is powerfully mediated by how a person reacts to living alone.

The error in equating living alone with loneliness is in assuming that people who live alone are socially isolated and lonely. Returning to our data, living alone, expectably, was strongly related to marital status, with never-married, widowed, and divorced respondents more likely to live alone than married respondents. Living alone, however, was related to only one of seven variables describing the individual's social environment. Elders living alone were less likely to name someone as a confidant, but had no fewer friends or relatives they could count on for help and were no less satisfied with the number of close friends they had, the quality of those friendships, or the quality of their social lives than older people living with others.

In contrast, all of the social environment variables were strongly related to reported loneliness among older people. The loneliest elders reported having fewer close friends or relatives they could count on and were less likely to have a confidant. What is more important is that they expressed a greater dissatisfaction with available relationships; correlations between loneliness and the variables measuring satisfaction with interpersonal relationships were much stronger than the correlations between loneliness and quantitative variables describing numbers of persons in the social network (see Revenson & Johnson, 1984). Structural features of interpersonal relationships (such as head counts of friends or relatives, geographical proximity to network members) may be poor indicators of the quality of the relationships.

Isolation or Desolation?

The *desolation hypothesis* proposes that a decrease in the quality or quantity of social relationships is the major cause of loneliness in old age (Gubrium, 1975; Townsend, 1968). "Rather than a certain level of isolation, per se, the argument is really one about the effects of changes in life-span isolation, i.e., the impact of persons becoming desolated in old age"(Gubrium, 1975, p. 31). Using marital status as an indicator of change in a primary social relationship, consistent evidence shows that widowed adults, particularly the recently widowed, report greater loneliness and depression and have less social contact than their married cohort across the lifespan (Berardo, 1970; Berg et al.,1981; Kivett, 1979; Lopata, 1969; Perlman et al., 1978). In one study (Gubrium, 1975), never-married elders were more (objectively) isolated than the widowed or divorced but reported lower levels of loneliness. In fact, they more closely resembled their married age-peers in reported loneliness.

Data from our study, too, confirm this. Combining widowed, separated, and divorced elders into a single group ("desolated"), the data indicated that desolated elders were slightly more lonely than either married or never-married older people (although this trend was not statistically significant at the conventional .05 level). Never-married elders were lonelier than the married but were less lonely than desolated elderly.

The desolation hypothesis also proposes that loneliness should be greater among those who have more recently suffered the loss of an intimate attachment. Dividing our sample into those who had lost their spouse or ended their marriage within the past two years and those who had lost their spouse longer than two years ago, a clear recency effect was obtained for loneliness: those who had more recently lost their spouse were lonelier. Although no studies could be located that test a similar desolation effect for close friends or relatives (e.g., siblings, parents), it logically follows that any significant interpersonal loss in late life may trigger increased loneliness. As suggested by Perlman and Peplau (1982), it is important to distinguish between the predisposing and precipitating (more immediate) causes of loneliness.

DIFFICULTIES IN DEBUNKING THE LONELINESS MYTH

This chapter has raised theoretical issues whose methodological implications are central to redefining loneliness in old age. In this section, I will briefly discuss several of the implications that lead to difficulties in debunking the loneliness myth.

Scrutiny of the Data

Data on older populations are subject to the same sampling errors and response biases as (self-report) data of any age group. However, the data are often more closely evaluated for older populations. This issue has been discussed in detail (see Carp & Carp, 1981; Nydegger, 1977) and will not be elaborated here.

Age versus Cohort Effects

Many of the fallacies that support stereotypes of the aging process arise because these stereotypes are based on data that are cross-sectional rather than dynamic or longitudinal. Age differences in any cross-sectional study may be representative of a developmental process or may reflect cohort effects due to historical differences of the different age groups. Cohort effects cannot be ignored, as there are likely to be powerful differences in socialization, life-style, and culturally accepted norms for social behavior across age groups.

Disparity in the Definition of "Old Age"

There is no clear-cut distinction as to what *old* is. Many studies, including the one detailed in this chapter, have used a standard cutoff of age 65, based on the old Social Security criterion. However, studies have sampled individuals as young as 50 to constitute elderly samples. Whatever criteria are used, few studies have included samples of defined elderly large enough to detect small effect sizes. More importantly, these small sample sizes of elderly do not allow researchers to distinguish between the young-old (ages 55–70), the old (ages 70-80), and the old-old (ages 80 and older)(Neugarten, 1975). Although loneliness does appear to decrease with age, there may be a sharp rise in very old age (Dean, 1962; Tunstall, 1966). Research examining age distinctions is crucial and may be even more important as the population ages. What we currently know about what very old age is like is based almost wholly on descriptive and anecdotal accounts (Blythe, 1979; Cowley, 1980; Myerhoff, 1978; Skinner, 1983).

Age Segregation

Negative old-age stereotypes may also have developed because of the isolation of older people from younger generations in living, social, and work environments. Age-segregated retirement housing has flourished in the past decade; the old neighborhood where old and young mingled on brownstone stoops is literally and metaphorically gone. Many younger people do not have the chance to get to know older people.

Media Coverage

Popular culture serves to reflect the values and stereotypes held by the culture; it also, intentionally or unintentionally, perpetuates them. Of partic-ular concern to gerontologists has been the images of aging and the aged in television, cartoons, and newspaper coverage. Although one recent study

(Buckholz & Bynum, 1982) indicated that the elderly are not presented as negatively and passively in the print media as they were 10 years ago, the portrait of aging we receive through the mass media does not convey accurately what to expect as we grow older. There has been a tendency to overlook the emergence of older people as a major segment of the population and to ignore the fact that the elderly have as varied a range of demographic, social, and economic characteristics as any age group. As suggested by Hess (1976), the myths and stereotypes portrayed in the popular media fail to capture the reality of old age precisely because there is no typical aged person nor any one successful way to age.

THOUGHTS AND QUESTIONS FOR RESEARCH

In attempting to debunk the myth of predictable loneliness in old age (as well as other myths of aging) we need to consider whether we are asking the right questions. Many of the early questions tended to focus on delineating characteristics of old people as if they possessed one constellation of personality traits or one role in society. We have come a long way in the past decade. Research has provided evidence of a wide variety of personality and adaptational styles among older people (Binstock & Shanas, 1976).

The entrenched assumptions of gerontological research have limited the types of questions gerontologists are willing to ask. Some questions we should be asking ourselves include the following: What are our purposes in attempting to measure the prevalence of loneliness among elderly populations? Are there consistent age-related changes in loneliness? To what extent are these changes reflective of age-related social conditions, such as widowhood, lowered income, or poorer quality housing versus natural sequelae of inherent biological processes?

A Life-Span Perspective

Although the well-being of the elderly has become the subject of great concern recently, the issue of loneliness is embedded in a life-span developmental framework. Empirical evidence describes gradual psychological changes in conjunction with biological aging, as opposed to sharp discontinuities in personality with age (Neugarten, 1968, 1977). Personality and adaptive styles are continuously shaped by the situational life events, both "on-time" and "off-time," that occur during adulthood. Such evidence suggests that it is important to examine to what extent loneliness in late life reflects lifetime attitudes in forming and maintaining relationships.

The results of our study and others suggest that loneliness changes not simply in prevalence with increasing age but in definition and meaning. Differential expectations for interpersonal relationships at various stages of the life span are most likely a strong explanatory factor of age differences in loneliness. Older and younger people may use different standards to evaluate their social lives. Although opportunities for social and intimate relationships are more numerous for younger people, they are accompanied by high (and often unattainable) expectations for those relationships. The greater prevalence of reported loneliness among young adults found in several studies could result from the failure of current relationships to meet expectations. In one study (Rubenstein, 1979), young adults rated having a spouse or love relationship as much more important than did respondents over 65. More young people also cited "being unattached" as the cause of their loneliness.

Given the somewhat expectable physical changes of aging and a more limited set of age peers to socialize with, older persons may have more realistic expectations for their current and future relationships. They may have experienced enough social losses over their lifetime to have acquired a greater equanimity over them. They may anticipate the "on-time" loss of a spouse, confidant, or colleague and thus, cope with it more successfully than younger people when it does occur, even though such losses do appear to be linked to feelings of loneliness.

As suggested by Blau (1981), the shared-loss experiences by older people may lessen their impact and provide additional coping resources. For example, older widows may report feeling less lonely than young widows because many of their age peers are also widowed. Lopata, Heinemann, and Baum (1982) provide empirical evidence for Blau's social structural theory in a study of Chicago-area widows. Using Neugarten's (1975) terminology of middle-aged, young-old and old-old, they found that 27% of the young and middle-aged widows and 23% of the young-old reported some degree of loneliness as compared to 15% of the old-old widows.

Taking an interactionist approach (Weiss, 1973), loneliness is neither a sole function of personality factors nor of situational factors, but is a product of their combined effect. Because the so-called problems of aging have no single or simple cause, it is necessary to approach them through multiple levels of analysis in a life-span framework, stressing the interplay between personal and environmental factors. It is impossible to understand the aging process without consideration of the connections between biological and psychological aging and the social or cultural milieu. Many of the social problems of old age are not in themselves directly attributable to biological aging processes but to age-related life transitions that frequently occur in later life, such as widowhood, and to social policies and social constructions of aging (Benjamin & Estes, 1983). This distinction is important because it suggests more focused loci for targeting interventions.

SOCIAL INTERVENTIONS

Two different approaches for remedying the so-called social problem of loneliness in old age immediately come to mind. One, an individual-level strategy, is to treat the symptoms of a social problem by treating the stigmatized individuals. In essence, this solution targets interventions at helping older persons cope more effectively with loneliness and compensate for age-related losses. Although the effects of such interventions are often visible and immediate, inherent in this intervention is the assumption that aging is a process of deterioration and decline.

The second approach is to develop educational or legislative interventions to change the social and economic factors that foster our definition of loneliness as a social problem. One mandate of the 1981 White House Conference on Aging was "to mount an education program for the general public to combat the deleterious effects of negative stereotypes about aging and the aged" (H. Johnson, 1982, p. 126). Underlying this approach is the goal of educating society as a whole and not just the "stereotyped" group. Deciding which intervention route(s) to choose requires balancing of short-and long-range effects, cost-effectiveness, and so forth. Although individually-oriented services provided to the elderly have the potential to improve the quality of life for today's elders, they sidestep the issue of larger-scale change based on redefining our social constructions.

The lion's share of current intervention strategies has been targeted toward the lonely individual. But questions regarding the designation of loneliness in old age as a mental health problem remain. Arguments have been presented against age-specific services in light of the impact such services would have on perpetuating negative attitudes toward the aged (cf. Felton, 1982), as loneliness may be more strongly rooted in social problems such as poverty or poor health than in a "lonely personality." For many older individuals, loneliness occurs in response to a particular interpersonal loss, such as death of a spouse (Weiss, 1973). This "situational" loneliness may result in decreased social interaction and/or morale, but appears to be both acute and fairly short-lived (Revenson & Johnson, 1984). As a result, in many cases, it may not require psychological intervention.

The loneliness that results from desolation raises different intervention issues than loneliness that results from lack of social ties or social skills (see Rook & Peplau, 1982). Although many loneliness interventions may be directed toward changing the individual's self-perceptions or attributional set (e.g., Young, 1982), interventions targeted for desolated individuals would focus on helping them adjust to the stressful transition. For example, mutual help groups for newly bereaved or separated persons may facilitate adaptation by providing new opportunities for social contact as well as emotional support and guidance during the transitional period following the loss of an intimate attachment (e.g., Bankoff, 1979; Bloom, Hodges, & Caldwell, 1982; Weiss, 1976). Natural support systems composed of others who are facing or who have faced the same transition have been shown to enhance coping with major life changes (Bankoff, 1983; Hirsch, 1980; Silverman, 1969). As help-seeking behavior declines with age and increases at times of crisis (e.g., Brown, 1978; G. Caplan, 1964; Veroff, Kulka, & Douvan, 1981), consideration of such alternative treatment modalities for loneliness requires a thorough evaluation of the role of social support and mutual help organizations in promoting adaptation to loneliness-inducing life transitions. However, we should not loose sight of the fact that professionals often overidentify issues as problems (e.g., Seidman, 1983). *Non*intervention by professionals may in itself be a better preventive "intervention" for loneliness in late life.

Aging itself is often viewed as a process of deterioration and decline; any deviations from complete physical and emotional well-being are regarded as unsuccessful aging. These deviations, however minor, underly our social construction of most elderly, although truly deviant behavior may accurately depict only a small proportion of older persons. Unfortunately, these overly general social contructions guide social policy. As Seidman has written,

> Uniform solutions are usually applied to many who are labeled elderly, thus reifying and perpetuating the initial problem definition that aging is inherently a process of deterioration and decline and therefore that those "afflicted" must receive special designation so that they can be cared for in segregated and protective settings. Such a social construction of aging is accepted, and consequently fostered by elderly individuals, family, friends, policymakers, and others. (1983, p. 55)

It may be that the most meaningful and far-reaching change will be in the public image of what it means to be an older adult. The increasing political activism, better education, and greater visibility on the part of older people should contribute to this social change by softening the image people hold of aging as an extremely negative part of life.

SUMMARY

What does existing research tell us about loneliness in late life? On the one hand, the popular notion that old people are lonely is a dangerous blanket statement that has not been substantiated by research. On the other hand, the current state of knowledge urges us to go beyond social myth, to investigate the social, economic, and emotional factors that may be linked to loneliness and that may be amenable to educational interventions aimed at social change.

Using the myth of loneliness in late life as an example, I have shown that social myths persist despite convincing and repeated research evidence to the contrary. I have raised many issues in this chapter without giving them full consideration in order to stimulate thinking about them from a somewhat different perspective. Careful consideration of these issues in both the academic and policy realms is critical if we are to understand the complexity of the aging process and design appropriate social interventions. The realization that current attitudes toward aging and the treatment of the elderly are often deeply rooted in social myth should encourage us to work toward systems-level and not individual-level change. We must strike a balance of designating the elderly as a special needs group, in order to provide the health and social services many require, while preventing that designation from leading to potentially harmful stereotyping and discrimination.

ACKNOWLEDGMENTS

I would like to thank David Altman, Barbara Brown, and Howard Friedman for helpful comments on an earlier version of this chapter.

REFERENCES

Achenbaum, W. A. (1978). The obsolescence of old age in America: 1865–1914. In M. M. Selzer, S. L. Corbett, & R. C. Atchley (Eds.), *Social problems of the aging* (pp. 26–35). Belmont, CA: Wadsworth.

Antonucci, T. C., & Beals, J. (1980, November). *Attachment in the aging process: A life span framework.* Paper presented at the Annual Meeting of the Gerontological Society, San Diego.

Atchley, R. C. (1978). Aging as a social problem: An overview. In M. M. Selzer, S. L. Corbett, & R. C. Atchley (Eds.), *Social problems of the aging* (pp. 4–21). Belmont, CA: Wadsworth.

Austen, J. (1976). *Emma. The Complete Novels of Jane Austen* (Vol. 2). New York: Vintage Books. (Original work published 1816)

Bankoff, E. A. (1979). Widow groups as an alternative to informal social support. In M. A. Lieberman, L. D. Borman, & Associates (Eds.), *Self-help groups for coping with crisis,* (pp. 181–193). San Francisco, CA: Jossey-Bass.

Bankoff, E. A. (1983). Aged parents and their widowed daughters: A support relationship. *Journal of Gerontology, 38,* 226–230.

Benjamin, A. E. & Estes, C. (1983). Social interventions with older adults. In E. Seidman (Ed.), *Handbook of social intervention* (pp.438–454). Beverly Hills, CA: Sage Publications.

Berardo, F. M. (1980). Survivorship and social isolation: The case of the aged widower. *Family Coordinator, 19,*11–23.

Berg, S., Mellstrom, D., Persson, G., & Svanborg, A. (1981). Loneliness in the Swedish aged. *Journal of Gerontology, 36,* 342–349.

Binstock, R. H. (1983). The aged as scapegoat. *The Gerontologist, 23,*136–143.

Binstock, R. H., & Shanas, E. (Eds.). (1976). *Handbook of aging and the social sciences.* New York: Van Nostrand Reinhold.

Blau, Z. S. (1981). *Aging in a changing society* (rev. ed.). New York: Franklin Watts.

Bloom, B. L., Hodges, W. F., & Caldwell, R. A. (1982). A preventive intervention program for the newly separated: Initial evaluation. *American Journal of Community Psychology, 10,* 251–264.

Blythe, R. (1979). *The view in winter: Reflections on old age.* New York: Harcourt Brace Jovanovich.

Brown, B. B. (1978). Social and psychological correlates of help-seeking behavior among urban adults. *American Journal of Community Psychology, 6,* 425–440.

Brubaker, T. H., & Powers, E. A. (1976). The stereotype of "old": A review and alternative approach. *Journal of Gerontology, 31,* 441–447.

Buckholz, M., & Bynum, J. E. (1982). Newspaper presentation of America's aged: A content analysis of image and role. *The Gerontologist, 22,* 83–88.

Buhler, C. (1969). Loneliness in maturity. *Journal of Humanistic Psychology, 9,* 167–181.

Burnside I. M. (1971). Loneliness in old age. *Mental Hygiene, 55,* 391–397.

Butler, R. N. (1969). Age-ism: Another form of bigotry. *The Gerontologist, 9,* 243–246.

Butler, R. N. (1975). *Why survive? Being old in America.* New York: Harper & Row.

Butler, R. N. (1980). Ageism: A foreword. *Journal of Social Issues, 36,* 8–29.

Caplan, A. L. (1984). Is aging a disease? In S.F. Spicker & S. R. Ingman (Eds.), *Vitalizing long-term care* (pp. 14–28). New York: Springer.

Caplan, G. (1964). *Principles of preventive psychiatry.* New York: Basic Books.

Carp, F. M. & Carp, A. (1981). It may not be the answer, it may be the question. *Research in Aging, 3,* 85–100.

Cowley, M. (1980). *The view from 80.* New York: Viking Press.

Cumming, E., & Henry, W. E. (1961). *Growing old: The process of disengagement.* New York: Basic Books.

Dean, L.R. (1962). Aging and the decline of affect. *Journal of Gerontology, 17,* 440–446.

Durkheim, E. (1951). *Suicide: A study in sociology.* New York: Free Press. (Original work published 1897)

Estes, C. L. (1979). *The aging enterprise.* San Francisco: Jossey-Bass.

Felton, B. J. (1982). The aged: Settings, services and needs. In L. R. Snowden (Ed.), *Reaching the underserved: Mental health needs of neglected populations* (pp. 23–42). Beverly Hills, CA: Sage Publications.

Fisher, C., & Phillips, S. L. (1982). Who is alone? Social characteristics of people with small networks. In L. A. Peplau & D. Perlman (Eds.), *Loneliness: A sourcebook of current theory, research, and therapy* (pp. 21–39). New York: Wiley.

Gordon, S. (1976). *Lonely in America.* New York: Simon & Schuster.

Gottlieb, B. H. (Ed.). (1981). *Social networks and social support.* Beverly Hills, CA: Sage Publications.

Gray Panthers. (1976). Statement of principles. Reprinted in B. B. Hess (Ed.), *Growing old in America* (pp.462–465). New Brunswick, NJ: Transaction Books.

Gubrium, J. F. (1975). Being single in old age. *International Journal of Aging and Human Develoment, 6,* 29–41.

Harris, L., & Associates (1976). *The myth and reality of aging in America.* Washington, DC: National Council on Aging.

Harris, L., & Associates (1981). *Aging in the eighties: America in transition.* Washington, DC: National Council on Aging.

Havighurst, R. J., Neugarten, B. L., & Tobin, S. S. (1968). Disengagement and patterns of aging. In B. L. Neugarten (Ed.), *Middle age and aging* (pp.161–172). Chicago: University of Chicago Press.

Heltsley, M. E., & Powers, R. C. (1975). Social interaction and perceived adequacy of interaction of the rural aged. *The Gerontologist, 15,* 533–536.

Hess, B. B. (1976). Stereotypes of the aged. In B. B. Hess (Ed.), *Growing old in America* (pp. 449–461). New Brunswick, NJ: Transaction Books.

Hirsch, B. J. (1980). Natural support systems and coping with major life changes. *American Journal of Community Psychology, 8,* 159–172.

Johnson, H. R. (1982). Three perspectives on the 1981 White House Conference on Aging: Education. *The Gerontologist, 22,* 125–126.

Johnson, J. L. (1981). *An attributional model of loneliness.* Unpublished doctoral dissertation, New York University, New York.

Johnson, R. L., & Revenson, T. A. (1981, November). *Life-span perspectives on loneliness: A model and empirical test.* Paper presented at the Annual Meeting of the Gerontological Society of America, Toronto.

Kalish, R. A. (1979). The new ageism and the failure models: A polemic. *The Gerontologist, 19,* 398–402.

Kalish, R. A., & Knudtson, F. W. (1976). Attachment versus disengagement: A life-span conceptualization. *Human Development, 19,* 171–181.

Kivett, V. R. (1979). Discriminators of loneliness among the rural elderly: Implications for interventions. *The Gerontologist, 19,* 108–115.

Kuhn, T. S. (1962). *The structure of scientific revolutions.* Chicago, IL: University of Chicago Press.

Larson, R. (1978). Thirty years of research on the subjective well-being of older Americans. *Journal of Gerontology, 33,* 109–129.

Lawton, M. P. (1982). Competence, environmental press, and the adaptation of older people. In M. P. Lawton, P. G. Windley, & T. O. Byerts (Eds.), *Aging and the environment: Theoretical approaches* (pp.33–59). New York: Springer.

Lemon, B. W., Bengston, V. L., & Peterson, J. A. (1972). An exploration of the activity theory of aging: Activity types and life satisfaction among in-movers to a retirement community. *Journal of Gerontology, 27,* 511–523.

Lerner, R. M., & Ryff, C. D. (1978). Implementation of the life-span view of human development: The sample case of attachment. In P. Baltes (Ed.), *Life-span development and human behavior* (Vol. 1, pp. 1–4). New York: Academic Press.

Levin, J., & Levin, W. C. (1980). *Ageism: Prejudice and discrimination against the elderly.* Belmont, CA: Wadsworth.

Lopata, H. Z. (1969). Loneliness: Forms and components. *Social Problems, 17,* 248–261.

Lopata, H. Z., Heinemann, G. D., & Baum, J. (1982). Loneliness: Antecedents and coping strategies in the lives of widows. In L. A. Peplau & D. Perlman (Eds.), *Loneliness: A sourcebook of current theory, research, and therapy* (pp. 310–326). New York: Wiley.

Lowenthal, M. F. (1964). Social isolation and mental illness in old age. *American Sociological Review, 29,* 54–70.

Lowenthal, M. F., & Haven, C. (1968). Interaction and adaptation: Intimacy as a critical variable. *American Sociological Review, 33,* 20–30.

Lowenthal, M. F., & Robinson, B. (1976). Social networks and isolation. In R. H. Binstock & E. Shanas (Eds.), *Handbook of aging and the social sciences* (pp. 432–456). New York: Van Nostrand Reinhold.

Lowenthal, M. R., Thurner, M., & Chiriboga, D. (1975). *The four stages of life.* San Francisco: Jossey-Bass.

Lynch, J. J. (1977). *The broken heart: The medical consequences of loneliness.* New York: Basic Books.

Moustakas, C. E. (1961). *Loneliness.* Englewood Cliffs, NJ: Prentice-Hall.

Myerhoff, B. (1978). *Number our days.* New York: Simon & Schuster.

Neugarten, B. L. (Ed.). (1968). *Middle age and aging.* Chicago, IL: University of Chicago Press.

Neugarten, B. L. (1975). The future of the young-old. *The Gerontologist, 15,* 4–9.

Neugarten, B. L. (1977). Personality and aging. In J. E. Birren & K. W. Schaie (Eds.), *Handbook of the psychology of aging* (pp.626–649). New York: Van Nostrand Reinhold.

Nydegger, C. N. (Ed.). (1977). *Measuring morale: A guide to effective assessment.* Washington, DC: Gerontological Society.

Palmore, E., & Luikart, C. (1972). Health and social factors related to life satisfaction. *Journal of Health and Social Behavior, 13,* 68–80.

Peplau, L. A., Bikson, T. K., Rook, K. S., & Goodchilds, J. D. (1982). Being old and living alone. In L. A. Peplau & D. Perlman (Eds.), *Loneliness: A sourcebook of current theory, research, and therapy* (pp.327–347). New York: Wiley.

Perlman, D., & Peplau, L. A. (1982). Theoretical approaches to loneliness. In L. A. Peplau & D. Perlman (Eds.), *Loneliness:; A sourcebook of current theory, research, and therapy* (pp.123–134). New York: Wiley.

Perlman, D., Gerson, A. C., & Spinner, B. (1978). Loneliness among senior citizens: An empirical report. *Essence, 2,* 239–248.

Revenson, T. A. (1981). Coping with loneliness: The impact of causal attributions. *Personality and Social Psychology Bulletin, 7,* 565–571.

Revenson, T. A., & Johnson, J. L. (1984). Social and demographic correlates of loneliness in late life. *American Journal of Community Psychology, 12,* 71–85.

Rook, K. S., & Peplau, L. A. (1982). Perspectives on helping the lonely. In L. A. Peplau & D. Perlman (Eds.), *Loneliness: A sourcebook of current theory, research, and therapy* (pp. 351–378). New York: Wiley.

Rosow, I. (1962). *Social integration of the aged*. New York: Free Press.

Rubenstein, C. M. (1979). *A questionnaire study of adult loneliness in three U. S. cities.* Unpublished doctoral dissertation, New York University, New York.

Rubenstein, C. M., & Shaver, P. (1982). The experience of loneliness. In L. A. Peplau & D. Perlman (Eds.), *Loneliness: A sourcebook of current theory, research, and therapy* (pp. 310–326). New York: Wiley.

Ryan, W. (1971). *Blaming the victim.* New York: Vintage Books.

Seidman, E. (1983). Unexamined premises of social problem solving. In E. Seidman (Ed.), *Handbook of social intervention* (pp.48–67). Beverly Hills, CA: Sage Publications.

Shanas, E. (1979). Social myth as hypothesis: The case of the family relations of older people. *The Gerontologist, 19,* 3–9.

Shanas, E., Townsend, P., Wedderburn, D., Friis, H., Milhoj, P., & Stehouwer, J. (1968). *Old people in three industrial societies.* New York: Atherton Press.

Shaver, P., & Rubenstein, C. (1983). Research potential of newspaper and magazine surveys. In H. T. Reis (Ed.), *Naturalistic approaches to studying social interaction. New Directions for methodology of social and behavioral science,* (No. 15, pp.75–91). San Francisco: Jossey-Bass.

Sheppard, H. L. (1976). Work and retirement. In R. H. Binstock & E. Shanas (Eds.), *Handbook of aging and the social sciences* (pp.286–309). New York: Van Nostrand Reinhold.

Silverman, P. R. (1969). The widow-to-widow program: An experiment in preventive intervention. *Mental Hygiene, 53,* 333–337.

Skinner, B. F. (1983). Intellectual self-management in old age. *American Psychologist, 38,* 239–244.

Sullivan, H. S. (1953). *The interpersonal theory of psychiatry.* New York: W.W. Norton.

Townsend, P. (1968). Isolation, desolation, and loneliness. In E. Shanas, P. Townsend, D. Wedderburn, H. Friis, P. Milhoj, & J. Stehouwer (Eds.), *Old people in three industrial societies* (pp.258–287). New York: Atherton Press.

Tunstall, J. (1966). *Old and alone.* London: Routledge & Kegan Paul.

United States Bureau of the Census. (1983). *America in transition: An aging society.* Washington, DC: U.S. Government Printing Office.

Veroff, J., Kulka, R. A., & Douvan, E. (1981). *Mental health in America: Patterns of help-seeking from 1957 to 1976.* New York: Basic Books.

Weiss, R. S. (1973). *Loneliness: The experience of emotional and social isolation.* Cambridge, MA: MIT Press.

Weiss, R. S. (1976). *Marital separation.* New York: Basic Books.

Young, J. (1982). Loneliness, depression, and cognitive therapy: Theory and application. In L. A. Peplau & D. Perlman (Eds.), *Loneliness: A sourcebook of current theory, research and therapy* (pp.379–405). New York: Wiley.

PART 3

Rethinking Systems for Action

The five chapters in this part discuss systems for action and service delivery. Each system is carefully examined with close attention to its underlying assumptions. These assumptions are questioned, and alternative systems for action are proposed, such as empowerment and primary prevention. We see how several premises described in the first chapter unfold and constrain the nature of the resulting intervention. The premise of individualism surfaces repeatedly.

In the first chapter, Julian Rappaport underscores the fact that the most important and interesting aspects of social and community life are, by their very nature, paradoxical. He describes what he sees as the fundamental paradox for viewing people in trouble—the conflict between a "rights" and "needs" model of service delivery. Both are described as one sided, and Rappaport goes on to state:

> What we require is a model which allows us to play within the dialectic and to pursue paradox, first to see one side, then the other; one which allows us to welcome divergent reasoning that permits many simultaneous, different, and contradictory answers, rather than a single solution to every social problem.

Rappaport concludes by suggesting an empowerment model as a contemporary social policy to transcend the rights–needs dialectic. It is based on a different set of assumptions and goals. In particular, it questions the aim of public policy and professionals' role relationship to dependent people. The objective of the empowerment model is the enhancement of possibilities for people to control their own lives.

In the next chapter, Linda K. Girdner develops the theme of paradox in the context of an historical and contemporary analysis of child custody issues. She demonstrates how the underlying ideology has changed during the last century, and with it, the custody assignment for children of divorce. Prior to 1880, a father's right was considered natural and legal. As the economic structure of society changed, the father's rights began to erode, and until very recently had become virtually nonexistent. The courts' changing decision and implicit problem redefinition were clearly related to the ideology of the time.

The roles of gender and individualism are two fundamental ideologies underpinnng the child custody debate. That is, in recent decades, the nurturance and "maternalness" of women were sacrosanct, and the assignment of custody, in most cases, automatic. Girdner points out that more recently there has been an ascendancy of the role of individual behavior (that is, the performance of instrumental and responsible behavior) over gender. With this change the emergence of divorce mediation and joint custody has begun to appear. Girdner sees these as forms of empowerment that symbolize "the increasing emphasis on divorce as a normative critical transition and parental self-determination as the appropriate decision-making process," in contrast to the earlier pathological view of divorce with its concomitant exclusive judicial determination.

The next chapter by Dan A. Lewis and Stephanie Riger turns the issue of dealing with crime on its head. They focus not on the criminal act, but on the fear, distrust, and isolation that victimization causes. Victimization leads to increasingly disintegrative processes in communities, like weakened cohesion, and consequently to greater vulnerability to future criminal acts. The outcome of this argument is also an empowerment, or equal security, model. It is suggested that this can best be achieved by a social policy that makes aid available to local groups and residents who are obliged to solve the problems through collective action.

The suggestions of an equal security model and collective action result from Lewis and Riger's critical analysis of existing models. Other models are advocated by those with relevant vested interests. For example, the coercive model, although sharing the common goal of reducing stress and community disintegration, reserves all actions for policing practices.

The subsequent chapter by Ronald Roesch and Denise J. Foisy also concerns criminal justice system interventions. They suggest that the viewpoint that criminal justice system reforms have failed is premature. They argue that the reforms themselves have been more myth than reality because insufficient attention has been paid to inherent assumptions of previous "reforms."

Reframing the issues is a consistent theme throughout the Roesch and Foisy chapter. One issue that arises consistently is the need for research on long-term effects of interventions. (This issue receives considerable attention in Part 4 of this volume.) Reframing underlying assumptions of criminal justice system interventions leads away from an individual and toward a societal level of analysis, away from rehabilitation and toward early intervention and primary prevention.

In the final chapter of this section, Cary Cherniss turns our interest to delivery system personnel *per se*. "Burnout" is a problem frequently described as characteristic of human service system personnel. This description stems from the dominant scientific-technical paradigm; in fact, such a conceptualization increases the likelihood of burnout. Cherniss suggests an alternative, a moral-religious paradigm, that implies that the prevalent loss of caring should be regarded as a loss of moral commitment rather than as a maladaptive reaction to stress. The latter redefinition directs our thinking toward the development and implementation of institutional and system factors needed to create social commitment mechanisms and practices.

CHAPTER 9

In Praise of Paradox
A SOCIAL POLICY OF EMPOWERMENT OVER PREVENTION

JULIAN RAPPAPORT

The thesis of this chapter is that the most important and interesting aspects of community life are by their very nature paradoxical; and that our task as researchers, scholars, and professionals should be to "unpack" and influence contemporary resolutions of paradox. Within this general theme I will argue that in order to do so we will need to be more a social movement than profession, regain our sense of urgency, and avoid the tendency to become "one-sided." I will suggest that the paradoxical issue that demands our attention in the foreseeable future is a conflict between "rights" and "needs" models for viewing people in trouble.

For those who are concerned with social/community problems, the idea of prevention is the logical extension of a needs model that views people in difficulty as children; the idea of advocacy is an extension of the rights model of people as citizens. I will conclude that both of these are one-sided and propose an empowerment model for a social policy that views people as complete human beings, creates a symbolic sense of urgency, requires attention to paradox, and expects divergent and dialectical rather than convergent solutions.

Originally presented in part as the presidential address, Division 27, 88th Annual Meeting of the American Psychological Association, Montreal, Canada, September 3, 1980. It appeared in the *American Journal of Community Psychology*, 9, 1981. Copyright 1981 by Plenum Press. Reprinted by permission.

JULIAN RAPPAPORT · Department of Psychology, University of Illinois at Urbana-Champaign, Champaign, Illinois 61820.

THE PARADOXICAL NATURE OF SOCIAL/COMMUNITY PROBLEMS

Basic to my argument is an assumption that unlike other (i.e., nonhuman, inanimate, or purely biological) systems, human social systems for living are paradoxical in nature. In order to make my case I will need to dabble in bits of philosophy and history, both social and psychological, and to define some terms. The terms are *paradox, antinomy, convergent and divergent reasoning,* and *dialectic.* I begin with a definition of paradox.

Paradox

A paradox, according to the *Oxford English Dictionary* 1971, (p. 450) is

> 1. A statement or tenet contrary to received opinion or belief...discordent with what is held to be established truth. 2. A statement or proposition which on the face of it seems self contradictory, absurd or at variance with common sense, though on investigation or when explained, it may prove to be well-founded...often applied to a proposition or a statement that is actually self contradictory...essentially absurd and false.

Notice that in this definition there are two possibilities when confronted with paradox: one is that we have discovered an essentially true phenomenon, a reality that at first seems to be self-contradictory but on investigation proves to be well founded. The second possibility is that the paradox is more apparent than real, or a false paradox. I am going to suggest in a moment that one of our tasks as social scientists is to discover the difference between true and false paradox. But first I need to introduce a related term: *antinomy.*

Antinomy

Basic to the idea of paradox is the notion of *antinomy,* "a contradiction in a law, or between two equally binding laws." This idea originates from conflict in authority or in canon or civil law wherein "whatever of the alternative solutions we adopt we are led to absurdity and contradiction"(*Oxford English Dictionary,* 1971, p. 371).

Antinomy is in many respects the rule rather than the exception in social and community life. As Schumacher (1977) points out, the frequently encountered opposites in education and politics, two major fields of social life, are freedom and equality. These are two equally positive values that when mistakenly viewed one at a time, lead us to maximize one and ignore the other. Because they are intimately intertwined they constitute an antinomy and present us with phenomena that are true paradoxes. That is, the very nature of education and politics is paradoxical. The problems do not simply appear to be paradoxical; they actually are paradoxical problems because they are made up of real antinomies.

Using the example of freedom and equality in government: If we maximize one we find that the other is necessarily minimized. Allowing total freedom will lead the strong (in whatever form strength is found—social power, money, physical prowess) to dominate the weak and equality to be obliterated. Equality will require constraints on freedom, which will necessarily impose limits on certain people. This is of course a classical problem, but we tend to think that its solution will be similar to solutions in the physical sciences and can be found by convergent reasoning. The problem requires divergent thought. I will discuss the difference between convergent and divergent thought in a moment.

A crucial task for anyone interested in social/community problems is to look for paradox so as to discover antinomies, such as the one I have just described, in social and community relationships. Once discovered, we will often find that one side or the other has been ignored and its opposite emphasized. To discover which paradoxes of social life are founded on antinomy and which are founded on absurdity and false reasoning is part of our job. That is the understanding part. The action part of our job is then to confront the discovered paradoxes by pushing them in the ignored direction. To take this seriously means that those who are interested in social change must never allow themselves the privilege of being in the majority; else they run the risk of losing their grasp of the paradox. That is one reason why social change is not an end product but rather a process. This leads me to immodestly suggest, only in part facetiously, Rappaport's Rule: *When most people agree with you, worry.*

Dialectic

The idea of the dialectic is central to what this chapter is about. The point is simply that much of what underlies the substance of our field requires us to recognize that we are being pulled in two ways at once and that we often need to pay attention to two different and apparently opposed poles of thought.

The picture of the dialectic that I like best is one portrayed in a modest book called *The Simple Life* by Vernard Eller (1973). Eller likens the dialectic to a department store demonstration of a vacuum cleaner with its hose pointed upward and the machine turned to "blow." In the jet of air above the nozzle there is a Ping-Pong ball caught between two opposing forces. Gravity pulls it down to the air jet, which has the effect of blowing it up. As it goes up it gets out of the range of the force of the air, and gravity pulls it back down.

"Thought or action that operates out of this sort of dynamic tension, giving attention to one truth in such a way that attention must then immediately be given to its counterpart—this is what we mean by dialectic" (Eller, 1973, p.11).

The tendency to become focused on one side of a dialectical problem, that is, to pay attention to one side of the truth so as to fail to take into account an equally compelling opposite, is what I refer to as being *one-sided*.

Joseph E. McGrath, when he was the editor of the *Journal of Social Issues*, reviewed the history of that journal and came to the conclusion, rightly I think, *"that most of the social issues of our time are fundamentally of this form: a basic opposition of two or more 'valid'* (that is morally correct) *principles"* and that *"most social issues of this form have at least two 'decent' solutions* (i.e., morally justifiable) *sides to them (often more than two)"* (p. 36, italics in original).

An example from content in our domain of interest may help to demonstrate the dialectic. In order to implement a social policy decision one must confront the organizational level of analysis, yet as soon as we turn away from individual persons, either the target people or the administrators, we begin to lose our ability to be effective.

When we try to implement a social policy such as Public Law 94-142 (the right to education for all handicapped persons), unless we pay a great deal of attention to the individual teachers who implement such policy at the face-to-face level, we are likely to find the intention of the policy distorted in practice. On the other hand, to deal only with the individual teachers would be very ineffective as a means to alter public policy. Either strategy alone is one-sided.

Another example: the development of compensatory education in our public schools was a step that rejected the notion of stable IQ as the determinant of school performance in favor of direct instruction to enhance performance for high-risk, that is, minority, children. Yet, as benign as was this intention, and indeed there is much reason to assume that direct instruction is useful and has its place, the development of a widespread policy of compensatory education led to what Herbert Ginsburg (1972) so rightly called *the myth of the deprived child.* It became so one-sided that it sanctioned the belief that minority children lack not only the content of middle-class knowledge but the ability to learn, because it refused to acknowledge what they do know and how they acquire it (cf. Hunt, 1969). We, quite mistakenly, as Baratz and Baratz (1970) pointed out a decade ago, institutionalized our heretofore personalized racism. No one intended to do that; we simply paid attention to one side of the dialectic as opposed to the other. We forgot that just because these children could benefit from direct instruction in the content of middle-class knowledge it did not mean that they did not already have a great deal of knowledge and skill. We forgot that change in the schools as well as the children is essential. We allowed ourselves to be content to show a statistical gain on achievement test scores in second grade without bothering to ask if that meant real success in school or in the world. Most such programs have simply ignored the strengths and assets of the children and their families and failed to change the schools, or the opportunity structure of the society, so that program effects simply fade away (e.g., Gray & Klaus, 1970; Rappaport, 1977, Chaps. 7 and 8). What we say is that the effects fail to generalize; what it means is that they do not make any difference in the real world of life.

The same may be said for desegregation. The national policy was intended to equalize educational opportunity. Busing children for racial balance in schools has, in many areas, effectively helped to destroy already decaying black neighborhoods. Respecting and fostering minority culture, preparing children for the majority culture, integration of minority and majority, strengthening local neighborhoods: these are equally compelling values with *opposite* poles. One does not necessarily lead to the other; one may hinder the other. It is by nature a dialectical problem and requires many divergent solutions.

Convergent and Divergent Reasoning

For a description of convergent and divergent reasoning I turn to the work of E. F. Schumacher, best known as the author of *Small is Beautiful* (1973). In his lesser known book, *A Guide for the Perplexed* (1977), Schumacher argues that there are two very different kinds of problems in the world. One type, convergent problems, are those characteristic of inanimate nature. For such problems many solutions are offered that gradually, over time, converge toward *the* right answer, one that turns out to be stable, if improvable, over time. Problems of this type are either solved or "as yet" unsolved. There is no reason, in principle, why unsolved convergent-type problems should not one day be solved forever. It is obvious that this attitude is very effective in the material world, where by choice of problem, exact measurement, and quantification, all problems chosen can and will be solved. In fact, one selects only problems one believes to be solvable.[1] It is far from obvious that social problems are of this type .

What if, rather than converging, we find that equally clear, logical answers, which are exactly the opposite of one another, are developed by equally clear, logical people; that is, the solutions diverge rather than converge?

This is, in fact, the case in social science over time (Cronbach, 1975; Gergen, 1973). That is, as new solutions are developed and institutionalized they become one-sided, and other solutions not seen before, and contradictory

---

[1] Whether or not the physical sciences and engineering, fields more likely than ours to work on convergent problems, do solve all of their problems is actually irrelevant to my argument, which is less that social problems are not solvable and more that they are solvable in many different ways.

to the first, emerge (Takanishi, 1978). The juvenile court is one of my favorite examples (Rappaport, 1980); originally developed as a means to divert children from the evils of the adult court, today we see many diversion programs aimed at diverting children from the evils of the juvenile court itself.

If we are dealing with problems that are dialectical by nature, then they will necessarily yield many divergent rather than one convergent solution, not only over time but even at the same moment in time. That may be one reason why social science seems to have no single dominant paradigm in the Kuhnian sense. Usually we lament this diversity of conflicting paradigms. It may be that the nature of the phenomena are such that diversity of paradigms is a true reflection of the things studied, which may be *best* understood in more than one way.

If by convergent reasoning we act as if there can be *the* solution, we will become one-sided and necessarily create unintended negative consequences by ignoring the other side. This is exactly what we have done when we have tried to implement community mental health policy by taking people out of mental hospitals without paying attention to them, or to the people who would need to interact directly with them, as individuals. The results have often been not only disastrous but inhumane (cf. *New York Times*, 1974, October 20). Unfortunately, some will argue that this means we never should have allowed such people to leave the hospital. That is simply a one-sided solution in the other direction.

In fact, what is wrong is that we acted as if this were a convergent rather than a divergent problem, and we ignored its dialectual nature. The problem of chronic patient status has a variety of solutions, some of which are contradictory, and both sides of the contradiction need to have attention paid to them. This is an example of a problem with a paradoxical nature. When we pay attention to paradox we are more likely than otherwise to find ourselves being useful.

CONFRONTING PARADOX: TWO EXAMPLES FROM OUR PAST

Perhaps one of the most important sources stimulating the origins of community psychology emerged from those who confronted the paradox that demand for human services infinitely expands to meet the services available and that we can never train enough professional mental health manpower to meet the needs (Albee, 1959; Cowen, Gardner, & Zax, 1967). Analysis of the paradoxical relationship between professional training, supply of services, demand and need, not only stimulated the nonprofessional movement, which gave vigor to both community mental health and community psychology, but also provided a kind of urgency to our work.

There are now enough studies of nonprofessionals (Rappaport, 1977) so that even if one is more conservative than to argue that they are better than professionals for certain problems (Durlak, 1979), neither can one argue that there is better evidence for the effectiveness of professionals. In fact, nonprofessional interventions have been subjected to more rather than less scrutiny than those of professionals, especially for service delivery other than psychotherapy *per se*. The fact that the American Psychological Association wishes to ignore this by exclusion and demanding licensing and credentialing is far more of a guild than an effectiveness issue (Gross, 1978; Koocher, 1979). But my aim here is not to convince you of that; it is rather to point out that confronting paradox led to more useful work and new ideas than most research programs.

Another outstanding example of confronting paradox is William Ryan's (1971) classic work, *Blaming the Victim,* and the brief but brilliant paper by Caplan and Nelson (1973) that pushes forward the implications of our individual "person blame" ideology. They presented us with an antinomy, a contradiction. It hurt our moral sensibilities and created a sense of urgency. It has served to fuel excitement in our field. When we see a glimpse of paradox we become charged with urgency because once the opposite to a one-sided solution is seen it burns to be said. Blaming the victim has been a major symbolic and ideological cry for community psychology as a social movement.

COMMUNITY PSYCHOLOGY AS A SOCIAL MOVEMENT

Partly because community psychology has had the character of a social movement (Killian, 1964), it has been able to contribute to the pursuit of paradox, a task that involves emotionality, ideology, the symbolic, and the ideational (Zald, 1980) as well as the logical and the concrete. As Lilly and Smith (1980) have recently shown for the field of special education, to the extent that a discipline becomes more a profession and less a social movement its practitioners are likely to become more defensive, conservative, and lose their sense of "urgency" (Hiller, 1975).

To hold on to urgency requires a cause that transcends ourselves, one that holds symbolic power. To burn with fervor for some higher purpose, be it expressed in understanding or in action, is to be alive and to push ourselves to create the possibilities for change. The most important contributions from community psychology have been fueled with a sense of urgency. To give up such urgency is to live with mediocrity.

A decade ago, in his presidential address to this division, Jim Kelly (1980) proposed an "antidote for arrogance" as the ecological view of man and the role of the psychologist in the community rather than as simply a student of the community. Murray Levine's (1980) recent writing on investigative reporting pleads a similar case for the researcher who immerses one's self in the phenomena of interest. The psychologist of this variety is one who is deeply involved, "dotes" on the environment, and has a "love of community" (Kelly, 1970).

In the decade following Kelly's plea we have seen much of psychology become concerned with establishing itself as a legitimate profession. We have also seen a nation turn from a time of urgency in its search for corporate justice to a desire for individual protection of personal, especially economic, interests.

The context for doing community psychology has changed, and we are being affected by that change in a way that runs the risk of pushing us away from our sense of urgency about the really important questions in the life of the community, toward a consolidation of our own position and a temptation to settle for the security and the mediocrity of fitting in (Special issue on licensing and accredidation, 1979).

If the antidote for arrogance is the ecological view of man, the medicine for mediocrity is the pursuit of paradox. Pursuit of paradox means looking for the contradictions of life. It means finding those places in social and community institutions that have become what I have referred to as *one-sided* and trying to turn them around. When I say "have become one-sided" I am implying that there is more than one side to the ways in which our social institutions can operate to do their job. Partly because institutions have a tendency to become one-sided, many social problems are ironically and inadvertently created by the so-called helping systems—the institutions and organizations developed by well-meaning scientists and professionals—and often "solutions" create more problems than they solve.

I now see such problem creation as a function of convergent reasoning about divergent problems that leads to an inability to think dialectically and causes us to create one-sided monolithic and institutionalized solutions requiring the pursuit of paradox in order to make change possible. Such pursuit can be accomplished only by those who carry a sense of urgency into their work, because all the pressures of professionalism will ask one to ignore the paradox and to keep on doing what is "acceptable."

But fortunately there are always those who fight against such pressures. The anthropologist Jules Henry (1963, p. 10) put it this way: "The strong inherent tendency of Homo Sapiens to search for solutions to problems he himself creates ranges from...therapy...to social revolution...although culture is for man, it is also against him." This statement, presented as a characteristic of human nature, is the prototype. If it is correct that solutions create problems that require new solutions this should be of some interest to us, but not because we can expect to find a solution once and for all. Rather, it is the paradox itself that should be of interest because that should tell us something about the fact that *a variety of contradictory solutions will necessarily emerge* and that we ought not only expect but welcome this, because the more different solutions to the same problem the better, not the worse.

That social institutions and professions create as well as solve problems is *not* a call for working harder to find the single best technique or for lamenting the failure of our best minds to be creative. Quite the opposite. *It is a problem to be understood as contained in the basic nature of the subject matter of our field.* It will always be this way. There can never be a now-and-for-all-time single scientific "breakthrough" that settles and solves the puzzles of our discipline. Today's solution must be tomorrow's problem. And even today we need many different solutions to the same problem, not one monolithic answer. To seek *the* answer may be more than wrong; it may be dangerous. Thomas Merton (1968) put it this way:

> Knowledge expands man like a balloon, and gives him a precarious wholeness in which he thinks that he holds in himself all the dimensions of a truth the totality of which is denied to others. It then becomes his duty, he thinks, by virtue of his superior knowledge, to punish those who do not share his truth. How can he love others he thinks, except by imposing on them the truth which they would otherwise insult and neglect. (p. 44)

This reality when pointed out by others such as Sarason (1978) has, I think, sometimes been misinterpreted to suggest that there are no solutions to social problems and that if we follow this view to its logical conclusion we must give up trying (McGrath, 1978). It is as if human problems can only be handled by positivistic convergent science or not at all. I do not believe that there are no solutions, only that given the nature of social problems there are no permanent solutions and no single this-is-the-only-answer-possible solutions, even at any moment in time. Divergent, dialectical problems must have many solutions that, like the Ping-Pong ball in Eller's example, change with the currents. The challenge for our discipline is to continue to fuel the fires of urgency by seeking out the paradoxical, by finding those places where one-sided solutions have developed, and pushing the institutions toward the other side. To do this requires that we pay some attention to social history.

SOCIAL HISTORY AND THE RIGHTS/NEEDS DIALECTIC

When the community mental health movement began to impact on psychology we believed that we were entering an era of exciting social change, and to some extent we may have been. What the community mental health movement did was to confront the fact that the mental health system had gone too far to one side and become an institutional warehouse for the poor and an existential philosophy for the wealthy. Confronting this one-sidedness was both necessary and useful. It had the character and urgency of a social movement; it pushed the dialectic within the mental health professions in an ignored direction, that is, toward deinstitutionalization and extending the reach of viable services to the unreached.

For the profession of psychology the period between mid-1960 and mid-1970 was the community mental health decade, and many American psychologists were greatly influenced by and contributed to it; but taken out of historical time it is not well understood. To understand what we were experiencing requires historical context other than the purely professional.

Those in the community mental health movement may not have fully appreciated the extent to which they were riding on the cusp of a change between two essentially different eras—each on opposite sides of a dialectic formed between a "rights" and a "needs" view of dependent people. Community mental health was, I now believe, the last breath of a dying age that social historians call the Progressive Era (Bremner, 1956; Chambers, 1963; Davis, 1967; Gaylin, Glasser, Marcus, & Rothman, 1978; Lubove, 1969). I will rely heavily for my brief description of this era on the work of historian David Rothman (1971, 1980) and others in *Doing Good: The Limits of Benevolence* (Gaylin, Glasser, Marcus, & Rothman, 1978).

The mainstream reform position in the United States between 1900 and 1965 was largely an attempt to translate the biological model of the caring parent into a program for social action. The prime-moving rationale was belief in the state as parent, not simply as metaphor but literally. This belief informed both the questions and the answers. For the first two-thirds of this century the legislative, governmental, and administrative social policymakers built an apparatus to provide services to the needy with little concern about the possibility of abuse and loss of rights. In this scheme of things the helping professions were the frontline soldiers in an army that would benevolently care for the poor, the retarded, the mentally ill, and the downtrodden. Those in need were more or less like children, to be helped, told what to do, and kept off the streets. The liberal mind was captivated by this idea which Rothman (1980) sees as a union of "conscience and convenience."

By mid-1960, just as this progressive era was about to give way to a new ideology, the community mental health movement (together with the "war on poverty") began to emerge. The thrust of community mental health came as a last-ditch effort to parent the entire society by means of the noble ambition of extending the reach of services via catchment areas to the heretofore unreached. What is ironic is that the community mental health movement believed itself to be a new benevolence when in fact it was a dying twitch of a beheaded organism.

The helping professions themselves have been shaped out of the era of progressivism. Partly because the progressive era social programs and their community mental health offspring had promised too much and compromised too much, and partly because of the experience of the civil rights movement and the war on poverty, and partly because of economic factors and an overbloated beauracracy, and partly because of generalization from the perceived energy crisis and the movement toward conservation of material resources, there has now developed a seemingly strange alliance between fiscal conservatives and social reformers. The reformers want to break down what they see as the negative effects of the "helping" social control institutions; the fiscal conservatives want to save money.

As the community mental health movement is transformed and dies out (of course I do not expect the words or the places named community mental health centers to die out so much as the intellectual vigor and social power of the idea), we are witnessing the rise of the idea of rights over needs. The paradox for the remaining years of this century will be encapsulated in a struggle between opposing views of the poor, the physically disabled, the mental patient, the retarded person, the juvenile, the elderly, and so on, as dependent persons to be helped, socialized, trained, given skills, and have their illnesses prevented, or as citizens to be assured of rights and choices. Symbols and imagery will be very important in this struggle. It makes a great deal of difference if you are viewed as a child or as a citizen, because if you believe it you are quite likely to act the part (Snyder & Swann, 1978; Swann & Snyder, 1980), and if those in power believe it they are likely to develop programs, plans, and structures that will help you to believe it.

The elderly are perhaps a case in point because of their relatively new status as either a "class to be represented" or as a population "at risk," depending on a rights or a needs point of view. There is already a struggle between those who see being old as a disease that requires services and those who see it as a period of life that requires assurance of citizen rights. Although neither view is a panacea, the images they conjure up do have an impact on us as well as them. Likewise, for the physically and mentally handicapped there is a struggle between aims of normalization and protection.

Now is a time when there is great pressure for the courts and the legislatures, through law, social, and administrative policy to offer fewer services and more rights. This has led to some strange bedfellows. We see them come together in the deinstitutionalization movements in mental health and child welfare, systems that are currently under fire on all sides, from radical noninterventionists through group-home advocates, from advocates of due process for children through advocates of benign neglect. The era of rights and fiscal conservatism is with us as its supporters compete with the more established help-centered agencies for symbolic, material, and social power (Glasser, 1978; Knitzer, 1980; 1978; Koocher, Webber & McCall, 1978).

Given our tendency to look for solutions as if we have convergent nondialectical problems, we can expect to see two developments in the helping fields' reaction to the changing sociopolitical and economic atmosphere. Many of the helpers will try to maintain control and services, basically standing by the progressive era notion of the expert as parent giving benign treatments on an individualized basis to the downtrodden, albeit now outside the institution. We will see new and optimistic arguments for the effectiveness of therapy and other social services for the poor combined with economic arguments to refocus our gaze on doing treatment for those who want it and to ignore as "not our job" the social conditions under which many people live their lives (Buck & Hirschman, 1980).

Others, still unable to let go of the needs model of the progressive era, but dissatisfied with programs that only treat people after they are in obvious trouble, will maintain that our task is to assist high-risk populations to adjust to the reality of social institutions. We may now prefer to call this *teaching competencies* rather than doing psychotherapy, but the crucial element of "expert–helper," or the "doctor–patient relationship," or at least the "student–teacher relationship," will be maintained. There will be no question about who is "up" and who is "down." Even programs aimed at so-called structural change, when framed in terms of *prevention*, create a metaphor that despite intentions, when adopted by our social institutions, yields all the wrong symbols, images, and meta messages.

Frankly, I am beginning to suspect that as it grows in popularity among mental health professionals, even to the point where the National Institute of Mental Health makes it a training grant priority for clinical psychology training programs, the whole idea behind prevention will somehow lose out to the image it creates. Prevention programs aimed at so-called high-risk populations, especially programs under the auspices of established social institutions, can easily become a new arena for colonialization, where people are forced to consume our goods and services, thereby providing us with jobs and money. Rothman (1980) observed that the progressives did not reduce the use of institutions; they added on new programs for more people while the supposed target groups continued to languish in institutions. Prevention programs may not change our current social institutions, but rather add on to them, and in turn to the therapeutic state (Kittrie, 1974); and I might add, with little evidence that they actually prevent anything.

This underlies much of what is called *prevention*: find so-called high-risk people and save them from themselves, if they like it or not, by giving them, or even better, their children, programs that we develop, package, sell, operate, or otherwise control. Teach them how to fit in and be less of a nuisance. Convince them that a change in their test scores is somehow the same as a change in their life. Operating our interventions through the professionally controlled educational and social agencies developed during the progressive era fosters this attitude, because it is consistent with the culture of these settings. Thus, we are consultants, not to people, but to agencies, schools, and other sanctioned social agents. Our role relationships to people need never change (Fairweather, 1972).

On the other side, equally convergent nondialectical in their thinking, stand both those who are saving money wasted on programs of unproven value and those who push for "freedoms" and "rights," including the right to be different to the point of missing the freedom to be the same as others, to obtain help, education, or services. Having rights but no resources and no services available is a cruel joke. Although ostensibly motivated out of a great deal of respect for the individual right not to be socialized or controlled so long as one hurts no one but one's self and by the desire to limit the arbitrariness of the therapeutic state, or the arrogance of prevention programs that I have just criticized, this position easily becomes one of "benign neglect." Just as easily as helpers can slip from a real desire to prevent mental illness into a social control mentality that obliterates legitimate differences or to mistake change on test scores for change in the conditions of life, advocates and fiscal conservatives can slip from a critique of naive helpers and concern over the violation of the rights of dependent people into their own naive belief that help will somehow emerge from the private sector, or that it is not needed at all, or mistake a change in law for a change in the conditions of life. We can, in our overreaction to the failures of progressivism, be led to allow the state (i.e., the citizenry) to ignore its moral and social (as opposed to simply legal) obligations.

Stier (1978), calling on the work of Hart (1955), has suggested that if we rely on the courts to provide as "rights" conditions of living that are actually human "needs," we run the risk of confusing the rights of children with the moral duty of the state, and she reminds us that "inspiring society to meet its duties to children [I would say to all dependent persons] involves the creation of a sense of moral and social imperative" (p. 57). To the extent that we accept the notion that advocating for legal rights is *the* solution to problems in living we will settle for a one-sided solution that misses the dialectal relationship between rights and needs. What good is the right to be in the community with no role, no respect, and no resources?

History seems to show that as society becomes more politically conservative we turn to a social science explanation favoring the intra-psychic as opposed to the environmental (Levine & Levine, 1970). It would be naive to think that in conjunction with our current swing toward conservative politics this will mean a simple return to older theoretical views of personality and psychodynamics, although that in part will be true. Rather, we will see an increased emphasis on *cognitive* (in-the-head) behavior modification and self-control, on socio-*biology*, on *individual* rights, and on changing the *person* side of person–environment fit as in so-called competency training as a form of socialization. These trends run counter to the behaviorism that helped to free us from our predetermined genetic background, the sociology that overturned the eugenics movement, the ecological view of context that has emphasized social change, and the civil liberties movement that sought corporate (class action) freedoms on the basis of moral imperatives.

There is now emerging a new kind of conservative intrapsychic and individual responsibility ideology that will blame victims in new and more clever ways. We will even be made to feel righteous about it. We will be asked to ignore the needs that do not fit into our social agencies, schools, and consulting rooms, as too costly a waste of resources on ineffective programs of unproven value. Those we ignore will be described as obtaining their right not to be coerced. This will salve our consciences as we collect money and prestige from the others. We will be told to become more of a profession (like real doctors) so we can qualify for certain social rewards by limiting our activities to those that are proper for licensed and accredited people and programs, that is, those that are reimbursable by insurance or supportable by grants or by established social agencies.

Because this is a paradoxical, dialectical problem, they will be partly correct. There are people who benefit from a needs-oriented human service system, and there are those who benefit from rights-oriented controls on that system; but there are a great many people, including the real social disasters of our society, who require both rights and needs. If we hope to be useful to them, *we will need to find a renewed symbolic and ideational goal and a renewed sense of urgency.* We must be a social movement that confronts with divergent reasoning the antinomies in the paradox of helping others. Many of us have placed our bets on the ideology of prevention. It is my contention that this ideology has outlived its usefulness and is one-sided at its core. It is a product of our failed social history, and it creates the wrong symbolism. In the final part of this chapter I will make the case that empowerment rather than prevention is far more promising both as a plan of action and as a symbolic ideology for the social movement called *community psychology.*

By *empowerment* I mean that our aim should be to enhance the possibilities for people to control their own lives. If this is our aim, then we will necessarily find ourselves questioning both our public policy and our role relationship to dependent people. We will not be able to settle for a public policy that limits us to programs we design, operate, or package for social agencies to use on people, because it will require that the form and the metacommunications as well as the content be consistent with empowerment. We will, should we take empowerment seriously, no longer be able to see people as simply children in need or as only citizens with rights, but rather as full human beings who have both rights and needs. We will confront the paradox that even the people most incompetent, in need, and apparently unable to function, require, just as you and I do, more rather than less control over their own lives, and that fostering more control does not necessarily mean ignoring them. Empowerment presses a different set of metaphors upon us. It is a way of thinking that lends itself to a clearer sense of the divergent nature of social problems.

THE LOGIC AND THE IMAGERY OF EMPOWERMENT

There are at least two requirements of an empowerment ideology. On the one hand, it demands that we look to many diverse local settings where people are already handling their own problems in living, in order to learn more about how they do it. This demand is obviously consistent with, indeed requires, divergent reasoning. On the other hand, it demands that we find ways to take what we learn from these diverse settings and solutions and make it more public, so as to help foster social policies and programs that make it more rather than less likely that others not now handling their own problems in living or shut out from current solutions, gain control over their lives.

Newbrough (1980) concluded his presidential address with a vision of what he called the participating society. He suggested, from review of a variety of writers on justice, values, society, bureaucracy, politics, and community life, that "the public interest is the empowerment of people" (p. 15). Riger (1980) has also commented on the logic behind empowerment. I suggest that this be our call to arms and that it replace "prevention" as our aim because the connotations, the metameanings, and the implications are different.

The idea of prevention is derived from a needs model of dependent people; it is a legacy of the progressive era and of the one-sided development of social service institutions. Within the context of social service agencies and a needs/dependency model, which views people as children, prevention is the most sensible logical alternative to clinical services for all the reasons of efficiency its adherents have argued (Caplan, 1964; Cowen, 1980; President's Commission on Mental Health, 1978).

Advocacy is an alternative based on a rights model of social responsibility (Webber & McCall, 1978). It is a logical approach based on the assumptions derived from a legal/due process ideology that views people as citizens rather than as children. It is just as logical as prevention and just as one-sided. Both advocacy and prevention suggest professional experts as leaders who know the answers and provide them for their clients. Despite many obvious differences this similarity in role relationships is striking.

What we require is a model that allows us to play within the dialectic and to pursue paradox, first to one side, then the other; one that allows us to welcome divergent reasoning that permits many simultaneous, different, and contradictory answers, rather than a single solution to every social problem. But we cannot afford to be dilettantes. We require social action and genuine involvement in the world. That, in turn, requires symbolic imagery to fuel the flames of urgency and to energize a movement. The imagery of empowerment has a very different feel than the imagery of prevention. Prevention suggests professional experts; empowerment suggests collaborators.

Empowerment implies that many competencies are already present or at least possible, given niches and opportunities. Prevention implies experts fixing the independent variables to make the dependent variables come out right. Empowerment implies that what you see as poor functioning is a result of social structure and lack of resources that make it impossible for the existing competencies to operate. It implies that in those cases where new competencies need to be learned, they are best learned in a context of living life rather than in artificial programs where everyone, including the person learning, knows that it is really the expert who is in charge (cf. Rappaport, Davidson, Wilson, & Mitchell, 1975).

If a problem is by nature divergent, it must have many solutions. If a problem can have many solutions, then it can have a diversity of people with a diversity of experiences who work out the solutions. Empowerment lends itself to the possibility of a variety of locally rather than centrally controlled solutions, which in turn fosters solutions based on different assumptions in different places, settings, and neighborhoods. The criterion shifts from a single one-sided standard of competence to genuine recognition that social problems have many different definitions as well as answers (Seidman, 1978), and that might (holding social power and material resources) does not necessarily make right; it simply allows one's solution to be acceptable.

As Illich (1976) has so well pointed out in the domain of physical health, the pervasive belief that experts should solve all of our problems in living has created a social and cultural iatrogenesis which extends the sense of alienation and loss of ability to control life even to one's own body. This is the path that the social as well as the physical health experts have been on, and we need to reverse this trend. We must begin to develop a social policy that gives up the search for one monolithic way of doing things according to *the* certified expert (i.e., the symbolic parent). Quality control from the central authority becomes a silly idea in this view. Rather than a top-down or forward mapping of social policy it is a bottom-up or backward mapping that starts with people and works backward to tell officials what social policies and programs are necessary (Elmore, 1979). This means that empowerment will not only look different depending on what sort of problems in living one is confronting, but it may even look different in each setting that it operates. Diversity of form rather than homogeneity of form should dominate if the operating process is empowerment.

As Naparstek and Cincotta (National Commission on Neighborhoods, 1979) have suggested with regard to the problem of decaying cities:

> [One] reason for the persistent failure of... programs has been the tendency to perceive the problem on a grand scale. Virtually all efforts to halt the decline of

our cities are marked by a failure to define national policy initiatives which serve the varied needs of differing neighborhoods. If we are to speak realistically of preconditions required for effective change, it must be recognized that the neighborhood—not the sprawling, anonymous metropolis—is the key. In real terms, people live in neighborhoods, not cities. In real terms, their investments, emotional as well as economic, are in the neighborhoods, not cities. And the city cannot survive if its neighborhoods continue to decline. (p.1)

With regard to the poor, Berger and Neuhaus (1977) put it this way:

Upper-income people already have ways to resist the encroachment of megastructures. It is not their children who are at the mercy of alleged child experts, not their health which is endangered by miscellaneous vested interests, not their neighborhoods which are made the playthings of utopian planners. Upper-income people may allow themselves to be victimized on all these scores, but they do have ways to resist if they choose to resist. Poor people have this power to a much lesser degree...empowering poor people to do the things that the more affluent can already do aims at spreading the power around a bit more—and to do so where it matters, in people's control over their own lives. (pp. 7-8)

It is not only the poor and the local neighborhoods that would benefit from a public policy of empowerment. Even traditional clinical populations stand to benefit from a goal that tends to foster more rather than less control over their own lives. There is no doubt that we lack a great deal of direct experimental data on the wonderful mental health outcomes when we collaborate with grass roots people. However, there is also no doubt that the same may be said for prevention programs (Novaco & Monahan, 1980) or advocacy. On the other hand, programs that foster what I have called elsewhere (Rappaport, 1977) *autonomous alternative settings,* obviously consistent with an empowerment ideology, such as the work of Fairweather (1972, 1979; Fairweather, Sanders, Cressler, & Maynard, 1969; Fairweather, Sanders, & Tornatzky, 1974) and of the Mendota group (Marx, Test, & Stein, 1973; Stein, Test, & Marx, 1975) with chronic patients, or the work of Goldenberg (1971) with "hard core" delinquents, have presented data that are as compelling as we are likely to find from programs for these populations.

Moreover, it is not clear to me why the criterion should be a measure of mental health in the narrow disciplinary sense. I am, frankly, willing to argue that programs and policies that make it more possible for people to obtain and control the resources that affect their lives are *per se* what empowerment is all about. This is based, in part, on my social values, but also in part on a variety of social science data bases.

There is ample psychological evidence from the study of normal (i.e., nonclinical) populations to safely conclude that the felt sense of internal control or alienation (Phares, 1973; Phares & Lamiell, 1977; Rotter, 1975; Seaman, 1972), learned helplessness (Seligman, 1975; Seligman & Maier, 1967; Sue & Zane, 1980), ascribed and achieved status (Sarbin, 1970), expectancy for success (Gurin & Gurin, 1970; Seidman & Rappaport, 1974), attributions

(Strickland & Janoff-Bulman, 1980), the impact of perceived labels (Rappaport & Cleary, 1980), and of the beliefs of powerful others (Snyder & Swann, 1978; Swann & Snyder, 1980) matters a great deal to people. It also seems safe to conclude that most people are likely to benefit psychologically from more rather than less control over their lives and resources. In addition, laboratory studies and historical analysis of group cohesiveness (Guttentag, 1970) as well as the obvious outcomes and popularity of self-help groups, labor unions, community organizations, and community development projects (Hampden-Turner, 1975; National Commission on Neighborhoods, 1979) must lead us to the same conclusion: Empowerment is a sensible social policy, but one that requires a breakdown of the typical role relationship between professionals and community people. Empowerment needs to be based on divergent reasoning that encourages diversity through support of many different local groups rather than the large centralized social agencies and institutions which control resources, use convergent reasoning, and attempt to standardize the ways in which people live their lives.

The implications of an empowerment ideology force us to pay attention to the mediating structures of society, that is, those that stand between the large impersonal social institutions and individual alienated people. For Berger and Neuhaus (1977), these include the family, the neighborhood, the church, and voluntary organizations. These are the places where people live out their lives, and the more control they have over them the better.

As researchers, our obligations are to study and understand more about how such settings actually work to provide niches for people that enhance their ability to control their lives and allow them both affirmation and the opportunity to learn and experience growth and development. On the action side, it is clear to me that we have been far too willing to intervene, label, and tell others how to cope with life without understanding how the diversity of settings in which people actually do live well operate. Most of our advice is drawn from a very limited set of personal or professional experiences in settings designed and controlled *by* professionals *for* others.

It is now quite obvious that for many people their network of friends, neighbors, church relationships, and so on, provide not only support, but genuine niches and opportunities for personal development. How can we learn to help to create new settings, or to assist those who are isolated from such settings or those who are trapped in settings that are harmful rather than helpful, if we do not spend a great deal of time observing, describing, and collaborating?

The recent interest in so-called natural support systems (Gottlieb, 1976, 1979; Gottlieb & Todd, 1979; Hirsch, 1980; Maton, 1979, 1980; Riessman, 1976) and in social support as a moderator of stress (Cobb, 1976; Dohrenwend, 1978; Lin, Simeone, Ensel, & Kuo, 1979; Sandler, 1980) has the potential to serve as an impetus for research and action of a different variety than the traditional convergent, one-sided sort, which I have criticized in this chapter, *only* if we are willing to see it as descriptive of how a variety of people are able to find a variety of means to solve their own problems in living. We can learn a great deal about how this works when it works well if we are willing to observe the process of empowerment when it is taking place, even if that is in settings which we typically ignore and over which we have no control. We need to recognize that many settings that are successful in the creation of opportunities, niches, and resources for empowerment will not concern themselves with mental health in our rather narrow disciplinary sense, and that not only are these genuine solutions of local people to their problems in living likely to be diverse, but the very behavior, attitudes, and life-styles that are useful to people will also differ from place to place. We need to learn from them what the range of solutions is really like and then to encourage social policies that enable more people to develop their own solutions.

Unfortunately, psychologists, and particularly mental health professionals, have a tendency to exclude *a priori* solutions to problems in living about which they know very little. For example, recent research comparing charismatic and mainline churches (McGaw, 1979) finds evidence that growth of so-called conservative congregations may be as much a function of a social structure that fosters a sense of community as is doctrinal appeal. Given what we know about the influence of organizational social structure on people in work settings (e.g., Hackman, 1976) or communes (Kanter, 1972), such findings in religious organizations are hardly surprising. Yet despite the fact that some two-thirds of Americans have formal membership in a church or synagogue (Jacquet, 1972) and that such settings provide a wide variety of important functions in people's lives (cf. Bergin, 1980; Pargament, 1982) these settings are likely to be either ignored by the mental health establishment or conceptualized as if they were second-rate mental health agencies in need of psychological consultation, rather than as places for us to learn from. This, despite the fact that one of our professed goals is to enhance the psychological sense of community. The same may be said for a variety of other local groups and organizations in neighborhoods, voluntary associations, clubs, and so on.

This is not an argument for any single solution such as developing more churches, block organizations, or tenants' councils. It is an argument for our work, at both the local and the social policy level, to recognize and foster the legitimacy of more rather than fewer, different rather than the same, ways to deal with problems in living. To the extent that we try to force our understanding of community settings into a prevention of mental illness or a social adjustment model, or our preconceived notions of how people ought rather than how they do solve their own problems, we will misunderstand both the nature of social problems and the meaning and value of settings for living. We will thereby cut off the possibility that we can learn a variety of divergent solutions from them. As Jacob Bronowski (1956, p.10) warned some 25 years ago: "Man masters nature not by force but by understanding. This is why science has succeeded where magic failed: because it has looked for no spell to cast over nature."

I conclude where I began. The most important and interesting aspects of community life are by their very nature paradoxical. Social problems, paradoxically, require that experts turn to nonexperts in order to discover the many different, even contradictory, solutions that they use to gain control, find meaning, and empower their own lives. From such study, which will require genuine collaboration fueled by a sense of urgency, we may be able to help develop programs and policies that make it possible for others to find niches for living and gain control over their lives. At this time in our history I believe that empowerment encapsulates the symbolic message required to bring a new sense of urgency and to transcend the rights/ needs dialectic. Should empowerment become dominant as a way of thinking I have no doubt that it too will force one-sided solutions. I come, not to bury paradox, but to praise it.

ACKNOWLEDGMENTS

In a chapter such as this one there are many intellectual debts. Those of which I am most aware are to the works of social historian David J. Rothman and economist and philosopher E. F. Schumacher. Perhaps less obvious but more direct is the influence of two colleagues whose papers (Sarason, 1978; Seidman, 1978) I deem to be among the more important written in this field, and that force me to see this one as a sequel. In addition, I am intellectually indebted to my friend, Ronald Simkins, who quite directly gave me many of the ideas presented here, and to conversations with and the influence of many others including Thom Moore, Ken Maton, Fern Chertok, Bruce Rapkin, Ann Jolly, Kathy Roesch, and Arlene Rappaport.

REFERENCES

Albee, G. W. (1959). *Mental health manpower trends.* New York: Basic Books.
Baratz, S., & Baratz, J. C. (1970). Early childhood intervention: The social science base of institutional racism. *Harvard Educational Review, 40,* 29–50.
Berger, P. L., & Neuhaus, R. J. (1977). *To empower people: The role of mediating structures in public policy.* Washington, DC: American Enterprise Institute for Public Policy Research.
Bergin, A. E. (1980). Psychotherapy and religious values. *Journal of Consulting and Clinical Psychology, 48,* 95–105.
Bremner, R. (1956). *From the depths: The discovery of poverty in the United States.* New York: New York University Press.

Bronowski, J. (1956). *Science and human values.* New York: Harper.

Buck, J. A., & Hirschman, R. (1980). Economics and mental health services: Enhancing the power of the consumer. *American Psychologist, 35,* 653–661.

Caplan, G. (1964). *Principles of preventive psychiatry.* New York: Basic Books.

Caplan, N., & Nelson, S. D. (1973). On being useful: The nature and consequences of psychological research on social problems. *American Psychologist, 28,* 199–211.

Chambers, C. (1963). *Seedtime of reform: American social service and social action.* Minneapolis: University of Minnesota Press.

Cobb, S. (1976). Social support as a moderator of life stress. *Psychosomatic Medicine, 38,* 300–314.

Cowen, E. L. (1980). The wooing of primary prevention. *American Journal of Community Psychology, 8,* 258–284.

Cowen, E. L., Gardner, E. A., & Zax, M. (Eds.). (1967). *Emergent approaches to mental health problems.* New York: Appleton-Century-Crofts.

Cronbach, L. J. (1975). Beyond the two disciplines of scientific psychology. *American Psychologist, 30,* 116–127.

Davis, A. F. (1967). *Spearheads for reform: The social settlements and the progressive movement.* New York: Oxford University Press.

Dohrenwend, B. S. (1978). Social stress and community psychology. *American Journal of Community Psychology, 6,* 1–15.

Durlak, J. A. (1979). Comparative effectiveness of paraprofession and professional helpers. *Psychological Bulletin, 86,* 80–92.

Eller, V. (1973). *The simple life: The Christian stance toward possessions.* Grand Rapids: Eerdmans.

Elmore, R. F. (1979). Backward mapping: Implementation research and policy decisions. *Political Science Quarterly, 80,* 601–616.

Fairweather, G. W. (1972). *Social change: The challenge to survival.* Morristown, NJ: General Learning Press.

Fairweather, G. W. (1979). Experimental development and dissemination of an alternative to psychiatric hospitalization: Scientific methods for social change. In R. F. Munoz, L. R. Snowden, & J. G. Kelly (Eds.), *Social and psychological research in community settings.* San Francisco: Jossey-Bass.

Fairweather, G. W., Sanders, D. H., Cressler, D. L., & Maynard, H. (1969). *Community life for the mentally ill: An alternative to institutional care.* Chicago: Aldine.

Fairweather, G. W., Sanders, D. H., & Tornatzky, L. G. (1974). *Creating change in mental health organizations.* New York: Pergamon Press.

Gaylin, W., Glasser, I., Marcus, S., & Rothman, D. (1978). *Doing good: The limits of benevolence.* New York: Pantheon.

Gergen, K. J. (1973). Social psychology as history. *Journal of Personality and Social Psychology, 26,* 309–320.

Ginsburg, H. (1972). *The myth of the deprived child: Poor children's intellect and education.* Englewood Cliffs, NJ: Prentice-Hall.

Glasser, I. (1978). Prisoners of benevolence: Power versus liberty in the welfare state. In N. Gaylin, I. Glasser, S. Marcus, & D. Rothman (Eds.), *Doing good: The limits of benevolence.* New York: Pantheon.

Goldenberg, I. I. (1971). *Build me a mountain: Youth, poverty and the creation of new settings.* Cambridge: MIT Press.

Gottlieb, B. H. (1976). Lay influences on the utilization and provision of health services: A review. *Canadian Psychological Review, 17,* 126–136.

Gottlieb, B. H. (1979). The primary group as supportive milieu: Applications to community psychology. *American Journal of Community Psychology, 7,* 469–480.

Gottlieb, B. H., & Todd, D. (1979). Characterizing and promoting social support in natural settings. In R. F. Munoz, L. R. Snowden, & J. G. Kelly (Eds.), *Social and psychological research in community settings.* San Francisco: Jossey-Bass.

Gray, S. W., & Klaus, R. A. (1970). The early training project. A seventh year report. *Child Development, 41,* 909–924.

Gross, S. J. (1978). The myth of professional licensing. *American Psychologist, 33,* 1009–1016.

Gurin, G., & Gurin, P. (1970). Expectancy theory in the study of poverty. *Journal of Social Issues, 26,* 83–104.

Guttentag, M. (1970). Group cohesiveness, ethnic organization and poverty. *Journal of Social Issues, 26,* 105–132.

Hackman, R. J. (1976). Group influences on individuals. In M. P. Dunnette (Ed.), *Handbook of industrial and organizational psychology.* New York: Rand McNally.

Hampden-Turner, C. (1975). *From poverty to dignity.* Garden City, NY: Anchor Press/Doubleday.

Handler, J. F. & Zatz, J. (Eds.).(1982). *Neither angels nor thieves.* Washington, DC: National Academy Press.

Hart, H. L. A. (1955). Are there any natural rights? *The Philosophical Review, 44,* 289–298.

Henry, J. (1963). *Culture against man.* New York: Random House.

Hiller, H. H. (1975). A reconceptualization of the dynamics of social movement development. *Pacific Sociological Review, 18,* 342–360.

Hirsch, B. J. (1982). Natural support systems and coping with major life changes. *American Journal of Community Psychology, 8,* 159–172.

Hunt, J. McV. (1969). *The challenge of incompetence and poverty.* Urbana: University of Illinois Press.

Illich, I. (1976). *Medical nemesis: The expropriation of health.* New York: Pantheon.

Jacquet, C. H. (Ed.). (1972). *Yearbook of American churches.* Nashville: Abingdon.

Kanter, R. M. (1972). *Commitment and community: Communes and utopias in sociological perspective.* Cambridge: Harvard University Press.

Kelly, J. G. (1970). Antidotes for arrogance: Training for a community psychology. *American Psychologist, 25,* 524–531.

Killian, L. M. (1964). Social movements. In R. E. L. Faris (Ed.), *Handbook of modern sociology.* Chicago: Rand-McNally.

Kittrie, N. (1974). *The right to be different: Deviance and enforced therapy.* Baltimore: Johns Hopkins Press.

Knitzer, J. (1980). Advocacy and community psychology. In M. S. Gibbs, J. R. Lachenmeyer, & J. Sigal (Eds.), *Community psychology: Theoretical and empirical approaches.* New York: Gardner.

Koocher, J. (1978). *Children's rights and the mental health professionals.* New York: Wiley.

Koocher, J. (1979). Credentialing in psychology: Close encounters with competence? *American Psychologist, 34,* 696–702.

Levine, M. (1980). Investigative reporting as a research method: An analysis of Bernstein and Woodward's *All the president's men. American Psychologist, 35,* 626–638.

Levine, M., & Levine, A. (1970). *A social history of helping services: Clinic, court, school and community.* New York: Appleton-Century-Crofts.

Lilly, M., & Smith, P. (1980). Special education as a social movement. *Education Unlimited, 2(3),* 7–11.

Lin, N., Simeone, R. S., Ensel, W. M., & Kuo, W. (1979). Social support, stressful life events, and illness: A model and an empirical test. *Journal of Health and Social Behavior, 20,* 108–119.

Lubove, R. (1969). *The professional altruist: The emergence of social work as a career, 1880–1930.* New York: Antheneum.

Marx, A. M., Test, M. A., & Stein, L. I. (1973). Extrohospital management of severe mental illness. *Archives of General Psychiatry, 29,* 505–511.

Maton, K. I. (1979, September). *Participant inhabitant observation, empirical investigatin and social ecology.* Paper presented at the annual meeting of the American Psychological Association, New York.

Maton, K. I. (1980). *Empowerment in a religious setting: An exploratory study.* Masters thesis, University of Illinois at Urbana-Champaign.

McGrath, J. E. (1978). *Social science and social action: A retrospective look through the pages of the* Journal of Social Issues. Mimeograph, University of Illinois at Urbana-Champaign.

McGaw, D. B. (1979). Commitment and religious community: A comparison of a charismatic and a mainline congregation. *Journal for the Scientific Study of Religion, 18,* 146–163.

Merton, T. (1968). *Conjectures of a guilty bystander.* Garden City, NY: Doubleday-Image.

National Commission on Neighborhoods. (1979). *Report to the President.* Washington DC: U.S. Government Printing Office.

Newbrough, J. R. (1980). Community psychology and the public interest. *American Journal of Community Psychology, 8,* 1–17.

Novaco, R. W., & Monahan, J. (1980). Research in community psychology: An analysis of work published in the first six years of the *American Journal of Community Psychology. American Journal of Community Psychology, 8,* 131–146.

Oxford English Dictionary. (1971). (Compact ed.). New York: Oxford University Press.

Pargament, K. (1982). The interface among religion, religious support systems, and mental health. In D. E. Biegel & A. J. Naparstek (Eds.), *Community support systems and mental health: Research, policy and practice.* New York: Springer.

Phares, E. J. (1973). *Locus of control: A personality determinant of behavior.* Morristown, NJ: General Learning Press.

Phares, E.J., & Lamiell, J. T. (1977). Personality. *Annual Review of Psychology, 28,*113–140.

President's Commission on Mental Health. (1978). *Report of recommendations* (Vol. 1). Washington DC: U. S. Government Printing Office.

Rappaport, J. (1977). *Community psychology: Values, research and action.* New York: Holt, Rinehart & Winston.

Rappaport, J. (1980). *Standards for juvenile justice as an example of fundamental change in social attitudes, law and social policy: Opportunities and dangers for psychologists.* Mimeograph, University of Illinois at Urbana-Champaign.

Rappaport, J., & Cleary, C. P. (1980). Labeling theory and the social psychology of experts and helpers. In M. S. Gibbs, J. R. Lachenmeyer, & J. Sigal (Eds.), *Community psychology: Theoretical and empirical approaches.* New York: Gardner.

Rappaport, J., Davidson, W. S., Wilson, M.N., & Mitchell, A. (1975). Alternatives to blaming the victim or the environment: Our places to stand have not moved the earth. *American Psychologist, 30,* 525–528.

Riessman, R. (1976). *The inner-city child.* New York: Harper & Row.

Riger, S. (1980, May). *Toward a community psychology of empowerment.* Paper presented at a symposium, "Community Psychology in Times of Scarcity," Midwestern Pychological Association meeting, St. Louis.

Rist, R. C.(1970). Student social class and teacher expectations: The self-fulfilling prophecy in ghetto education. *Harvard Educational Review, 40,* 411–451.

Rothman, D. J. (1971). *The discovery of the asylum.* Boston: Little, Brown.

Rothman, D. J. (1980). *Conscience and convenience: The asylum and its alternatives in progressive America.* Boston: Little, Brown.

Rotter, J. B. (1975). Some problems and misconceptions related to the construct of internal versus external control of reinforcement. *Journal of Consulting and Clinical Psychology, 56*– 57.

Ryan, W. (1971). *Blaming the victim.* New York: Random House.

Sandler, I. N. (1980). Social support resources, stress, and maladjustment of poor children. *American Journal of Community Psychology, 8,* 41–52.

Sarason, S. B. (1978). The nature of problem solving in social action. *American Psychologist, 33,* 370–380.

Sarbin, T. R. (1970). A role theory perspective for community psychology: The structure of social identity. In D. Adelson & B. L. Kalis (Eds.), *Community psychology and mental health: Perspectives and challenges.* Scranton: Chandler.

Schumacher, E. F. (1973). *Small is beautiful.* New York: Harper & Row.

Schumacher, E. F. (1977). *A guide for the perplexed.* New York: Harper & Row.

Seaman, M. (1972). Social learning theory and the theory of mass society. In J. B. Rotter, J. Chance, & E. J. Phares, *Applications of a social learning theory of personality.* New York: Holt, Rinehart & Winston.

Seidman, E. (1978). Justice, values and social science: Unexamined premises. In R. J. Simon (Ed.), *Research in law and sociology* (Vol. 1). Greenwich: JAI Press.

Seidman, E., & Rappaport, J. (1974). You have got to have a dream, but it's not enough. *American Psychologist, 29,* 569–570.

Seligman, M. E. P. (1975). *Helplessness: On depression, development and death.* San Francisco: W. H. Freeman.

Seligman, M. E. P., & Maier, S. F. (1967). Failure to escape traumatic shock. *Journal of Experimental Psychology, 74,* 1–9.

Snyder, M., & Swann, W. B. (1978). Behavioral confirmation in social interaction: From social perception to social reality. *Journal of Experimental Social Psychology, 14,* 148–162.

Special issue on licensing and accreditation. (1979, Summer). *Division of Community Psychology Newsletter, 12,* 1–16.

Stein, L. I., Test, M. A., & Marx, A. J. (1975). Alternative to the hospital: A controlled study. *American Journal of Psychiatry, 132,* 517–522.

Stier, S. (1978). Children's rights and society's duties. *Journal of Social Issues, 34,* 46–58.

Strickland, B. R., & Janoff-Bulman, R. (1980). Expectancies and attributions: Implications for community mental health. In M. S. Gibbs, J. R. Lachenmeyer, & J. Sigal (Eds.), *Community psychology: Theoretical and empirical approaches.* New York: Gardner.

Sue, S., & Zane, N. (1980). Learned helplessness theory and community psychology. In M. S. Gibbs, J. R. Lachenmeyer, & J. Sigal (Eds.), *Community psychology: Theoretical and empirical approaches.* New York: Gardner.

Swann, W. B., & Snyder, M. (1980). On translating beliefs into action: Theories of ability and their application in an institutional setting. *Journal of Personality and Social Psychology, 38,* 879–888.

Takanishi, R. (1978). Childhood as a social issue: Historical roots of contemporary child advocacy movements. *Journal of Social Issues, 34,* 8–28.

Webber, G. H., & McCall, G. J. (Eds.). (1978). *Social scientists as advocates: Views from applied disciplines.* New York: Sage Publications.

Zald, M. (1980). *The federal impact on the deinstitutionalization of status offenders: A framework.* Working paper commissioned by a Panel on Public Policy Contributions to the Institutionalization and Deinstitutionalization of Children and Youth. National Academy of Sciences.

CHAPTER 10

Child Custody Determination

IDEOLOGICAL DIMENSIONS OF A SOCIAL PROBLEM

LINDA K. GIRDNER

INTRODUCTION

The determination of the custody of children subsequent to marital dissolution emerged as a social problem in the 1970s. What criteria should be used to determine "the best interests of the child?" Who should have input in the decisions? What process should be used? Judges, lawyers, policymakers, mental health practitioners, and behavioral scientists as well as interest groups supporting men's, women's, and children's rights entered the social arena to address these questions.

In this chapter, I place child custody determination practices in historical context, examine child custody determination as a social problem, and the practices that have developed to treat it. Then I address the paradoxical nature of divorce and custody and demonstrate its complexity through an analysis of empirical research on contested child custody cases. I examine alternative practices that have emerged and the new social problems they are likely to spawn. The emphasis throughout is on the ideological dimensions of the child custody determination problem.

According to Althusser (1971, p. 153), an ideology "represents the imaginary relationship of individuals to their real conditions of existence." Ideologies "interpellate," or address, subjects; thus, "to conceive of a text or an utterance as ideology is to focus on the way it operates in the formation and transformation of human subjectivity" (Therborn, 1980, p. 2). Therborn (p. 18) defines three modes of interpellation. Ideologies tell (1) what exists and

---

LINDA K. GIRDNER • Institute for Child Behavior and Development, University of Illinois at Urbana–Champaign, Urbana, Illinois 61820.

what does not, including "who we are, what the world is, what nature, society, men and women are like"; (2) what is good, right, just, and so forth, and its opposites; and (3) what is possible and impossible; what can be changed and what cannot.

Ideologies do not exist as separate entities except for analytical purposes. They are materialized in social practices. Three areas of social practice have been critical in defining the custody determination problem and in proposing solutions. The *legal system* is a particular institutional site where ideologies are articulated. *Social science* contains ideological dimensions in defining problems, conducting research, and interpreting results. Practitioners in the *mental health field*, in the services they offer, in their notions of what is healthy and unhealthy, in their views of what children and parents need, and how families function and change are involved in defining what exists, what is good, and what is possible.

Contested child custody cases between divorcing and divorced parents became a battleground in the 1970s over competing ideologies of the family. This is not the first time that custody determination practices have shifted reflecting changing ideologies of the family and changing family forms.

Custody Determination in Historical Perspective

Courts have been making decisions involving the custody and guardianship of children throughout American history. These cases not only include disputes between mothers and fathers but also those between parents and other relatives, parents and "strangers," and parents and public agencies.

Prior to the 1880s the father's primary right to his children was considered natural as well as legal. The development of "modern" criteria for awarding custody is often traced back to a case in 1881 involving a dispute between the natural father and the man who raised the child (*Chapsky v. Wood*, 1881). The "welfare of the child" was raised in the case as the primary consideration to be weighed against the father's legal right.

The preference for fathers in these cases slowly eroded after the turn of the century as the emphasis on the economic aspects of the child's future were superseded by the psychological and emotional welfare of the child. This shift coincided with the continuing transition of the family from a unit of production to a unit of consumption, laws regulating the work of women and children, the development of women's domestic "calling," and the emergence of psychology as a field of knowledge. Children were no longer regarded as little adults but rather as emerging personalities needing to be formed in the care of the nurturing mother.

By the 1920s, the interpretation of "the best interests of the child" had shifted to a preference for mothers when young children or daughters were involved in custody cases. By the 1940s the maternal preference, or tender age presumption, was firmly entrenched in custody practices. This was consistent with and reinforcing of the cultural beliefs and social roles of the middle-class American family in the postwar era.

In the 1960s and 1970s the feminist movement pushed for a reformulation of these beliefs and roles. A new subjectivity developed redefining what it meant to be male and female. The struggle by women against the sexual discrimination in the public domain was taken up by men in the private domain of the family. States that had adopted the Equal Rights Amendment found it especially difficult to justify the preference for mothers in custody cases because it clearly was a preference based on sex. The tender age presumption was overturned in state after state, leaving few clear guidelines to define "the best interests of the child."

The legal concept of "the best interests of the child" has existed in child custody law for over a century. Its interpretation has changed over time reflecting the ascendency of different ideologies of the family and changing family and social organization. However, custody determination had not been defined heretofore as a social problem. What is different about this particular historical juncture that has led to the definition of child custody determination as a social problem and what are the ramifications of it being perceived as such?

CUSTODY ADJUDICATION

Custody determination emerged as a social problem in the 1970s as children of divorce were seen as a significantly growing "at-risk" population. In 1953 there was a total of one and a half million children of divorced parents in the United States (Duquette, 1978). Since 1972, about 1 million children *every year* experience the divorce of their parents. By 1990 it is projected that one-third of the children under 18 will have parents who divorce (Glick, 1979).

The judicial system became increasingly burdened in the 1970s with the responsibility of settling custody disputes between divorcing and divorced parents. The legal presumption of maternal preference and the notion of fault as a sign of unfitness, which had facilitated custody dispute settlement, were being overturned. The trend in custody determination practices was an increasing emphasis on the totality of the evidence rather than on any one overriding factor for determining the best interests of the child. Although states vary in the particulars of case law, many have adopted Section 402 of the Uniform Marriage and Divorce Act (1970, p. 197), which provides the following guidelines:

> The court shall determine custody in accordance with the best interests of the child. The court shall consider all relevant factors including:

1. the wishes of the child's parent or parents as to his custody;
2. the wishes of the child as to his custodian;
3. the interaction and interrelationship of the child with his parent or parents, his siblings, and any other person who may significantly affect the child's best interests;
4. the child's adjustment to his home, school, and community; and
5. the mental and physical health of all individuals involved.

The court shall not consider conduct of a proposed custodian that does not affect his relationship to the child.

The lack of legal presumptions allowed for far greater judicial discretion in custody cases. With few guidelines, judges needed to ascertain the interests of the children from the evidence presented to further the cause of the mother and father. The judicial dilemma led to the conclusion that: "The behavioral scientist has essentially been given a societal mandate for involvement and must be prepared to function appropriately in child custody determinations" (Woody, 1977, p. 7). Solutions to the problem of child custody determination focused on closer collaboration between the legal and mental health fields.

Some of these efforts have been in the direction of social-science-based policy recommendations. The most well-known work of this kind has been Goldstein, Freud, and Solnit's *Beyond the Best Interests of the Child* (1973). Their recommendation that custody should be awarded to the "psychological parent" has been embraced by many in the mental health field. Judges have been sensitized to the concept but have rejected its use as the single determining factor in favor of greater flexibility on a case-by-case basis. The authors also recommend that the custody placement be final and that the custodial parent have the authority to determine when and if the other parent sees the child. The former suggestion would mean that courts abdicate their responsibility to children once an award is made. The latter would involve the abrogation of the legal rights of noncustodial parents. Consequently, these policy recommendations have been considered untenable (Crouch, 1979).

Other efforts have involved the direct participation of mental health professionals in contested child custody cases. These include the often overlapping roles of mental health professionals as evaluators (Benedek & Benedek, 1972; Chasin & Grunebaum, 1981; Gardner, 1982; Swerdlow, 1978; Trombetta, 1982), child advocates (Westman, 1971; Woody, 1978), and expert witnesses (Brodsky, 1972; Goldzband, 1982; Slovenko, 1973). These roles function to assist the judge in determining the best interests of the child by injecting supplementary information about the child's needs and the parents' capacities into the proceedings.

The solutions proposed by the mental health professionals share the definition of the problem as the need for an authoritative third party to decide postdivorce parent–child arrangements. They advocate the primacy of the psychological dimension in determining "the best interests of the child" and, consequently, the indispensability of their input.

One assumption underlying the role of mental health professionals in custody determination is that they are able to make objective, reliable assessments and predictions of parental capacities and children's needs in the context of divorce. In evaluating, advocating, or providing testimony relating to the needs of the children and/or the fitness of parents, the personal and professional biases of the mental health professional or behavioral scientist influence the choice of "objective" criteria and its interpretation. Differences frequently center around the criteria for assessing normal healthy male and female roles. For example, when Richard Gardner, whose work probably has had greater impact on present custody evaluation practices than any other individual's, evaluates "parental capacity," he examines *maternal* capacity in mothers that is based on different behaviors and attitudes than *paternal* capacity is for fathers. In his book on how to be an impartial expert in custody litigation, Gardner (1982, p. 103, emphasis in original) states that

> the homemaking interests and identifications are an important factor to be considered in determining custody. If she [the mother] hated it, or *her* mother hated it, and she most often did it begrudgingly then this would be a negative factor.

His tape presentation on the same topic (Gardner, 1974) has been severely criticized by feminists for inferring maternal capacity from "the degree to which the woman conforms to traditional stereotypic sex roles" (Hare-Mustin, 1976, pp.219–220). The notions expressed in professional assessments of children's needs after divorce, parental capacities, and appropriate custodial arrangements arise out of the different views of sex roles and family that are intrinsic to the paradoxical nature of divorce.

The Paradox of Divorce

Child custody determination as a social problem is intricately connected with the paradoxical nature of divorce. In American culture, individual freedom and the right to the pursuit of happiness are strongly held beliefs at the same time that commitment to family and sacrifice for one's children are cherished values. Ideally one finds room for self-expression and happiness within marriage, and, thus, there is no apparent contradiction. The antinomy between freedom and commitment is at the base of the paradox of divorce. This paradox reflects the contradictory interests between the individual and the family. Presently there are two competing ideological definitions of divorce, each privileging one side of the antinomy.

The ideological definition of divorce as pathology was pervasive until the 1970s. Earlier in the century divorce was an indication of sin and immorality. The definition of deviance changed to a medical model of pathology by the 1930s (Halem, 1980). Putting one's own needs and goals before commitment to the family was seen as selfish and a sign of psychological disturbance. Divorce was considered contrary to public policy and was only granted to an "innocent" party who could prove the other guilty on specific fault grounds. Marriage counseling developed to "save" marriages and help individuals adjust to the family. The belief in the necessity of a traditional intact nuclear family for the healthy development of children inspired research on the occurrence of mental illness (Gregory, 1965, 1966; Harper & Harper, 1961; Herzog & Sudia, 1973), juvenile delinquency (Gibson, 1969; Glueck & Glueck, 1950), antisocial behavior (Felner, Stolberg, & Cowen, 1975; Loeb & Price, 1966; Tuckman & Regan, 1966), and sex role problems (Biller, 1974; Reed, 1970) among children from "broken homes."

Implicit in the pathological definition of divorce is the superiority of the nuclear family and traditional sex roles. Divorce was seen as ending family relationships. Sole custody to mothers was the preferred custodial arrangement. Fathers were viewed as marginal and sometimes replaceable through remarriage. Stability for the child was connected with "sleeping in the same bed every night," a phrase accepted as common wisdom among parents and professionals.

The definition of divorce as pathology was challenged in the late 1960s and 1970s by the alternative definition of divorce as a legitimate path to individual growth and self-fulfillment. These values were reflected in "the culture of narcissism" (Lasch, 1978), the spread of self-growth therapies and movements, and the increasing emphasis on individual rights. Within this definition, priority was given to individual freedom over commitment to the marital unit. Staying in a "bad marriage" was seen as unhealthy rather than responsible and moral. No-fault divorce laws gave legal validation to the notion that spouses should be able to terminate their marriage if they so chose without necessitating a finding of fault. Divorce counseling and groups emerged to assist adults and children through the emotional process of divorce. Social scientists and helping professionals focused on divorce as a critical transition in families identified by normative stages leading to a new stable family system (Hetherington, Cox, & Cox, 1978; Ricci 1980).

This definition of divorce accepted the postdivorce family as a legitimate "alternative life-style." Divorce was viewed as restructuring rather than ending family relationships. Commitment to family was redefined as commitment to one's children, for example, "You divorce your spouse, not your child." The father's role in the child's development assumed greater significance (Biller & Meredith, 1975; Green, 1976; Lynn, 1974). Maintaining a relationship with both parents was considered important for the children's emotional stability (Hetherington *et al.*, 1978; Wallerstein & Kelly, 1980). Co-parenting and joint custody emerged as appropriate and desirable arrangements (Ricci, 1980; Roman & Haddad, 1978).

These ideological views of the family and divorce are in contestation at the present time for primacy in defining what exists, what is good, and what is possible for parents and children of divorce. This struggle and its underlying paradox are reflected in the ambivalence and ambiguity with which divorce is handled in the society and is experienced by divorcing men and women.

The Paradox of Custody

Divorce represents an individual decision by one or both partners that is imposed on the children. Although the decision to divorce is increasingly viewed as a private matter between individuals, the state retains the ultimate authority over children. The doctrine of *parens patriae* gives the state the right and the duty to protect children and, consequently, to intervene in the internal functioning of the family. Nuclear families are not normally subjected to this intervention unless there is suspicion of child abuse or neglect. Divorce opens up the family to the scrutiny of the state because the act of divorce itself is seen as putting children at risk.

The custody issue brings to the fore the paradoxical relationship between the autonomy of parents and the responsibility of the state. Divorcing parents are encouraged to arrive at their own custody agreements without appealing to the courts. However, these agreements are never considered final and are not binding on the court. Parents have the right to ask the court to make the custody decision for them, but when they do ask, the interests of both parents are relegated to secondary importance relative to the interests of the child as perceived by the court. This antinomy between the empowerment of the parents and social control by the state is at the root of the custody determination problem.

In sum, one dimension of the custody determination problem relates to the degrees of parental empowerment and social control afforded by different solutions to resolving custody disputes. The other dimension of the problem relates to the changing views of the family, the individual, and sex roles, which are seated in the paradoxical nature of divorce and which affect what types of custodial arrangements are considered appropriate and desirable. A closer examination of custody adjudication reveals the interconnections between these dimensions of the problem.

IDEOLOGIES OF THE FAMILY IN CUSTODY ADJUDICATION

An ethnographic research project on contested child custody cases conducted by the author addressed the following two questions: (1) What is the relationship between legal and extralegal categories in contested child custody cases that arise out of divorce proceedings? (2) In what ways does the interrelationship of the legal and extralegal categories invoked in such proceedings express an ideology of the family and formulate a code for conduct for family members? *Legal categories* include rules and concepts, which derive from procedural and substantive law and which serve to structure and limit the discourse. *Extralegal categories* refer to the norms and symbols about family and sex roles that are expressed in the discourse.

Background

The fieldwork took place in the circuit and family courts in Wiltshire County, a largely affluent suburban county in the eastern United States.[1] Fieldwork involved immersing myself in the "legal culture" of the courts for 18 months in 1978–1979. I carried out the traditional ethnographic tasks of gaining entrée, establishing rapport, talking with informants, observing and recording behavior, and examining records. The primary methods of data collection were the direct observation and recording of contested child custody hearings, interviews with judges, commissioners, and attorneys, and the examination of legal documents and court records. Additional data came from informal talks with parents, witnesses, and attorneys while they waited in the courthouse prior to the hearing and during recesses, observations of their interactions during these times, and a concurrent year of participant observation at weekly meetings of a fathers' advocacy group (Girdner, 1983). The particular aspect of research that is examined here derives primarily from the analysis of the legal records and observations of court hearings involving the adjudication of child custody.

The study of law is conducive to a case approach, and the "trouble case" method has been used extensively in the anthropology of law. The method for selecting cases was primarily to find those that involved the adjudication of the issue of custody, no matter how the case was labeled on the docket. Disputes over custody involve conflicting norms, and situational analysis was used to examine how these norms "are ultimately manipulated by individuals in particular situations to serve particular ends" (Van Velsen, 1967, p. 136). The extended case method was used to place the particular hearing in the context of the parties' ongoing legal dispute; especially in cases involving modification of custody, public records were often quite extensive, including transcripts of former proceedings, pleadings, orders, and depositions.

The analysis of the data first involved the identification of categories and properties. Constant comparison of these categories and their properties across cases served to expand and refine them and to develop an understanding of

[1] The actual location of the fieldwork is not identified in conformance with the requirements for protection of human subjects established for this research. The research was funded by a National Research Service Award from the National Institute of Mental Health and a Doctoral Dissertation Award from American University, Washington, DC.

their interconnections. Collection, coding, analysis, and interpretation were ongoing and interconnected processes. Emerging interpretations led to choices of data collection that would maximize differences and possibly bring out the weaknesses of the interpretation. In this manner concepts were refined and the interpretation was deepened. Sampling was guided by theoretical sensitivity and was stopped when theoretical saturation was reached (see Glaser & Strauss, 1967).

The discourse of a custody hearing is structured by legal categories, which are intrinsic to the practice of litigation. These include rules and concepts that derive from procedural and substantive law. Procedural rules establish the adversarial structure of the proceedings. These categories define turn taking, who can be spoken to, by whom, when, and how. Not only do they structure what can be said but also what cannot. The lawyers and judges have a shared knowledge and understanding of these categories. The complex reality of the particular family is transformed and interpreted through these categories for presentation in the courtroom.

Evidence in custody cases needs to relate to the legal concept of "the best interests of the child." Legal categories derived from rules of evidence are manipulated by each attorney to present evidence in support of his or her case, to discredit the other side, and to prevent the other attorney from doing the same.

The rules of evidence found in the discourse have an existence independent of the issue of custody because they are part of procedural law. Legal concepts derived from substantive law are put into operational form in the discourse through the rule-governed and manipulated presentation of the particular family's situation.

The Code for Conduct

The evidence that is presented in the hearings relating to the child's best interests or to parental fitness is information about how people raise children and act as parents. The questions asked by attorneys and the responses of witnesses indicate what is considered to be appropriate behavior and what are breaches of norms (e.g., a mother is asked: "Is it true that you did not serve your children breakfast when you were living in the marital home?"). Comments and questions by the judges during the hearing often make explicit what the behavior of a parent should be and how children should be raised (e.g., "Children should have a certain hour to get up in the morning."). From a systematic recording and analyses of these sources, a particular code for conduct was extracted (Girdner, 1983).

The code for conduct abstracted from the data consists of two different and yet interconnected sets of norms. The first set relates to parents' responsibilities to their children; the second relates to the parents' fitness.

The code for conduct relating to how children should be raised involves the successful fulfillment of three major types of parental duties: (1) meeting the children's basic needs, (2) supervising the children, and (3) providing a home for the children. Each of these categories is defined by specific behavioral prescriptions.

The second code for conduct abstracted from the data relates to how a person should behave as a parent. Each parent must show that he or she is a "fit and proper person" to have custody of the children. The qualities of parental fitness involve the way in which parental duties are carried out, the way in which the parent has adapted his or her life to parenting, and how well the parent conforms to the standards of appropriate behavior. Prior to the separation, mothers show this by having the primary care of the children and fathers by having worked to provide for the children.

The code for conduct reflects an ideal model of the family against which the divorcing parents are measured. Norms define appropriate behavior of persons occupying specific roles. Father and mother are seen as complementary rather than identical roles; thus the appropriate behavior of fathers and mothers is different, although overlapping. Determining custody involves choosing who will be the parent to care for the children on a daily basis and be responsible for them, which is more closely associated with the normative role of mother in the intact family. The articulation of this in custody cases leads to different strategies and consequences for mothers and fathers.

In testifying, fathers frequently justify their lower level of past participation in child rearing by stating that they did "as much as any normal father would do." To strengthen his case, a father attempts to show that the mother has not performed the role of mother adequately and/or that he has excelled beyond the normative expectations of being a father. Lawyers representing fathers frequently characterize their clients as unusual or abnormal in their behavior and their desire to have their children, for example:

> A man, surprisingly enough, provides the maternal and paternal care for this child....To be honest, I am very surprised when men are capable of raising little children. It's hard for me to imagine cooking, cleaning, etc. He has that commitment.

However, too much deviation from the norm can work against the father. In one case, the judge said that he felt that the father might have "too much love" for the children, which was a "warning signal" for the future.

Because the role expectations of mothers are high, it is not difficult to find occasions when mothers have deviated from them (e.g., "Is it true that you said to your husband that you wanted a vacation away from your children?"). Mothers' attorneys seek to show that the woman has excelled as a mother, whereas the fathers' attorneys seek to indicate how she has fallen below the ideal standards. The role of mother is portrayed at a level of primacy in the divorcing or divorced woman's life in a way which fatherhood is not for a man. Thus, a woman's performance in other roles (e.g., employee, friend) appears as detracting from or weakening her role as mother, whereas other roles for men appear frequently as either neutral or supportive of their father role.

On one level, the code for conduct defines the duties and proprieties of nongender-specific parenthood. On another level it differentiates between parents on the basis of gender and judges them against normative constructs of mother and father. An examination of the ideologics of the family, which are the symbolic dimensions of the code, will further highlight this contradiction.

The Gender-Based Ideology

Gender-based ideology has held a dominant position in the ideological discourse in contested child custody cases since the 1930s, but it has been increasingly challenged by the individual-based ideology since the 1970s. The gender-based ideology of the family privileges the "natural order" in relating what exists, what is good, and what is possible. It is a cultural construct of the nuclear family, which is brought to bear on a situation arising from divorce, and consequently throws into relief certain elements within it.

Husbands and wives are connected to one another by their love, which is expressed through the natural act of sex. Marriage is the only proper place for its expression. Fathers and mothers are connected to their children through their shared biological substance (blood), which results from sexual act between the spouses. The natural tie between mothers and children is somewhat stronger than that between fathers and children due to the primordial tie of pregnancy, the maternal attachment during infancy, and the mother's day-to-day involvement in child rearing. Divorce ends the relationship between the husband and wife and breaks the natural bond of sex between them. The blood tie of each with the children remains, which is irreducible and permanent.

Actions carried out by the female as mother/wife/woman are mutually reinforcing within the nuclear family and are "naturally" female. The acts of the mother/wife in the household, such as cleaning, cooking, and childcare are women's activities. They are done out of love and as expressions of love for her husband and children. The home symbolizes love and is the woman's domain.

The role of mother embodies a level of sacrifice and selflessness, which places it in conflict with any other role once divorce necessitates the differentiation of mother/wife/woman. Other roles and activities outside of the home indicate selfishness and a lack of sacrifice that are "unmotherly." Sexual acts outside of the marital relationship are self-gratifying animal acts and, thus, are especially contradictory to the role of mother. In one case this was made quite explicit. The mother's therapist testified as an expert witness about the mother's "warm supportive" relationship with her boyfriend, which the judge later characterized as "meeting her carnal needs." The father's sexual activities were overlooked. The identity of mother, then, takes primacy and is often in contradiction to other roles of women.

The actions carried out by the male as a father/husband/man are also mutually reinforcing within the nuclear family. The primary role is of provider to the wife and children, which involves earning money in the public sphere of work outside of the home. Although men are able to learn the tasks women do in the home, these do not "come naturally" and are done instrumentally rather than as expressions of love.

With divorce, the identity of man takes primacy over other roles the male has but it does not affect those roles in the way that the mother's role is affected. However, if the man is performing a mother's role, he is in conflict with that role because as a man it is axiomatic that he cannot be a mother. Thus, although the tasks associated with motherhood can be performed by him, they do not carry the same meaning because they are not "natural."

These are several of the more salient features of the gender-based ideology of the family that emerged from the analysis of the symbolic dimension of the discourse observed in the custody cases. Both attorneys manipulate elements of this ideology to denigrate the other party, while building the case of their client.

The Individual-Based Ideology

The individual-based ideology privileges the "rational order" in relating what exists, what is good, and what is possible. The unit of focus is the individual as a goal-directed actor. Equality and achievement are the cornerstones of the ideology.

The parental duties of the code for conduct are instrumental tasks to be done competently, efficiently, and rationally. The appropriate behavior of a fit parent is consistent with the rational behavior of a self-controlled individual showing good judgment.

A person is responsible for his or her own actions and has considerable control over his or her own life. In one case, the judge told an abused wife who lost custody of the children to her husband, "You have no one to blame but yourself," referring to her inconsistent behavior.

Striving toward goals, even if they are not successfully reached, emerged as an important factor in the observed cases. In one case, for example, the father explained how he had "tried to make a go of it" under difficult circumstances. Until his testimony, the judge was seriously considering putting the children in a foster home rather than award them to either parent because the children's circumstances were very much wanting. Instead, the judge stated that the father "deserved" to be able to keep them because it was clear that he had tried and was trying to care for them. In another case, the father was characterized by two expert witnesses as not able to give the children what they needed emotionally, whereas the judge saw him in a positive light because he was "a gung-ho type," willing to do anything for his children.

In addition, problem solving and seeking expertise appeared as important characteristics in the custody hearings. Parents should be able to work out solutions for themselves, but when they cannot, they should seek out the appropriate expert.

Neither the gender-based nor the individual-based ideologies exist in isolation. All cases involve interwoven aspects of both ideologies; judges, attorneys, and parents articulate elements of both. A synthesis of the two that reflects their interconnection with one another is as follows: Marriage is like a business partnership. When the partners want to split they have to decide who gets what and what happens with the ongoing business they have. Raising children is the ongoing business which remains after a husband and wife end their marriage partnership. A decision needs to be made on whom the responsibility falls. They ask the state, a hidden partner in their marriage, to make that decision. The state has an interest in seeing that the job is done correctly. The parents appear before the judge, who is an equal opportunity employer when it comes to the job of raising children. The judge looks at how they handled the job in the past and how they intend to do it if they retain it. He or she listens to how they handled other jobs, keeping in mind that the applicants are not important; the crucial factor is furthering the best interests of the child. It is the judge's responsibility to figure out who is the better person to handle that job.

The two people before the judge have an equal right to be there, but they are not the same. They are individuals with different strengths and weaknesses. One is male/husband/father; the other female/wife/mother. The female is more naturally adapted to the task, but then has she shown that she has put her natural capacities to the best use? The man is not so naturally qualified for the task, but has he learned how to do it and can he do it adequately? Who will put this job as the top priority and carry it out competently?

The way in which the two ideologies articulate with one another in the records and courtroom interaction that I observed reflects the possible receding of the gender-based ideology and the ascendency of the individual-based ideology. Because law is "a collection of ideologies, sanctioned in the correct manner by the institutionalized executors of social power, which define the socially permissible modes of social intercourse" (Sumner, 1979, p. 266), the significance of the custody determination problem goes beyond the managing of disputes between parents and the placement of children. It relates to the process of legitimization of certain meanings of parenthood, family, love, and duty and of a particular code for conduct about how children should be raised and how parents should behave.

THE PROBLEM REDEFINED

The parents who appear before the court have abdicated their decision-making power, and the judge's determination is imposed on them. The impact of the sanctioning power of the courts reaches beyond the parents who contest custody to other divorcing and divorced parents because a noncustodial parent can threaten court action as a means of regulating the custodial parent's behavior. Thus, custody adjudication functions directly and indirectly as a mechanism of social control of single-parent households subsequent to divorce.

Although divorced men and women are often cognizant of the social control function of the courts, this function has received little attention by professionals as a dimension of the custody determination problem. The emphasis has been placed on the courts' functions in protecting the interests of the children and in resolving disputes between parents. The importance given to these functions reflects the perception that the source of the problem is in the family. Efforts to "humanize" custody adjudication by increasing the impact of social science knowledge and mental health expertise are based on the notion that authoritative third parties are needed to determine the proper custodial arrangements for these families. This perception is shifting as the inadequacy of the courts to carry out these functions is recognized and the definition of divorce as pathology decreases in significance.

The source of the problem is increasingly defined as the legal system. The procedure for determining "the best interests of the child" is in contradistinction to its stated purpose. Children experience their parents' litigation over custody as a form of psychological child abuse. The win-lose structure of custody proceedings exacerbates conflict between parents and, consequently, is more likely to lead to further disputes rather than to resolve the extant one. The input of mental health professionals has not altered the adversary nature of the proceedings. Removing custody determination from the courtroom is now advocated by many as the solution to the problem.

Mediation and Joint Custody

Divorce mediation emerged as an alternative to the adversary system in the mid-1970s, although it is still not widely recognized or available in most states. The development of divorce mediation coincides with the trend toward alternative means of dispute resolution in other types of disputes, such as neighborhood, environmental, labor, and international. Mediation has been heralded by its proponents as "the wave of the future" (Vroom, Fassett, & Wakefield, 1981). During the early 1980s the U.S. Congress passed the Dispute

Resolution Act which encouraged the development of alternative means of dispute resolution. Supreme Court Chief Justice Warren Burger (1982) called for the propagation of mediation and arbitration to help alleviate the burdened judicial system.

In divorce mediation, a third party assists the spouses in making mutual decisions about the division of marital property, spousal maintenance, child support, and child custody and visitation. Presently, most divorce mediators are lawyers and therapists who develop a mediation practice alongside their traditional professional practice. Custody mediators are primarily mental health professionals who focus on the parenting issues relating to divorce, especially conflicts over custody and visitation. Although some are in private practice, their numbers are increasing in court-connected custody mediation services (Brown, 1982).

Although mediators are supposed to be neutral and nonjudgmental, they have notions about what is appropriate for postdivorce families. Most believe that co-parenting is the best arrangement for parents and children and tend to favor joint custody over sole custody (Haynes, 1981; Trombetta, 1981; Vanderkooi & Pearson, 1983). Mediators do not impose their own ideas, but because "the mediator is seen by the parents as a reliable and trustworthy source of information, the mediator can have considerable influence in the development of their custody arrangements, although the decision making is done by the parents" (Girdner, 1985, p.42).

Divorce and custody mediators see themselves at the cutting edge of social change. The development of custody mediation and the preference for joint custody is intrinsically connected to a shift along three ideological dimensions reflected by mediation proponents. First, they favor the definition of divorce as a normative critical transition rather than as pathology. Second, they believe that the solution of the custody problem is to empower parents. Third, they tip the balance more toward the individual-based ideology of the family than the gender-based ideology, the former of which is elaborated in the redefinition of the parental relationship as based on contract rather than status.

Some of their colleagues in the mental health and legal professions are the severest critics of mediation. Although part of the criticism is based on the ideological differences stated before, part of it focuses on issues relating to standards of practice. Lawyers are concerned that the needs emphasis of many therapist-mediators may mean that clients are not adequately informed of their rights. Separating custody from the financial issues is criticized by some as unrealistic and detrimental to women, who have little to bargain with in the economic settlement. Some mental health professionals are concerned that the needs of the child will be overshadowed by the desire for parental compromise. Many are extremely wary of the rapid growth of a profession that is new, ill defined, unregulated, and in which training is unequal.

The Social Control of Empowerment

In 1980, California became the first state to enact a statute making joint custody the presumption in custody cases. Twenty-six other states have passed new laws relating to joint custody, although none is as "extreme" as California's (Freed & Foster, 1983). The social policy debate over joint and sole custody as preferred custodial arrangements is ongoing and reflects ideological divisions within the legal profession, social science, and the mental health field. Men's groups have strongly advocated joint custody, whereas women's groups have largely opposed it.

In 1981, California enacted a statute mandating mediation in child custody disputes, and several other states are considering similar legislation. Many courts across the country have instituted local court-connected mediation programs requiring parents to mediate their disputes. Mandatory mediation operates as an agent of social control, partially regulating the internal functioning of these families. Parents may find that they are empowered within the limits established by the mediator, who educates them as to what is desireable and possible for postdivorce families. For parents who share similar values with the mediator, this does not present a problem. In fact, most clients who enter mediation voluntarily are white and upper middle class as are their mediators. Mandatory mediation involves a much broader population, representing different life-styles and values relating to sex roles and child rearing. The judicial system has become increasingly supportive of mediation because it is seen as an efficient and economical means of "disposing of cases." The definition of success that appears to be emerging in mediation is the percentage of mediated cases that reach agreement. The needs of the judicial system to get cases settled together with the interests and values of the newly created profession of mediators place constraints on the degree of empowerment parents actually have in mediation.

Mediation is based on the assumption that disputants have relative equality. In cases where the parents are of relative unequal power, the emphasis on agreement may be at the expense of fairness. If the less powerful party does not agree to a settlement in mediation, he or she risks being labeled "uncooperative." This has the potential of leading to a new way of "blaming the victim," while upholding the positive values of empowerment and cooperation. Because women are often the less powerful parties in divorce, several feminist groups are active in lobbying against the institutionalization of mediation (National Center on Women and Family Law, n.d.).

SUMMARY AND CONCLUSION

In this chapter, custody determination of children of divorce has been examined as a social problem. The definitions of the problem and its solutions have favored different aspects of the paradoxical character of custody and divorce. Custody involves the antinomy between parental autonomy and the responsibility of the state regarding the welfare of children. Intrinsic to divorce is the antinomy between individual freedom and family commitment. The adjudication of custody disputes as a primary means of handling custody determination emphasizes the pathological view of divorce and the need for authoritative decision making to regulate postdivorce families.

The shifting from gender-based to individual-based ideologies of the family has been affected by and has facilitated the increasing emphasis on divorce as a normative critical transition and parental self-determination as the appropriate decision-making process. Mediation and joint custody are emerging as new solutions, emphasizing empowerment with social control maintained in a more diffuse and implicit manner.

An old social problem that reemerges in these new solutions relates to the relations of power between men and women. The ideology of mediation with its focus on parental empowerment and cooperative conflict resolution obfuscates power imbalances that sometimes exist between couples and potentially can lead to agreements reflecting relations of dominance and acquiescence. Is joint custody sometimes a compromise solution that allows the mediator to avoid confronting this? Mediation treats the problem on the microlevel as between two individuals. What will be the consequences for men and women on the macrolevel? The issue of gender and power in divorce and in mediation is complex and multidimensional, meriting further investigation.

At the present time, courts and public and private agencies are interested in research that emphasizes outcome variables in mediation, such as cost-effectiveness, efficiency, and rates of agreement and compliance. These studies favor a positivist and quantitative approach to research. The small amount of funding available on this topic appears to reflect the same priorities. The process of mediation is little understood and virtually unexamined by researchers. Research is needed that will focus on the roles of power, norms, and ideology in the development of consensus. The relationships between mediation and other processes of dispute settlement, such as legal negotiation and adjudication, need to be understood to further our knowledge of how decisions are reached in mediation. Researchers should be cognizant of the social and legal context in which mediation exists as a social practice. Because the field is in its infancy, research especially needs to focus on the use of grounded theory, the development of hypotheses, and the creation of models. Phenomenological and positivist approaches are both needed to build a sound body of research and to make wise policy decisions.

REFERENCES

Althusser, L. (1971). Ideology and ideological state apparatuses. In *Lenin and philosophy and other essays* (pp. 121–173). London: NLB.

Benedek, E. P., & Benedek, R. S. (1972). New child custody laws: Making them do what they say. *American Journal of Orthopsychiatry, 42,* 825–834.

Biller, H. B. (1974). *Paternal deprivation*. Lexington, MA: Lexington Books.

Biller, H. B., & Meredith, D. (1975). *Father power*. New York: McKay.

Brodsky, S. L. (1972). Special applications of psychology to judiciary. In S. Brodsky (Ed.), *Psychologists in the criminal justice system* (pp. 93–101). Urbana: University of Illinois Press.

Brown, D. O. (1982). Divorce and family mediation: History, review, and future directions. *Conciliation Courts Review, 20 (2),* 1–44.

Burger, W. E. (1982). Isn't there a better way? *American Bar Association Journal, 68,* 274–277.

Chapsky v. Wood, 26 Kan. 650, 40 Am. Rep. 321 (1881).

Chasin, R., & Grunebaum, H. (1981). A model for evaluation in child custody disputes. *The American Journal of Family Therapy, 9,* 43–49.

Crouch, R. D. (1979). An essay on the critical and judicial reception of "Beyond the Best Interests of the Child." *Family Law Quarterly, 13(1),* 49–103.

Duquette, D. N. (1978). Child custody decision-making: The lawyer–behavioral scientist interface. *Journal of Clinical Child Psychology, 12 (3),* 192–195.

Felner, R. D., Stolberg, A., & Cowen, E. L. (1975). Crisis events and school mental health referral patterns of young children. *Journal of Consulting and Clinical Psychology, 43(5),* 305–310.

Freed, D. J., & Foster, H. H. (1983). Family law in the fifty states: An overview. *Family Law Quarterly, 16 (4),* 289–383.

Gardner, R. A. (Speaker). (1974). *The mental health professional and divorce litigation* (Cassette Recording). New York: Psychotherapy Tape Library.

Gardner, R. A. (1982). *Family evaluation in child custody litigation.* Cresskill, NJ: Creative Therapeutics.

Gibson, H. B. (1969). Early delinquency in relation to broken homes. *Journal of Child Psychology and Psychiatry, 10,* 195–204.

Girdner, L. K. (1983). Contested child custody cases: An examination of custom and family law in an American court (Doctoral dissertation, American University, 1981). *Dissertation Abstracts International, 43,* 08A.

Girdner, L. K. (1985). Adjudication and mediation: A comparison of custody decision-making processes involving third parties. *Journal of Divorce, 8 (3/4),* 33–47.

Glaser, B., & Strauss, A. (1967). *The discovery of grounded theory.* Chicago: Aldine.

Glick, P. C. (1979). Children of divorced parents in demographic perspective. *Journal of Social Issues, 35 (4),* 170–182.

Glueck, S., & Glueck, E. (1950). *Unraveling juvenile delinquency.* Cambridge: Harvard University Press.

Goldstein, J., Freud, A., & Solnit, A. J. (1973). *Beyond the best interests of the child.* New York: The Free Press.

Goldzband, M. G. (1982). *Consulting in child custody: An introduction to the ugliest litigation for mental-health professionals.* Lexington, MA: Lexington Books.

Green, M. (1976). *Fathering.* New York: McGraw-Hill.

Gregory, I. (1965). Anterospective data following childhood loss of a parent: I. Delinquency and high school dropout. *Archives of General Psychiatry, 13,* 99–109.

Gregory, I. (1966). Retrospective data concerning childhood loss of a parent: II. Category of parental loss by decade of birth, diagnosis, and MMPI. *Archives of General Psychiatry, 15,* 362–367.

Halem, L. C. (1980). *Divorce reform: Changing legal and social perspectives.* New York: The Free Press.

Hare-Mustin, R. T. (1976). The biased professional in divorce litigation. *Psychology of Women Quarterly, 1(2),* 216–222.

Harper, M., & Harper, F. V. (1961). Lawyers and marriage counseling. *Journal of Family Law, 1(1),* 73–88.

Haynes, J. M. (1981). *Divorce mediation: A practical guide for therapists and counselors.* New York: Springer.

Herzog, E., & Sudia, C. E. (1973). Children in fatherless families. In E. M. Caldwell & H. H. Ricciuti (Eds.), *Review of child development research* (Vol. 3, pp. 141–232). Chicago: University of Chicago Press.

Hetherington, E. M., Cox, M., & Cox, R. (1978). The aftermath of divorce. In Y. H. Stevens & M. Mathews (Eds.), *Mother/child, father/child relationships* (pp. 149–176). New York: NAEYC.

Lasch, C. (1978). *The culture of narcissism.* New York: Norton.

Loeb, J., & Price, J. R. (1966). Mother and child personality characteristics related to parental status in child guidance cases. *Journal of Consulting Psychology, 30,* 112–117.

Lynn, D. B. (1974). *The father: His role in child development.* Monterey, CA: Brooks/Cole Publishing.

National Center on Women and Family Law. (n.d.). *Mediation hurts women* (Resource packet available from National Center on Women and Family Law, 799 Broadway, Room 402, New York, New York 10003).

Reed, A. (1970). *The women on the verge of divorce.* London: Thomas Nelson & Sons.

Ricci, I. (1980). *Mom's house, dad's house: Making shared custody work.* New York: Macmillan.

Roman, M., & Haddad, W. (1978). *The disposable parent: The case for joint custody.* New York: Holt, Rinehart & Winston.

Slovenko, R. (1973). *Psychiatry and law.* Boston: Little, Brown.

Sumner, C. (1979). *Reading ideologies: An investigation into the Marxist theory of ideology and law.* New York: Academic Press.

Swerdlow, E. L. (1978). Mental health services available to the bench and bar to assist in resolving problems to custody and visition in family law cases. *Journal of Clinical Child Psychology, 7,* 174–177.

Therborn, G. (1980). *The ideology of power and the power of ideology.* London: Verso and NLB.

Trombetta, D. (1981). Joint Custody: Recent research and overloaded courtrooms inspire new solutions to custody disputes. *Journal of Family Law, 19* (2), 213–234.

Trombetta, D. (1982). Custody evaluation and custody mediation: A comparison of two dispute interventions. *Journal of Divorce, 6,* 65–77.

Tuckman, J., & Regan, A. (1966). Intactness of the home and behavioral problems in children. *Journal of Child Psychology and Psychiatry, 7,* 225–233.

Uniform Marriage and Divorce Act, § 402, 9 U.L.A. (1970).

Van Velsen, J. (1967). The extended case method and situational analysis. In A. L. Epstein (Ed.), *The craft of social anthropology* (pp. 129–149). London: Tavistock.

Vanderkooi, L., & Pearson, J. (1983). Mediating divorce disputes: Mediator behaviors, styles, and roles. *Family Relations, 32,* 557–566.

Vroom, P., Fassett, D., & Wakefield, R. (1981). Mediation: The wave of the future? *American Family, 4(4),* 8–13.

Wallerstein, J. S., & Kelly, J. B. (1980). *Surviving the breakup: How children and parents cope with divorce.* New York: Basic Books.

Westman, J. C. (1971). The psychiatrist and child custody contests. *American Journal of Psychiatry, 127,* 1687–1688.

Woody, R. H. (1977). Behavioral science criteria in child custody determinations. *Journal of Marriage and Family Counseling, 3,* 11–18.

Woody, R. H. (1978). Fathers with child custody. *Counseling Psychologist, 7,* 60–63.

CHAPTER 11

Crime as Stress

ON THE INTERNALIZATION OF A SOCIAL PROBLEM

DAN A. LEWIS and STEPHANIE RIGER

At the beginning of their book *Constructing Social Problems,* Spector and Kitsuse (1977) ask a question that they never answer: "What is it that makes crime a social problem?"

> Is it the absolute number of crimes? Is it the types of crimes committed? Is it the increase in the rate of some crimes or of crime in general? Does crime become a social problem when "the streets are no longer safe at night?"

The short answer to the question is that it depends on the way one looks at crime. A social problem takes its shape from the theoretical "container" that holds it (Gusfield, 1975). If we think of a social problem as defined by its container and its content, then to understand what makes a crime a social problem, we must look at the various containers or theoretical perspectives that hold the problem.

The fact that there are so many different ways to think about crime speaks more to the intense competition among groups for the "ownership" of the issue than it does to the complexity of the issue. Social problems are defined and analyzed by individuals who represent the interests of various constituencies. Those constituencies have a stake in how particular problems are "solved." Most of those who produce crime containers have an interest in managing individuals who commit criminal acts. They share a common focus on the offender and the offender's motivations. Sociologists and psy-

DAN A. LEWIS • Center for Urban Affairs and Policy Research, Northwestern University, Evanston, Illinois 60201.   STEPHANIE RIGER • Department of Psychology, Lake Forest College, Lake Forest, Illinois 60045.

chologists have focused on the formation of the disposition to commit criminal acts, the former accounting for it through the collective experience of groups located at different points in the social system; the latter through individual experiences. To understand criminal behavior, they both argue, is to grasp the motivation that triggered the act.

In this chapter we will describe the emergence of a new container for the crime problem that has significant consequences for how we think about crime. That container, which we call the *victimization perspective,* treats crime as a source of stress. It emphasizes the experience of the victim rather than the offender. We will describe the victimization perspective, compare it to other approaches, and then discuss both positive and negative implications of defining crime in this way.

We show that, although the victimization viewpoint shifts the focus from the criminal to the victim, it fails to shift the focus of power and responsibility from traditional holders of that power. Thus, those who represent traditional constituencies with an interest in crime as a social problem continue to maintain their dominance. Finally, as equal security advocates, we offer an alternative that shifts that power and responsibility.

STRESS AND INTEREST GROUPS

Gusfield (1975) has made a useful distinction between the *cognitive* and *political* responsibility for a social problem. By the former, he means explaining why the problem occurs and by the latter, who is obliged to solve it.

We now turn our attention to the question of political responsibility and to the relationship between the cognitive and political dimensions. As Gusfield points out, there is no necessary logical link between the cognitive and political dimensions, that is, a problem may be caused by factors that are independent of the political responsibility for its solution (e.g., inflation and the federal government's responsibility). We believe, however, that cognitive and political responsibility are closely associated, each supporting the other's claim to legitimacy. We argue that the link between the cognitive and political dimensions is made by the various criminal justice interest groups that tie the two dimensions together in theory as well as practice. The cognitive and political dimensions are produced by actors whose values and interests link the two spheres. The cognitive dimension contains the suggestion of where the political responsibility for the problem ought to be located. Those interests that, at any given point in time, either hold or seek to hold that political responsibility will be selective in promoting the construction of problems that strengthens their claim. The mechanism for creating that association is the interest groups who benefit from the particular picture of cognitive and political responsibility presented.

We are speaking here of the "competing public positions" about a social problem, not the almost infinite variety of private opinions, personal preferences, and academic musings that surround social problem debate. These "positions" are put forth in public and taken seriously by others; they shape how elites think about the issue and what they propose to do about it. Although the origins of the cognitive aspect of the problem can be manifold, the extent to which that approach emerges in public discussion depends upon the uses to which it can be put by the interest groups who seek to control the policy agenda. Indeed, policy that develops from various approaches to social problems is not a "natural" consequence of objective investigation but rather an ideological tool in the hands of those who seek control over the remedies to the problem. The definition of the social problem flows from that set of interests as the interests congregate around the definitions that best suit their understanding of the problem.

We see three major interests groups with competing public positions on the crime issue. Those groups are loose-knit associations of individuals who represent the "structural interests" in criminal justice. Our typology borrows heavily from Alford's (1975) analysis of health care policy where the alignment of interests is much the same. Each of these interest groups has developed a position on the threat of crime that combines cognitive and political responsibility for the problem in a way that places that group in the pivotal position to manage the crime problem. Each interest group represents a set of political, economic, and social institutions whose maintenance depends on their ability to control resources and absorb social problems into their orbit of responsibility.

Alford argues that "professional monopolists" and "corporate rationalizers" represent the structural interests in the health care arena. The monopolists argue for leaving the decision to professionals (mostly doctors) and the market; and the rationalizers seek to regulate both doctors and markets to distribute health care more "rationally." There is much accommodation and compromise between these groups that leaves the basic economic, professional, and political relationships among the interest groups intact but may shift power relations marginally among the competing actors. "Equal health advocates" often criticize the reliance on the market system in health care, but they have had little success in challenging its dominance. They represent lower class groups who are the least competitive in the marketplace.

The criminal justice system and the health care system are parallel systems. Both distribute a value as a supplement to the market system. Health and security, in the main, are a function of one's position in the class system. Although members of the upper classes can become seriously ill or experience serious victimization, one's class position determines one's resources in maintaining health and security. Indeed, two of the main benefits of upward mobility are increased health and safety. The two "care" systems (medical and criminal justice) supplement those market relations and the distribution that follows from them. Both are *reactive,* responding to individual requests for service when a health or safety deficiency is reported. Both systems declare themselves to be "in crisis" regularly, particularly concerning the issue of how they distribute their services. And both "solve" those crises by bringing representatives of the interest groups together. Generally speaking, the monopolists in criminal justice seek to manage these crises by pumping more resources into police, courts, and corrections—that is, into the institutions they represent. The rationalizers look to coordination and planning to improve services, and to improve the bargaining position of the institutions (in particular the now-defunct Law Enforcement Assistance Administration) they represent.

As we will show later, each of these interest groups developed a public position on the cognitive and political responsibility for reducing the stress of victimization; that is, each adapted the victimization perspective to reflect its own interests.

The monopolists and rationalizers fix the cognitive responsibility for stress upon the experience of the victimization event and the individual's reaction to it, yet they differ in their attribution of political responsibility. John Conklin made the important connection between event and individual response in *The Impact of Crime* (1975). Rejecting Emile Durkheim's concept of the *functionality of deviance* in strengthening communities, Conklin argues that the stress of crime robs citizens of the capacity to trust, isolates them, and thus contributes to the decline of community:

> Little of the material we have examined...suggests that Durkheim was correct in arguing that crime brings people together and strengthens social bonds. Instead, crime produces insecurity, distrust, and a negative view of the community. Although we lack conclusive evidence, crime also seems to reduce social interaction as fear and suspicion drive people apart. This produces a disorganized community that is unable to exercise informal social control over deviant behavior. (Conklin, 1975, p.99)

Rather than collectively sanctioning the criminal behavior, as Durkheim would anticipate, citizens react to fear individually and seek to protect themselves (e.g., buying guns and locks, not going out), thus breaking community cohesion.

Conklin's discussion of community hinges on the distinction he makes between *individual* and *collective* responses to crime. The importance of this distinction stems from his use of the victimization perspective, for the logic of responding individually hinges on the salience of the victimization experience. Individual responses are assumed to be the normal reactions to the fear, or experience, of victimization. Thus, the conclusion that individual responses have negative consequences for the community hinges on the imputed salience of victimization. Interestingly, this line of reasoning makes the *response* to victimization, rather than victimization itself, the central phenomenon. Conklin goes on to argue that when a community can respond collectively, crime does integrate:

> Crime weakens the fabric of social life by increasing fear, suspicion, and distrust. It also reduces public support for the law, in terms of unwillingness to report crime and criticism of the police. However, under certain conditions people will engage in collective action to fight crime. They may work for a political candidate who promises to restore law and order. They may call meetings of community residents to plan an attack on crime. Sometimes they may even band together in a civilian police patrol to carry out the functions that the police are not effectively performing for them. Since people who perceive high crime rates often hold the police responsible for crime prevention, we would expect such patrols to emerge where people feel very threatened by crime, believe that the police cannot protect them, and think from past experience with community groups that the people themselves can solve the problem. (Conklin, 1975, p.185)

The political responsibility for the problem rests on the kind of response a community produces. The result for the rationalizers is a strategy for crime prevention postulating that to build a collective response is to deter crime and reduce fear. For the monopolists, however, the individual response is anticipated, and the police are responsible for reducing crime and fear through their activities. In contrast, the rationalizers seek to reduce the number of victimizations in a neighborhood by increasing the capacity of that neighborhood and the criminal justice system to respond collectively. For both approaches, the cognitive responsibility for the problem of stress rests with how the individual responds to victimization. The political responsibility for controlling that stress rests with those who can increase collective responses (i.e., coping resources).

The *victimization perspective*, as we have called this approach, defines crime as an *event* produced by the interaction of offender, victim, and environment rather than as an *act* produced by a criminal. A victimization (crime) is produced by the behavior of both offender and victim, and these in turn depend upon a social and physical environment that supports their victimization-producing behaviors. All of these elements are necessary if the victimization is to take place. The victim himself or herself becomes one of the sources of the crime problem. His or her reports of victimization experiences (made independently of criminal justice agencies' reporting mechanisms) are the basis for judgments about the types of crimes committed and their disbution within a population.

From the victimization perspective, then, crime is a problem because it disintegrates communities and distresses individuals. This disintegration is produced by the fear, distrust, and isolation that victimization causes. Typically, people react to crime individually. They develop mechanisms to cope with the problem independent of and in isolation from others. This increases the disintegrative process. If people could react together, that is, collectively, crime's devastating impact on communities might be mitigated.

Figure 1 illustrates the shape of the crime problem from this perspective. Whether crime becomes a problem depends on how one *reacts* to it (Lewis & Salem, 1981). Crime is important to communities because it serves to weaken their cohesion. Crime is important to the individual because it taxes the individual's adaptive resources. As Monat and Lazarus (1977) have defined it, any event that has this effect can be viewed as a source of stress. Crime is thus a problem because it produces stress in those who experience it directly or who are "stressed" by the threat of the experience.

THE STRESS MODEL OF CRIME

The model of psychological stress developed by Lazarus (1966), McGrath (1977), and others (e.g., Baum, Singer, & Baum, 1981) emphasizes transactions between individuals and situations, rather than each of these elements separately. This emphasis is characteristic of ecological psychology, a perspective that considers the interaction of people and environments as its basic unit of analysis. If crime produces stress, then its emergence as a social problem draws our attention to how the individual appraises the threat of crime and what coping mechanisms are used to mitigate its impact.

Lazarus (1966) defines *threat* as the *appraisal of possible future harm.* People first assess the extent and nature of danger. Once a stimulus is judged to be threatening, then alternative means of dealing with that threat are evaluated. The major elements of the stress model of crime thus consist of factors that influence the assessment of danger and the strategies that are used to mitigate threat (Riger, 1985). Individual factors such as belief in control affect the cognitive processes that mediate stress, resulting in substantial differences among people in the way that stressors are perceived (Lazarus & Launier, 1978; McGrath, 1977). What is a threat to some may be inconsequential or even a challenge to others.

One of the antecedents that affect the process of appraisal is the nature of the stimulus configuration. Being confronted with a group of unknown teenaged boys, for example, will evoke a different response than if the boys are known (Merry, 1981). The psychology of the individual will also affect the appraisal process. Those who believe they can influence the outcome of a criminal encounter may see such a situation as less threatening than those who feel powerless in the face of danger. Additionally, previous experiences may have learning effects that influence responses, whereas adaptation processes may lessen the impact of cues of danger (McGrath, 1977).

Responses to threat may vary as a function of what Lazarus (1966) called

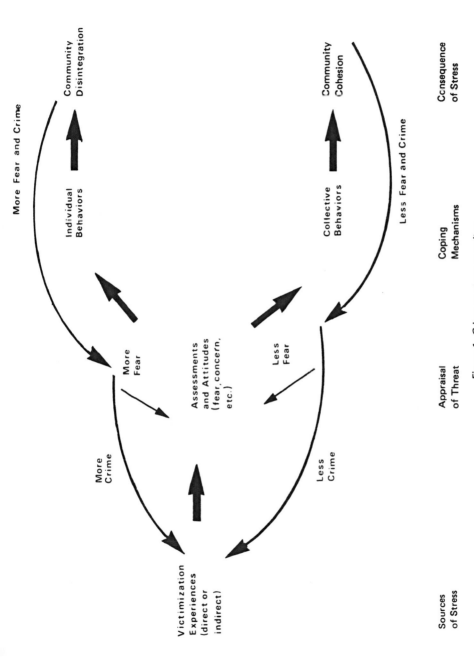

Figure 1. Crime as stress paradigm.

secondary appraisal: the assessment of coping resources to deal with threat. Once again, factors within the stimulus, such as the source of danger, and factors within the psychological structure of the perceiver affect the appraisal process. Yet the cues that affect the appraisal of coping strategies may differ from those that affect assessment of the threat itself (Lazarus, 1966; McGrath, 1977). Graffiti or groups of teenagers "hanging out" may signal that crime is likely to occur (Lewis & Maxfield, 1980), whereas the outcome of past experience with criminal attack may determine choice of strategies for reducing the likelihood of such an attack in the future.

Appraisal of coping resources leads to a choice among two kinds of strategies, problem oriented (or instrumental) and emotion oriented (Folkman & Lazarus, 1980). *Instrumental strategies* seek to alter the troubled transaction between person and environment, whereas palliative techniques such as denial seek to regulate the emotions. The target of instrumental coping actions can be either the environment, the self, or both. Two types of instrumental strategies for coping with the threat of criminal victimization have been identified (Skogan & Maxfield, 1981). *Risk-avoidance* tactics seek to minimize contact with threatening situations, whereas *risk-management* tactics aim to reduce harm in the fact of possible attack. The time element varies between the two strategies: risk avoidance wards off future harm, whereas risk-management attempts to reduce harm once a perceived danger is present.

If crime is defined as the stressful events with which individuals have to cope, then it is a problem for those who are taxed by its effects, not for those who produce the events through their behavior. The victimization container literally reshapes the meaning of crime as a problem. Crime is a problem because some people have difficulty coping with its effects (fear, isolation, personal harm). Just as some people get depressed, become alcoholic, or fail to adapt to relocation, others are negatively affected by crime. The key factors in determining the impact of crime are how it is appraised, how it is coped with, and what resources are brought to bear on its consequences. Thus, the psychological factors that distinguish potential victims become central to understanding the social problem of crime (Pearlin, Lieberman, Menaghan, & Mullan, 1981).

This container looks very different from the others used to study crime during this century. First, it does not focus on the offender and his or her motivation, but rather on the victim and his or her responses. Most theories of crime as a social problem have sought to explain why certain people violate norms, customs, and laws. It is the deviant nature of their behavior that is to be explained. The stress container is less concerned with why one breaks rules and more concerned with how certain experiences tax the victim's ability to cope. This change of emphasis to the victim is in itself revolutionary.

Second, our interest is drawn to the differences among victims in their responses to the various criminal events, particularly negative psychological reactions. This orientation has a long honorable history in psychology where the "stress process" is seen as the explanation for a variety of individual pathologies, but it shifts our attention still further away from the offender.

LIMITS OF THE STRESS PARADIGM

The stress paradigm is not without its critics. For example, it does not take social organization very seriously; that is, it does not consider how individual behavior is shaped by membership in groups or one's position in the social structure. That membership shapes not only the meaning and intensity of the life events experienced but also the options available in response to them.

> From one social position to another, people are dispersed or aggregated. If they are dispersed, individualistic forms of deviation are more likely; if aggregated, collective modes of deviation become possible. The isolation or solidarity in the one world tends to be reproduced in the other world. Thus, in some age and sex categories people are aggregated; in others they are dispersed. (Cloward & Piven, 1979, p. 659)

People with the same motives will behave differently because the normative structure of their groups differ (Barton, 1970). This collective dimension of human action is lost in the stress paradigm, as it is in other psychological theories. The "internalization" of crime problem in the stress paradigm thus ignores the social processes that produce crime-related attitudes and behaviors.

The stress model treats the victimization event as *constitutive* rather than *regulative,* suggesting that adaptation to crime shapes self-concepts and has a profound effect on identify and self-esteem. The person is changed rather than merely constrained by criminal victimization. Changes in behavior then become self-imposed and psychological, suggesting fundamental and often negative shifts in self-concept. Adaptation is coming from within (Wrong, 1961). Indeed, the emphasis on individual disposition follows from the internal focus of the stress process. The stress model accounts for how the disposition of the victim is formed rather than for the criminal's behavior. The formation and maintenance of the victim's disposition replaces the criminal act itself as the phenomenon to be explained and modified. When such theories inform prevention strategies they focus on changing the victim; thus, changing victims becomes synonymous with preventing crime. The cognitive and emotional processes of the individual remain at center stage. The individual and his or her motivational pattern are the key concepts, reducing the complexity of individual action to assessments of the environment and the coping strategies employed by those taxed by the events they experience. The problem of crime has been internalized.

If crime is a source of stress, then the victimization event is the stimulus to which individuals must respond. The context in which those events take place can be either hospitable or inhospitable to those events. The environment (both physical and social) "hosts" the event. Conflicts between classes, ethnic groups, and generations may be reduced to stress, in which the superordinate groups are stressed by the activities of the subordinates. Power differentials between groups are left unexplored in descriptions of the environment, and the competitive claims of groups are lost in the cognitive processes of individuals. It is here that the ideological consequences of the stress paradigm begin to surface. Which structural interests would benefit from treating crime as stress? Who gains resources and legitimacy as the definition achieves hegemony?

THE STRESS MODEL AND PUBLIC POLICY

The internalization of the crime problem expands the class of people affected by the phenomenon because everyone is a potential victim of crime. If crime is a source of stress and if that stress is linked to, but not equivalent to, victimization (because people may be stressed by the anticipation of crime), then whole new constituencies are "in need" of services. This applies especially to the elderly and middle-class groups who are not generally served by offender-oriented programs. Reducing stress through crime prevention rationalizes programming for groups not directly served by traditional criminal justice agencies.

From a political perspective, the stress model achieves the elusive result of producing benefits for new constituencies while at the same time protecting the interests of those who control criminal justice policy. In simple terms, the stress model allows for innovation without fundamental change.

The policy issue can be put succinctly: Who has the political responsibility for reducing the stress caused by crime? The victimization perspective was developed during the late 1960s and was nurtured throughout the 1970s. The bureaucratic rationalizers used the victimization perspective and Conklin's refinement of it to claim the crime problem for themselves. In the simplest terms, they broke the professional monopolists' hold on the crime problem, by offering a picture of crime that was politically and methodologically independent of the police, courts, and corrections. However, because the rationalizers at the Law Enforcement Assistance Administration (LEAA) depended upon the monopolists for much of their support at budget times, their demands for reform were tempered by restraint. The "dark figure" of victimization was illuminated by the victimization perspective (Skogan, 1977), but in a way to create a supplemental rather than alternative picture of the problem. This alternative picture created a knowledge base from which rationalizers could propose management changes in how the monopolists performed their jobs.

In order not to strain relations too much, the rationalizers defined new groups in need of service. Much of the victimization perspective research was utilized to expand services to those who were eligible because they felt afraid. These efforts (victim–witness programs, crime prevention for the elderly, rape prevention, etc.) appeared to be responsive to current problems without challenging the distribution of power within the criminal justice establishment. Various groups were funded to develop programs that supplemented, rather than challenged, the criminal justice constituencies. LEAA could thereby produce innovation without disturbing the status quo. Professional monopolists needed "innovations" to secure federal support for local efforts. Within local jurisdictions, professional reformers (local corporate rationalizers) could demand new programs that appeared to be alternatives but that were in fact supplemental in function.

In this respect, LEAA behaved no differently than other federal agencies. That agency had the difficult charge of changing a system on which it depended for its very existence. Thus the actions of the agency had to have the appearance of altering the status quo, while being acceptable to its central constituencies. This leads to what Wilson (1975, p.xviii) has called *criminal justice syndicalism*: "the tendency for decisions to be unduly influenced by the organized interests of those whose behavior is to be changed." Consequently, there has been a high premium on programs and policies that seemed to change but that enhanced the position and authority of the institutions to be reformed. The rationalizers simply expanded the service field to allow new programs to be established without upsetting the status quo. A few examples should illustrate this point.

The Hartford Crime Prevention Program was one of the first federally funded demonstration projects. The rationale of the Hartford Crime Prevention Program was as follows:

1. The crime rate in a residential neighborhood is a product of the linkage between offender motivation and the opportunities provided by the residents, users, and environmental features of that neighborhood.
2. The crime rate for a specific offense can be reduced by lessening the opportunities for that crime to occur.
3. Opportunities can be reduced by (a) altering the physical aspects of buildings and streets to increase surveillance capabilities and lessen target/victim vulnerability, to increase the neighborhood's attractiveness to residents, and to decrease its fear-producing features; (b) increasing citizen concerns about and involvement in crime prevention and the neighborhood in general; and (c) utilizing the police to support the above.
4. Opportunity-reducing activities will lead not only to a reduction in the crime

rate but also to a reduction in fear of crime. The reduced crime and fear will
mutually reinforce each other, leading to still further reductions in both. (Fowler,
Mangione, & McCalla, 1979, p.2)

The Hartford approach sets in motion a series of interventions that
literally reshape the targetted community and, if they are successful, will
reshape the potential vulnerability of citizens to victimization. Although this
approach indirectly affects the motivation of offenders by increasing their risk
of apprehension and decreasing the benefits to be obtained through illegal
activities, the emphasis has shifted away from changing offenders' personalities
or economic opportunities. Rather we see a utilitarian, rationalistic approach
to reshaping social relations among residents. Motivation still remains central,
but it is the motivation of the offended rather than the offender that becomes
pivotal to the success of the intervention. Individuals must be *motivated* to
act collectively rather than individually. Organizations are developed to give
individuals options when they respond to crime. The success of this program
as described by its evaluators lay in its reduction of fear and distrust, rather
than a significant decline in crime (Fowler & Mangione, 1979).

The Community Anti-Crime Program (CACP) offers a slightly different
approach to utilizing the victimization perspective in a stress-reduction strategy. Introduced in the summer of 1977, and sponsored by LEAA, the CACP
was authorized to spend $30 million in direct grants to community organi-
zations

> to assist community organizations, neighborhood groups and individual citizens
> in becoming actively involved in activities designed to prevent crime, reduce the
> fear of crime and improve the administration of justice. (U.S. Department of Justice,
> 1977, p.58)

The program's guidelines also describe the problems that the grants are meant
to alleviate

> the increasing social isolation of neighborhood residents, resulting from a fear of
> crime, which has destroyed the feelings of community necessary for social control.
> (U.S. Department of Justice, 1977, p.58)

And the program guidelines are equally clear about what types of activities the program is meant to foster

> the mobilization of community and neighborhood residents into effective self-help
> organizations to conduct anti-crime programs within their communities and neigh-
> borhoods and to encourage neighborhood anti-crime efforts that promote a greater
> sense of community and foster social controls over crime occurrence. (U.S. De-
> partment of Justice, 1977, p.58)

Victimization experiences are assumed to create fear. Fear, in turn, generates
isolation because citizens react individually to threat. Crime consequently

disintegrates community. "Crime occurrences" and fear can be reduced if the citizens react collectively to that threat. Crime events are seen as promoting the decline of community, and federally funded collective action to prevent those events is seen as the solution to the fear problem.

In both these cases, the political responsibility for controlling the problem is diffused. If the problematic situation is the stress of victimization, then it is not clear who is charged with stimulating the collective response. Although a variety of agencies have funded these efforts, the actual intervention is often left to the local agencies and groups receiving the aid. Those local groups are obliged to solve the problem, usually in cooperation with other agencies, both public and private. These solutions have been temporary because they depended upon categorical grants and the approval of local officials, both of which can be short lived.

Although useful innovations developed from the LEAA perspective, they offered no lasting challenge to the monopolists. Community organizations have neither the political muscle nor the formal authority to monopolize the "ownership" of the fear problem (Gusfield, 1975). Thus, their early success in assuming the political responsibility for the problem lay in the benefits accruing to the sponsoring federal agencies.

The policy of increasing the likelihood of collective responses served the rationalizers well. Rather than attempting to alter the predispositions and motivations of the criminal, as progressive reforms throughout the century had sought to do, rationalizers sought to prevent crime and reduce fear by altering the relations among the criminal, victim, and environment, and by reducing the opportunity for victimization. Crime is to be prevented and fear reduced not by changing perpetrators, but rather by educating potential victims, limiting the opportunities for victimization, and thus reducing fear. This was an innovation. For the first time in this century, a crime prevention policy has emerged that aims at changing the behavior of community residents and the structure of urban communities, not because they produce criminals but rather because they produce victims.

Community crime prevention (as we call the rationalizers' approach) placed the cognitive responsibility in the victim and his or her environment and the political responsibility with the "collective response" of community groups. But this attribution of political responsibility to community groups came in a context that demanded no change in the control of criminal justice decision-making resources.

If we can thank the corporate rationalizers at LEAA for the emergence of community crime prevention, we should also expect that the other "structural interests" involved would develop "competing public positions" on the issue of fear of crime. To fail to do so, or to deny that victimization is a problem, would leave the field to the one public position supported by the federal bureaucrats.

Perhaps the most important competing position comes from the professional monopolists who have recently redefined the political responsibility for the problem. The clearest and most important articulation of this position comes from Wilson and Kelling in *Broken Windows* (1982). They argue that fear of crime can be reduced through policing practice. Their approach hinges on the elaboration of the "high road" sketched in Figure 1. They focus in particular on the way community disintegration affects the production of crime, and they suggest that police-patrolling strategies can mitigate that production process by forestalling the disintegration of community.

> The citizen who fears the ill-smelling drunk, the rowdy teenager, or the importuning beggar is not merely expressing his distaste for unseemly behavior, he is also giving voice to a bit of folk wisdom that happens to be a correct generalization—namely that serious street crime flourishes in areas in which disorderly behavior goes unchecked. The unchecked panhandler is, in effect, the first broken window. Muggers and robbers, whether opportunistic or professional, believe they reduce their chances of being caught or even identified if they operate on streets where potential victims are already intimidated by prevailing conditions. If the neighborhood cannot keep a bothersome panhandler from annoying passersby, the thief may reason, it is even less likely to call the police to identify a potential mugger or to interfere if the mugging actually takes place. (Wilson & Kelling, 1982, p. 34)

By policing against "incivilities," crime and fear can be curtailed. There are two important points about this approach. First, it assumes the victimization perspective but suggests that successful intervention pivots less on how individuals react to crime and more on influencing the conditions that produce the crime. Crime produces fear, and if crime is curtailed fear will be too. The connection between disorderly behavior, crime, and fear is asserted. In this scenario, it is only the *coercive* power of the police that has the potential to curb disorderly behavior. "The police are plainly the key to order maintenance" (Wilson & Kelling, 1982, p. 36). This is the case because they are the only group who can force an end to disorderly behavior that stimulates criminality. This brings us to the second point, which is that solving the fear problem rests with traditional criminal justice agencies. Through this analysis, the professional monopolists can reassert their ownership of the fear issue. Informal social control may be the key to maintaining order, but the police are alone in being able to directly affect the behavior that challenges that order. Thus, fear of crime can be lessened to the extent that disorderly behavior is reduced. Community organizations have little capacity to reduce the incidence of disorderly behavior. Police can solve the problem through changes in their practice. The cause of the disorderly behavior does not have to be addressed in its solution. Coercion can go a long way to reducing crime and fear, especially if the coercion supports the conventional standards of the community.

In contrast, equal security advocates (and we count ourselves in this camp) place the cognitive responsibility for the problem in the lack of social control in some communities. Paralleling the equal health advocates in both their analysis and constituency, this perspective focuses on altering the balance within the criminal justice policy community. To ameliorate the stress problem, social control must be reasserted by local groups. Community organizations are the appropriate vehicle for that solution, given their capacity to enforce neighborhood standards. If the community is *empowered* through its local organizations to assert that control, then stress will be reduced.

Each of the three positions discussed here has a different notion of the "motor" for stress-reduction control. That is, the reduction of stress follows from the process each interest group puts into action through its analysis and strategies. The professional monopolists rely on *coercion*; the corporate rationalizers on bureaucratic *cooperation*; and the equal security advocates on *empowerment*. Each position offers a vision of how stress might be reduced, and each serves the interests of a constituency in the criminal justice arena. Those interests are served by suggesting that the problem can be ameliorated by placing the issue in the hands of one of the constituencies.

The central point which we want to emphasize in conclusion is not so much that there are problems with the stress model when it is applied to crime but rather that we must find ways to improve the model, especially if one is to develop a competing public position. The issue is how to make the model work for the groups with which one is aligned. The key to that improvement, if one adapts the empowerment idea, is to link the impact of crime to the capacity of groups and individuals to improve the situation in which they find themselves. Bandura (1982) suggests that the concept of efficacy might serve well as the link between the acquisition of knowledge and the execution of response patterns—the classic concern of psychologists. The research on efficacy would show the process through which an individual comes to act in ways that lead to empowerment. In our case, the stress of crime could be mitigated by looking at the sense of efficacy that individuals feel. What is more important, if personal and collective efficacy were the focus of research, policy efforts might focus on increasing the coping resources available to the individual or the community. The stress model could be employed to realign relations between groups and classes. This would involve "externalizing" the stress process, showing what factors increased both personal and collective efficacy, and translating that knowledge into policy development.

REFERENCES

Alford, R. (1975). *Health care politics*. Chicago: University of Chicago Press.

Bandura, A. (1982). Self-efficacy mechanism in human agency. *American Psychologist, 37,* (2), 122–147.

Barton, A. H. (1970). *Communities in disaster*. Garden City, NY: Doubleday.

Baum, C., Singer, J. E., & Baum, C. S. (1981). Stress and the environment. *Journal of Social Issues, 37,* 4–35.

Cloward, B. A., & Piven, F. F. (1979). Hidden protest: The channeling of female innovation and resistance. *Signs, 4,(4)*, 651–669.

Conklin, J. (1975). *The impact of crime.* New York: Macmillan.

Folkman, S., & Lazarus, R. S. (1980). Coping in an adequately functioning middle-aged population. *Journal of Health and Social Behavior, 21*, 219–239.

Fowler, F., Mangione, T., & McCalla, M. E. (1979). *Reducing residential crime and fear.* Washington, DC: National Institute of Justice.

Gusfield, J. (1975). Categories of ownership and responsibility in social issues: Alcohol abuse and automobile use. *Journal of Drug Addiction, 5*, 285–303.

Lazarus, R. S. (1966). *Psychological stress and the coping process.* New York: McGraw-Hill.

Lazarus, R. S., & Launier, R. (1978). Stress-related transactions between person and environment. In L. A. Pervin & M. Lewis (Eds.), *Perspectives in interactional psychology* (pp. 287–327). New York: Plenum Press.

Lewis, D. A., & Maxfield, M. G. (1980). Fear in the neighborhoods: An investigation of the impact of crime. *Journal of Research in Crime and Delinquency, 17*, 160–189.

Lewis, D. A., & Salem, G. (1981). Community crime prevention: An analysis of a developing strategy. *Crime and Delinquency, 27*, 405–421.

McGrath, J. E. (1977). Settings, measures, and themes: An integrative review of some research on social-psychological factors in stress. In A. Monat & R. S. Lazarus (Eds.), *Stress and coping: An anthology* (pp. 67–76). New York: Columbia University Press.

Merry, S. E. (1981). *Urban danger: Life in a neighborhood of strangers.* Philadelphia: Temple University Press.

Monat, A., & Lazarus, R. S. (Eds.). (1977). *Stress and coping: An anthology.* New York: Columbia University Press.

Pearlin, C. I., Leiberman, M. A., Menaghan, E. G., & Mullan, J. T. (1981). The stress process. *Journal of Health and Social Behavior, 22*, 337–356.

Riger, S. (1985). Crime as an environmental stressor. *Journal of Community Psychology, 13*, 270–280.

Skogan, W. G. (1977). Dimensions of the dark figure of unreported crime. *Crime and Delinquency, 23*, 41–50.

Skogan, W. G., & Maxfield, M. G. (1981). *Coping with crime: Individual and neighborhood reactions.* Beverly Hills, CA: Sage Publications.

Spector, M., & Kitsuse, J. I. (1977). *Constructing social problems.* Phillipines: Cummings.

U.S. Department of Justice. (1977). *Guidelines manual: Guide to discretionary grant programs* (M4500.IE). Washington, DC.

Wilson, J. Q. (1975). *Thinking about crime.* New York: Basic Books.

Wilson, J. Q., & Kelling, G. L. (1982, March). Broken Windows. *Atlantic Monthly*, pp. 29–38.

Wrong, D. (1961). The oversocialized view of man. *American Sociological Review, 26*, 347–361.

CHAPTER 12

Examining Criminal Justice Interventions
THE MYTH OF REFORM

RONALD ROESCH and DENISE J. FOISY

The need to redefine social problems and examine social myths is certainly evident when one reviews interventions in the criminal justice system. Criminals have been variously defined as *mad* or *bad* and sometimes as both, but usually with little or no empirical support. Several decades ago, prominent mental health professioals like Menninger (1968) argued for the appropriateness of a mental illness perspective on criminal behavior (see Lehman, 1972, for an historical review). This perspective reinforced the notion that criminals should be treated rather than punished and led to the development of a variety of treatment programs, including the creation of a treatment-oriented prison, Patuxent Institute, in which prisoners were sent for an indeterminate time until they were rehabilitated. The treatment perspective gained popularity despite the fact that there were no empirical studies attesting to the validity of claims of effectiveness.

There were, however, a number of writers who voiced concerns about the appropriateness of a treatment model in criminal justice. Kittrie (1971) argued that individual rights were increasingly threatened by what he termed *the therapeutic state* which justifies a variety of treatment programs even against the individual's wishes as well as allowing indeterminate confinement. Szasz (1963) has made similar arguments. But the more recent shift away from rehabilitation programs had perhaps less to do with these civil libertarian concerns than with the concern that rehabilitation programs cost the state a considerable amount of money (see Scull, 1981, for similar arguments about

RONALD ROESCH and DENISE J. FOISY • Department of Psychology, Simon Fraser University, Burnaby, British Columbia, Canada V5A 1S6.

treatment in mental hospitals), and encouraged the acceptance of the results of a major review of treatment programs by Lipton, Martinson, and Wilks (1975). Their work reinforced a growing sense that rehabilitation programs based on a mental illness model of criminal behavior were dismal failures and should be abandoned in favor of a punishment model, or that treatment should at least be noncoercive and not linked with release from prison (e.g., Fogel, 1975; Morris, 1974). Again, the empirical basis of this shift in policy (which, incidentally, meant that policy had come full circle with a return to the practices of the early 1900s) was not substantial as many writers pointed to the flaws in Martinson's work (Palmer, 1975) and to the distinct lack of available treatment in most correctional facilities (Silber, 1974).

There have been, of course, numerous other attempts to create change in the criminal justice system. In general, most reforms have ultimately been considered failures. It is the thesis of this chapter, however, that the reforms have failed because they have not been genuine reforms. There has been, to be sure, an *appearance* of reform because we have countless examples of new programs that have been tried. But upon close examination of the various reforms, it is possible that a primary reason for the perceived failure is not the reforms themselves but rather problems in the manner in which the issues have been framed that has led to specific difficulties. Reforms in the criminal justice system have failed or have been prematurely abandoned because the system has not paid sufficient attention to or examined critically the assumptions inherent in the following questions: (1) What should the expected and actual reach of an intervention be? (2) How should the focus of interventions be defined? (3) What psychological treatments should be applied to offenders? (4) What is the expected impact of an intervention on other parts of the criminal justice system or on other systems? The failure to address these questions has contributed to the current view that reform is impossible to achieve. It will be argued that true reform can be achieved by examining these questions and reframing the assumptions that have been made about the nature of reform. In the remainder of this chapter, these questions will be considered in detail.

THE REACH OF REFORM

One of the more popular myths of criminal justice reform is that most individuals in the system are provided some form of treatment or support. The fact is that most do not. Many criminal justice reforms began with quite laudable goals and expectations that the intervention would have an impact on a large number of persons in the system. Yet many of these reforms have had far less impact. We believe this is the case, at least in part, because of the implicit desire of criminal justice officials to minimize risks and avoid negative publicity. For example, it is much more desirable for the system to detain a potentially dangerous person even at the cost of a high false-positive rate. The public knows little of a defendant who was retained incorrectly as being dangerous, but becomes quite alarmed and outraged when a released person commits a violent act. As a consequence, decision makers are pressed to err in the false-positive direction (i.e., detain an individual incorrectly because of predicted dangerousness) in order to minimize the risk of incorrectly releasing dangerous persons.

The tendency to minimize risk is also quite evident when the pretrial diversion literature is examined. Diversion began as a liberal reform based on the view that avoiding the negative consequences (e.g., labeling; association with more serious offenders) of involvement in the criminal justice system and of providing some form of early treatment would be beneficial to first-time offenders. The practice of diversion allows selected offenders to have charges dismissed upon successful completion of specified terms of the treatment program. The initial intention of many programs was to have fairly broad selection criteria that would allow the diversion of defendants with a range of criminal charges. The actual practice, however, has been quite different as the majority of programs have focused on defendants charged with minor crimes. For example, in some programs, the predominant charge of selected participants is shoplifting. There is persuasive evidence that many of the selected defendants would not have been prosecuted anyway (Austin, 1980; Baker & Sadd, 1981; Blomberg, 1980). If this is so, diversion programs may result in an increase in the amount of social control over individuals who otherwise would be released. This suggests that diversion has been used inappropriately with some individuals and has failed to involve defendants for whom there might be benefits (i.e., those charged with more serious crimes *and* who might benefit from treatment). This issue will be discussed again later in the chapter when the area of treatment integrity is treated.

It is possible that if reformers approached the issue of diversion with a different set of assumptions, then the form of diversion might well have been different. If we asked, "Do pretrial defendants need treatment?", we might have answered in the negative. In other words, it may have been as effective and likely more cost-efficient to simply have left these defendants alone (a "warn-and-release" strategy), as Schur (1973) has suggested we do with certain juvenile offenders. Politically, however, it was perceived as necessary to do something more with these defendants. Simply leaving them alone did not seem right to prosecutors and others in the criminal justice system. So we established diversion programs with various forms of treatment to make the programs more palatable. Recent reviews of diversion programs suggest that diversion has not been effective because the programs have been too conservative and the interventions have cost much (Baker & Sadd, 1981; Roesch & Corrado, 1983). One of the reasons, we believe, for the limited success is that reformers naively assumed that the programs would be used by the system in the way they envisioned. Baker and Sadd (1981), for example, demonstrated that charges against many defendants in a control group (that was not diverted and thus presumed to be prosecuted) were dismissed. As Baker and Sadd (1981) have concluded,

> Simply providing court decision-makers with an alternative for handling cases does not assure that the new option will be used in the way preferred by its advocates....Existing diversion programs cannot assume they are diverting defendants from conviction and harsh sanction. (pp. 44–45)

How should reformers have approached the creation of diversion programs, and what should be done in the future to ensure that they would have a greater impact on the criminal justice system? One of us has argued the following:

> First, projects should follow procedures that ensure that diversion occurs only after the filing of charges, so that diversion is a genuine alternative to the criminal justice system....Second, the scope of diversion should be expanded to include, and perhaps emphasize, defendants charged with more serious crimes. Third, diversion programs should try true diversion, in which defendants are simply diverted out of the system, with no services from a diversion program. Charges would be dismissed immediately and individuals would not be required to participate in any program. Fourth, the type of program offered by a diversion program should have a firm gounding in theory. A program should justify why a selected intervention, such as counseling, should be presumed to have an effect on recidivism, the participants's quality of life, or any other outcome variable....Programs with an emphasis on employment may be more supportable given the high rates of unemployment among many arrested persons. Finally, more research on the effects of diversion programs is needed. (Roesch & Corrado, 1983, p. 392)

Another example of the limited reach of interventions is bail reform. One of the early attempts to change the manner in which pretrial defendants were released from jail was initiated by Herbert Sturz (see Feeley, 1983, for an historical review). Sturz was critical of the bail practice that required defendants to post a cash bail in order to secure release prior to trial. He argued that this was discriminatory against indigent defendants. As an alternative, he created a program designed to increase the use of an alternative to bail, referred to as *release on recognizance*. Sturz and his colleagues (Ares, Rankin, & Sturz, 1963) argued that the strength of a defendant's ties to a community would be a good way of predicting whether he or she would appear in court. Thus, if a defendant had resided in a neighborhood for a extended time, had a family, and was employed or attending school, then he or she was considered a good risk. Ares *et al.* (1963) converted these factors to a point system and used this as a basis for making recommendations to the court to release a defendant without a cash bail.

There is little doubt that point systems, which after the initial demonstration spread rapidly throughout the country, were successful in terms of increasing the use of release on recognizance (Thomas, 1976). However, if the reform is examined in light of the questions raised in this section about the reach of reform, the results may not be as dramatic. It is possible that the point systems simply replaced the use of cash bail for defendants who could have posted the cash bail. Bynum and Massey (1977) have reported data showing that the increase of release on recognizance in one jurisdiction was associated with a decrease in defendants who posted a cash bail. It may be that the criteria employed, community ties, are just as discriminatory against indigent defendants as was cash bail.

These examples suggest that greater attention has to be paid to the extent to which reforms have an impact on the intended populations, or indeed even reached the population. In the case of diversion and bail reform, there *appeared* to be significant change, and this may have limited attempts at real change. If early reformers had looked at the impact in the way Bynum and Massey (1977) later did for bail reform, or Baker and Sadd (1981) did for diversion, the nature of the reform might have been altered before the reforms were implemented throughout the country.

FOCUS OF THE INTERVENTIONS

A second myth of criminal justice reform is that the focus of change should be on the individual, and that psychological treatment is appropriate for all, or nearly all, offenders. There is an implicit assumption in criminal justice reform that the individual is the source of the problem and, consequently, should be the focus of attempts at reform. If one examines the nature of reform, it is clear that the predominant focus of interventions in the criminal justice system is the individual. This is the case regardless of whether the model has been a rehabilitation one or a punitive one. Furthermore, the individual is seen as responsible for the criminal behavior, which is often based on an assumption of psychological deficit (Reppucci & Clingempeel, 1978). Thus, the primary question has been, "What is wrong with this person who has committed a crime?"

Once the problem has been defined in this manner, there is a tendency to view all criminals in the same way and to treat all offenders the same. For example, Kassebaum, Ward, and Wilner (1971) had all prisoners participate in a group therapy session. Countless other examples can be found. The primary point that should be considered is whether it was reasonable to expect that all prisoners would benefit from a particular treatment or from any treatment at all. It may well be the case that only 10% of a given prison population would benefit from treatment. If this is true, it is not surprising that most treatments do not show significant changes in the experimental group when compared to a control group. Martinson's findings and conclusions about the effectiveness of various attempts at rehabilitation would be expected if most offenders were inappropriately given treatments that simply do not address the reasons or circumstances that brought them to prison in the first place.

With respect to psychological treatment, it is clear that its application should be more narrowly focused. If the correctional treatment research had heeded the more specific psychotherapy research questions (Kiesler, 1966; Paul, 1967), the field might be in a better position to consider which types of offenders would benefit from particular treatments. Assuming that the appropriate population in need of psychological treatment is a relatively small percentage of the total offender population, as Lehman (1972) and Silber (1974) have suggested, then we must ask what other theories or explanations would account for the behavior of the remainder of the population. This would necessitate asking other questions about the nature of criminal behavior, and it is likely to involve a consideration of factors other than those at the individual level (e.g., employment, socioeconomic status).

It is much easier, of course, to look at the individual offender as the target of change or punishment. Explanations at the individual level, regardless of whether they are based on rehabilitation or punishment models, allows society to maintain the status quo. If the individual is responsible and in fact can be blamed for the criminal behavior (Ryan, 1971), then it is easy to justify individually oriented interventions. This also allows us to avoid examining more difficult social structural forces that affect crime, such as the distribution of wealth and power in society, unemployment and underemployment, and education. Furthermore, placing a large amount of resources on individual interventions (including the maintenance of high-cost prisons) results in little or no resources left over for prevention programs. It is also likely that administrators find it difficult to invest in prevention programs that may have primarily long-term payoffs and little in the way of short-term impact. Because they do not see these benefits immediately, there is a tendency not to believe in them. Thus, society continues to pour more and more money into after-the-fact rehabilitation or punishment of offenders rather than try to understand and change the circumstances that brought those offenders to the attention of the criminal justice system.

Reframing the questions about the appropriate focus of interventions might lead to substantially different attempts to reform the criminal justice system. In fact, this reframing might take us beyond the criminal justice system to address the problem more adequately. Drawing on the work of

Caplan and Nelson (1973) and Rappaport (1977), Roesch and Corrado (1979) argued that

> much of our efforts are directed at person-centered interventions, while many of the problems faced by offenders may be more directly relevant to system centered interventions, including such activities as the creation of new settings and programs which will increase the power, autonomy, and self-control of disenfranchised groups. (p.540)

For example, how much do unemployment rates contribute to the level of crime? What is the relationship between economics and stress (Seidman & Rapkin, 1983)? How does undereducation or lack of job or vocational training effect crime rates? Reform within the criminal justice system that paid attention to the issues raised by these questions might take a different approach. Instead of putting substantial resources into dealing with individual offenders after a crime has been committed, greater resources might be placed in prevention efforts aimed at reducing the rates of crime.

A clear example comes from examining the issue of violence. How successful is a policy that focuses much of its energies on detention of individuals, most of whom have already been violent at least once, as a method of preventing violence. We would argue that it is not likely to be very effective. Rather, it might be more productive to examine other factors that are likely to produce or facilitate violence. There is now a growing body of literature, for example, that suggests there is a relationship between television watching and aggression (Garofalo, 1981; Lefkowitz, Eron, Walder, & Huesmann, 1977). If a greater share of our efforts were put into research on the causes of violence, it might lead to more effective policies than is presently the case. Reframing the questions to allow the possibility of system-level explanations and changes (Kushler & Davidson, 1981) would be a step in that direction.

PSYCHOLOGICAL TREATMENTS

Another myth of criminal justice reform is that psychological treatments, when appropriate, were provided in sufficient strength to have an impact. One interpretation of the conclusions reached about the failure of the rehabilitation model is that the treatment programs were never given a reasonable chance to succeed. This interpretation would suggest that the programs were never delivered on a sufficient scale by properly trained individuals to have had the desired impact. Silber (1974) points out that the ratio of prisoners to mental health professionals is so high that individual and even group treatment is virtually impossible to deliver. Some programs have used guards or other nonprofesionals (e.g., Kassebaum, Ward, & Wilner, 1971), but unfortunately the persons delivering the program have not typically been well trained or supervised; thus, the quality as well as quantity of treatments offered under a rehabilitation model would have to be questioned.

Quay (1977) has discussed this issue in an article in which he argued that an assessment of program integrity is essential when one evaluates the effectiveness of any intervention. Treatment or program integrity refers to the degree to which the treatment addresses the following areas: (1) the specificity of the program and the extent to which the treatment can be accurately and specifically described; (2) the degree to which the program is delivered in the manner specified; (3) the expertise, training, and supervision of the treatment personnel; and (4) the match of treater, treatment, and client. He criticizes the lack of attention paid by reviewers of research to this issue who tend to focus on adequacy of design and outcome data. Reviews of this type, which would include Martinson's, may well reach misleading conclusions because they fail to consider the issue of treatment integrity. It matters little that a study was well designed if the treatment was ill conceived, delivered to too broad a group of offenders, or improperly or poorly given. Furthermore, Quay (1977) is critical of the inattention given to program and offender match. He argues:

> There is a great deal of evidence for the proposition that neither juvenile nor adult offenders are homogeneous with respect to characteristics related to responsiveness to differing kinds of interventions. In no other areas of human services are all clients expected to react equally well to all treatment approaches, and the case of corrections is certainly no different. The extent to which the intervention is appropriate to the needs of its clients should be addressed; blanket applications of almost any treatment without regard for client characteristics are doomed to failure at the outset. (p. 346)

Anyone familiar with the psychotherapy research literature is aware that questions about the match between therapist, treatment, and client are of critical importance when evaluating the effects of treatment (Kiesler, 1966; Paul, 1967). Yet, implicit in criminal justice interventions is that it is possible to develop a treatment package applicable to all offenders or a large subpopulation of offenders. To date, the application of psychotherapy to offenders has followed what Kiesler (1971) has referred to as *uniformity myths.* That is, offenders have been viewed as a homogeneous group with similar treatment needs. This myth was first recognized in work with psychotherapy clients and it has persisted when psychotherapy has been used with offenders. It is not that psychotherapy with offenders is inappropriate but rather its indiscriminate application to a group without giving thought to the underlying assumptions that govern the appropriate application of an intervention. The first question that should be asked is, "Is psychotherapy appropriate for this individual?"

Quay (1977) uses the group therapy study by Kassebaum et al. (1971) to illustrate how this issue has been ignored in criminal justice. In the Kassebaum *et al.* study, it was found that group therapy with prisoners had no significant effects on later recidivism rates—the major dependent variable of concern in the study. The research was well-designed, but Quay points to several aspects that would raise questions about treatment integrity. For example, the majority of the group counselors did not believe the treatment would have any effect on recidivism, the amount and type of counselor training was not adequate, especially in view of the fact that many of the counselors were previously untrained prison guards or clerical staff, participation by inmates was not voluntary, and "there was no attempt...to select, or even identify, those most likely to have benefitted from the treatment, nor was there any attempt to compose the counseling groups in any systematic way" (Quay, 1977, p. 351).

Another example can be found in pretrial diversion. This has already been discussed in this chapter as an example of a conservative intervention. It is also the case that diversion has been applied inappropriately to defendants who had little need for the type of services offered by the program. This is because the programs have selected "safe" cases that would likely not recidivate no matter what was done to them. At the same time, diversion programs may have failed to accept defendants for whom the intervention would be useful. As Austin (1980) concluded after presenting data on the San Pablo (California) Adult Diversion Project:

> Pre-trial diversion programs should be faulted for what they became and not what they were supposed to do. The problem of diversion lies not in its assumptions about the negative effect criminal justice actions have upon offender attitudes and criminal careers. Hypotheses derived from them remain to be empirically tested. This study and others have shown that current diversion programs bear little correspondence with a theory premised on reducing criminal justice intervention. Instead of diversion, there has been organizational extension and expansion within the pre-trial court processes. (p. 237)

Given these and other problems, Quay suggests that it is not surprising that the Kassebaum *et al.* study did not have an impact on recidivism. What is surprising, however, is that one would realistically expect it to have an impact on the behavior of inmates after release. There is a need for a more narrow focus of psychological interventions as well as ensuring that treatment integrity questions are addressed. If the nature of interventions was reformed with these issues in mind, the psychological treatments might be more appropriately and effectively applied to some offenders.

Another possible outcome of reframing the question about the nature of intervention is that it would allow us to consider the advantages of focusing on the strengths rather than the deficits of individuals. This is more than simple rhetoric; it involves a significant change in how offenders are regarded once they enter the criminal justice system. It will have an impact on the nature of reforms for, as Rappaport and Seidman (1983) have put it,

Underlying the search for competence and strengths is the notion of diverse
standards of adjustment. Once we begin to look for strengths in our clients, we
are more likely to see a wider variety of ways in which people may find solutions
to their problems in living. Thus, reframing the questions about intervention has
important implications for the future of psychological treatment in the criminal
justice system. (p. 1093)

ANTICIPATING EFFECTS OF REFORM

A final myth of criminal justice reform is that the criminal justice system
is actually a system and that it can function independently of other systems.
The parts of the criminal justice system (police, courts, jails, prisons) actually
function semiautonomously. This fact makes true reform difficult because the
parts do depend upon each other but often do not cooperate. As a consequence, a reform implemented in part of one system often fails because it did
not obtain the necessary support from other parts of the system. For example,
if a prosecutor decides to no longer refer first offenders charged with serious
offenses to a diversion project, there is little the project can do (see Seidman,
1981, for a case history and analysis). It is also the case that interventions
in any large system (e.g., mental health, criminal justice) often do not take
into account radiating effects of those interventions within other parts of the
system and rarely consider implications for other systems. This tendency
might be characterized as a narrow within-system perspective on reform. This
has been true in terms of the manner in which pretrial defendants who appear
to have mental health problems are handled by the police, the jails, and the
courts. In the past, police who encountered such individuals would simply
refer them to the local mental hospital and have civil commitment proceedings
initiated. Because of changes in the commitment laws, this avenue was blocked
or at least its use lessened. Once these individuals were brought to the jail,
they occasionally presented problems for the jailers. As an easy solution, the
courts used the existing procedures for evaluating defendants' competency to
stand trial as a method of getting them out of jail and into the mental health
system. This is an example of how reform in a seemingly separate system—
namely the mental health system—ultimately had an impact on the criminal
justice system (see Roesch & Golding, 1980, for a review).

Originating, in part, from a somewhat narrowly focused attempt to make
civil commitment more difficult to justify, deinstitutionalization of state mental hospitals has been occurring over the past 20 years. As civil libertarians
fought to secure the release of the mentally ill from institutions, a number
of legal decisions and mental health policy changes led to the discharge of a
substantial number of patients into the community. This movement toward
deinstitutionalization has seen the inpatient census of state mental hospitals

declining steadily for the past 20 years (Steadman & Morrissey, 1984). In one sense, therefore, the mental health reform appears to have been successful. On the other hand, when other considerations are taken into account, deinstitutionalization can only be described as a dismal failure.

One method for dealing with the large number of persons who are no longer hospitalized but come to the attention of the police is to use other institutions to detain them. Steadman and Morrissey (1984) use the term *transinstitutionalization* to describe the trend of patient flow from one institution to another. They regard it to be somewhat more revealing than the misused term of *deinstitutionalization*, and it can be used to describe movement within one system as well as between systems.

Kiesler and Sibulkin (1983) illustrate transinstitutionalization within a system when describing that, contrary to popular belief, the proportion of inpatient days for mental disorders had actually increased between 1969 and 1978, during the height of so-called deinstitutionalization. They argue that when general hospital psychiatric units, residential treatment centers, private hospitals, and community mental health centers are taken into account, "total inpatient psychiatric episodes have increased in excess of the general population increase, despite a substantial decrease in episodes at VA and state psychiatric hospitals" (p. 610). Further, a study conducted by Luckey and Berman (1979) found that rates of involuntary readmission to mental health centers after change in the Nebraska commitment laws reversed a downward trend and began to increase. These authors also provide evidence to support data by Lamb, Sorkin, and Zusman (1981) who reported findings from California that although the rate of involuntary admission remained fairly stable over time, the length of commitment decreased. The decrease in length of stay has resulted in a significantly reduced mental health census even though the admission rates have not changed. Thus, this population appears not to have been deinstitutionalized at all. More realistically, they are often merely being reinstitutionalized in the same or similar settings.

We turn now to an examination of transinstitutionalization as it occurs between the mental health and criminal justice systems. To ascertain the extent to which the criminal justice system has been affected by the release of mental patients into the community, a number of studies have focused on state prison populations (see Steadman & Morrissey, 1984, for a review). The result of such examinations led to the conclusion that there were simply no consistent patterns of released mental patients contributing to the U.S. prison population. But as Steadman and Morrissey (1984) argue, the state prison is only one of several facets of the criminal justice system through which deinstitutionalized mental patients could become involved. A far more likely place for this population to appear would be the local jails that serve as initial holding and booking sites, pretrial detention centers, and as placement for those convicted of crimes with sentences of less than one year (i.e., misdemeanors). However, as these authors report, very little data exist that measure the impact of deinstitutionalization on local jails apart from Steadman and Ribner's (1980) very limited study on the Albany County Jail that revealed an increase of inmates with prior mental hospitalization of 9% to 12% from 1968 to 1975.

It is possible, however, that the police may be arresting a number of individuals who in the past would have been hospitalized. Evidence for this comes from the research on competency to stand trial. One of us has conducted a number of studies of competency procedures and has proposed reforms (Roesch & Golding, 1980). Two of the major problems identified as part of this research were that a large number of defendants were being inappropriately referred for evaluations and that most evaluations took place in forensic facilities. With respect to the former, it was learned that attorneys, jailers, and the courts were using competency evaluations as a means to obtain mental health treatment. The lengthy institutional evaluations were seen as unnecessary for most defendants in that most decisions could be made in a brief period of time and could take place in a local jail or on an outpatient basis if the defendant had been released on bail. The proposed reform called for a community-based screening evaluation (Golding, Roesch, & Schreiber, 1984) and minimal use of institutional evaluations. Although this would solve the immediate problem of inappropriate uses of competency evaluations, it does not deal with the larger question of how these defendants should be dealt with by the jails.

What this reform also fails to address is the very issue that prompts members of the criminal justice system to use competency proceedings; namely as a route to obtain mental health treatment for individuals who come to their attention but are viewed as needing help rather than punishment. In describing information from a study of three Wisconsin mental health institutions, Dickey (1980) found that incompetency commitments rose 42% from the year before Wisconsin revised its Mental Health Act compared to a year after. A substantial percentage of all incompetency commitments were for misdemeanors, a significant proportion of which were for the charge of disorderly conduct. Furthermore, the charges against these individuals were frequently dropped at the end of commitment.

Bearing in mind that police would prefer to hospitalize rather than incarcerate when confronted with a seemingly mentally ill individual, coupled with the fact that this alternative is becoming increasingly difficult to utilize, it is not surprising that the criminal justice system has instituted new programs to deal with the situation. An example of this appears in South Carolina where, in 1976, funds were appropriated to create a psychiatric unit consisting of 48 cells in the Kirkland Correctional Center (Gearing, Heckel, & Matthey, 1980). Referrals to this unit are received from state correctional centers.

Inmates deemed appropriate for referral are described as *those fit for the state hospital*. If a referral is considered questionably appropriate, the inmate may be transferred to Kirkland for an evaluation. Perhaps nowhere is transinstitutionalization portrayed more clearly than in this type of situation where the criminal justice system has taken over the role and function of the mental health system.

It is clear that reformers need to pay attention to the potential larger within and between-system effects of the changes made in any one system. It may be possible to anticipate some of the negative consequences of reform and to propose methods for avoiding problems created by reform. If this is achieved, it may minimize the tendency of a system to subvert reform.

SUMMARY AND DISCUSSION

This chapter has reviewed four myths that operate in the criminal justice system. It was argued that in order for true reform to be achieved, these myths and their underlying assumptions must be critically examined. It was acknowledged that many previous attempts to create new programs in the criminal justice system have met with failure. Four possible explanations to account for this failure were discussed. These explanations were not intended to account for all failures but, rather, were used to present some basic problems in the manner in which problems and potential solutions have been identified in the criminal justice system. It was suggested that the problem definitions are often too narrow in scope and inappropriately focus almost entirely on the individual as the target of change. The solutions are typically offered in insufficient quantity and quality, which makes successful outcomes unlikely. Finally, the interventions often fail to take into account the effects of the intervention on other parts of the criminal justice system, or indeed, on other systems such as the mental health system.

Possible ways to reframe the questions related to criminal justice system reform were addressed in this chapter and need not be reviewed again here. One issue that is relevant across all four areas is the need for research on the immediate and long-term effects of an intervention. There are very few examples of reforms that, from the planning stage and throughout the implementation of an intevention, included research as part of the process of introducing an intervention. One good example is the work of Rappaport and Seidman who created and evaluated a juvenile diversion project (Rappaport, Seidman, & Davidson, 1979). In this project, attention was paid to both process and outcome variables so that the impact of the program on the juveniles as well as on the system could be monitored. Furthermore, the intervention itself as well as the research design was guided by a concern that the problems identified in this chapter would be addressed. The criminal justice system needs more examples of this type. To accomplish this, it must adopt an experimental attitude about reforms (Campbell, 1969) as well as question the underlying values and expectations of proposed or existing interventions.

Another possible consequence of reframing the questions posed in this chapter is that a more preventive philosophy would emerge. It should be evident from the discussion in this chapter that the focus on individual psychological treatment is often inappropriate. Reframing the questions opens up a number of other strategies of change, including the larger societal-level changes as well as individual strategies that focus on strengths rather than deficits. It was suggested that the dominant strategy of the criminal justice system has been to put most of its resources into dealing with offenders *after* a crime has been committed. This is not only a costly strategy, but it is one that is ultimately ineffective because it has not correctly identified the problems and potential solutions.

REFERENCES

Ares, C., Rankin, A., & Sturz, H. (1963). The Manhattan Bail Project: An interim report on the use of pre-trial parole. *New York University Law Review, 38,* 67–95.

Austin, J. (1980). *Instead of justice: Diversion.* San Francisco: National Council on Crime and Delinquency Research Center.

Baker, S. H., & Sadd, S. (1981). *Diversion of felony arrests: An experiment in pretrial intervention.* Washington, DC: U.S. Department of Justice.

Blomberg, T. G. (1980). Widening the net: An anomaly in the evaluation of diversion programs. In M. W. Klein & K. S. Teilmann (Eds.), *Handbook of criminal justice evaluation* (pp. 571–592). Beverly Hills, CA: Sage Publications.

Bynum, T., & Massey, C. (1977). Implementing community based corrections: An exploration of competing goals of equality and efficiency. In C. R. Huff (Ed.), *Contemporary corrections: Social control and conflict* (pp. 34–48). Beverly Hills, CA: Sage Publications.

Campbell, D. T. (1969). Reforms as experiments. *American Psychologist, 24,* 409–429.

Caplan, N., & Nelson, S. D. (1973). On being useful: The nature and consequences of psychological research on social problems. *American Psychologist, 28,* 199–211.

Dickey, W. (1980). Incompetency and the nondangerous mentally ill client. *Criminal Law Bulletin, 8,* 22–40.

Feeley, M. M. (1983). *Court reform on trial.* New York: Basic Books.

Fogel, D. (1975). *We are the living proof: The justice model for corrections.* Cincinnati: Anderson.

Garofalo, J. (1981). Crime and the mass media: A selective review of research. *Journal of Research in Crime and Delinquency, 18,* 319–349.

Gearing, M., Heckel, R. V., & Matthey, W. (1980). The screening and referral of mentally disordered inmates in a state correctional system. *Professional Psychology, 11,* 849–854.

Golding, S. L., Roesch, R., & Schreiber, J. (1984). Assessment and conceptualization of competency to stand trial. *Law and Human Behavior, 8,* 321–334.

Kassebaum, G., Ward, D. A., & Wilner, D. M. (1971). *Prison treatment and parole survival.* New York: Wiley.

Kiesler, C. A., & Sibulkin, A. E. (1983). Proportion of inpatient days for mental disorders: 1969–1978. *Hospital and Community Psychiatry, 34,* 606–611.

Kiesler, D. J. (1966). Some myths of psychotherapy research and the search for a paradigm. *Psychological Bulletin, 65,* 110–136.

Kiesler, D. J. (1971). Experimental designs in psychotherapy research. In A. E. Bergin S. L. Garfield (Eds.), *Handbook of psychotherapy and behavior change: An empirical analysis* (pp. 36–74). New York: Wiley.

Kittrie, N. N. (1971). *The right to be different: Deviance and enforced therapy.* Baltimore: Johns Hopkins.

Kushler, M. G., & Davidson, W. S. (1981). Community and organizational level change. In A. P. Goldstein, E. G. Carr, W. S. Davidson. P Wehr (Eds.), *In response to aggression: Methods of control and prosocial alternatives* (pp. 346–401). New York: Pergamon Press.

Lamb, H. R., Sorkin, A. P., & Zusman, J. (1981). Legislating social control of the mentally ill in California. *American Journal of Psychiatry, 138,* 334–339.

Lefkowitz, M. M., Eron, L. D., Walder, L. O., & Huesmann, L. R. (1977). *Growing up to be violent.* New York: Pergamon Press.

Lehman, P. E. (1972). The medical model of treatment: Historical development of an archaic standard. *Crime and Delinquency, 17,* 204–212.

Lipton, D., Martinson, R., & Wilks, J. (1975). *The effectiveness of correctional treatment: A survey of treatment evaluation studies.* New York: Praeger.

Luckey, J. W., & Berman, J. J. (1979). Effects of a new commitment law or involuntary admissions and service utilization patterns. *Law and Human Behavior, 3,* 149–161.

Menninger, K. (1968). *The crime of punishment.* New York: Viking Press.

Morris, N. (1974). *The future of imprisonment.* Chicago: University of Chicago Press.

Palmer, T. (1975). Martinson revisited. *Journal of Research in Crime and Delinquency, 12,* 133–152.

Paul, G. L. (1967). Stragegy of outcome research in psychotherapy. *Journal of Consulting Psychology, 31,* 109–118.

Quay, H. (1977). The three faces of evaluation: What can be expected to work. *Criminal Justice and Behavior, 4,* 341–354.

Rappaport, J. (1977). *Community psychology: Values, research, and action.* New York: Holt, Rinehart & Winston.

Rappaport, J., & Seidman, E. (1983). Social and community interventions. In C. E. Walker (Ed.), *The handbook of clinical psychology* (1089–1122). Homewood: IL: Dow Jones-Irwin.

Rappaport, J., Seidman, E., & Davidson, W. S. (1979). Demonstration research and manifest versus true adoption: The natural history of a research project to divert adolescents from the legal system. In R. R. Munoz, L. R. Snowden, & J. G. Kelly (Eds.), *Research in social context: Bringing about change* (pp. 101–144). San Francisco: Jossey Bass.

Reppucci, N. D., & Clingempeel, W. G. (1978). Methodological issues in research with correctional populations. *Journal of Consulting and Clinical Psychology, 46,* 727–746.

Roesch, R., & Corrado, R. (1979). The policy implications of evaluation research: Some issues raised by the Fishman study of rehabilitation and diversion services. *The Journal of Criminal Law & Criminology, 70,* 530–541.

Roesch, R., & Corrado, R. (1983). Criminal justice interventions. In E. Seidman (Ed.), *Handbook of social intervention* (pp. 385–407). Beverly Hills, CA: Sage Publications.

Roesch, R., & Golding, S. L. (1980). *Competency to stand trial.* Urbana: University of Illinois Press.

Ryan, W. (1971). *Blaming the victim.* New York: Random House.

Schull, A. (1981). Deinstitutionalization and the rights of the deviant. *Journal of Social Issues, 37,* 6–20.

Schur, E. M. (1973). *Radical non-intervention: Rethinking the delinquency problem.* Englewood Cliffs, NJ: Prentice-Hall.

Seidman, E. (1981). The route from the successful experiment to policy formation: Falling rocks, bumps, and dangerous curves. In R. Roesch & R. R. Corrado (Eds.), *Evaluation and criminal justice policy* (pp. 81–103). Beverly Hills, CA: Sage Publications.

Seidman, E., & Rapkin, B. (1983). Economics and psychosocial dysfunction: Toward a conceptual framework and prevention strategies. In R. D. Felner *et al.* (Eds.), *Preventive psychology* (pp. 175–198). Elmsford, NY: Pergamon Press.

Silber, D.E. (1974). Controversy concerning the criminal justice system and its implications for the role of mental health workers. *American Psychologist, 29,* 239–244.

Steadman, H. J., & Morrissey, J. P. (1984). *The impact of deinstitutionalization on the criminal justice system: Implications for understanding changing modes of social control.* Paper presented at the symposium, "The Decentralization of Social Control," Simon Fraser University, Vancouver, BC.

Steadman, H. J., & Ribner, S. (1980). Changing perceptions of the mental health needs of inmates in local jails. *American Journal of Psychiatry, 137,* 1115–1116.

Szasz, T. S. (1963). *Law, liberty and psychiatry.* New York: Macmillan.

Thomas, W. H. (1976). *Bail reform in America.* Berkeley: University of California Press.

CHAPTER 13

Different Ways of Thinking about Burnout

CARY CHERNISS

The term *burnout* refers to a phenomenon in the human services that is not new. Over 30 years ago, Schwartz and Will (1969) described essentially the same process as they observed it in a nurse on a psychiatric ward. But they did not call it *burnout*; instead, they used the term, *low morale syndrome*. They used terms such as *anxiety, guilt,* and *withdrawal.* In this chapter, I shall propose that how we label and conceptualize the social problem of burnout reveals much about the underlying values and assumptions of our culture. Our labels and conceptualizations also dictate how we study and attempt to solve the problem. And finally, new ways of thinking about burnout ultimately could lead to a fundamental rethinking of human service delivery systems in our society.

The metaphors that we have chosen to illuminate the burnout phenomenon are mechanistic. Both *burnout* and *stress* are terms lifted directly from engineering. Why have we chosen to conceptualize a disturbing personal experience in terms used by engineers when they work with bridges and rocket engines? Why have we abandoned other terms, phrases, and conceptual frameworks that might be equally appropriate, terms and phrases such as *loss of commitment* or *alienation* or *weakening of moral purpose*? More important, how does the engineering metaphor, and the scientific-technical paradigm from which it comes, influence the way in which we approach the problem of burnout?

CARY CHERNISS · Graduate School of Applied and Professional Psychology, Rutgers, State University of New Jersey, Piscataway, NJ 08854.

THE MORAL-RELIGIOUS AND SCIENTIFIC-TECHNICAL PARADIGMS

By now most of us are familiar with Kuhn's (1962) idea of a paradigm in science. In studying the history of science, Kuhn found that normal science typically is conducted within the rather rigid limits imposed by a paradigm — that is, a particular way of viewing the world based on untested assumptions and biases. The prevailing paradigm begins to weaken when its theories and methods no longer can account for observed phenomena. However, there must be numerous discrepancies and challenges before the prevailing paradigm is abandoned. Also, there must be a new paradigm to replace it, one that need not be rational at its foundation but that better accounts for the world as it then is known.

If one looks at the history of social science and related, applied fields (social welfare, mental health, education) during the last 150 years, one can identify two different paradigms that have been used to guide research and practice: the moral-religious and the scientific-technical (e.g., Bockoven, 1963; Krantz, 1981). The moral-religious paradigm was dominant during the 19th century. In mental health and mental retardation, it took the form of the "moral treatment" movement. In sociology, there were the Christian sociologists and the moralistic, social reformist impulses characteristic of the early social workers.

During the latter part of the 19th century, the moral-religious paradigm was challeneged by the work of sociologists and psychologists who used the values and strategies of natural science in probing the mysteries of the human psyche and social life. Marx, Freud, and Durkheim were probably the most influential. Gradually, the scientific-technical paradigm became dominant, replacing the moral-religious in numerous areas. For instance, social work rejected the social reformist approach and adopted the professional and scientific approach associated with psychoanalysis (Levine & Levine, 1970). Psychiatry purged the moral treatment approach in mental health and replaced it with the mechanistic, organic models of medicine (Bockoven, 1963; Grob, 1966). In education, the romantic and progressive theories of Dewey, Pestalozzi, and others gradually gave way to the more scientific approach associated with learning theory. In their organization, schools increasingly were bureaucratized, with the factory used as an explicit model (Callahan, 1962).

Not surprisingly, the recently "discovered" problem of burnout quickly was defined in terms that reflect the now-dominant scientific-technical paradigm. Researchers in the field increasingly have conceptualized burnout as a stress reaction. Studies and interventions focus on (a) stressors in the environment (e.g., role overload); (b) individual dispositions that make people more vulnerable to stress or more likely to create it for themselves (e.g., a strong need for control); and (c) coping mechanisms (e.g., jogging, social support groups). The stress formulation is appealing in at least two ways. First, it is mechanistic in the extreme. Second, it is a legitimate concept that has been studied by biologists as well as experimental psychologists (e.g., Lazarus, 1966; Selye, 1956).

But we also could conceptualize the problem of burnout in terms derived from the other major paradigm—the moral-religious. If we did so, we would begin to see the phenomenon in a new light. This change in perspective would suggest new ideas for research and intervention.

USING THE MORAL-RELIGIOUS PARADIGM TO RECONCEPTUALIZE BURNOUT

Viewed from the moral-religious perspective, the problem now referred to as *burnout* might be regarded instead as the loss of commitment. For instance, those who followed the moral treatment approach in the treatment of the mentally ill believed that a crucial ingredient in the helping process was the caregiver's kindness, and his or her commitment to a moral-religious perspective that supported this kindness. If caregivers began to lose their commitment, especially if they did so in large numbers, the response would not have been to hire a special type of professional who would use a readily packaged "technology" such as relaxation training (the preferred intervention style of the scientific-technical approach). Instead, one might have examined the external frame of reference on which helping was based in order to find ways of making it more valid, meaningful, and compelling.

Thus, the moral-religious paradigm suggests that what we often refer to as *burnout is really a symptom of the loss of social commitment.* Experiences that we label as *stress* or *burnout* occur when institutional supports for commitment are weak. This conception is very different from the one that is found in most current formulations of the problem. It probably is most at odds with the view that burnout is a response to "overcommitment" (Freudenberger & Richelson, 1980). However, the apparent contradiction is not as great as it seems because we are talking about two different ways of defining *commitment.* When Freudenberger refers to a *committed person,* he seems to be thinking of an individual who becomes overextended, works too long and too hard, at an exaggerated pace. Freudenberger also seems to be referring to an individual whose commitment is primarily egotistic, career-oriented achievers whose self-esteem is strongly affected by how well they perform and how quickly they rise up the career ladder. However, I am referring to *social* commitment, by which I mean *belief in a transcendent body of ideas and strong identification with a group, institution, or method that is based on those ideas.* In other words, socially committed people believe in something greater than themselves; and when their work is based on this commitment, they are less likely to experience the phenomena associated with burnout.

Thus, intense absorption in work need not lead to burnout when the worker is truly committed to that work. As Marks (1979, p. 31) has noted,

> Our energy tends to become fully available for anything to which we are highly committed, and we often feel more energetic after having done it. We tend to find little energy for anything to which we are *not* highly committed, and doing these things leaves us feeling "spent," drained and exhausted.

In the 19th century, the eventual "remedy" for the loss of social commitment might well have been a revival meeting. Today, we might do better to study why certain kinds of settings are capable of generating high levels of commitment. What social structures and practices seem to promote the kind of enduring commitment to a set of beliefs that reduces the likelihood of burnout?

In trying to answer this question, I have studied two rather unusual human service programs. One was a residential institution for mentally retarded people operated by a Catholic order of nuns. The core "staff" were the sisters who lived and worked in the institution. Although I did not measure commitment, discussions with some of the sisters, turnover rates, and the bright, clean, and attractive physical appearance of the facility all suggested that commitment was unusually high. This is not to say that there were no commitment problems in this facility, but the level of commitment did seem high compared to other residential settings I have observed. (I arranged to interview a former member of this community who had left because of dissatisfaction with it, but her concerns turned out to be philosophical; she had not experienced a loss of caring, emotional exhaustion, or other changes usually associated with burnout.)

What was most interesting about this setting was that there *should* have been more commitment problems, according to prevailing ideas about the burnout phenomenon. For instance, the staff's work is not just part of their lives; it is their whole life. They literally have no life outside of the religious order and their work with retarded people. They are in almost continual contact with the residents 7 days a week, 52 weeks a year.

Furthermore, the sisters' autonomy is almost nonexistent. They are expected to obey any command given by their superior. Their religious order and the church impose a plethora of rules which govern almost every aspect of their lives. Objectively, many of these rules appear onerous, trivial, and unnecessary. Secular human service workers in the most bureaucratized settings seem to enjoy more freedom of thought and action than do these sisters.

The content of the work also should weaken commitment. Many of the jobs performed by the sisters are not particularly varied or interesting. In fact, intelligent and well-educated individuals with professional credentials sometimes were required to do the most menial and demanding chores, such as working in the kitchen or doing janitorial work. Yet, these women willingly, even joyfully, submitted themselves to this work, defying much of the prevailing wisdom concerning commitment.

Intrigued by this apparent aberration, I looked for another setting in which there was a strong, guiding ideology and found one that was secular rather than religious. This was a school for mentally retarded and emotionally disturbed children who lived in one of the most notorious slums in Chicago (which also was where the school was located). The children had been excluded from the public schools as too difficult to teach. This school was committed to taking any child that the public school decided to reject. It was situated in a former church plagued by bad plumbing, erratic heat, no air conditioning (the school operated all year), and junkies sprawled all over the street right outside the front door. Loss of commitment did occur here, but turnover rates and interviews with staff suggested that it was much lower than was the case for other schools in the city serving this type of population. For instance, in nine other schools serving a similar population with which I worked, the turnover rate was close to 50% annually, whereas at this school the rate was only 10%.

Staff at the school pointed out that the director was one factor contributing to the sustained caring and commitment found among the teachers. She had been in charge for 15 years and was described as warm, nurturant, and supportive. She believed that it was as important to care for the staff and their needs for growth as it was to do so for the children. However, about five years before I visited the school, this positive leadership no longer seemed to be enough to keep them going. They increasingly were working with students who were much more serious behavior problems, and the strain on everyone was intense. At this point, they decided to become a Montessori school. Within two years, every teacher remaining on the staff received training and certification as a Montessori teacher; and new staff were expected to begin Montessori training shortly after they were hired, if they did not already have their certification. The school's problems did not magically disappear, but they became more tolerable and morale was restored.

INSTITUTIONAL SOURCES OF SOCIAL COMMITMENT

Commitment in the two settings I have just described was high, even though the work was difficult and stressful. What was it about these settings that generated such strong commitment? How were they different from more typical human service settings? Certainly there was strong social support, and much research has suggested that social support can provide a buffer from stress (e.g., Gottlieb, 1981). But this is not a real answer to the question, for the social support in these settings comes from strong, shared commitment. From where does this commitment come?

Examining the voluminous literature on stress and burnout does not provide even a shred of an answer to the question of commitment. The research on stress has come out of the scientific-technical paradigm; social commitment is a concept that is more compatable with the moral-religious perspective. Fortunately, sociologists such as Kanter (1972) and Clark (1970) have deviated from the prevailing paradigm and studied institutional sources of social commitment. Their work has dealt with communes and small liberal arts colleges, and they were not concerned specifically with burnout. However, their findings have revealed several sources of social commitment that also can be found in human service programs.

Ideology

One source of social commitment identified by Kanter and Clark was a clear, explicit, formal ideology. In the human services, a formal ideology seems to be particularly useful as means of promoting commitment. An ideology literally provides "moral support" for human service providers. To know that the Catholic church or Montessori sanctions a particular action reduces much of the ambiguity and self-doubt that can lead to lowered motivation and morale.

One of the Montessori teachers I interviewed explicitly identified the ideology as a factor that helped her in her work. When she began her teaching career in another school, there was no formal ideololgy. She had her own values and ideas, but they were not reinforced by the setting. Thus, they tended to be vague, general, and weak. When she finally changed jobs and joined this school, which followed one coherent approach, she felt a great sense of relief. Now there was a single, clear, consistent model, a beacon to which she always could turn if she became uncertain or discouraged. This teacher reported that after she adopted the Montessori approach, she found herself becoming more confident and relaxed. Her attitudes toward teaching and children became more positive.

A single, explicit ideology also seems to be a factor that enhances social support. When most of the staff in a program share an ideology, when that, in fact, becomes a basis for membership, a major barrier to the development of social support is removed (Cherniss, 1979). One of the Montessori teachers confirmed this when she compared her current school with two others in which she had taught. After noting that there was less isolation, more "togetherness," and more "watching out for each other" among teachers at her current school, she said:

> Because there is a sameness in the philosophy and everyone knows what we're trying to do and how we're trying to go about it, we can help each other much more. We have a common bond. Montessori is a common ground.

Many programs have an ideology, but only a few emphasize the ideology to the extent that the Montessori school and religious residential program do. Kanter (1972) found that successful communes, compared to unsuccessful ones, had ideologies that were stronger, more comprehensive, and more elaborated. Clark (1970) found that the successful liberal arts colleges reinforced their guiding ideologies through extensive publicity (e.g., articles about the college and its ideology written for numerous magazines). Thus, a strong, clear, explicit ideology seems to be one way in which institutions such as human service programs can build strong social commitment.

Guidance

"Guidance" is a second important way in which institutions can increase social commitment. *Guidance* refers to a specific program of behavioral norms, linked to the guiding ideology. Kanter found that "by providing members with minutely detailed instructions for dealing with specific situations, nineteenth century communities rendered meaningful in terms of their values even the most minute and mundane behaviors and acts" (Kanter, 1972, pp. 120–121).

The Montessori "method" provides a good example of guidance in a human service context. The method is based on a clear set of values and principles that are translated into an elaborate, standardized curriculum. The curriculum specifies the materials to be used, the arrangement of the classroom, and directions concerning the role of the teacher. Also, each lesson or unit is broken down into small, preordained steps.

Highly structured curricula are not uncommon in education. What is unique about the Montessori method is that there is a single, comprehensive curriculum (not many different ones for teaching different subjects) based on a strong ideology, and the curriculum and ideology are supported by the school. All of the teachers are expected to follow the same curriculum. Thus, unlike most other curricula, the Montessori method exists in a social context that infuses the curriculum with meaning and makes it a powerful vehicle for enhancing social commitment.

Communion

Communion refers to practices that bring "members into meaningful contact with the collective whole" (Kanter, 1972, p. 73). One example is communal sharing of resources. Another communion practice used in the Montessori school was regularized group contact: each morning before school the teachers would assemble for coffee and conversation, group exercise, or some other kind of shared activity. Communal labor through job rotation is yet another communion practice contributing to social commitment. The Residential Youth Center (RYC), a human service program for inner city youth described by Goldenberg (1971), used this approach. At some point every month, every staff member performed every job in the program. Thus, the counselors took a turn as secretary, the director cooked one meal, and everyone was required to spend at least one night at the facility as a live-in counselor during the month. The purpose of this practice was to provide each staff person with a clear sense of, and appreciation for, the work experience of every other staff person. Social barriers among staff thus were reduced.

Investment

According to Kanter, many communal settings enhanced social commitment through investment: "A process whereby the individual gains a stake in the group, commits current and future profits to it, so that he must continue to participate if he is going to realize those profits" (Kanter, 1972, p. 72). The Montessori school used this mechanism in requiring all staff to return to school and invest a considerable amount of time and effort toward securing Montessori training and certification. L'Arche, a residential program for mentally retarded persons (Shearer, 1976), requires anyone who wishes to start a new community to first spend three years in an existing community. Such an investment creates a strong sense of commitment in those who make it.

Mortification

One other relevant set of practices identified by Kanter is *mortification*, which involves the "submission of private states to social control, the exchanging of a former identity for one defined and formulated by the community" (Kanter, 1972, p. 74). The formal probationary period for novices used in the religious order would be a specific example of mortification. Another example from that setting is the policy of making no status distinctions among members on the basis of skill or educational attainment. Everyone was expected to submit to the most menial and unpleasant tasks if the need arose.

Thus, several human service programs in which demands on staff were great, yet morale and motivation remained high, employed institutional mechanisms for generating strong social commitment. Perhaps we can enhance caring and morale in the human services by increasing social commitment through the use of strong service ideologies, guidance, investment, and mortification, rather than, or in addition to, reducing the sources of stress. But what would this mean for professional training and practice?

RETHINKING TRAINING AND PRACTICE IN THE HUMAN SERVICES

To summarize, we have seen that there have been two paradigms in the social sciences and helping fields during the last 150 years: the moral-religious and the scientific-technical. When the loss of caring is viewed from the perspective of the first, it is more likely to be regarded as the loss of moral commitment rather than a maladaptive reaction to stress. This distinction is meaningful for research and action because a social commitment conception leads us to analyze ways in which social systems generate and sustain commitment. The other perspective leads us to think about how social systems create stress. Obviously both perspectives are valid and useful. Both can be used to guide future thought and action.

However, there is one problem with relying on the scientific-technical paradigm: this mode of thinking actually contributes to burnout in the human services. It does so in at least two ways. First, it weakens our ability to form strong commitment to any external frame of reference by encouraging a cool, critical attitude toward the world. Objectivity is a worthy value, but it is the antithesis of strong social commitment. Second, it develops a culture of professionalism that weakens the bonds between caregivers and the settings in which they work. Or, to put it another way, the culture of professionalism dilutes the sense of community, and burnout is one manifestation of this.

When the scientific-technical paradigm replaced the moral-religious one in the human services, it did not simply substitute one dogma for another; it weakened the legitimacy and power of any dogma to generate social commitment.

As Lasch (1979) and Krantz (1981) have pointed out, behavioral scientists have not simply replaced the religious and familial authorities of the past with a new system of authority. The new "religion" in the Age of Psychology (Sarason, 1977) is essentially antireligious and antiauthority. As Krantz (1981) put it:

> The moral guides of the past, the religious leaders and family heads who provided recipes for living with a truth bred from an embeddedness in authority, are now suspect. In their place, a clergy of apparent and actual social scientists has arisen in a truly modern fashion; in their claimed authority of science and proessionalism, they preach that all authority is suspect and ultimately to be dismissed for the sake of unfettered expression.

One consequence of this weakening of moral authority in the human services is that there is increasing pressure not to embrace any method or theory not strongly supported by empirical research. Unfortunately, no educational, social welfare, or mental health approach has been able to pass such a stringent test. For instance, psychoanalysts can argue that clinical work since Freud has demonstrated the validity of their method, but hard-headed skeptics can easily point out the weaknesses of the clinical encounter as a method for generating valid knowledge. Psychoanalysts can respond to these challenges with their own, but the end result is a weakening of the veracity that this approach can have for most practitioners. And even if there were empirical research that one could point to that supports one's methods, this would be a rather weak basis for commitment compared to the higher, more absolute, and symbolic system associated with a moral-religious perspective.

Because skepticism has become so strong, and no approach is able to claim the absolute moral authority of the past, the number of different methods has proliferated. A new practitioner in mental health, for instance, can choose from numerous different systems of psychotherapy and counseling (e.g., ego psychology, behavior modification, transactional analysis, and Gestalt), each claiming to do the job better. In such a chaotic marketplace of ideas, it is difficult for any approach to generate the kind of strong social commitment that buffers the individual from the stress and burnout found in the helping field.

The culture of professionalism further weakens social commitment in the human services. Professionalization is one of the consequences of the dominant scientific-technical paradigm. In fact, it epitomizes the paradigm to a great extent. As Bledstein (1976) has demonstrated, professionalism in the human services is a value system, and many of the values associated with the culture of professionalism actually would seem to encourage a loss of commitment. Rationalism and skepticism are two that I have already considered. Another is a strong emphasis on individualism and the insistence that the practitioner be granted a high degree of autonomy. This has the effect of isolating the professional from others; social support among members of a setting is weakened and thus everyone is more likely to experience stress and burnout (Cherniss, 1979; Pines & Aronson, 1981).

Another element of the professioal culture that generates stress for the practitioner is the notion that the professional is the "expert" who takes sole control and responsibility for the solution of the client's problem. This creates a high degree of dependency in the client, increasing the burden placed on the service provider. Also, the community increasingly looks to professionals to solve what are essentially unsolvable problems (at least unsolvable through the rational-technical methods of the professions, for the problems are essentially political and cultural in nature).

Despite these drawbacks, professional status is attractive: it is a primary route to social mobility in our society. For this reason, many fields strive to become more professionalized, and many young people enter them because they desire status, autonomy, and interesting work. Unfortunately, in the large, impersonal, bureaucratic world in which the professional must work, one rarely finds such rewards (Cherniss, 1980a). For instance, a new public health nurse who was taught that she is a professional and has the competence and "right" to develop health education programs as she sees fit soon met a school principal who told her she could not set up a sex education program as she had designed it. Not only does this limit her autonomy, but it also deflates whatever illusions she might have had about her professional status.

And the result in many cases is intense frustration, disillusionment, and burnout (Cherniss, 1980b).

Nonprofessionals in the human services also become disenchanted, and the culture of professionalism would seem to have less to do with this phenomenon. However, professionalization also plays a role here. First of all, the nonprofessional sometimes assumes the *role* of the professional, if not the *status*. So, for instance, in a mental health center, the nonprofessionals sometimes do individual counseling with clients; when they do so, both client and service provider are influenced by the same role expectations that exist when professionals engage in that relationship. Also, the nonprofessional in a professional system is a second-class citizen. Eventually, the nonprofessionals come to view themselves as less valuable people doing less valuable work, and then they act accordingly (Goldenberg, 1971). The result can be identical to burnout.

The subtle way in which professionalism undermines commitment was demonstrated by one of the nuns in the religious program that I described previously. I asked her why their facility seemed to be so much cleaner and more attractive than many others that I had seen, and she pointed out that in her order, every member is regarded as equally important and every task that contributes to helping children and serving God is deemed to be equally worthy. Everyone is expected to do anything that needs to be done; professional title or educational background does not exempt one from doing maintenance, or cleaning, or working in the kitchen. As the sister put it succinctly at one point, "We don't belong to a union here. There's not a rigid line of demarcation—this is your job, this is my job. We do a variety of things every day, and we're all willing to pick up garbage or clean the floors when it needs to be done." Whatever benefits professionalization in the human services may have given us, it has encouraged invidious distinctions to be made among practitioners based on role, function, or professional credential. Interpersonal conflict and role strain are the inevitable results. The sense of community is weakened, vulnerability to stress is increased, and burnout becomes both a buzzword and a significant social problem in the human services.

SOME IMPLICATIONS FOR RESEARCH AND PRACTICE

One important task for future research is to test the validity of the social commitment interpretation presented here. Specifically, if the theory is valid, there should be greater commitment and morale in human service programs that employ many of the commitment practices described earlier in this chapter. Conversely, human service workers who receive a typical professional education, based on the scientific-technical paradigm, working in settings with weak ideologies, little guidance, minimal investment and mortification, and so forth should be particularly vulnerable to excessive demands and frustrations.

If the presence of social commitment mechanisms does, in fact, lead to reduced caring and morale, another important task would be to study methods for introducing social commitment practices in human service programs. For instance, what are the most effective strategies for developing a strong, unifying ideology in a public school or a day treatment program for ex-mental patients? How can guidance be increased without excessively reducing the staff's sense of autonomy? This chapter has suggested some promising leads, based on actual human service programs, but much more research is needed.

In conclusion, I have identified two paradigms that have guided thought and action in the social sciences. During the last century, the scientific-technical paradigm has become the dominant one. It truly is a paradigm in the sense that it influences how we think about any social problem. In the case of burnout, the paradigm has encouraged us to adopt a stress-coping conception of the problem. Although this approach has been useful, there is another way of thinking about the phenomena, one that sees them as symptoms of the loss of social commitment.

In the social sciences, paradigms not only influence how we conceptualize problems, they also may be part of the problems. I have argued that this has been the case with burnout. The emphasis on rational skepticism and professionalism inherent in the scientific-technical paradigm has underminded the social supports and commitment mechanisms that could protect caregivers in the human services from the many demands and frustrations. Unfortunately, we are more comfortable with technology than with moral belief, especially within the context of our work roles. Thus, no matter how much we strive to develop techniques for alleviating burnout, the cultural conditions that contribute to it will remain until their hold on us is lessened.

REFERENCES

Bledstein, B. J. (1976). *The culture of professionalism.* New York: W. W. Norton.

Bockoven, J. S. (1963). *Moral treatment in American psychiatry.* New York: Springer.

Callahan, R. E. (1962). *Education and the cult of efficiency.* Chicago: University of Chicago Press.

Cherniss, C. (1979). Institutional barriers to social support among human service staff. In K. A. Reid & R. A. Quinlan (Eds.), *Burnout in the helping professions* (pp. 80–93). Kalamazoo: Western Michigan University.

Cherniss, C. (1980a). *Staff burnout: Job stress in the human services.* Beverly Hills, CA: Sage Publications.

Cherniss, C. (1980b). *Professinal burnout in human service organizations.* New York: Praeger.

Clark, B. R. (1970). *The distinctive college.* Chicago: Aldine.

Freudenberger, H. J., & Richelson, G. (1980). *Burn-out.* New York: Anchor Press-Doubleday.

Goldenberg, I. I. (1971). *Build me a mountain: Youth, poverty, and the creation of new settings.* Cambridge, MA: MIT Press.

Gottlieb, B. (1981). *Social networks and social support in community mental health.* Beverly Hills, CA: Sage Publications.

Grob, G. N. (1966). The state mental hospital in mid-nineteenth century America: A social analysis. *American Psychologist, 21,* 510–523.

Kanter, R. M. (1972). *Commitment and community: Communes and utopias in sociological perspective.* Cambridge, MA: Harvard University Press.

Krantz, D. L. (1981). *The psychologist as moralist.* Unpublished manuscript, Lake Forest College.

Kuhn, T. (1962). *Structure of scientific revolutions.* Chicago: University of Chicago Press.

Lasch, C. (1979). *The culture of narcissism: American life in an age of diminishing returns.* New York: Norton.

Lazarus, R. S. (1966). *Psychological stress and the coping process.* New York: McGraw-Hill.

Levine, M., & Levine, A. (1970). *A social history of helping services.* New York: Appleton-Century-Crofts.

Marks, S. (1979, Summer). Culture, human energy, and self-actualization: A sociological offering to humanistic psychology. *Journal of Humanistic Psychology, 19,* 27–42.

Pines, A., & Aronson, E. (1981). *Burnout.* New York: Free Press.

Sarason, S. B. (1974). *The psychological sense of community: Prospects for a community psychology.* San Francisco: Jossey-Bass.

Sarason, S. B. (1977). *Work, aging, and social change: Professionals and the one-life, one-career imperative.* New York: Free Press.

Schwartz, M. S., & Will, G. T. (1969). Intervention and change on a mental hospital ward. In W. G. Bennis, K. D. Benne, & R. Chinn (Eds.), *The planning of change* (pp. 564–683). New York: Holt, Rinehart & Winston.

Selye, H. (1956). *The stress of life.* New York: McGraw-Hill.

Shearer, A. (1976). L'Arche. In President's Committee on Mental Retardation, *Changing patterns in residential care for the mentally retarded* (pp. 355–369). Washington, DC: U. S. Government Printing Office.

PART 4

Alternative Research Agendas

The final part of this volume consists of four chapters. Individually and collectively these chapters help to sensitize us to the specific nature of the social research questions we pose and also enable us to begin to rethink the "nuts and bolts" of how we address them. Implementation of these suggestions would fundamentally alter the face of social problem research. Each chapter highlights the issues in a different content domain. The lead chapter by Edward Seidman employs criminal justice system interventions as illustrative; the next two chapters by Jean Ann Linney and Richard R. Scott are anchored in the desegregation literature; and this part closes with a chapter focused on ethnic research by Nolan Zane and Stanley Sue.

Seidman demonstrates how a number of implicit premises in our Western construction of social reality comingle to unwittingly predetermine both the social problems we identify and the research design and methods we employ. Many of these unexamined premises were reviewed in the introductory chapter of this volume, but several additional constraints unique to the research endeavor are highlighted in the next chapter—funding agency, university administration, and paradigm constraints, or what Moore (1973) has called the *research organization set. Funding agency constraint* refers to social scientists need to define research problems in terms familiar, and too often consistent with, public officials' social values. *University administration constraint* refers to demands on researchers to publish, acquire large grants, and avoid potentially negative controversy, whereas *paradigm constraint* refers to social scientists proclivity for unidirectional cause–effect and person-causal attribution models. Consequently, Seidman argues that the fruits of this research can do little more than reify the initial problem definition and the eventual solution.

Seidman suggests a set of dialectial mechanisms (e.g., radically distinct philosophical models, disciplines, and kinds of conceptualizers) to help social scientists struggle with these implicit premises. It is recommended that these mechanisms be employed in research problem selection and formulation as well as at each successive choice point in the research process.

In the next chapter, Linney examines the research on desegregation, pointing out that the inconsistency and weak explanatory power in desegregation findings is, at least in part, a function of the restricted set of assumptions that focus almost exclusively on change in individual student outcomes that stem directly from change in school racial composition. Employing a systems/ecological perspective, she suggests three intriguing and salient research questions: (1) Does desegregation bring about a change in the *relationship* between blacks and whites as groups? (2) Are these changes relatively stable over time? and (3) Is there evidence of organizational change in the operating premises that define the relationship between the groups? The importance of these questions is highlighted with several examples, including data from Linney's own probing investigation of court-ordered desegregation. Methods consistent with these alternative questions and assumptions are presented. Change and its measurement *between*, as opposed to *within*, groups becomes paramount. Linney points out that without critical examination and subsequent alteration of the underlying assumptions, both our research methods and policy interventions will continue to validate the adage that "the more things seem to change, the more they really stay the same."

Scott, like Linney, argues that direct, short-term effects of desegregation at the individual level are less meaningful. He refers to this as a microfocal approach. This is contrasted with a macrofocal approach that is concerned with indirect, long-term effects at a group or global level of analysis. (The relationship beteen racial groups is again salient.) Here, the participation of racial minority groups in the social, political, and economic mainstream of American life becomes the critical criterion. Thus, the source of the difficulty is seen as structural barriers as opposed to individual deficits.

Three research approaches are described that reflect a macrofocal focus—national studies of impact, the use of community or structural variables, and what is most important, a status attainment framework. "Status attainment is concerned with how individuals acquire both material and nonmaterial resources, and how those resources are translated into other resources and socially desirable attainments such as education, occupation, and income."

Utilizing this status attainment framework Scott documents the channeling effect of a desegregated/segregated schooling history on subsequent education, occupation, and income. In other words, desegregated education cumulatively produces skills for coping in desegregated situations. These indirect, long-term effects of desegregation that result from addressing macrofocal research questions also imply different intervention strategies than does a microfocal approach.

The final chapter by Zane and Sue stresses the fact that research, consistent with the larger societal values, has helped to perpetuate an incomplete and one-sided assessment of most ethnic minority issues. Thus, they identify the dominance of etic (the search for universals) over emic methods (the search for cultural specificity) as a major problem for ethnic minority research. For researchers, they see this one-sidedness as perpetuating the Anglo model as the standard of comparison. A misleading belief in timeless solutions also results from such a "mindscape." Their thesis builds on the earlier discussion of paradox (and antinomies) by Rappaport (see Chapter 8), in which two or more equally valid but opposing and cherished values are pitted against each other.

In a vein similar to the dialectical mechanisms suggested by Seidman (Chapter 13), Zane and Sue see the goal as the achievement of balance betewen opposing perspectives and levels of analysis. En route to this objective they describe the evolution of three research strategies: point, linear, and parallel. The salient aspect of both point and linear research for our purposes is that they have a single reference point and thus can only be logically derived from one culture. Though linear is an improvement over point research, in that it employs a sequence of studies rather than a single isolated study, it, too, fails to address the question of whether a construct developed from an alternative perspective can better explain the phenomena under investigation. Parallel research strategies, on the other hand, are precisely suited to address this question. They consist of two linear approaches, each based on an alternative cultural viewpoint. Rich exemplifications of parallel strategies are presented.

Individually and collectively, the chapters in the last part of this volume have illustrated how many of our underlying societal premises predetermine the nature of our specific research strategies that are employed, thereby inhibiting the production of truly novel knowledge. Alternative and novel research conceptualizations, strategies, and methods are sorely needed, and several are presented in this part of the volume.

CHAPTER 14

Justice, Values, and Social Science
UNEXAMINED PREMISES

EDWARD SEIDMAN

Reviewing contemporary social science research literature and participating in recent meetings and discussions of social policy with regard to law and criminal justice, I have experienced a gnawing feeling of discomfort and disillusionment. As I have attempted to pin down the source of my emotional reaction, I have come to recognize that most of the research and theorizing perpetuates the status quo. Specifically, it seems to do little more than reify existing legal and criminal justice policies, practices, and inherent values. Often the process is both insidious and unwitting. This chapter is an initial effort to understand the nature of that process by unraveling its intertwining elements.

To begin, the process itself will be more clearly explicated through the use of several intriguing notions developed by other writers (Mitroff & Turoff, 1973; Watzlawick, Weakland, & Fisch, 1974) which separately and together provide a metaperspective to understand the selection and formulation of the "wrong" problem. I shall refer to such problem selection and definition as an *error of conceptualization*. In the second section, the determinants or unexamined premises facilitating the selection and formulation of the "wrong" problem will be analyzed. In the third and final section, an initial set of guidelines will be put forth as an attempt to move social scientists toward awareness of the multitude of pathways available to us even at the point of

Originally published in R. J. Simon (Ed.), *Research in Law and Sociology, 1,* 175–200. Copyrighted by JAI Press, 1978. Reprinted by permission.

EDWARD SEIDMAN • Research, Demonstration and Policy Division, Bank Street College, New York, New York 10025. This work was supported in part from Grant #MH 22336 from the National Institute of Mental Health.

problem selection and definition. I hope this will stimulate development of a more refined set of guidelines that will eventually force us to make our choices more wittingly.

In an effort to concretely demonstrate the points discussed in each of the following sections, I will employ two contemporary areas of legal and criminal justice research—behavior modification and social indicators. A third fully encapsulated example concerning juvenile delinquency is presented later in the chapter to highlight and further clarify the issues, processes, consequences, and alternatives being discussed (see Table 1, later). I have chosen these examples both for the diversity of their content and because I have some familiarity with them. Their selection is not meant to cast aspersions on investigations of the particular type they exemplify, any more than numerous others that I have not chosen as examples of which I am uninformed. One important thesis of this chapter is that if one were to critically examine the bulk of research on law and criminal justice in the ways being discussed here, the identification of unwitting errors of conceptualization would be seen to occur frequently.

PROBLEM SELECTION, FORMULATION, AND ITS CONSEQUENCES

At the most general level, one salient set of intended goals and objectives for social scientists engaged in law and criminal justice research is the enhancement of social welfare, equity, and justice. The major thesis put forth for examination is that although this set of objectives may ostensibly represent the *intended* outcomes, more often than not the functional result is quite the opposite. A number of writers, for example Runkel and McGrath (1972), have conceived of the scientific process as akin to the process of problem solving. Based on this notion, the alternatives at each successive choice point in the scientific enterprise following problem selection and definition (i.e., design, operational plan, observations, and so on) are increasingly curtailed. Because the manner in which an issue is addressed is seriously circumscribed by its initial selection and formulation (Caplan & Nelson, 1973; Mitroff & Turoff, 1973; Rappaport, 1977; Sjoberg & Miller, 1973) the focus of this chapter is on that first step. As Caplan and Nelson (1973) have so aptly stated:

> The social scientist who becomes "relevant" seldom questions already established problem definitions, or the wisdom behind the process that leads to the identification of so-called social problems. Nor does he question whose ends are served by the entire definitional process and by his participation in that process. Instead he waits in the wings until the problems have been selected for attention. Only then does he become involved, as if accepting as given that (a) whatever becomes

identified publicly as a social problem is a genuine problem, derived from universally recognized truths; and (b) the problem is of such priority that it deserves attention over other problems that go unattended or unrecognized. (pp. 206–207)

Those who formulate research and social policy in criminal justice are not immune from the influences described by Caplan and Nelson. Blumberg (1974) has delineated 12 properties that he sees as characteristic of modern criminology. Among these, one and its corollary are of particular interest in this context:

Criminologists recognize that they constitute an interest group that seeks access to funds, resources, and official patronage of the very groups they wish to study, and that a price will be exacted for this institutional respectability. As a corollary...they recognize that they have a vested interest to some degree in existing social arrangements in that they share some of the benefits along with the police, prison, parole, probation, and other crime control functionaries. (p. 31)

What Blumberg (1974) makes clear is that the values and goals of the parenting criminal justice organization contribute a great deal to the selection and definition of a problem, even before the criminologist enters the picture. What I am suggesting is that the social scientist in collaboration with representatives of the judicial or crime control organizations agree, often unwittingly and usually for unexpressed reasons, to solve some problem before they have considered if it is the "right" problem. This situation increases the likelihood that the scientist will, almost before realizing it, select the "wrong" problem. Mitroff and Turoff (1973) have aptly titled this mistake an *error of the third kind* or E_{III}. They discuss E_{III} as an error of conceptualization, one of the most important errors associated with the problem-solving process.

From what at first appears to be a dramatically different perspective (i.e., psychotherapy and behavior change), Watzlawick *et al.* (1974) utilize several mathematical theorems to understand the solution of the "wrong" problem.[1] Following their lead let me present a classical illustration. Figure 1 shows an arrangement of nine dots. Your task is to connect the nine dots with four straight lines without lifting the pencil from the paper. If you have never done it before, try it.

Almost everybody who first tries to solve this problem introduces as part of his problem solving an assumption which makes the solution impossible. The assumption is that the dots compose a square and that the solution must be found *within* that square, a self-imposed condition which the instructions do not contain. His failure, therefore, does not lie in the impossibility of the task, but in his attempted solution. Having now created the problem, it does not matter in the least which combination of four lines he now tries, and in what order; he always finishes with at least one unconnected dot. (Watzlawick *et al.*, 1974, p. 25)

---

[1] For a more detailed explanation of these mathematical theorems, the interested reader is referred to their exciting book, *Change: Principles of problem formation and problem resolution.*

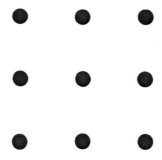

Figure 1. Nine-dot problem.

Whether through the self-imposed or implicit acceptance of the premise that the nine dots compose a square, the problem solver is inhibited from examining this very salient premise. Thus, the problem solver has accepted and addresses the "wrong" problem. There is no way out of this bind until one alters or questions what appears to be the "given." Ignoring, failing to accept, or changing the assumption that the nine dots need compose a square might lead one to the solution presented in Figure 2.

Solutions that accept implicit but unnecessary assumptions are referred to as *first-order change* and are derived from the mathematical theory of groups. This refers to change that can occur within a system that itself stays invariant. But as we have seen in the nine-dot problem, the solution cannot be found within the system as it first appears. *One must instead ask what the rules, assumptions, or premises of the game are. Now seen from outside the system, the solution requires a change of the premises, rules, or assumptions governing the system as a whole.* This is referred to as *second-order change,* derived from the mathematical theory of logical types. The theory of logical types is not concerned with what goes on inside a class, that is, between its members (dots), but gives us a frame for considering the relationship between member and class and the peculiar metamorphosis that is in the nature of shifts from one logical level to the next higher. These authors go on to point out that if we accept this basic distinction between the two theories, it follows that there are two different types of change: one that occurs within a given system that itself remains unchanged, and one whose occurrence changes the system itself, that is, the body of rules governing the system's strucure. The rhetoric of most policy studies suggests that criminal justice policy analyses should be aimed at second- not first-order change. This requires that the social policy analyst step outside the system. When the distinction between member and class is obscured or ignored, an *error of logical typing* is committed. Consequently, the attempt might be to solve the "wrong" problem (e.g., a first- versus a second-order solution).

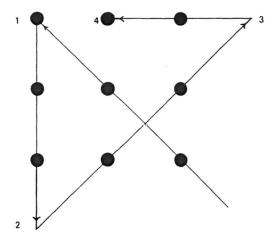

Figure 2. The solution of the nine-dot problem.

Let us refer to this error of logical typing or error of the third kind more simply as an *error of conceptualization.* If we try to understand the precise nature of an error of conceptualization with regard to a legal or criminal justice research problem, we will quickly realize that unlike the nine-dot problem there is no single simplistic premise to uncover or expose. Here there are numerous unexamined rules, values, and premises originating from multiple sources that create and/or maintain an error of conceptualization. Several important domains of unexamined premises or determinants will be more closely analyzed in the following section. But first, let us return to the areas of exemplification noted earlier in order to illustrate what is meant at the most general level by an error of conceptualization and how the understanding of a first- versus a second-order solution helps to clarify the nature of such an error.

Behavior modification, conducted in either a penal institution or a community-based setting, is avowedly aimed at the rehabilitation of the convicted or alleged offender. Although rehabilitation is presumably the goal of those involved in the practice of and research on behavior modification, the society as a whole views our correctional system with mixed objectives. Some see its primary objective as punishment, others deterrence or rehabilitation, and still others as varying combinations of these attributes. Rehabilitation implies the reshaping of the prisoner to live and work independently in the community on his/her return, without repeated criminal offenses. The focus of change is seen as the individual offender. Furthermore, it follows logically from the prior statement that the individual is implicitly assumed to be the source of the problem—criminal activity. Centuries of theorizing and decades of research have neither definitively confirmed nor refuted this implicit, philosophical, and value-based premise, nor should we realistically expect it to. In any case, the implicit assumption of either a rehabilitative, punishment, or deterrent view is the same; that is, crime is viewed as caused by individual "deviants." The functional outcome of this view can only be more of the same, or a first-order solution in which new techniques are employed to attain old ends—social control—more effectively (Davidson & Seidman, 1974). (For example, even within a correctional facility it is not uncommon that behavior modification research and practice are only conducted on the most recalcitrant inmates.) Thus, behavior modification and other therapeutically oriented schools of research and practice have and continue to function as "benign" agents of social control. Functionally, they agree with the often implicit premise that the individual is the source of the problem; this is the error of conceptualization. Parenthetically, it is particularly paradoxical that behavior modification research functionally treats the individual as the source of the difficulty and as the focus of change, because it is theoretically based on an environmental conception of human behavior.

Without a struggle to break out of our usual modes of thinking and acting, it is quite difficult to understand how or why this might not be the problem to address (as the square seemed to be in the nine-dot problem). If we were to ask whether there are other conceptualizations possible regarding the rules, assumptions, or premises of criminal activity, we are on the road to developing different conceptualizations, including, perhaps, one that addresses the "right" problem. As I see it, the intended outcome of policy-oriented research should be an alteration of the social system itself. Attempting to change individual "deviants" helps maintain the social system in an unchanged fashion; it is a first-order change. If one were to step outside the system and look, as Watzlawick et al. (1974) imply, at the relationship between the identified target group of individual "deviants" and the larger society, instead of exclusively within the group of so-called deviants, a novel conceptualization might become apparent. This could lead to a second-order change. A specific example of such a reformulation will be presented in the final section.

As a second specific example, consider the research on social indicators. The ostensible goal of social indicators research is to improve the quality of life of individuals and the social well-being of the community. Researchers in this area generally seek to understand the effects of various types of public investment upon the latter objectives. Social indicators research, as it pertains to the area of law and criminal justice, has public safety, a euphemism for crime control, as its major goal. When we move to the actual use of this research for social policy formulation, the objective of establishing an optimal relationship between public safety and expenditures overshadows the more diffuse and general objectives. Herein lies the fundamental unexamined premise and consequently an error of conceptualization. Striving for the optimal point of maximization, if successful, guarantees the long-run maintenance of homeostasis and the status quo. Such a negative feedback mechanism insures only within-system variations (first-order changes), simultaneously precluding change of the system itself. No significantly new answers are likely to occur from framing the question based on the rule of optimal maximization. Again, in the final section a reformulated conception will be presented.

Although the specific errors of conceptualization identified in each of the preceding examples differ somewhat, they can each be culled from an analysis of the unexamined premises, assumptions, values, or rules. On occasion, these premises receive some attention, but it appears to be only pro forma consideration; they are rarely seriously questioned or challenged. One negative long-range consequence common to both areas is that the process of continually investigating each area based on the preexisting problem formulation reifies that endeavor and the error of conceptualization in particular. In this society, that usually serves to preclude the investigation of alternative conceptualizations.

DETERMINANTS FACILITATING AN ERROR OF CONCEPTUALIZATION

What are the assumptions, rules, premises, and/or antecedents that lead to an error of conceptualization and make it difficult to recognize such an error in the field of criminal justice policy analysis? Two key sources of the error of conceptualization have been highlighted by Caplan and Nelson (1973) in an article primarily addressed to the discipline of psychology, but which is equally applicable to other disciplines.

> By investigating a social problem in terms given him, a *mutually beneficial exchange relationship* is established: the researcher is rewarded both materially and in terms of prestige (in addition to remaining a "proper member of the group") by using the tools of his trade; while on the other side of the exchange, officialdom stands to have its preferred interpretation buttressed by the respectability of "scientific data." (p. 206)

This quotation highlights the mutual interdependence of two determinants—the researcher and officialdom (i.e., the parenting agency of the social policy research)—involved in an error of conceptualization. In addition, two other determinants need consideration: the dominant values of our society and constituents (or recipients) of criminal justice policies (or programs). The researcher will be considered more broadly under the subheading of *Social Science*. These four major determinants will be presented in the following order: dominant societal values, officialdom, social science, and constituents. Despite the obvious fact that the determinants are mutually interrelated and causal, they are presented separately for ease of explication. The discrete and sequential structure of this presentation should not obscure these interrelationships.

Dominant Societal Values

Sjoberg (1975) has noted that social scientists have too often accepted the power structure's definition of what is right and what is wrong. Both social science and officialdom naturally embody this value system in their daily functioning. Consequently, these societal values constrain the problem formulation. For example, the notion of individual motivation and responsibility has always been a cherished, dominant, and pervasive value in this society. It is at the root of our legal and constitutional structures. It has led to what Caplan and Nelson (1973) and Ryan (1971) among others have referred to as a person-centered causal attribution bias or "victim blaming" ideology. This refers to the tendency to find individuals responsible for their own problems, despite the antecedent and contextual economic, social, and political factors. This is part of a larger set of social processes in which our institutions work toward the socialization of almost everyone to a "single standard," and those who fail to behave in conformity with the norm are labeled as deviant (Rappaport, 1977; Ryan, 1971). As we shall see, neither the scientist, decision maker, nor anyone else is immune from these values and biases.

In addition to the tendency toward victim blaming, the dominant cultural groups in Western society hold in high esteem the value of pragmatism and raionality with regard to personal, organizational, and institutional functioning. This is accomplished by a quantitative supply-and-demand orientation with a tendency to convert cultural, social, and psychological considerations into monetary values.

As indicated in the earlier discussion of behavior modification in corrections, the premise that the individual is not only the culprit, but also the proper focus of change, is central to research and practice in the area. As expressed by the man on the street, it reads, "I did it the hard way (i.e., worked, did not steal) and made it." If one is only minimally familiar with behavior modification research, its pragmatism should be apparent. In many token economy programs "good" behavior is rewarded by tokens having direct monetary purchasing power.

Although superficially the premise of individual responsibility seems less apparent in the social indicators research, one need only recall that a goal of such policy research is to more effectively control crime via increased police power, hardware, and so forth. The pragmatism, quantitative suppy-and-demand orientation, and conversion of social and psychological factors into monetary values by such research, is based to a large extent on economic models and needs no further elaboration. These illustrations have crystallized how the dominant societal values substantially determine and curtail the selection and formulation of social science research problems.

Officialdom

The stated goals and values of an organization established for the enhancement of criminal justice usually have to do with improving human and social welfare, equity, and so forth. This goal may be expressed in attempts to adequately or efficiently achieve certain program objectives; but it is implicitly assumed that the attainment of such objectives would in no way bring the death of that agency. This is not hard to understand, in that entertainment of such a possibility threatens the very administrators who have, to say the least, a vested interest in maintaining their jobs, status, and power. The question of how an agency can attain its lofty objectives usually means, "How can we more adequately or efficiently, by doing what we already know how to do, attain these objectives and maintain, or better yet increase, the quantity and quality of our jobs, status, and power?"

Any organization will find it inordinately difficult to change, if change implies an alteration in the nature of its role relationship with clients or constituents (Fairweather, 1972; Watzlawick et al., 1974). A change in role relationship means a change in the ongoing pattern of transactions; thus, if one party consistently made the decisions and the other party conformed, an altered role relationship would result if they now alternately shared the decision-making role. An analysis of the functioning of any social system from a general system's theory perspective would lead us to a similar recognition (Buckley, 1967, 1968). In this way, a hidden agenda severely constrains the scope of the particular problem formulation, from the point of view of agency officials. Consequently, a second-order solution, one that requires a shift in relationships, will not be logical or feasible from their point of view. Parenthetically, we cannot ignore the fact that this publicly funded organization may only be interested in collaborating with the social scientist to "improve" their functioning in order to appease or, more specifically, to get the funding source "off their back." This also enables the organization to appear "accountable," to have its preferred mode of operation buttressed by the respectability of scientific data.

Beyond the question of vested self-interest, there is a second more subtle factor that contributes to an error of conceptualization. Most program managers and decision makers, as previously indicated, hold to the dominant cultural theme of attributing responsibility to individuals. The acceptance of person-blame explanations for deviance tends to turn the program managers away from a social policy that looks outside the individual and focuses on the social system. This, then, interacts with their own vested interests to allow first-order change and prohibit second-order change.

Most individuals receiving correctional services have endured a powerless role, in terms of access to and availability of material and psychological resources, for most of their life. Placement in a behavior modification program maintains the representatives of authority in a position of dominance and concomitantly keeps the prisoner in his/her place, that is, down, but more systematically and effectively. It is not unlikely that such programs reinforce, as opposed to change, the already powerless feelings and actions that may lead the person to further criminal activity. The unfortunate consequence of this process is that the victims are again blamed and with greater vehemence— "See how bad they are; we invested all this money...; just lock 'em up." The system remains invariant because role relationships between different social statuses remain unchanged.

Aside from providing officialdom with increased control, power, and easier jobs, their involvement in avowedly rehabilitative programs make them appear committed to the rehabilitation of offenders and their successful return to the community. Returning prisoners to the community in any substantial number would jeopardize the very jobs of these employees. This unlikely desire has occasionally been exposed for what it is when the intention to close such an institution has been made public. In such instances, the political and economic issues maintaining the institution raise their "head" and guarantee the institution's continued existence. Thus a continual influx of prisoners is essential. The result must be first- rather than second-order change.

For the salient institutional structures, research on social indicators permits them the luxury of appearing accountable, being concerned about the improvement of human welfare, and requires little additional effort on their part. Often, the outcome of such research is not unlikely to be demonstrative of their need for additional resources to "control crime."

In summary, we have seen how the self-interests, threat of altered role relationships, and dominant societal values converge to severely restrict the research questions an agency is willing to collaboratively address.

Social Science

The social scientists themselves are no less immune, nor value-free, than the program managers or policy makers (for one discussion of this, see Gouldner, 1969). They often share the same person-centered causal attribution biases, as well as a concern with their own vested interests. More often than not, they accept as given the premise that individual peformance is a function of individual motivation and responsibility. In fact, the outcomes of many research investigations have, implicitly or explicitly, given credence and scientific respectability to such biases among the lay public, program managers, and politicians, precisely because of the assumptions inherent in problem definition. That is, the assumptions inherent in the social scientist's definition of a particular problem cause one to structure the question in a fashion that frequently leads to a verification of those inherent biases—victim blaming. Thus, as Green (1971) has indicated, officialdom's "sponsorship can only emphasize the existing tendency in the social sciences to concentrate attention on the personality structures of the least influential of all constituents" (p. 18).

At this point it would be helpful to recall the behavior modification and social indicator illustrations of how the dominant societal values of pragmatism, rationality, quantitative supply-and-demand orientation, and tendency to convert cultural, social, and psychological consideration into monetary values are accepted by the social scientist and consequently constrain problem selection and formulation.

What additional factors interact with these societal values to further constrain the definition of problems addressed by the social scientist? Several major factors can be culled from what Moore (1973) has called the *research organization set* in her discussion of sociological research on minorities. Two of these factors are the funding agency and university administration constraints, and what we shall call *paradigm* constraint.

Funding Agency Constraint. Most funding exists through some governmental agency. "It seems obvious that if social science is to have a practical short-run application, a given research problem must be defined in terms which are familiar to public officials" (Green, 1971, p. 15). In fact, Galliher and McCartney (1973) have recently demonstrated how funding patterns have affected the use of certain research strategies and methods as well as the emphasis on individuals in the sociological literature on juvenile delinquency. Moore and Nay (1977) provide similar documentation for research in the social sciences more broadly conceived. A special issue of the *Annals of the American Academy of Political and Social Science* was devoted to an extensive discussion of this general topic entitled, "Social Science and the Federal Government" (Lyons, 1971). It is not difficult to imagine the ramifications of governmental funding patterns on formulating problems of study by social scientists. For example, at the technical level one may accept governmental statistics, definitions, and categories of criminal behavior. This is precisely what has occurred with regard to social indicators research with such government agencies as the Law Enforcement Assistance Administration requesting scientists to make use of the data banks they have compiled, for example, victimization surveys and Uniform Crime Reports, for policy analysis. Results of such investigations can only support inherent biases, already existing in their definitions and categories of criminal behavior. As long as we allow funding agencies to determine the type and formulation of research problems we address, we are bound to continue making errors of conceptualization.

University Administration Constraint. Moore (1973) indicates that the academic researcher is constrained by the administration's demand that one publish, acquire large grants, and "avoid generating controversy that would 'offend' the nonuniversity public" (p. 69). Anyone remotely associated with academia knows the salience and potency of these issues.

For example, funding agencies and universities have, until recently, been supporting and encouraging behavior modification research. It was held in considerable esteem throughout the 1960s and early 1970s. It also provided the investigator with a captive population over which one had a great deal of control, mimicking the rigor of the idealized experimental laboratory situation and at the same time being "relevant" by presumably improving social well-being. Such a course produced numerous publications (in fact, the creation of many new journals) and a resultant increase in academic status and prestige for these scientists, individually and collectively.

The social indicators movement seems to be following a similar course in terms of growth, funding, and prestige, although it began much later.

Paradigm Constraints. Perhaps the most difficult of all constraints on problem formulation for the social scientist to recognize are those rooted in the scientific models subscribed to by most contemporary social scientists. Maruyama (1974) delineates the structures of reasoning, or as he labels them, *paradigms* that lie beneath different cultures, professions, and disciplines. Scientists and others seem unaware of these structures of reasoning. Maruyama explicates a dimension of paradigms ranging from a unidirectional causal paradigm to a mutual causal paradigm. The unidirectional causal paradigm is essentially a traditional cause-and-effect model. This paradigm appears to be uncritically employed most often by social scientists in an apparent attempt to emulate the physical sciences. It is heavily based on a classificational logic. The assumptions of this classificational logic are:

1. The universe consists of material substances (and in some cases also of power substances).
2. These substances persist in time.
3. They obey the law of identity and the law of mutual exclusiveness, except that in power substance may penetrate into things.
4. The substances are classifiable into mutually exclusive categories. The classification is unambiguous. The categories persist in time and space. (The categories are believed to be uniformly and universally valid.)
5. Categories may be divided into subcategories, and categories may be combined into supercategories. Thus, categories are a hierarchy.
6. The categories can be constructed a priori, i.e., they can preexist before the things are to be put into them. They have their reality independent from things, and higher than things. (Maruyama, 1973, p. 136)

From a different perspective, Watzlawick *et al.* (1974) have commented on the negative consequences of such classificational logic:

> For instance, the handling of many fundamental social problems—e.g., poverty, aging, crime—is customarily approached by separating these difficulties as entities unto themselves, as almost diagnostic categories, referring to essentially quite disparate problems and requiring very different solutions. The next step then is to create enormous physical and administrative structures and whole industries of expertise, producing increased incompetence in ever vaster numbers of individuals. We see this as a basically counterproductive approach to such social needs, an approach that requires a massive deviant population to support the raison d'etre of these monolithic agencies and departments. (p. 159)

A major, but subtle, reason why behavior modification issues have been readily addressed is that the formulation of the problem is consistent with most social scientists' underlying theoretical framework—a unidirectional causal model. Because behavior modification research sees the environmental contingencies as causing an individual's behavior, it meshes well with a unidirectional causal framework. Furthermore, the usual behaviors monitored are consistent with the classificational logic assumptions previously delineated. Finally, behavior modification has itself become an industry, with its own conventions, professional and paraprofessional training programs, journals, degrees, and certificates. Consequently, we can expect more and more problems to be framed as in need of behavior modification, perpetuating errors of conceptualization.

Coming from a different, but somewhat similar, vantage point, Mitroff and Turoff (1973) describe how different methodologies stem from different philosophical premises or inquiring systems (Churchman, 1971). These different inquiring systems (e.g., Lockean, Leibnitzian, Kantian, Hegelian) may be ill-suited to the conceptualization of a particular problem, but are employed without a thorough analysis of their fit and concomitant constraints on problem definition, methodology and outcome.

The indices employed in the Unified Crime Report are frequently employed in social indicators research on public safety. Included in this research are categories regarding specific kinds of crime and related public expenditures for personnel, hardware, and the like. The specific nature of these indices is consistent with the statements by Maruyama (1973) concerning classificational logic. What enters the equation is a small number of very select variables. Although passing reference may be given to the inadequacy and unreliability of such measures, they nevertheless appear to be enthusiastically employed. The employment of such static, hierarchical, and mutually exclusive indices demands and is well suited to a unidirectional causal paradigm. This traditional cause and effect model restricts the possibility of novel conceptualizations of research problems. A novel set of indices and assessment devices that defy the simplistic classificational logic would have to be developed if, for example, we intended to build our research on the assumptions of a mutual causal paradigm. Questioning this body of research as peformed will not be easily heard, because it possesses all the prestigious elegance and trappings of mathematics and science. Nevertheless, if we seek solutions other than more or less public expenditures for one method of crime control over another, we need to select and formulate problems differently; that is, based on different premises, scientific and otherwise.

Caplan and Nelson (1973) have again cogently stated the issue:

> If social scientists choose to be morally indifferent social bookkeepers and leave the selection of indicators and their use in the hands of others, then, to use Biderman's (1966) term, social "vindicators" would be a better name for such measures. If our apprehensions are confirmed, these vindicators will take the form of person-blame data collected for the political management of guilt and culpability. (p. 207)

Unfortunately, such research has the additional face value and congruence with the dominant value structure in this country: they are pragmatic, accounting-like, and so on.

Integration. To buck the tide of the societal, funding agency, university, and discipline-based underlying rules, premises, pressures, and assumptions described previously would seriously jeopardize an individual investigator's understandable striving for academic and material success. Nevertheless, not to at least question them forces the researcher into a number of predetermined actions that are taken for granted, and may inhibit desirable social changes. This is not meant to imply that most researchers do not also exhibit a genuine quest for knowledge, but rather that social scientific activities have multiple determinants, not all of which are encompassed by the search for "truth." Furthermore, all of these determinants commingle in a complex fashion with those of the host organization to form a mutually beneficial exchange relationship. The frequent but unwitting consequence may be an error of conceptualization or the investigation of the "wrong" problem. Paradoxically, the "real" problem goes unaltered and is, in fact, often perpetuated. Successive phases in the research process are subject to similar determinants, but the selection and formulation of the problem is most critical.

Unfortunately, the social scientist's acceptance of preselected and preformulated research problems adds credibility and legitimation to the values inherent in such conceptualizations. Individually and collectively social scientists must take a much more active role in the process of problem selection and formulation, and institute mechanisms—to the largest extent possible—to maximize diversity in the conceptualization of research problems.

Constituents or Recipients

It may appear from the analysis to this point that one major determinant has been omitted—the constituents or clients of the judicial or criminal justice policy/program. This is not an oversight. They are often ignored or exert little if any pressure on the formulation of the problem and are most often themselves labeled as the problem. Because the ostensible goal is the constituents' welfare or the clients' rehabilitation, would it not make sense to incorporate their views into problem selection and definition in a central fashion? We shall return to this later.

MECHANISMS FOR VALUE CONFLICT GENERATION

Having followed the line of reasoning presented to this point, the reader may feel quite powerless in dealing with the multitude of forces and pressures impinging upon selection and formulation of a research problem. The convergent values inherent in many of these determinants make it quite difficult for the social scientist to address a research problem other than one to which the answers will most likely perpetuate the status quo, rather than to foster an increase in justice and human welfare.

Given this situation, how can the social scientist cope, that is, how can one more effectively select, define, and address research problems, the potential answers to which have a greater possibility of enhancing justice, equity, and social welfare? Obviously, there is no simple answer. In some ultimate sense what is required for social scientists, individually and collectively, is a heightened level of consciousness and responsibility which transcends personal and social pressures and needs. The fact that few of us, if any, are such "superpersons" necessitates a set of guidelines, for what I am referring to as *value-conflict-generating mechanisms*, to minimize the likelihood of our falling into these "traps." This tentative set of guidelines is offered in the hope that it will make it more difficult to unwittingly select, conceptualize, and address the "wrong" problem. Nevertheless, each scientist *must not* shirk his individual responsibility in actively seeking to achieve the essential message conveyed by these guidelines through yielding to the omnipresent personal, social, and organizational constraints and pressures.

The precursor to any actual steps needs to be what Maruyama (1974) has called *demonopolarization*. Monopolarization is the tendency of persons, particularly of Western heritage, to develop a dependency on *one* right theory, *one* truth, and so forth (Maruyama, 1966). Consequently, demonopolarization is necessary, that is, we have to become aware that there are other ways of thinking. Similarly, Johnson (1975, pp. 90–91) has discussed the importance of including criticism *per se* as a formal step in public policy evaluation. He defines criticism as including "both the examination and advocacy of alternative policies, based upon alternative outcomes," and goes on to state that "doing criticism means exposing the implicit values that guide our research and recognizing that research which precludes implications for alternative policy choices is not worth doing." Sjoberg (1975) further suggests that "criticism alone will not advance the cause of human dignity. We must formulate research orientations that emphasize the development of alternative structural arrangements that transcend some of the difficulties inherent in the present-day social order" (p. 45).

To begin in this direction, it is useful to return to the metaperspective offered throughout this paper, that is, the notions regarding first- versus second-order change. In the example presented earlier, despite the often expressed intent of the social policies they represent, the problem selected, formulated, and addressed could only lead to solutions of a first-order nature, in that the solution was sought given the extant rules of the game. It is precisely the rules of the game that need to be seriously questioned as a precondition to further action. As was apparent with the nine-dot problem presented earlier, failing to question the implicit rules precluded solution of the real problem; and only through a reconceptualization of the rules and premises could a second-order solution be discovered. The way most people approach the nine-dot problem is analogous to the social scientists addressing legal, judicial, and criminal justice issues by accepting the problems as defined, with all their inherent values, and without questioning the appropriateness of the problem definition *per se*, or its selection. Given the pressures against questioning our most basic premises, how might we proceed?

Watzlawick *et al.* (1974) suggests that the major means of extricating ourselves from this bind is a *reframing of the question*. To reframe means to place the "facts" within an alternative conceptual framework. Although the "facts" should fit equally well, their new context should change the entire meaning attributed to the situation (i.e., its underlying premises) and therefore its consequences. An important key to this reframing is to look at the pattern of transactions or relationships *between* levels, for example, group, organization, institution, that represent the rules governing the game (Seidman, 1976). To stay within a level accepts the premises or the rules of the game as they exist.

Let us concretize the process of reframing by returning to the behavior modification example. The goal is to rehabilitate individual offenders, based on the premise that they are the source of the problem and the proper locus of change. However, the social scientist's acceptance of this premise, along with the notion that these individuals need to be taught to conform to the culturally valued norm, is unlikely to lead to anything but a reification of age-old values and conceptions, and as a social policy this approach does little to curb crime, or for that matter to alter the behavior of individuals once released from the control of the therapeutic agents. At best, this is a first-order solution in that it only leads to within-group changes (differential changes within the group of "deviants"). If one were to try to reframe the question one might begin by looking at the relationship *between* these identified groups of "deviants" and the organizations and institutions with which they must interact (Seidman, 1976). These transactions are characterized by their one-up, one-down (or powerful, powerless) nature with regard to access and availability of environmental resources (Davidson & Rapp, 1976). From this perspective the research problem to be addressed might be conceptualized as the alteration of a relatively stable pattern of transactions between employment opportunities and a high-risk crime group (i.e., a group having a high probability of being apprehended for criminal activities). Interventions, if successful, would be expected to increase the variability in the existing pattern of transactions where members of the high-risk crime group have repeatedly failed to be given access to jobs, or at least to jobs associated with a modicum of dignity, respect, and financial renumeration. However, such a reformulation of the problem requires the development and measurement of indices reflecting the pattern and nature of these transactions and mutually interdependent factors. Formulating the problem in this fashion will lead to the development of new interventions and social policies.

In dealing with a population of "hard-core" youth, all of whom had been "given up" on by existing social service agencies, Goldenberg (1971) reframed, both at the conceptual and action levels, the rehabilitation or treatment issue. He developed an autonomous alternative residential setting. A direct attempt was made to alter the one-up, one-down pattern of relationships that characterizes the daily transactions in superficially similar correctional facilities. Goldenberg (1971) characterizes this as a function of a vertical organizational structure. Seeing this as a central problem, he reframed the issue and developed a program emphasizing a horizontal organizational structure as a vehicle to facilitate the "growth" of staff as well as clients. It was a genuine collaborative venture in which residents and staff were all directly and equitably involved in all aspects of life in the setting, including decision making. Thus, the aim was precisely an alteration of the nature and pattern of transactions between "treater" and "treated." The richness and excitement conveyed in *Build Me a Mountain* can only be captured by reading the detailed descriptions and examples provided by Goldenberg. Although the venture seemed to be successful by traditional criteria, Goldenberg failed to measure or develop assessment devices reflecting the pattern and nature of the transactions.

Sjoberg and Cain (1971) describe what they term *countersystem analysis* that can similarly produce a significant reformulation of the research problem to be addressed. The countersystem analysis is described as a form of dialectical reasoning in which the existing social order (or social structure) is negated and a logical alternative is suggested. Pertaining to the behavior modification example, one could negate the need for rehabilitation and postulate an alternative of the need to accept and reward, via material and psychological resources, diverse personal and social competencies, and not simply attempt to standardize all to a single culturally valued norm of the dominant society (Rappaport, 1977). One can easily imagine the potentially diverse consequences resulting from the latter problem formulation as opposed to the one originally posed.

How can we reframe the research question pertaining to our second example, that is, social indicators research on public safety? You will recall that the fundamental unexamined premise or error of conceptualization depicted was the objective of establishing an optimal relationship between public safety and expenditures. Striving to accomplish this objective was viewed as simply perpetuating the existing homeostatic balance. Consequently, reframing or negating this implicit premise should lead the social policy analyst to question its utility and suggest an alternative formulation. One such alternative premise might be to disrupt the homeostatic balance or equilibrium. To change the system, deviation-amplifying positive feedback mechanisms must be employed (Maruyama, 1968). Only through such deviation-amplification, as contrasted with negative, feedback, can the calibration of the system itself be eventually altered. Thus a different system with a new equilibrium could be created.

In a further attempt to concretize the issues discussed in this chapter — the error of conceptualization, its consequences and determinants, and a reframing of the unexamined premise(s) — a self-contained example concerning juvenile delinquency research (and based heavily on the writing of Schur, 1973) is portrayed in Table 1. Hopefully, this will help the reader in thinking about other illustrations, for example, diversion and incompetency to stand trial.

In order to put these metaperspectives in their appropriate context, I must state emphatically that questions resulting from a reframing or negation of the original problem have no greater priority on truth or justice than those traditionally posed, despite an implicit preference of the author. What is imperative is that we *examine the premises underlying the selection and formulation of research problems, generate alternative conceptualizations, evaluate each empirically, and thoroughly examine their respective intended and unintended social consequences.*

Thus, we are led to the posing of a set of dialectical mechanisms that force the generation and examination of value conflicts. In order to do this systematically, I shall borrow, adapt, and add to a set of guidelines suggested by Mitroff and Blankenship (1973) with regard to the conceptualization of large-scale social experiments.

1. *At least two "radically distinct" philosophical models must be brought to bear on the formulation of any potential research problem.* What is implied here are two philosophical systems like a unidirectional causal paradigm, that is, a traditional cause and effect model, versus a mutually interdependent causal paradigm (Maruyama, 1974) or a Leibnitzian inquiring system, that is, an abstract formal, mathematical, or logical system versus a Hegelian inquiring system, that is, a conflictual system (Churchman, 1971). Additionally, two less formal philosophical models, previously discussed, can be employed. A first- versus second-order formulation (Watzlawick *et al.*, 1974),

as well as the system and countersystem conception (i.e., negation; Sjoberg & Cain, 1971), can be brought to bear on problem selection and definition, as previously exemplified.

2. *At least two radically distinct disciplines must be brought to bear.* This point is also supported by Johnson (1975), who states, "The internal standards of a discipline are inadequate guidelines for making research choices and encourage perpetuation of fraudulent academic claims on scarce societal resources" (p. 77). Mitroff and Blankenship (1973) go so far as to suggest that these must not simply be two diverse social science disciplines, but, for example, a behavioral and physical science. Two different behavioral science disciplines alone would still view the problem primarily in behavioral and human terms. "Both are valid; each is required" (p. 345).

3. *At least two "radically distinct" kinds of conceptualizers must be brought to bear.* As Johnson (1975) has pointed out everyone, including the self- or other-appointed critic, is in a sense trapped within his own conceptual framework. What is most frequently needed here is someone who formulates problems contrary to the traditional expectancies of mainstream social science. Such mavericks or critics are often viewed with disdain and go unrewarded by their own disciplines. We really need to cultivate a group of persons who are able to walk with only one foot in our camp. This remains a major challenge for each discipline, university, funding agency, and the like.

Mitroff and Blankenship (1973) indicate a much narrower interpretation of this guideline. They are referring to conceptualizers with convergent versus divergent cognitive styles. Mechanisms number one, two and three are obviously not mutually exclusive and derive primarily from our discussion of the social science constraints.

One likely consequence of the actualization of this mechanism is what Maruyama (1974) has called *transpection*, the process of getting into the head of the other, and secondly, letting the other person transpect one's own paradigm.

4. *The constituents, participants, or the ultimate beneficiaries or victims of the research endeavor must be incorporated into the selection and formulation of the research problem.* Those people whom the research is presumed to benefit in the short or long run can no longer be excluded or incorporated in only a token fashion if research is to be truly meaningful and beneficial to them. They may have a dramatically different conceptualization. These individuals rightfully deserve a major role of influence in problem selection and formulation. The ultimate value of research must be with "the human population on whom policy consequences are perpetrated" (Johnson, 1975). In another context Goulet (1971) has indicated that our "subjects" must actively define the ground rules by which they are studied. Although this is a threatening and uncomfortable position for the social scientist to enter, it is nevertheless crucial. It may curtail some potentially fruitful research, along

Table I. Conceptualizations of Delinquency and Their Consequences[a]

Issue				Comments
Facts	Youth violating societal rules. Oftentimes, the rules violated are those that apply solely to youth, i.e., status offenses.			
Social science orientation	(A) Individual treatment	(B) Liberal reform	(C) Radical nonintervention	These are ideal types; they are not mutually exclusive. They also represent a historical progression from A to C.
Basic underlying assumption (conceptualization)	Offenders are *different* from nonoffenders and differences are assumed to be a function of *individual* variables.	Offenders are *different* from nonoffenders, but differences are assumed to result from *social conditions* to which they've been exposed.	*Reactions* to certain behaviors largely determine their social meaning (i.e., "deviance") and consequences (i.e., further rule-violations).	Orientation C's frustration with the lack of efficacy of orientation A and B's policies led them to reframe the basic underlying research problem (or error of conceptualization) of A and B. A and B are basically similar because of the common assumption or concern with differences. A and B are heavily influenced by dominant societal values.
Favored research	Comparison samples of delinquent and nondelinquent	Comparison of rate of rule violations in different social	Self-reports, observations, and legal analyses focused upon	In A and B one or the other is the focus (individual or social

methodology and focus	youth matched on demographic and other social variables. Thus, social system variables are held constant and *personological-like factors are free to vary* (∴ the focus).	classes, neighborhood settings, group and subcultural contexts. In a sense, holds constant individual variability, leaving *social and cultural variables free to vary* (∴ the focus).	*pattern of interactions between* "deviants" and social control agents.	system variables) while the focus of orientation C is on the pattern of interactions between the two. Reframed conceptualization of C leads to a different methodology and focus.
Implicit causal perspective	*Unidirectional causality;* individual difference variables, by the nature of methodology employed, are "set up" to be the cause of rule-violating behavior.	*Unidirectional causality;* environmental or social parameters, by the nature of methodology employed, are "set up" to be the cause of rule-violating behavior.	*Mutual causality;* patterns of interactions, by the nature of methodology employed, is "set up" to be cause of rule-violating behavior.	A and B's causal perspective is similar in attempting to emulate the physical sciences. The reframed conceptualization of C implies a different causal model than A and B.
Social policies created (or implied)	*Treatment and rehabilitation of "deviants";* agents of social control must act on behalf of the violators' "best" interest.	*Treatment and rehabilitation of "deviants";* increased attention to social factors and causes.	*Narrowed scope of juvenile court jurisdiction;* decriminalization of status offenses; treatment only on a voluntary basis.	Social policies stem directly from prior issues.
Long-range effect on the "facts"	Increased numbers viewed as "deviant" and in need of treatment or rehabilitation. Problem has reached crisis proportion.	Increased numbers viewed as "deviant" and need for social reform is emphasized. However, functionally reform is translated to increased services. Problem has reached crisis proportion.	Increased tolerance of diversity. Fewer individuals viewed as problematic.	The manner in which C reframed the basic assumption of A and B leads to drastically different long-range consequences.

* *Source:* This table is adapted from Table 1 (p. 20) of Schur (1973).

with reducing the number of trivial studies, but in the long run I am confident that it will benefit the populations whose welfare is central as well as benefitting our mutual relationships. Viable mechanisms for the genuine incorporation of these populations, with decision-making power and not of a token nature, need to be developed. This guideline derives primarily from our discussion of the fact that the constituents (or recipients) of social policies (or programs) are rarely, if ever, a meaningful determinant in the selection and formulation of social policy research questions.

5. *Autonomy from the organizations and institutions we evaluate and/or serve should be maximized.* Although complete independence is not feasible in many instances, Glaser (1974) has pointed out that autonomy is critical not only for the increased theoretical grounding of criminal justice research, but also with regard to the unadulterated release of potential findings. The development of such autonomy would hopefully increase the diversity of problem selection and formulation. This suggestion is derived primarily from the discussion of officialdom as a determinant and other funding constraints on social science research.

Even if all these conflict generating mechanisms were implemented, there is obviously no assurance that problems would not be conceptualized in such a way that their results would not simply perpetuate, directly or indirectly, what is. Furthermore, the guidelines may be viewed as impractical. However, the point to be emphasized is that we should not ignore or sidestep their importance because they are not foolproof or practical. Rather, we must, individually or collectively, strive to actualize as much as possible for the ultimate benefit of society and the quality of knowledge. At a minimum, they should make us more aware and cautious of the "traps" in a problem selection and formulation.

Several closing comments seem warranted. Although this chapter emphasizes an examination of the unexamined premises and their determinants with regard to problem selection and conceptualization, it should be recalled that this is primarily because the initial stage in the process is viewed as the most influential. However, similar concerns could be raised about each successive choice point in the research process. The mechanisms for generating value conflict can and should be applied at each successive choice point, although the phase of problem selection and formulation remains most essential.

The general issues and guidelines discussed in this chapter are applicable to other areas of social science research—education, mental health, public welfare—even though the chapter is addressed to scientists interested in social policy research with regard to law and criminal justice. Furthermore, I am not only referring to applied research, but also to what is often called *basic* research with direct or indirect implications for the developmenht of social policy. The traps in such research are even more subtle and potentially dangerous.

ACKNOWLEDGMENTS

   The author expresses his gratitude to Philip L. Berck, Guy Desaulniers, James Lamiell, Thom Moore, Julian Rappaport, Ronald Roesch, Evelyn N. Seidman, and Rita J. Simon for their helpful comments on an earlier draft of this manuscript. I am especially grateful to Thom Moore for continually suggesting pertinent references.

REFERENCES

Blumberg, A. S. (Ed.). (1974). *Current perspectives on criminal behavior.* New York: Alfred A. Knopf.

Buckley, W. (1967). *Social and modern systems theory.* Englewood Cliffs, NJ: Prentice-Hall.

Buckley, W. (Ed.). (1968). *Modern systems research for the behavioral scientist: A sourcebook.* Chicago: Aldine.

Caplan, N., & Nelson, S. D. (1973). On being useful: The nature and consequences of psychological research on social problems. *American Psychologist, 28,* 199–211.

Churchman, C. W. (1971). *The design of inquiring systems.* New York: Basic Books.

Davidson, W. S., & Rapp, C. (1976). Child advocacy in the justice system. *Social Work, 21,* 225–232.

Davidson, W. S., & Seidman, E. (1974). Studies of behavior modification and juvenile delinquency: A review, methodological critique, and social perspective. *Psychological Bulletin, 81,* 998–1011.

Fairweather, G. W. (1972). *Social change: The challenge to survival.* Morristown, NJ: General Learning Press.

Galliher, J. F. & McCartney, J. L. (1973). The influence of funding agencies on juvenile delinquency research. *Social Problems, 21,* 77–90.

Glaser, D. (1974). Remedies for the key deficiency in criminal justice evaluation research. *Journal of Research in Crime and Delinquency, 11,* 144–154.

Goldenberg, I. I. (1971). *Build me a mountain.* Cambridge: MIT Press.

Gouldner, A. W. (1969). Anti-minotaur: The myth of a value-free sociology. In W. G. Bennis, K. D. Benne, & R. Chin (Eds.), *The planning of change.* New York: Holt, Rinehart & Winston.

Goulet, D. (1971). An ethical model for the study of values. *Harvard Educational Review, 41,* 205–227.

Green, P. (1971). The obligations of American social scientists. *The Annals, 394* (The American Academy of Political and Social Science), 13–27.

Johnson, R. .W. (1975). Research objectives for policy analysis. In K. M. Dolbeare (Ed.), *Public policy evaluation,* Beverly Hills, CA: Sage Publications.

Lyons, G. M. (Ed.). (1971). Social science and the federal government. *The Annals, 394* (The American Academy of Political and Social Science), 1–120.

Maruyama, M. (1966). Monopolarization, family, and individuality. *Psychiatric Quarterly, 40,* 133–149.

Maruyama, M. (1968). The second cybernetics: Deviation amplifying mutual causal processes. In W. Buckley (Ed.), *Modern systems research for the behavioral scientist: A sourcebook.* Chicago: Aldine.

Maruyama, M. (1973). Cultural, social and psychological considerations in the planning of public works. *Technological Forecasting and Social Change, 5,* 135–143.

Maruyama, M. (1974). Paradigms and communication. *Technological Forecasting and Social Change, 6,* 3–32.

Mitroff, I. I., & Blankenship, L. V. (1973). On the methodology of the holistic experiment: An approach to the conceptualization of large-scale social experiments. *Technological Forecasting and Social Change, 4,* 339–353.

Mitroff, I. I. & Turoff, M. (1973). Technological forecasting and assessment: Science and/or mythology. *Technical Forecasting and Social Change, 5,* 113–134.

Mitroff I. I. & Turoff, M. (1974). On measuring the conceptual errors in large scale social experiments: The future as decision. *Technological Forecasting and Social Change, 6,* 389–402.

Moore, J. W. (1973). Social constraints on sociological knowledge: Academics and research concerning minorities. *Social Problems, 21,* 65–77.

Moore, T., & Nay, W. R. (1977). *Control of freedom in social research.* Unpublished manuscript, University of Illinois.

Rappaport, J. (1977). *Community psychology: Values, research and action.* New York: Holt, Rinehart & Winston.

Runkel, P. J., & McGrath, J. E. (1972). *Research on human behavior: A systematic guide to method.* New York: Holt, Rinehart & Winston.

Ryan, W. (1971). *Blaming the victim.* New York: Vintage Books.

Schur, E. M. (1973). *Radical non-intervention: Rethinking the delinquency problem.* Englewood Cliffs, NJ: Prentice-Hall.

Seidman, E. (1976). *Steps toward the development of useful social and public policies.* Paper presented at interdisciplinary seminar, "Public Policy in Industrialized Countries," Urbana, IL.

Sjoberg, G. (1975). Politics, ethics and evaluation research. In M. Guttentag & E. L. Struening (Eds.), *Handbook of Evaluation Research* (Vol. 2). Beverly Hills, CA: Sage Publications.

Sjoberg, G., & Cain, L. D., Jr. (1971). Negative values, countersystem models, and the analysis of social systems. In H. Turk & R. L. Simpson (Eds.), *Institutions and social exchange: The sociologies of Talcott Parsons and George C. Homans.* Indianapolis: Bobbs-Merrill.

Sjoberg, G., & Miller, P. J. (1973). Social research on bureaucracy: Limitations and opportunities. *Social Problems, 21,* 129–143.

Watzlawick, P., Weakland, J. H. & Fisch, R. (1974). *Change: Principles of Problem Formulation and Problem Resolution.* New York: Norton.

CHAPTER 15

Court-Ordered School Desegregation
SHUFFLING THE DECK OR PLAYING
A DIFFERENT GAME

JEAN ANN LINNEY

Research on student outcomes and changes associated with school desegregation has focused primarily on student achievement and personality variables (Hawley, 1981; St. John, 1975). Much of this research has assessed the degree to which school desegregation facilitates racial equality and "equal educational opportunity" in the public education setting. Reflecting a definition of equal opportunity as similarity in behavioral outputs (Mosteller & Moynihan, 1972), the research has most commonly compared the performance of desegregated black students with their white classmates and/or segregated black students. The assumption is that if equal opportunity is afforded, there will be no significant differences between the performance of black and white students. Conversely, this definition assumes that differences which do exist are the result of inequities in schooling.

Desegregation research has been plagued with methodological shortcomings that preclude or seriously limit causal inference. For example, Crain and Mahard (1981) gathered 93 published and unpublished studies that measured minority achievement. Less than half of those were judged methodologically strong enough to include in their meta-analysis of desegregation research. Bradley and Bradley (1977) felt that methodological problems precluded conclusions about the effects of desegregation. St. John's (1975) earlier review found similar methodological problems. Considering only those studies she judged methodologically "adequate," she concluded that the findings were

JEAN ANN LINNEY · Department of Psychology, University of South Carolina, Columbia, South Carolina 29208. Parts of this work were supported by a grant from the National Institute of Mental Health, MH22336.

mixed. Crain and Mahard's (1981) meta-analysis concluded that the studies showed a modest positive effect of desegregation on the achievement of black children.

Does desegregation effect a change in students? Are there significant improvements in black student achievement and self-concept? Do racial attitudes improve? These pre-post research questions stem from assumptions of change at the individual level, of parallel patterns of change and development for both black and white students, and linear, somewhat unidimensional change (premises reflected in the legal arguments and opinions as well). This is in sharp contrast to a multidimensional, interdependent systems-based set of assumptions that examine changes at the organizational level, patterns of change within groups and between groups, as well as the variables or mechanisms that contribute to the observed patterns of change. Despite dozens of studies, the existing literature fails to offer explanation or insight into the dynamics of desegregation, for example: What variables contribute to observed changes or the absence of change for students and schools? What kinds of change are effected in classroom interaction patterns? How does the school adapt to its new black students? What happens to interpersonal interaction patterns? In what ways does the school as an organization change or adapt to desegregation? These more ecological and systems-oriented questions have not been addressed except in isolated studies (e.g., Rist, 1978; Schofield, 1982). In general, the ecology of the schools and its functioning as a system have not been fully incorporated into research designs or implementation plans for desegregation.

There has been a growing recognition that desegregation may have effected changes that were unintended, perhaps not anticipated, and sometimes counterintuitive (cf. Schofield, 1982). Educational and psychological research has focused almost exclusively on outcomes for individual students and has been rooted in assumptions of linear, unidimensional change, that is, change in school racial composition effects change in individual student outcomes. It is suggested that these unexamined premises and their corresponding research strategies may be responsible for the inconsistency and weak explanatory power in desegregation findings to date. This chapter examines desegregation from a systems or ecological perspective, and suggests alternative research questions that stem from a systems model.

SCHOOL DESEGREGATION AND A SYSTEMS CONCEPTION OF CHANGE

Desegregation can be conceptualized as a system-level intervention intended to have "radiating impact" (Kelly, 1971) at several levels including individuals and organizations. Such a systems conception suggests alternative

constructs for considering and evaluating change accompanying desegregation, provides a framework for understanding the process at multiple levels,
and has important implications for research design and the units of analysis.

School desegregation can be considered a mechanism to bring about very
specific changes (e.g., elimination of school assignment by race), and some
less well-defined changes (e.g., change in the equality of opportunity in education available to minority children). As desegregation plans have been
implemented, a variety of other unintended changes have been observed. In
many situations, it has spawned new problems and conflicts beyond those it
was designed to ease. For example, busing plans have often precipitated
community opposition and protest leading to disruption in school functioning.
When this occurred, those activities became the concern of most of the actors,
overshadowing concern about enhanced educational outcomes. Some plans
have resulted in resegregation within the school through curricula based on
homogeneous groupings (Sager & Schofield, 1978). Rist (1978) describes the
phenomenon of black children becoming "invisible" in the integrated classroom. Schofield's (1982) ethnography of an integrated magnet school demonstrates the related "color blindness" syndrome in which school personnel
reduce the importance of race in understanding student behavior and performance and instead view "interracial education as an opportunity for class
assimilation" (Schofield, 1982, p. 49). The "outcomes" of desegregation would
seem to affect student achievement, well-being, and the like but have only
been researched when a descriptive, system-wide research model (e.g., ethnography) was adopted, and even then they have not been systematically
linked with individual-level outcomes. At some level, these "unintended outcomes" accomplish the same ends or serve similar functions as segregated
schooling. Resegregation at the classroom level through homogeneous grouping may be a quasi-replication of segregation by school. Being treated as
"invisible" may limit opportunities for involvement and learning in the interracial classroom in a manner not totally different from the limited opportunities of the de jure segregated setting. No less important, these outcomes
seem to reflect the adage, "the more things change, the more they remain
the same."

Watzlawick, Weakland, & Fisch's (1974) discussion of change offers a
useful way of considering the multiple outcomes of desegregation and the
types of change precipitated. They distinguish two types of change, first-order
change and second-order change. First-order change is "change that occurs
within a system which itself remains unchanged" (Watzlawick et al., 1974).
They hypothesize that when first-order change occurs alone, some change is
immediately apparent but the operating mechanisms of the system remain
unchanged. For example, in the 1970s there was concern about the labeling
and stigmatizing effects of ability grouping for reading in elementary school.
As on response to this, reading texts were no longer numbered consecutively

(e.g., Primer 1, 2, 3, etc.) reflecting difficulty level, but rather given color labels (e.g., red, green, blue). Students quickly learned which color was harder or better than others, and despite this apparent change, the basic procedure of graded reading instruction was maintained and children continued to know who was a better or worse reader. The system of ability grouping with differential evaluation placed on those groups was maintained despite some obvious changes. The adage, "the more things change the more they remain the same," aptly describes the impact in these circumstances. Oftentimes, a consequence of this type of change is that the solutions become part of the problem to which the change strategy was applied.

Second-order change involves "change in the body of rules governing the structure and internal order" of a system. This type of change involves a change in the premises of the operating system and redefines or "reframes" relationships among the groups or units involved in the system. For example, rather than disguise the gradations of ability grouping, a second-order change might redefine or reframe group relationships (in this example groups would be defined as good readers versus poor readers) by establishing a peer tutoring system in which "good" and "poor" readers jointly tutored each other in reading and another area (perhaps one in which the poor reader excelled). Alternatively, students might self-select into groups and choose reading materials on their own, inviting assistance from some "teacher" of their choosing. In these examples, the system procedure of ability grouping would be changed and its corollary mechanism of group definition eliminated. To the extent that such a change questioned the "rules of the system," second-order change would be predicted.

Watzlawick, et al.'s propositions are rooted in a system model of change. As such, the probability of systems adapting to change to maintain themselves must be recognized. They posit that system maintenance and change can be understood in the context of four principles from the mathematical theory of groups. These principles constitute operating mechanisms or defining functions for system maintenance, in essence, the "rules of the game."

The four principles are (1) the outcome of any combination of the members of a group is itself a member of the group, for example, in mathematical terms, if the group-defining characteristic is integers, then any combination of integers will result in an integer; (2) that combination of members of the group in varying sequence leads to the same outcome, for example, $2 + 3 + 4 = 9$ and $3 + 4 + 2 = 9$; (3) that an identity member exists such that combination with this member maintains the individual member's identity (the identity member in mathematics is zero for the operation of addition, e.g., $5 + 0 = 5$, and one for the operation of multiplication, e.g., $5 \times 1 = 5$); and (4) that every member has a reciprocal that in combination with a member gives the identity member, for example, $5 + (-5) = 0$ and $5 \times \frac{1}{5} = 1$.

In our society, groups are often defined by characteristics such as sex, age, race, role, and ethnicity. The theory of groups suggests that any change applied to the individual members of a group without changing the "rules of the game" will result in first-order change, and ultimately maintain group membership and the characteristic patterns of intergroup relations. Rappaport (1977) offers several examples of these principles and the effects of change strategies.

> If, for example, as in our society, groups are defined on the basis of race or role, any attempt to change a member of a given group so as to have him behave more like a member of another group will create change internal to the group, but the member will still not be placed outside the group of which he is a member. The black child who is a participant in a preschool education program will still be a black child, and to the extent that black children experience difficulty in public school as a function of being a group member, that difficulty will not be eliminated. (Principle 1).... The black child with a preschool education may initially do better in school than another member of his group (he may change his rank-order within the group) but the outcome for the group will remain the same. Most blacks will continue to experience more difficulty in school than most whites if the difficulty is a function of their group membership and resultant racial discrimination. (Principle 2).... In groups of blacks or whites in our society skin color is the identity member, and any combination of characteristics with skin color will not change one's indentity. (Principle 3).... In our examples white is the reciprocal of black (Principle 4). (pp. 133–134)

To effect second-order change, Watzlawick *et al.*'s principles require an analysis of the "rules of the game" that maintain relationships between groups. This necessitates a higher order level of analysis, stepping outside of the group identified as problematic, and examining the mechanisms or rules that maintain its status and relationships vis-à-vis other groups (e.g., the relationship defining black and white relative group status). The principles suggest that change applied to the members of one group or change within the system of rules underlies first-order change, and that second-order change will necessitate a redefinition of group maintenance mechanisms and differential patterns of change for the group might be expected.

Applying the principles of the theory of groups to desegregation suggests that, on the surface, desegregation focused on the members of the groups, combining them in a different way (e.g., student transfers, achieving racial balance). To the extent that the education system defined group membership by race, which seems self-evident under de jure segregation, desegregation further focused attention on group membership by making school placements by race, albeit mixing black and white individuals.

When school desegregation plans are implemented, there is clearly some observable change. Large numbers of children may be transferred to different schools so that the appearance of any classroom or school is quite different, that is, first-order change is apparent. If a second-order change is accomplished, then the desired outcomes of the system (i.e., education and socialization) should be unrelated to racial group membership, that is, group membership is no longer the source of difficulty, and the group and its reciprocal should change their relationship vis-àa-vis each other. In assessing the extent of second-order change following this framework, at least three alternative research questions become apparent: (1) Does desegregation bring about a change in the relationship between blacks and whites as groups? (2) Are these changes relatively stable over time? and (3) Is there evidence of organizational change in operating premises that define the relationship between the two groups?

SECOND-ORDER CHANGE AND DESEGREGATION

Change in Group Relationship

Studies of achievement in desegregated schools frequently examine the degree to which black and white student performance differs and the extent to which the desegregation has begun to "close the gap" in measured achievement between the groups. Change in academic performance, for example, is typically examined in terms of change in raw scores or standardized grade equivalent indexes for the individual students included. Examination of these differences offer one strategy for assessing relationship change, that is, change in group averages and distance between the groups. Most of the research indicates that desegregated black students make significant raw score gains on measures of achievement, although a significant gap between black and white student performance still remains (Hawley, 1981).

Watzlawick *et al.*'s model proposes that stable, second-order change occurs when group relationships within the system are redefined. This framework suggests that a student's relative position vis-à-vis peers is an additional unit of analysis for dependent measures. It is possible and perhaps likely that although transferred or desegregated black students make significant raw score gains in academic and behavioral measures following desegregation, at the same time they experience a decrease or no change in their relative position in the classroom. For example, consider a black child in the upper third of his class in a segregated school. This child's performance level compared with national norms places him at the 30th percentile. A year after his transfer to a predominantly white school he is performing at the 40th percentile by national norms, a substantial increase. Compared with his former classmates remaining in a segregated school, his achievement surpasses most of that class. Compared with his current classmates, however, he may now be in the lowest quintile of his class.

If these percentiles represented group means, then desite the absolute gains apparent for black students, the relative position of the two groups remains unchanged. That is, only the unit of comparison has changed. Instead of black schools performing less well than white schools, black students in desegregated classrooms would be performing less well than their white class-mates. In Watzalwick *et al.*'s terms, only first-order change has occurred. Group membership remains the prominent predictor of performance. In terms of absolute raw score change in achievement, the desegregation has obviously been beneficial to this student, although his relative standing in the classroom has decreased. Clearly, an absolute increase in achievement is important and should not be ignored or belittled. However, in isolation those absolute gains may be misleading as indicators of social change, equal opportunity, or integration. Relativistic measures provide a broader context for interpreting absolute changes and offer an index of outcomes that is more indicative of organizational or second-order change.

There is substantial theoretical precedent and empirical support for em-ploying relativistic measures. Pettigrew's (1967) integration of psychological research in social comparison theory and sociological constructs such as reference groups and relative deprivation leads to the conclusion that indi-vidual attitudes and behavior are products of comparisons between present personal circumstances and alternatives presented by other reference groups and social norms. In their study of mainstreamed handicapped students, Strang, Smith, and Rogers (1978) found that reference groups and relative position vis-à-vis the reference group was an important predictor of student self-concept. Similarly, Seidman and Rapkin (1983) have argued that the relationship between economic conditions and psychological dysfunction can be better understood by using indexes "which assess economic status relative to standards of comparison salient to the individual or group of interest" (p. 192).

In desegregation research, the question of change in relative position, the correlation between absolute change and relative change, and the effects of differing patterns are rarely addressed. Only a few studies have begun to examine these issues. For example, in a longitudinal study of a midwestern city's court-ordered desegregation, Linney (1978) examined both absolute change and change in relative standing in academic performance for a sample of transferred and nontransferred children in the primary grades during de-segregation. Raw scores on the achievement measures were used to assess absolute gains. To examine change in relative position, each child's score was standardized within the classroom unit and the Z score was used as an estimate of relative standing. The raw score means showed that the transferred black students gained slightly more than their former classmates two years after desegregation. However, their relative standing vis-à-vis classmates declined following desegregation. Weinberg (1975) compared change in school grades and standardized achievement test scores. Standardized achievement scores provide an assessmant of "absolute" performance, whereas grades are more likely to be based on relative class performance. He found that standardized achievement scores increased, whereas school grades decreased for black children transferred from majority black to majority white schools. Other research on social status in desegregated schools has shown that black high school males gain some status relative to peers in the integrated school through their performance in athletics. In contrast, black high school females may lose status relative to peers because they are less likely to be selected for high-status positions in the integrated school (e.g., homecoming queen, cheerleader, class officer) (cf. Patchen, 1982; Schofield, 1982).

These examples illustrate the potential for differences in absolute performance and relative position following desegregation. The psychological impact of these patterns remains to be determined. For example, decline in relative status may enhance motivation and increase expectations for students or it may create frustration, hostility, and a decline in self-worth. The specific effects will be the result of a complex set of variables both individual and situational. Research based on linear, univariate assumptions about the nature of change will overlook this complexity.

Change in absolute performance alone may indicate first-order change only. Analysis of both absolute and relative standing offers a more comprehensive analysis of changes for individuals experiencing desegregation and provides one overview assessment of the presence of second-order change. The Z transformation is suggested as an index of relative standing applicable to many different variables when individuals of several groups are being compared. Other measures such as grades, sociometric data, or teachers' rankings of student behavior are also indexes of relative standing. If the goals of second-order change are accomplished, over time any differences in relative standing between minority and nonminority students should diminish to the point that race or ethnic group is not correlated with relative position.

The Stability of Change

In any system-level intervention, time is a critically important variable. As Watzlawick *et al.* (1974) define first-order change, it is an "apparent change" that does not effect a change in the basic defining relationships (relative positions) among the groups in the system. Implicit in this definition is the transitory nature of first-order changes. The initial appearance of change may fool us into accepting the efficacy of the intervention only to realize shorly after that the original problem has not been resolved. The instability of some kinds of change is also discussed in cybernetics where it is proposed that the system's regulatory mechanisms function to maintain equilibrium. As such, cybernetic theory predicts that after intervention there is an immediate and visible change in outputs followed by oscillation in those outputs and an eventual stabilization at levels close to those prior to the intervention (Ashby, 1956; Buckley, 1969; Cadwallader, 1959).

Theories of change suggest that initial effects may dissipate in a relatively short time. To call for longitudinal research on desegregation is to repeat the recommendations of many methodologists and researchers in this area (e.g., Cook & Campbell, 1979; Schofield, 1978). However, the effects of desegregation, or any social policy change, may manifest themselves differently over time. If changes are unstable, then the selection of time points to be included in an evaluative analysis may dramatically alter conclusions regarding the intervention's effects.

Figure 1 illustrates this point. Data are presented for two nontransferring groups in a desegregation investigation (from Linney, 1978). The data were collected over a three year period in a moderate-sized midwestern city. Two assessments (Time 1 and 2) were completed in the year prior to desegregation. Time 3 and 4 assessments were completed during the first year following desegregation, and Time 5 twenty months after the implementation of desegregation. The students included in these two groups were not transferred within the desegregation plan but instead experienced a change in the racial balance of the school they attended. Prior to desegregation, their schools averaged 45% minority students. Postdesegregation, these schools averaged 28% minority children (approximately 21% of the community's citizens were minority). Figure 1 shows group means for aggressive behavior on the Peer Behavior Description Form—Aggressive factor (Seidman, Linney, Rappaport, Herzberger, Alden, & Kramer, 1979) scored to reflect each student's relative standing in his or her class (i.e., Z score transformation).

Figure 1a shows Times 1, 2, and 3 only (pre- and immediately postdesegregation). This assessment schedule is typical of early desegregation research. There appears to have been a dramatic change in the relative standing of these groups. Given that these are Z scores, the means postdesegregation (Time 3) are indicative of random nominations and suggest the occurrence of a change in the relationship between these racial groups.

Figure 1b includes a different combination of three assessments, that is, mean scores for the same groups immediately prior to the desegregation and two years post. This design is more common in later research, recognizing the need for longitudinal analysis. With the greater time interval between observations, quite a different picture emerges from that in Figure 1a. In Figure 1b, the data suggest that very little change in group relative standing has been effected by the desegregation (a finding not uncommon in studies including observations a year or more after desegregation).

With five observations included, a still different picture of the impact of desegreation on the groups relative status emerges (Figure 1c). This pattern of means provides evidence that the desegregation precipitated changes that were relatively unstable (Times 2 and 3) and dissipated within two years (Times 3 to 5). The pattern of change in Figure 1c is consistent with cybernetic predictions of change, (i.e., oscillation and stabilization at preintervention levels) and Watzlawick *et al.*'s notions of first-order change.

In the analysis of policy impact and organizational-level interventions, the importance of longitudinal investigation with multiple data points cannot

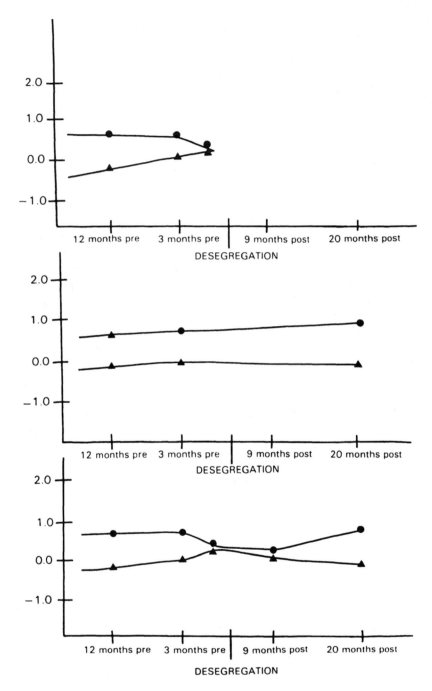

Figure 1. Change in peer rated aggression pre and postdesegregation.
● Black nontransfers (*N* = 11); ▲ White nontransfers (*N* = 21).

be underestimated. The short time series shown here illustrate three diverse evaluative conclusions depending on which components of the series are examined and when the intervention effects are measured. Time series designs examining policy change need to be based in systems theories of change, rather than assuming simple linear change. Most systems theories suggest that initial change (or disruption) is inevitable but that a system will adapt to maintain its equilibrium. In bringing about second-order change, that is stable change in group relationships and the rules defining those relationships, a new equilibrium needs to be found and maintained. Evaluations of desegregation and similar system-level interventions need to distinguish among simple disruption, adaptations to restore equilibrium, and stable systemic change. The patterns of change observed over time may provide hypotheses about the strength of an intervention and the countervailing forces operating within its system. Different systems may respond to the same intervention in different ways (e.g., rapid change in outputs sustained for several years followed by dissipation vs. no change initially, followed by dramatic improvement in student outputs). Comparisons of these differential responses can highlight the conditions necessary for the maintenance of desired changes. Implicit in the notions of adaptation and differential response is the likelihood that multiple dependent variables and subsystems may be affected by a policy intervention. Systems conceptions may guide the selection of dependent variables, analysis of change, and selection of assessment times.

Organizational-Level Change

Change is necessary at a systemic or organizational level to insure that desegregation effects have an impact for subsequent groups of children. Second-order change requires organizational change in the operating premises and rules defining group membership within the system. Changes in the operating premises should be reflected in (1) organizational practices or rules determining the range of acceptable input into the system and the routing of input through the system (Cadwallader, 1959), for example, placement in special education and remedial classes, and suspension and disciplinary action by race; (2) indexes of organizational functioning like quality of output, for example, standardized achievement levels of the schools including change in district means and standard deviations, graduation rates, and postgraduation education and placement success; and (3) the interrelationships in terms of distribution of resources among the components (schools) of the system, for example, if segregated schools are inferior, then eliminating segregated schools should lead to a redistribution of the remaining schools on indexes such as achievement levels and graduation rates.

Political scientists and sociologists have examined these types of changes in their analyses of the effects of desegregation (Rossell, 1978). However, their focus has been on identifying organizational impact alone rather than in the context of organizational change as it influences individuals. For example, there has been consideration of within-school resegregation practices as an organizational adaptation to desegregation. These changes have been studied as organizational indicators or effects of intervention with little analysis of the impact on student perceptions and relative position, or as processes reflecting basic system maintenance functions. Change at the organizational level and the individual level have not been conceptually integrated.

Multiple indicators of organizational processing and systemic functioning can be considered, for example, classroom racial composition, attendance rates, school achievement levels, student placement patterns, and school climate variables. These measures reflect characteristics of the school not specific to individuals, yet comprised of individual students. Each of the measures would be examined with individual schools constituting the units of analysis. Time series analyses and nonparametric analyses can test for systemic change in organizational characteristics following desegregation. For example, Linney (1978) examined patterns of racial composition for the schools of a desegregating district before and after desegregation. Spearman's rank-order correlations between school racial composition pre- and postdesegregation showed that the patterns of minority student enrollment throughout the schools of the district did not change following a desegregation/transfer plan that "racially balanced" each of the schools. The "whitest" schools before the desegregation remained the "whitest" schools after the transfers. In light of the correlation between school facilities and resources and the percentage of white students (Coleman *et al.*, 1966), relative access to resources and educational facilities appears to have been maintained at the more macrolevel of the school system. It might be expected, then, that patterns of student performance would similarly be maintained even though the overall level or mean performance for any single group might be elevated.

The distribution of black students throughout the classes of a school district following desegregation provides evidence of the nature of organizational change. Desegregation plans may enhance racial balance across the schools, while at the same time maintaining segregated classrooms through ability grouping or other class assignment practices (Sager & Schofield, 1978). Placement in special education classes, for example, may provide a way of "handling" transferred black students in formerly white schools and newly desegregated districts. Given the status of special education classes within the public school (Milofsky, 1974), disproportionate placement of black students in special classes further serves to maintain lower status in the school system and restricts access to educational opportunities.

Table 1 shows data on placements in classes for the educable mentally handicapped (EMH) for two years, one immediately prior to desegregation and the second during the first year of the desegregation plan in one school system (from Linney, 1978). The chi-square analysis suggests that following desegregation black children were more often placed in EMH classes than

Table 1. Patterns of Special Education Placement Following
Desegregation

Educable mentally handicapped classes	First year of desegregation	Second year of desegregation	
Number of white students	145	114	(259)
Number of black students	101	117	(218)
	(246)	(231)	

χ^2 (1) = 4.42 ($p < .05$).

white children. In view of the differences in performance between students in predominantly white and black schools, it is likely that the transferring black students might be less well prepared. Hence, these placement figures may represent an assessment of the "need for services" rather than any racially motivated activity and may seem to be an "educationally sound" practice. Nevertheless, because special education placements become relatively permanent and the placement *per se* may seriously limit further academic opportunities, such action can have detrimental side effects. Because the process of placement begins with a teacher referral, relative position in the classroom is that much more important for the potential referral. These data suggest that race has remained the identity member's defining membership in lower versus higher achieving groups. Should such a pattern of placement persist, it indicates no change in the "rules of the game."

A substantially longer time series is necessary for analysis of the degree to which the trend reflected in Table 1 represents a system change in the routing of students through the subsystems of the school district. The important point in these data is the need to examine systemic responses to policy changes and to investigate potential system adaptations that undermine or preclude the accomplishment of stable change.

RESEARCH DIRECTIONS AND POLICY IMPLICATIONS

Researchers considering longitudinal investigations of desegregation have concluded that "desegregation alone apears not to have disturbed the status quo"(Linsenmeier & Wortman, 1978, p. 31). Change in racial composition alone may not be sufficient to bring about the second-order changes implied by the goals of "equal educational opportunity." The transferring process of most desegregation plans is essentially a manipulation of the individual members of the groups without changing the "rule" defining the relationship between the groups, or the operating systems of the school. In essence, the desegregation mandate focuses attention on group membership and in so doing solidifies or exaggerates the identity rule.

Chesler, Crowfoot, & Bryant (1978) have said, that in the area of school desegregation,

> the first generation problem for lawyers, judges, social science researchers and educators was how to plan for and facilitate the physical reassignment of students. The second generation problem has been to determine what was required to advance beyond physical racial mixing toward integrated schooling—interracial learning environments of high quality. The third generation problem is how to implement hunches, research findings and practical lessons about what is important to do in desegregated schools. (p. 213)

Chesler *et al.* imply that "integrated schooling" or second-order change has yet to be accomplished, but that the first-order change of racial mixing was a necessary prerequisite to achievement of second-order change. Watzlawick *et al.* argue that the set of underlying assumptions for each of these types of change are mutually exclusive. First-order change gives the impression of change and, as such, diverts attention from second-order change issues, while at the same time precipitating additional problems that still further divert attention from the group relationship issues and prevalent rules of the game. There is ample evidence of this in the implementation history of desegregation. Because racial mixing was the goal, attention and conflict centered on methods of achieving that goal, for example, busing programs, which in turn created turmoil over who was to be transferred and how this was to be financed. Presently, we have seen that these issues are leading to exemptions and the rescinding of orders to establish racial balance in the public schools. As the "solutions" become the problem, the prospects of achieving the earlier goals of second-order change seem to diminish.

As researchers and practitioners become involved in "second and third, generation" implementation activities, research and evaluation designs and program development efforts should increasingly focus on the nature of group relationships, relative position, group changes, the stability of observed changes, systemic adaptations to imposed change, and system maintenance mechanisms. Adopting such a perspective not only focuses attention on the efficacy of change efforts but also directs activity toward understanding multilevel, ecological relationships and the generation of data useful in a more prescriptive way for the policy formation and program development process.

There are multiple factors affecting policy formation and policy impact (e.g., political and economic factors). This discussion has focused on elements as if they were in isolation. However, the histories of policy change and intervention outcomes are not inconsistent with the adage "the more things change, the more they remain the same." The prevalence of first-order changes points to the need for alternative conceptualizations of change efforts and reexamination of the premises underlying interventions. Both theoretical and empirical work is needed to explicate how prevailing ecological and systemic constraints determine the outcomes of policy-level intervention. Without these considerations, we may continue to simply shuffle the deck, without changing the rules to begin playing a different game.

REFERENCES

Ashby, W. R. (1956). *An introduction to cybernetics.* New York: Wiley.

Bradley, L., & Bradley, G. (1977). The academic achievement of black students in desegregated schools. *Review of Educational Research, 47,* 399–449.

Buckley, W. (Ed.). (1968). *Modern systems research for the behavioral scientist: A sourcebook.* Chicago: Aldine.

Cadwallader, M. (1959). The cybernetic analysis of change in complex social organizations. *American Journal of Sociology, 65,* 154–157.

Chesler, M. A., Crowfoot, J. E., & Bryant, B. I. (1978). Institutional changes to support school desegregation: Alternative models underlying research and implementation. *Law and Contemporary Problems, 42 (4),* 174–213.

Coleman, J. S., Campbell, E. G., Hobson, C. J., McPartland, J., Mood, A. M., Weinfeld, F. D., & York, R. L. (1966). *Equality of educational opportunity.* Washington, DC: U.S. Government Printing Office.

Cook, T. D., & Campbell, D. T. (1979). *Quasi-experimentation: Design and analysis issues for field settings.* Chicago: Rand McNally.

Crain, R. L., & Mahard, R. E. (1978). Desegregation and black achievement: A review of the research. *Law and Contemporary Problems, 42 (3),* 17–56.

Crain, R. L., & Mahard, R. E. (1981). Minority achievement: Policy implications of research. In W. D. Hawley (Ed.), *Effective school desegregation: Equity, quality and feasibility* (pp. 55–84). Beverly Hills, CA: Sage Publications.

Hawley, W. D. (Ed.). (1981). *Effective school desegregation: Equity, quality, and feasibility.* Beverly Hills, CA: Sage Publications.

Kelly, J. G. (1971). The quest for valid preventive interventions. In G. Rosenblum (Ed.), *Issues in community psychology and preventive mental health* (pp. 109–139). New York: Behavorial Publications.

Linney, J. A. (1978). *A multivariate, multilevel analysis of a midwestern city's court-ordered desegregation.* Unpublished doctoral dissertation, University of Illinois at Urbana-Champaign.

Linsenmeier, J. A., & Wortman, P. M. (1978). The Riverside School study of desegregation: A re-examination. *Research Review of Equal Education, 2 (2),* 3–36.

Milofsky, C. D. (1974). Why special education isn't special. *Harvard Educational Review, 44,* 437–458.

Mosteller, F., & Moynihan, D. P. (Eds.). (1972). *On equality of educational opportunity.* New York: Vintage Books.

Patchen, M. (1982). *Black–white contact in schools.* Lafayette, IN: Purdue University Press.

Pettigrew, T. F. (1967). Social evaluation theory: Convergences and applications. *Nebraska Symposium on Motivation, 15,* 241–311.

Rappaport, J. (1977). *Community psychology: Values, research and action.* New York: Holt, Rinehart & Winston.

Rist, R. C. (1978). *The invisible children.* Cambridge, MA: Havard University Press.

Rossell, C. (1978). School desegregation and community social change. *Law and Contemporary Problems, 42 (3),* 133–183.

Sager, H. A., & Schofield, J. W. (1978). *Integrating the desegregated school: Perspectives, practices and possibilities.* Unpublished manuscript, University of Pittsburgh.

Schofield, J. W. (1978, August). *Conceptual problems in desegregation research.* Paper presented at the meeting of the American Psychological Association, Toronto.

Schofield, J. W. (1982). *Black and white in school: Trust, tension or tolerance?* New York: Praeger.

Seidman, E., & Rapkin, B. (1983). Economics and psychosocial dysfunction: Toward a framework and prevention strategies. In R. D. Felner, L. A. Jason, J. N. Moritsugu, & S. Farber (Eds.), *Preventive psychology: Theory, research and practice,* (pp. 175–198). New York: Pergamon Press.

Seidman, E., Linney, J. A., Rappaport, J., Herzberger, S., Alden, L., & Kramer, J. (1978). Assessment of classroom behavior: A multiattribute, multisource approach to instrument development and validation. *Journal of Educational Psychology, 71,* 451–464.

St. John, N. H. (1975). *School desegregation: Outcomes of children.* New York: Wiley.

Strang, L., Smith, M. D., & Rogers, C. M. (1978). Social comparison, multiple reference groups, and the self concepts of academically handicapped children before and after mainstreaming. *Journal of Educational Psychology, 70,* 487–497.

Watzlawick, P., Weakland, J. A., & Fisch, R. (1974). *Change: Principles of problem formation and problem resolution.* New York: Norton.

Weinberg, M. (1975). The relationship between school desegregation and academic achievement: A review of the research. *Law and Contemporary Problems, 39,* 241–270.

CHAPTER 16

Indirect Effects of Desegregation

RICHARD R. SCOTT

In the years since desegregation has become national policy, little can be said about whether or not that policy has been successful. Many reasons have been cited as to why the evidence remains inconclusive. These reasons include such factors as the failure to conduct desegregation research within a theoretical framework, the frequent use of inadequate research methodologies, and the overblown or contradictory expectations of what desegregation could accomplish. Of these reasons, perhaps the most important are (1) the imprecise definition of desegregation and (2) the lack of agreement about the substantive areas desegregation might be expected to affect. Both of these problems stemmed from the same source: an inadequate conceptualization of desegregation. Desegregation was initially a legal phenomenon, and as a consequence the courts were at the forefront in providing a definition of that phenomenon.

Following the *Brown* decision (1954), indeed, in the footnote to the *Brown* decision written by social scientists, the implicit meaning of desegregation centered around the removal of legal barriers. It was not assumed that the removal of legal barriers would necessarily result in a change in the racial composition of the nation's schools (Graglia, 1980). But, by 1971, in *Swann v. Charlotte-Mecklenburg Board of Education*, the Supreme Court made racial composition the benchmark by which to determine if desegregation had been achieved (Read, 1975). Despite this change in the legal meaning of desegregation, the emphasis among researchers remained on the remedial effects of desegregation.

Nonetheless, the ultimate importance of desegregation as an educational social policy, rather than as a legal remedy, lies in its contribution to (or detraction from) equality of opportunity. Therefore, the question must be

RICHARD R. SCOTT · Quaker Oats Company, Merchandise Mart Plaza, Chicago, Illinois 60654.

raised as to whether or not the probability of increased interracial contact is at all related to an increase in the equality of opportunity for either blacks or whites.

The answer to this question cannot be found in a vacuum where interracial contact is the only factor. Rather, other factors that have been found to be important in the status attainment of individuals must be considered along with interracial contact. Although this line of research on the indirect or interactive effects of desegregation is still new and the findings hardly more than exploratory, it seems to be the most promising road for future "desegregation" research; it promises to determine the ultimate worth of desegregation as a national policy.

One consequence of the focus on the legal definition of desegregation was an approach that emphasized *individual outcomes* for students following desegregation. An approach more in keeping with an emphasis on the long-term goal of desegregation—equal opportunity—would have emphasized structural effects of desegregation such as community politics, conflict, economic outcomes and changes in the racial composition of social institutions.

The difference between these two approaches is reflective of the difference between a microfocal and a macrofocal approach. Here a microfocal approach will be used to indicate an individual level of analysis, whereas a macrofocal approach will be used to indicate a global or group approach. In addition, a microfocal approach will be used to connote an emphasis on direct short-term effects, and a macrofocal approach will be used to connote indirect long-term effects.

NEW APPROACHES TO DESEGREGATION RESEARCH

Newer approaches to desegregation research, which shift from the study of microfocal or direct effects to the study of macrofocal or indirect effects, are now more likely to lead to useful new information. Whereas the microfocal approach assumed the direct impact of desegrgation on individuals, the macrofocal approach is concerned with the indirect effects of desegregation. In particular, macrofocal approaches stress the impact of desegregation on the social, political, and economic participation of blacks in the American mainstream.

Following the judicial expectations of what effects were thought likely to be outcomes of desegregation, early desegregation research focused upon the direct effects for interracial attitudes, self-attitudes, and academic achievement. In fact, indirect effects may be more salient if the most important question about desegregation is considered to be whether or not it leads to opportunities for minorities to fully participate in the American mainstream. The focus on macrofocal or indirect effects has been most clearly stated by

McPartland and Braddock (1981). They note first, that support for desegregation based upon its effects on individual attainments has led to political disagreements. Some minority spokesmen, for example, have questioned whether or not optimal learning for minority students can only be accomplished when they are in classrooms with majority students. But second and what is more important, they note that many inequalities are not due to individual deficits but to structural barriers. As a consequence, not only does a focus on the indirect effects that reflect the structure of opportunity provide a rationale for desegregation, but a focus on those indirect effects is also more in keeping with the broader purpose of desegregation: the status attainment of blacks in America. Three approaches to desegregation research exemplify this new agenda: national studies of the impact of desegregation, the use of community or structural variables, and the use of status attainment as a framework in which to study desegregation.

National Studies

There has been a tendency for desegregation studies to be done on a school-by-school or system-by-system basis. Although this approach does allow greater control of those factors that mediate desegregation effects, such as contact, it has also made the conceptual integration of seemingly inconsistent desegregation effects more difficult (see Stephan, 1978; St. John, 1975).

One method that has been used to approximate a national evaluation of desegregation is to review the many local studies and attempt to place them within some meaningful framework. These efforts have demonstrated that first, schools vary greatly in terms of those factors that can mediate the effects of desegregation (e.g., the local history of race relations, the way in which desegregation was implemented, and the internal conditions of the schools). Consequently, desegregation can be expected to have different effects under different conditions. Second, these reviews demonstrate the difficulty of combining studies employing different methodologies, different methodological skills, and different conceptual frameworks. McConahay (1978), in a review of the literature, found only 5 of more than 100 studies that met minimal methodological standards. And, because these studies have not systematically varied the local conditions that might have affected the outcomes of desegregation, those effects are hopelessly confounded with local conditions.

As a consequence, little can be said about the effects of desegregation as a *national* policy. However, a different approach to the evaluation of desegregation as a national policy is to examine the effects of desegregation for a national probability sample of students. Because students are randomly sampled, the effects on such samples of students would reflect all types of desegregation (e.g., "natural," voluntary, court ordered, bused, etc.) as well as all types of local mediation. The use of national probability samples allows for the appropriate measurement of "national desegregation" (the predictor variable); it does not affect the assessment of those effects—either microfocal or macrofocal. This new approach not only involves a shift in the meaning of desegregation but is also methodologically more tractable and more in keeping with judicial limits affecting desegregation. That is, fewer desegregation orders can now be expected from the courts and thus, the most accurate meaning of desegregation is now one of racial composition regardless of how that composition is achieved (Scott & McPartland, 1982).

Community Response and Racial Isolation

The questions or effects that are of primary interest in this approach concern the effect of desegregation on various community-level responses, including racial composition. The areas that have been most researched are political responses, "white flight," and residential segregation. Additionally, racial composition operationalized as the probability for interracial contact has been studied. The most important aspect of this approach is the operationalization of desegregation and the identification of potential effects.

Desegregation in this approach typically refers to the type of desegregation plan implemented and the amount of parental choice in the reassignment of pupils (Rossell, 1978). Here, desegregation is clearly a structural variable, and, as such, focus is directed to social processes. Two political social processes that have received some attention are the level of protest and dissent voting that particular types of desegregation plans engender. Rossell (1978) found that community protest increases as the proportion of white students reassigned increases. Two studies of voting behavior following court-ordered desegregation found that voting turnout in school board elections decreased (Rossell, 1978). However, when the desegregation has been board ordered, the greater the pupil reassignment, the more the voter turnout increases (Rossell, 1978).

White flight refers to the potential for resegregation that is due to a system's loss of white students following desegregation, either by the movement from the district or the transferral of students from public to private schools within the district. The study of white flight has received the greatest amount of research attention within this approach (Coleman, Kelly & Moore, 1975; Giles, 1978; Giles, Cataldo, & Gatlin, 1976; Pettigrew & Green, 1976; Rossell, 1976). From this research and the controversy it has generated, several conclusions about white flight seem tenable. First, most white flight occurs in the transfer of students to private schools or the nonentrance of students to public schools, rather than in the residential movement of the parents. Second, the amount of white flight depends upon a number of factors such as the amount of white reassignment, the amount of negative media coverage, the distance of the receiving schools from the local school, and the amount of protest preceding desegregation. And third, despite the highest loss of white students in the year of implementation, the net effect of mandatory desegregation is still beneficial to the goal of reducing the racial isolation of students.

Although it might appear that this approach is similar to others in that it uses a measure of racial composition, it is different in one important respect. Earlier studies focused on the impact of racial composition on such things as student achievement or racial attitudes. This approach, in contrast, emphasizes racial composition as a consequence or outcome of a desegregation plan (e.g., student reassignment and parental choice). One aspect of this approach has been a greater reliance upon measures that reflect the opportunity for contact rather than the outcomes of that contact. In particular, Coleman's Index of Exposure (Coleman et al., 1975) are measures of the likelihood of exposure of a student of one race to a student of another race given a certain proportion of each race in the school.

Unfortunately, the conclusions from these studies must be tentative because they are few in number. Moreover, the reason why so few of these studies have been conducted is that for some combinations of student reassignment and parental choice, few, if any, cases exist. In addition, these studies are local studies and therefore confounded by local conditions. Nevertheless, certain points can be made about them. First, they illustrate that some of the methodological problems inherent in other approaches can be solved. A reasonably consistent definition of desegregation has been developed, with a set of dependent variables that are measured at the same level of analysis as the predictor variable—increased interracial contact. This, in part, solves the problem of specification error that has plagued earlier microfocal desegregation research. In addition, this approach demonstrates the importance of considering long-term rather than short-term effects of desegregation. Its basic fault seems to lie in the fact that it may miss assessing the objective that guided earlier research. Namely, does desegregation have a beneficial impact on the students affected? The third approach—status attainment—more directly addresses this issue.

Status Attainment

Status attainment is concerned with how individuals acquire both material and nonmaterial resources, and how those resources are translated into other resources and socially desirable attainments such as education, occupation, and income. In large part, developed from the work of Blau and Duncan (1967), status attainment models conceptualize later status attainments as the consequences of prior attainments and resources. Thus, certain critical experiences over the life cycle of the individual, beginning with origin status (i.e., family background), and including schooling, peers, and other factors, determine the probability that the individual will attain a particular destination status. Generally, the research in this area has found that one's destination status is primarily dependent upon origin status, but that this (dis)advantage is transmitted through schooling (Featherman & Hauser, 1978).

To the extent that desegregation is concerned with social and economic inequality (as opposed to legal inequality), then the relevance of this approach to desegregation is obvious (Wilson, 1979). Because the average status origin of blacks is lower than that of whites, then the same quality and amount of schooling for blacks as for whites will still result in a status disadvantage for blacks relative to whites (Duncan, Featherman, & Duncan, 1972). Two issues are raised by this consideration. First, in terms of eventual status destination, schooling—segregated or desegregated—is only one of the critical experiences in the life of the individual. And second, the relationship of one experience to another becomes crucial. That is, even if desegregation does increase the probability of one later critical experience, it may decrease the probability of another critical experience, with the net result that the eventual status destination is reduced.

Complementary to the status attainment approach is the input–output approach of educational productivity. This approach, adapted from economists, attempts to identify and measure how changes in educational inputs affect educational outputs (e.g., IQ, SAT scores, etc.). It is thus complementary to the status attainment approach in that it potentially can identify those inputs or critical experiences that affect the schooling experience. Moreover, it is characterized by large national studies, in which the specifics or local histories become input variables in the prediction of outputs (Cohn & Millman, 1975). In terms of desegregation, the independent variable is racial composition rather than student reassignment or parental choice.

From these two aproaches, several considerations become important. First, long-term, rather than short-term, effects are seen as crucial. Second, the identification of both school-related inputs as well as other types of critical experiences must be included in the consideration of the eventual outcomes of education. And finally, the benefits of any educational program or intervention, including desegregation, ought to be viewed in terms of both its costs and benefits. The status attainment approach can be seen in three promising lines of research in the desegregation area: the perpetuation of segregation in education, occupational attainments, and social effects.

Desegregation and Educational Attainments

The elementary and secondary desegregation of blacks affects their later attainments in higher education in two ways. First, early desegregation is positively related to the type of postsecondary education that blacks receive; second, desegregation is positively related to the overall amount of education that blacks receive.

Although methodologically flawed, Armor's (1972) study found that desegregated students in the METCO program were more likely to attend higher quality colleges than were those students who were not in the program. Braddock (1980) and Braddock and McPartland (1981) found that after controlling for differences in social class, ability, and college costs, black students who had attended desegregated high schools were more likely to attend predominantly white colleges. This relationship was even stronger for those black students who had also attended desegregated elementary schools. In addition, those black students who had attended desegregated elementary and high schools—controlling for differences in social class and ability— were more likely to continue in college and fare well academically than those students who had attended segregated schools (Braddock & McPartland, 1981). This research, conducted with a nationally representative sample (National Longitudinal Survey of the National Center for Educational Statistics) replicates the findings of an earlier study conducted with data collected in Florida (Braddock, 1980). Further, the data used in the later study represent the best currently available data; analyses made on these data can, to a large extent, rule out the possibility that the results hold only for a certain subset of students (i.e., those students especially sensitive to the effects of desegregation or those who were desegregated in some particular way).

The preceding research findings indicate that segregated elementary and secondary schools act to channel black students into either segregated postsecondary schools or lower quality postsecondary schools. And, when black students from segregated schools do go to predominantly white schools, regardless of their ability or achievement in high school, they tend to do less well academically than their counterparts from desegregated high schools. This last fact leads to the inference that one advantage of early desegregated education is that it cumulatively produces skills for coping in desegregated situations, thus increasing the liklihood of future positive desegregated experiences.

Desegregation and Occupational Attainments

Desegregation can affect the occupational attainments of blacks in two ways. First, educational desegregation is positively related to the jobs and occupations to which blacks aspire and for which they prepare themselves with specialized training. And second, desegregation positively affects the resources that blacks use to seek a job.

Although blacks as a group seriously lag behind whites as a group in level of income and rate of employment, the reason for this gap is not solely due to the level of education attained by blacks relative to that attained by whites. If blacks were to receive the same amount of education as whites, substantial differences in earned income and employment rate would still exist. The reasons for these persisting disparities would lie in the types of occupations in which blacks are employed and the ways in which blacks seek jobs. To the extent that segregation indirectly perpetuates this pattern of black occupational choice, then occupational choice is considered an appropriate dependent variable for desegregation research.

Occupation type. When occupations are categorized by the types of skills required, rather than the level of skills (i.e., managing a small store and a major national corporation both require the same types of skills albeit a different level of those skills), substantial white/black differences are found. Gottfredson (1977, 1978), in a national probability sample of highly educated men, found that 12% of the black men were in "enterprising" (e.g., business-related) occupations, whereas 39% of the white men were in enterprising occupations. Another 12% of the black men were in "investigative" (e.g., science-related) occupations, whereas 21% of the white men were in investigative occupations; 47% of the black men were in "social" (e.g., education-related) occupations as compared to 19% of the white men. A similar pattern of occupational channeling is found for lower educated blacks relative to lower educated whites.

Although a given income might be earned in any type of occupation, those in some occupations are more likely to earn high incomes than those in others. Because blacks tend to be located in those occupations that pay less, as a group blacks would earn less regardless of their educational level.

Besides the income disparity between blacks and whites that results from blacks being in certain occupations, income disparity also results from the different educational requirements of occupations. That is, in order to earn the same income in a social occupation as in an enterprising occupation, one would need about four years more education. Not only do those social occupations where blacks are located generally pay less, but it takes more education for them to yield a given return compared to some other occupations (Gottfredson, 1977, 1978).

Taken together, these findings illustrate the pivotal role of occupational aspiration and choice in the socioeconomic destiny of blacks. Those social occupations into which many blacks are today lumped are the same "traditional" occupations into which many blacks in the past were forced because of discrimination; current segregation continues to channel blacks into those same "traditional" occupations. If blacks are to achieve incomes comparable to those of whites, then the mechanisms that perpetuate black occupational aspirations and choices must be broken. Segregated education is a primary means by which blacks are channeled into "traditional" occupations. Crain (1970), in an important study of school desegregation and occupational achievement, found that desegregation was associated with the choice of nontraditional occupations for blacks. Segregation seems to exclude blacks from those information networks that are used in the formation of aspirations and choices that lead to nontraditional occupations.

Job Seeking. A second way in which desegregation affects occupational attainment is in job-seeking behavior. Obtaining a job is the elementary level of occupational attainment; it is at this level that black/white differences are greatest, especially for younger black males (Becker, 1979). Today only about one-third of all black males 16 to 17 years old have jobs; 20 years ago more than half of all black males 16 to 17 years old held jobs.

Here, it is important to note that as the educational attainments of black youth have been increasing, their employment rate has been decreasing. Moreover, despite the fact that differences do exist in the mean educational achievements of blacks and whites, there remain jobs for which employers find other intangible qualities, such as reliability, to be as, if not more, important than educational achievement. It is for these jobs that subjective employer judgments are most crucial. Additionally, employers make subjective judgments about the "worth" of educational credentials.

Rossi, Sampson, Bose, Jasso, and Passel (1968), in one of the few studies of how employers actually fill vacancies, found that employers rely most heavily on referrals from current employees, which appears to be the most widely used technique for hiring in lower level, blue-collar jobs. Consequently, one of the most important job sources for a job seeker will be relatives or friends who are currently employed. Because of the extent of segregation in all areas of our society, a black job applicant is likely to be dependent upon other blacks for job referrals. Obviously, because blacks are unemployed at a greater rate than whites, a black job seeker will be relatively disadvantaged compared to a white job seeker.

Becker (1980), in a study of the racial and sex compositions of the work forces of 35,000 employers, found that the racial composition of a particular place of employment (e.g., firm) is strongly related to the racial composition of the work force in that occupational category. In effect, as the number of black workers in a particular occupational category increases, a place of employment that hires from within that occupational category is increasingly likely to have black workers. Further, as the proportion of the workers in a place of employment is concentrated in a given occupational category, the proportion of black employees at that place of employment will be higher. Thus, for example, as the number of clerical workers at a given place on employment increases, the number of black clerical workers at that firm will also increase. It appears, therefore, that referrals from current black employees are also likely to further channel black job seekers into those occupations and jobs that perpetuate income disparity between blacks and whites.

Moreover, when employers evaluate job seekers to determine the best employee, even "objective" criteria are not immune from various forms of bias. Little research is available that directly addresses this point. But, given the amount of segregation that exists in society, it is likely that employers distrust references, credentials, and evaluations that are beyond their own cultural experiences. Put bluntly, there is considerable reason to believe that a black job seeker with credentials from a predominantly white referral system (e.g., school, employment agency, etc.) will be preferred to blacks with the same type of credentials from a black referral system. Thus, it can be inferred that desegregated education provides credentials that are more likely to be accepted at face value by white employers.

Desegregation in education directly affects not only the type of job obtained but also whether any job is obtained. First, desegregation increases the pool of contacts and informants from whom blacks can obtain information about available jobs. Such informational networks are highly important not only for providing specific job information and referrals but also for providing information about job-seeking strategies. Becker (1979) notes that black youth who do use employment services are much more likely to use public employment services or those provided by groups such as the Urban League. White job seekers, on the other hand, are more likely to use private employment services, which may be better able to place job seekers in higher paying occupations.

Social Effects of Desegregation

One concern often expressed is that desegregation has negative psychological effects on black students. Perhaps the most cited negative psychological consequences involve concepts related to the self (e.g., self-esteem and identity). Research has found that the experience of desegregation tends to lower the self-esteem of black students (Rosenberg & Simmons, 1971). Taken at face value, this appears to be a negative consequence. However, this same research also indicates that black students in segregated schools tend to have higher levels of self-esteem than do white students. Additionally, the magnitude of the relationship between self-esteem and academic achievement for black students in segregated schools is less than the magnitude of the relationship between self-esteem and achievement in desegregated schools. This suggests that the decrease in the self-esteem of desegregated black students may be due to the increased importance of academic achievement as a source of their self-esteem (Hare, 1979). If the observed change in self-esteem is due to the increased importance of academic achievement, then, perhaps, it should not simply be counted as a negative consequence.

Another possible psychological effect is that black students cannot develop positive identities in desegregated (and especially predominantly white) schools. Little direct evidence can be brought to bear on this issue. Armor (1972), in his study of the METCO program, however, did find that desegregation increased black racial consciousness and solidarity.

Some indirect evidence is available on the possible effects of desegregation on racial indentity. Simon and Alstein (1977) found that transracially adopted children had slightly more positive racial indentities than children with adoptive parents of the same race. Probably the strongest inference that can be made from these studies, however, is that empirical research does not indicate desegregation is harmful to the development of a positive racial indentity.

Besides raising questions about the possible psychological harm desegregation might cause, it should also be pointed out that desegregation has positive psychological benefits for black students. A considerable body of literature indicates that "personal efficacy" or "sense of control" is positively related to achievement and motivation in many different fields. Conversely, a low sense of control has been viewed as a disability (Gurin, Gurin, Lao, & Beattie, 1969). Several studies have previously found that desegregation, independent of social class, increases the personal efficacy of black students (Coleman, Campbell, Hobson, McPartland, Mood, Weinfeld, & York, 1966; McPartland, 1968), although some researchers have suggested that this finding may no longer be true (St. John, 1975). Hare (1979), however, using a (1975–1976) national probability sample (National Assessment of Educational Progress), found that the net effect of desegregation is positively related to personal efficacy. This is particularly meaningful when one considers the many ways — some quite traumatic—in which desegregation has been accomplished from one part of the country to another.

CONCLUSION

Desegregation has been surrounded by many myths involving its almost mystical powers over those who are touched by it. In fact, desegregation means taking affirmative action to make sure that there is interracial contact between black and white students. Most directly, the effect of this contact seems to be that interracial friendships and attitudes become more positive toward the other race. However, the most important effects may be indirect. It seems that, as a result of contact, the opportunities for blacks to become a part of the American mainstream are increased. This results not so much from changes in the blacks as from the addition of resources for them to enter the mainstream, such as information and credentials. This way of looking at desegregation encompasses a wholly new view, but it promises to hold more for both blacks and whites.

REFERENCES

Armor, D. J. (1972). The evidence on busing. *The Public Interest, 28,* 90–126.
Becker, H. J. (1979). *Personal networks of opportunity in obtaining jobs: Racial differences and effects of segregation.* Paper presented at the annual meetings of the American Educational Research Association, San Francisco.

Becker, H. J. (1980). Racial segregation among places of employment. *Social Forces, 58,* 761–776.

Blau, P. M. & Duncan, O. D. (1967). *The American occupational structure.* New York: Wiley.

Braddock, J. H. (1980). The perpetuation of segregation across levels of education: A behavioral assessment of the contact hypotheses. *Sociology of Education, 53,* 178–186.

Cohn, E. & Millman, S. D. (1975). *Input–Output analysis in public education.* Cambridge, MA: Ballinger.

Coleman, J. S., Campbell, E. G., Hobson, C. J., McPartland, J., Mood, A. M., Weinfeld, F. D., & York, R. L. (1966). *Equality of educational opportunity.* Washington, DC: U. S. Department of Health, Education, and Welfare, Office of Education.

Coleman, J. S., Kelly, S., & Moore, J. (1975). *Trends in school desegregation, 1968–1973.* Washington, DC: Urban Institute.

Crain, R. L. (1970). School integration and occupational achievement of Negroes. *American Journal of Sociology, 75,* 593–606.

Duncan, O. D., Featherman, D. L., & Duncan, B. (1972). *Socioeconomic background and achievement.* New York: Seminar Press.

Featherman, D. L., & Hauser, R. M. (1978). *Opportunity and change.* New York: Academic Press.

Giles, M. W. (1978). White enrollment stability and school desegregation: A two level analysis. *American Sociological Review, 43,* 848–864.

Giles, M. W., Cataldo, E., & Gatlin, E. (1976). *Determinants of resegregation: Compliance/rejection behavior and policy alternatives.* (Report RA–760179). Washington, DC: National Science Foundation.

Gottfredson, L. S. (1977). *A multiple-labor market model of occupational achievement.* Baltimore: John Hopkins University, Center for Social Organization of Schools.

Gottfredson, L. S. (1978). An analytical descrition of employment according to race, sex, prestige, and Holland type of work. *Journal of Vocational Behavior, 13,* 210–221.

Graglia, L. A. (1980). From prohibiting segregation to requiring integration: Developments in the law of race and the schools since *Brown.* In W. G. Stephan & J. R. Feagin (Eds.), *School desegregation* (pp. 69–96). New York: Plenum Press.

Gurin, P., Gurin, G., Lao, R. C., & Beattie, M. (1969). Internal-external control in the motivations of Negro youth. *Journal of Social Issues, 25,* 29-53.

Hare, B. (1979). *School desegregation variations in self-perception and achievement: An analysis of three national samples by race, SES, sex, and region.* Unpublished manuscript.

McConahay, J. B. (1978). The effects of school desegregation upon students' racial attitudes and behavior: A citical review of the literature and a prolegomenon to future research. *Law and Contemporary Problems, 42,* 77–107.

McPartland, J. (1968). *The segregated student in desegregated schools.* Baltimore, MD: Center for the Social Organization of Schools, Johns Hopkins University.

McPartland, J. & Barddock, J. (1981). *Desegregation: Equity, Quality and Feasibility* (pp. 141-154). Beverly Hills, CA: Sage Publications.

Pettigrew, T. F. & Green, R. L. (1976). School desegregation in large cities: A critique of the Coleman "white flight" thesis. *Harvard Education Review, 46,* 1–53.

Rosenberg, M, & Simmons, R. (1971). *Black and white self-esteem: The urban school child.* Washington, DC: American Sociological Association.

Rossell, C. H. (1976). School desegregation and white flight. *Political Science Quarterly, 90,* 675–695.

Rossell, C. H. (1978). The effect of community leadership and the mass media on public behavior. *Theory into practice, 17,* 131–139.

Rossi, P. H., Sampson, W. A., Bose, C. E., Jasso, G., & Passel, J. (1968). Measuring household social standing. *Social Science Review, 3,* 169–190.

Scott, R. R., & McPartland, J. M. (1982). Desegregation as national policy: Correlates of racial attitudes. *American Educational Research Journal, 19,* 397–414.

Simon, R., & Alsein, J. (1977). *Cross-racial adoption.* New York: Academic Press.

Stephan, W. G. (1978). School desegregation: An evaluation of the predictions made in *Brown v. Board of Education. Psychological Bulletin, 85,* 217–238.

St. John, N. (1975). *School desegregation.* New York: Wiley.

Wilson, K. L. (1979). The effects of integration and class on black educational attainment. *Sociology of Education, 52,* 84–98.

CHAPTER 17

Reappraisal of Ethnic Minority Issues

RESEARCH ALTERNATIVES

NOLAN ZANE and STANLEY SUE

Ethnic minorities often have been highly critical of research on problems concerning race relations. Controversy has occurred in areas such as intelligence (Jorgensen, 1973; Williams, 1974), personality and ethnic identity (Banks, 1976; Brand, Ruiz, & Padilla, 1974; Nobles, 1973), mental health (Gynther, 1972; Sue, Sue, & Sue, 1975), and family structure (Gordon, 1973; Trimble, 1976). Invariably, criticisms focus on the use of culturally biased measures, inattention to ethnic response sets, invalid interpretations of minority behavior from an Anglo-Saxon perspective, lack of norms for evaluating ethnic responses, and effects of the experimenter's race on subjects' behavior.

It is proposed here that these problems create a serious dilemma for ethnic research. Critics of previous research have maintained that business cannot be conducted as usual from a Western perspective. As a result they are often forced into the defensive position of having to demonstrate that the Anglo-Saxon model does not constitute a universal and that cultural differences do make a difference. This, itself, becomes a problem because ethnic minority issues are, by their very nature, paradoxical. Such issues involve two equally valid but contradictory viewpoints, one emphasizing the importance of differences between cultures and the other stressing the significance of their commonalities. Consequently, it is important not to become too one-sided; otherwise, one perspective dominates to the detriment of the other. The

Parts of this chapter were adapted from an article by Stanley Sue in the *American Psychologist*, *38(5)*, May, 1983. Copyright 1983 by the American Psychological Association. Adaptation was made by permission.

NOLAN ZANE and STANLEY SUE · Department of Psychology, University of California at Los Angeles, Los Angeles, California 90024.

dilemma occurs because one must reaffirm the validity of different cultural perspectives to expose the false universal based on a Western emic. However, in doing so ethnic research becomes skewed in the one-sided direction of focusing on cultural group differences that precludes the search for true commonalities and the appreciation of individual differences within a culture. It is our contention that the lack of appreciation for ethnic perspectives results in an incomplete and one-sided appraisal of ethnic minority issues. Moreover, this one-sided emphasis will continue until the process of reifying an Anglo-Saxon emic is directly challenged. The crucial task requires the development of parallel research to adequately address both sides of the cultural paradox.

PARADOX AND PROBLEMS

Rappaport (1981; Chapter 1 and Chapter 9 this volume) and McGrath (1980) believe that many issues facing behavioral scientists and practitioners consist of paradoxes in which two or more positive or cherished values are pitted against one another. Rappaport notes that some paradoxes consist of antinomies in which two or more laws, principles, or ideals are valid but contradictory. For example, freedom of expression and speech is a strong principle advocated by many Americans. Yet, a large segment of the population also values protection from exposure to unwanted or allegedly harmful materials. Should one, for instance, have the right under the principle of freedom of speech to expose others to pornographic materials or to express racial slurs? It is not uncommon to find individuals endorsing both principles in the abstract. The contradiction or paradox is most apparent when these two equally valid or morally justifiable positions are applied in a concrete situation.

In the case of true paradoxes or antinomies, Rappaport argues the futility of using convergent reasoning in an attempt to find *the* solution, namely a single and permanent resolution of the paradox. Efforts to find the true solution obscure the inherent and fundamental nature of the contradiction and lead to the strengthening of one principle at the expense of the other. The meaningful task is to engage in divergent reasoning whereby true paradoxes are identified and a number of diverse, limited solutions are utilized. These solutions may require change over time because single, overall solutions cannot be found. Otherwise, today's solutions may well become tomorrow's problems, as is illustrated later.

Our belief is that many ethnic minority issues are conflicts in which the clash of values and the fruitlessness of single solutions have not been clearly recognized. Moreover, in trying to resolve issues, one side has been dominant, often to the detriment of ethnic minority groups. Perhaps we can best illustrate this point by noting some value conflicts and the concomitant problems that arise in psychological theory, research, and practice.

Conflict 1: Etic versus Emic

Nearly all social scientists would agree that human beings are alike in some respects and are different in other respects. The etic approach in research and practice views human phenomena across cultures and emphasizes "universals" or core similarities in all human beings. In contrast, the emic approach utilizes a culture-specific orientation whereby the influence of sociocultural variables is stressed. In trying to find the "better" or more meaningful way of conceptualizing human beings, psychology has traditionally opted for an etic perspective, based upon an Anglo model (Brislin, Lonner, & Thorndike, 1973). Consequently, the etic is strengthened at the cost of the emic, and cultural relativity and diversity go largely unappreciated. Available research studies have typically assumed that ethnic minority behaviors should be judged according to established norms (APA Ad Hoc Committee on Minority Affairs, 1979). In a recent survey of APA accredited clinical programs, Bernal and Padilla (1982) found that program directors acknowledged the large variability of faculty opinion on the importance of ethnic minority training and indicated that little was actually being done to prepare their students to work with ethnic minority groups. The etic view is still dominant.

The issue is not over the validity of the etic or emic perspective. In fact, precisely because of the validity of each, we have a controversy. The problem resides in the strong dominance of one over the other.

Conflict 2: Mainstreaming versus Pluralism

Related to the etic–emic struggle is one concerning assimilation or mainstreaming versus pluralism. It involves the extent to which ethnic minorities should be mainstreamed (assimilated) or be permitted to maintain ethnic cultural and behavioral patterns in a multiethnic society (pluralism). This dilemma has been articulated for many years. In the past, the assimilation or Anglo conformity of ethnic groups was expected because, among other things, Anglo-Saxon culture was deemed superior (Gordon, 1978). Even though many persons have now rejected the notion that Anglo-Saxon culture is intrinsically superior, the goal of assimilation is resurfacing with a more complex face. Mainstreaming advocates now use practical or functional arguments rather than references to intrinsic superiority. For instance, bilingual education is attacked with the argument that a foreign tongue is not very functional in our society and may, in fact, be a handicap in classroom learning. It is asserted that education programs for immigrants should stress English rather than bilingual development.

As another example, we can look at the controversy over intelligence testing. Although many investigators no longer adopt a view that such tests are totally free from cultural biases, they may still advocate their use because these tests can moderately predict academic performance in schools. Because academic achievements are valued, such predictions is considered useful. Those who favor pluralism feel that under the guise of functionalism, ethnic cultural patterns may be eliminated and the superiority of Anglo-Saxon tradition reasserted. Again, there is a clash of fundamental values. How can one argue against acquisition of functional skills, development of good predictors, and some degree of "Americanization"? Similarly, how can one doubt that maintenance of pluralism, diversity, and respect for different cultures is also a valid principle? The one-sidedness of the mainstreaming effort is the problem.

Mainstream advocates often overlook the fact that consensus may be lacking on what constitutes functional skills. For instance, the ability to speak Spanish, Chinese, and so on may be an important asset and should be encouraged. Olmedo (1981) suggests that bilingualism does not interfere with the basic ability to learn. Moreover, in a society where racial discrimination and prejudice exist, ethnic minorities often have the experiences of being invited or coerced into the mainstream in some areas, only to be denied entry into other aspects of society (Gordon, 1978). Developing one's own cultural identity may be a useful and necessary step before one can engage the majority on an equal basis. The task ahead of us is to balance mainstreaming and pluralistic interests, to continually define what is meant by "functional," and to explore ways in which individuals can be free to pursue both assimilation and pluralism.

Conflict 3: Equal Opportunity versus Equality of Outcome

In attempts to foster equality, we have tried to discover instances of discrimination or differential treatment on the basis of race or ethnicity. Findings (Yamamoto, James, & Palley, 1968) that ethnic minority group clients actually did receive inferior forms of treatment compared to whites stimulated a movement to increase equity in service delivery. However, by equalizing opportunities for treatment, we did not necessarily equalize outcomes. In one study, Sue (1977) found that even when ethnic minorities received the same kinds of treatments as whites at 17 community mental health centers in the Seattle area, they tended to fare worse. Similarly, in the fields of educational admissions and employment, it may be that affirmative action is necessary if we are to obtain equality of outcomes. The dilemma here is quite apparent. Advocates of equal treatment opportunities run the risk of perpetuating unequal outcomes; those who argue for equal outcomes (e.g., seeing that minority groups are as likely as whites to benefit from educational, employment, or mental health services) may have to discriminate by treating some groups differently because of sociocultural differences. By emphasizing on principle, the other conflicting one may have to be sacrificed.

Conflict 4: Modal Personality versus Individual Differences

Even with awareness that cultural factors are important in personality development, problems arise in the conceptualization of the factors and their influences. These problems are similar to those that occur in the nomothetic-idiographic controversy: In discussing ethnic minority groups, should one stress between-group differences or within-group differences? The between-group approach largely ignores individual differences, whereas the within-group orientation often fails to deal adequately with actual cultural variations between groups. Investigators have typically employed the notion of modal personality in describing cultural patterns (Inkeles & Levinson, 1969). According to this formulation, cultures may vary in the extent to which their members exhibit certain average or modal scores on any particular personality attribute. The greater the difference, the more meaningful the attribute in differentiating cultures. In ethnic minority research, we have made white-nonwhite comparisons. If major differences are found between the groups, investigators frequently feel content that they have identified emics and have given due consideration to cultural relativity. At another level of analysis, however, such comparisons often ignore within-group variations. Campbell (1967) has warned that finding actual differences between groups often leads to exaggerated stereotyped images of these differences. The fact that blacks are more likely than whites to endorse items on a personality test indicative of suspiciousness and distrust (Dohrenwend & Dohrenwend, 1969) does not mean that all blacks are distrustful and that all whites have trust. This point may seem overly obvious and unworthy of mentioning. Nevertheless, although one may intellectually acknowledge within-group variations, in practice we often apply research findings between groups in an almost literal manner. Olmedo (1979) has stressed that within-group differences be more fully examined, and only recently has a trend in this direction emerged.

Conflict 5: Racism versus Self-Determinism

The final perplexing and complicated issue addressed concerns the current impact of racism. As indicated by Denton and Sussman (1981), national surveys reveal that both blacks and whites feel that race relations have greatly improved and the whites believe discrimination has all but disappeared (and now it is up to blacks to demonstrate their drive and motivation to take advantage of their opportunities). Blacks see persistent forms of discrimination while admitting to racial improvements. Do discrimination and prejudice exist or are they phenomena of the past? If ethnic minority groups fail to achieve equality, should we "blame the victims" in view of our belief that opportunities are now present to all? A self-determinism perspective praises society for changes and holds ethnic minorities solely responsible for their respective difficulties. A racism viewpoint claims that, despite changes, society is still largely implicated in racial problems. As in the preceding four conflicts, two positions can be taken. One can legitimately praise or condemn contemporary society.

The disturbing fact is that despite the popular belief, the notion that racism has all but disappeared has not received much empirical support. In a review of research studies on prejudice and discrimination, Crosby, Bromley, and Saxe (1980) tried to analyze whether the expression of attitudes of equality actually corresponds to a lack of prejudice and discrimination. They examined three types of unobtrusive studies. The first involved research on whether blacks or whites in need of assistance received the same amount of help from whites; the second examined whether race of victim was a factor in the extent of punishment received from whites in learning tasks; and the third noted whether whites' nonverbal behaviors varied as a function of the race of the person with whom they interacted. The investigators concluded that antiblack prejudice and discrimination still exist. Blacks tended to receive less aid, to receive more indirect punishment, and to be treated differently than whites in nonverbal interactions. The attitude change, although important, may reflect more of a change in what one ought to say in response to surveys rather than in what one really feels, or how one behaves.

McConahay and Hough (1976) also believe that the nature of prejudice and discrimination has changed. According to their theory of symbolic racism, the old-fashioned "redneck" variety with overt discriminatory acts and negative racial sterotypes has decreased. Now there is a more complicated form of racism in which the feeling is that deprived minority groups are too demanding and pushy and are getting more than they deserve. Much of this feeling is expressed in symbolic issues such as opposition to welfare, so-called black militance, and affirmative action programs. The theory suggests that direct antiblack or antiethnic sentiments are suppressed; what is expressed is opposition to factors of ideological symbols associated with blacks and other ethnics.

That racial prejudice may underlie opposition to ideological symbols was tested by Sears, Speer, and Hensler (1977). The researchers note that opposition to busing to achieve racial desegregation is substantial. Two major explanantions have been advanced for this antibusing sentiment—self-interest and symbolic racism. The former assumes that opposition is caused by fears that taxes will rise in order to support busing, that children may be sent to low-quality and distant schools, that social relationships among children will be disrupted, that children may be sent to high-crime areas, and so on. The symbolic racism explanation is that antibusing attitudes are frequently caused by racial prejudice directed toward a symbolic issue—in this case, busing. To test the two hypotheses, Sears et al. gathered data from a national survey sample on busing attitudes. They reasoned that self-interest in the busing issue would be reflected in respondents who had school-aged children, who had children in public rather than in private or parochial schools, who lived in all white neighborhoods, and who anticipated that busing might occur in their schools. According to the self-interest notion, antibusing sentiments would be strong among those who had the greatest threat. On the other hand, the symbolic racism hypothesis would be supported if antibusing attitudes were related to questionnaire items concerning racial intolerance and lower levels of education, factors traditionally associated with racial prejudice. Analysis indicated that opposition to busing was not related to the measures of self-interest, but was related to factors such as intolerance and education.

By describing the work of Crosby et al. and Sears et al., we are not suggesting that society has failed to make significant changes or that all antibusing sentiments reflect racism. The main point is that there are opposing views over race relations and that many racial issues involve value clashes. Ideally, it should be possible for one to agree that although progress has been made in improving race relations such that ethnic minorities can determine their own fates to a greater degree, racial equality has not been achieved. However, this is not the case, as is illustrated in the prevailing public belief that responsibility for the progress of ethnic minority groups is now up to the groups themselves.

Implications

What are the possible solutions in the etic–emic, mainstreaming–pluralism, opportunity–outcome, modal personality–individual differences, and racism–self-determinism issues? To repeat, there are not single, timeless solutions. What may apparently seem to be the solution today may become a problem tomorow. Diverse solutions should be sought. More often than not, the direction of our efforts has been one-sided, lacking the involvement and perspectives of ethnic minority groups. Consequently, many ethnic minority group individuals do not feel research and practice represent their viewpoints, interest, and their gestalts of society. Minority group status and the history of racism have made it difficult for minorities to have a strong voice in influencing directions.

Although each problem is posed as a separate issue, two general themes can be identified. Most ethnic minority problems involve either the etic–emic or the group–individual differences controversy or both. For example, the mainstreaming–pluralism issue is related to whether socialization practices should follow an emic (pluralism) or etic (assimilation) perspective. In the racism–self-determinism issue, racist conditions become evident when examined at the macrolevel of cultural groups but self-determined factors assume prominence when viewed at the individual level. The primary task is to achieve a balance between both sets of opposing perspectives. However, this becomes problematic when ethnic relations are conceptualized in terms of the Western emic that is then applied as an etic. Consequently, ethnic research becomes focused on demonstrating that the Anglo-Saxon model does not constitute a universal and that cultural differences are important. In this manner the appraisal of ethnic minority issues regresses to an emphasis on group differences between cultures that masks cultural commonalities and individual variation within a culture.

It should be noted that we are not suggesting that research emphasizing cultural differences is unimportant. On the contrary, there is no type of research that is more valuable in studying the influence of ethnicity. The main problem resides in the perpetuation of the Anglo-Saxon model as the standard to which all cultures are compared. It is this bias that steers research toward examining only one side of the cultural antinomy. Often the initial appraisal of a problem sets up several premises that subsequent reevaluations inadvertently follow in the process of questioning other premises. For example, in football during the 1970s extreme disagreement existed among coaches about the proportion of passing to running plays that a team should use in its offense. Many coaches assumed that to pass would incur a greater risk for error. Thus, although some coaches questioned the very conservative use of the pass, they continued to accept the premise that a pass-dominant attack would fail. Most of their time was spent debating what offensive formations would best enhance the running game. Not until the 1980s with the advent of the short-passing game was this assumption about the value of a passing game proved invalid. Along similar lines, in the process of directly challenging the superiority of the Anglo-Saxon emic, researchers have inadvertently stressed several one-sided perspectives in conceptualizing ethnic minority issues. Rather than to assert that things are not what they should be, let us be more specific in showing how one-sidedness has hampered ethnic research and the tasks that remain in diversifying solutions.

A Dilemma in Research

A brief overview of ethnic research illustrates the dilemma involved in attempts to balance research with minority group perspectives. Early research on blacks and other ethnic groups perpetuated the theme that they were socially and intellectually inferior to whites, largely because of hereditary or biological factors (Thomas & Sillen, 1972). Society was held unaccountable for the plight of ethnics because blame was attributed to the victims. As noted by Clark (1972), researchers and practitioners were not immune to racism by virtue of their values and training, and much of their work reflected this theme. Implicit in this failure to recognize the adverse impact of racism was the notion that minority and white psychosocial experiences were essentially similar. Consequently, given this false universal, the problems of ethnic minority groups were attributed to their inherent inferiority.

In an effort to correct these errors of overgeneralization, investigators studied institutional racism and its effects on ethnic minorities. The culprit was not the victims but the society at large. Allport (1954), in his classic book *The Nature of Prejudice*, laid the groundwork for the view that prejudice and discrimination could not be solely attributed to abnormal personalities or to evil persons. Rather, historical, economic, political, and sociopsychological processes were responsible, a theme reiterated and elaborated by Jones (1972) and Pettigrew (1973).

Research based on the deficit model proliferated. The deficit model assumption was that prejudice and discrimination created stress and decreased opportunities for minority groups. As a result, many minority group persons were considered deficient, underpriviledged, deprived, pathological, or deviant. Baldwin (1957) stated that "I can conceive of no Negro native to this country who has not, by the age of puberty, been irreparably scarred by the conditions of his life. The wonder is not that so many are ruined but that so many survive" (p. 71). Kramer, Rosen, and Willis (1973) took the position that "racist practices undoubtedly are key factors—perhaps the most important ones—in producing mental disorders in blacks and other underpriviledged groups"(p. 335). Studies documented the social and economic conditions and the mental health status of minority groups. Blacks were believed to have high rates of drug addictions and personality disorders; American Indians were prone to alcoholism and suicide; Hispanics were seeen as exhibiting tendencies toward drunkenness, criminal behavior, and undependability (see Fischer, 1969; Kitano, 1980; Padilla & Ruiz, 1973, for a discussion of these problems).

In many respects, the deficit model was helpful in furthering the cause of ethnic minority groups. It served to focus attention on society rather than on the victims in explaining the status of ethnic minority groups. What is more important, it documented how the socialization experiences of minorities were culture specific and, thus, different from those of whites. Research was directed to social factors, effects of racism on personality and mental health, the adequacy of psychological services to these groups, and the influence of institutional practices and policies. However, because of its one-sided emphasis on cultural group differences, use of the deficit model also produced negative effects. Even though "inferiority" was no longer viewed as a product of heredity, ethnic minority groups now were considered inferior, deficient, or permanently damaged because of societal practices. Most ethnic minorities were assumed to have potential problems involving self-identity and self-esteem because of culture conflicts and negative social sterotypes.

That current solutions can become tomorrow's problems is well illustrated by the use of the deficit model in the 1954 U.S. Supreme Court decision of *Brown v. Board of Education*. In that decision, which relied in part on social science research and argued that blacks were harmed by institutional policies, the court declared that the separate-but-equal practice in schools was detrimental to black children. Otto Klineberg (1981), who was highly involved in that court case, noted that the joy felt over the Supreme Court decision was later tempered by the unexpected controversy over the replacement of nature by nurture in explaining the inferiority of blacks. By implicating educational-segregation policies as the cause for black deficiencies, desegregation was deemed necessary—a desirable outcome. Yet, in so doing, the image of inferiority was perpetuated. Neglected were the strengths, competencies, and skills found in ethnic families, communities, and cultures.

This neglect was not intentional. Nor did it result from poor research. Rather, positive qualities were ignored because cultural commonalities and individual differences were forgotten. People across cultures vary in their reaction to stressful and adverse conditions. Not only do they vary, but most individuals within a culture do not succumb to such conditions; otherwise, pathology would be the norm. With respect to the effects of an oppressive society on the self-esteem of blacks, Thomas and Sillen (1972) have observed that

> the threat to self-esteem does not have uniform consequences. Some individuals may be overwhelmed. Others become aware of the source of threat, develop appropriate anger at the injustices they suffer, and focus their energies on the struggle against oppression. Still, others may show a mixture of healthy and unhealthy responses. (p. 52)

It is important to consider the adverse effects of racism without overgeneralizing this impact by stereotyping ethnic individuals' responses to these conditions.

RECOMMENDATIONS FOR RESEARCH

Examination of Trends

Studies on ethnic minorities can be categorized according to the degree to which they have developed and tested explanatory constructs reflecting different cultural perspectives. We have identified three trends that we call (1) *point research*, (2) *linear research*, and (3) *parallel research*. Point research refers to isolated group comparisons on one construct or set of constructs derived from one culture. The empirical focus is from one reference point that logically can only be derived from one culture. Almost always this research is based on a Western perspective. Ethnic minorities have been compared to whites in areas such as self-concept and ethnic identity (Connor, 1974; Powell, 1973), psychopathology (Brown, Stein, Huang, & Harris, 1973; Pasamanick, Roberts, Lemkau, & Kreuger, 1959), and personality (Costello, Fine, & Blau, 1973; D. Sue & Kirk, 1973). When found, cultural differences can be considered to indicate that ethnic individuals actually differ from whites on the given dimension.

Researchers have exercised caution in accepting this Western emic interpretation. For example, Gynther (1972) found that blacks consistently score higher than whites on several pathological scales of the MMPI. However, he notes that these results do not necessarily reflect a greater degree of maladjustment on the part of blacks because conceptual equivalence of many MMPI items across cultures does not exist. Although valuable in generating a large array of rival hypotheses, the information yield of such research is limited. This is because, given the monocultural approach using monocultural measures, alternative explanations based on cultural differences in values and behaviors are always post hoc.

In response to these problems, a linear research model has developed. Linear research involves a sequence of studies aimed at systematically testing the set of hypotheses predicted by the theory underlying the single construct of interest. Like point research, this construct is usually developed from a Western emic. However, rather than one isolated study, there are two or more empirical points of reference on which to compare cultural groups. If the pattern of cultural differences (or similarities) manifests according to the construct's theory, the construct is considered to be a universal that allows for meaningful cultural comparisons.

As an illustration, let us examine studies conducted by Dohrenwend and Dohrenwend (1969), who were interested in determining if certain ethnic groups differed in psychopathology. After administering the Midtown 22-item sympton questionnaire, they did find ethnic differences: Puerto Ricans scored higher in psychological disturbance than did Jewish, Irish, or black respondents in New York City. To test whether the higher score among Puerto Ricans indicated higher actual rates of disorders, patients matched in types of psychiatric disorders from each ethnic group were administered the same questionnaires. Because patients were matched on type and presumable severity of disorders, one would expect no differences in symptom scores. However, Puerto Ricans again scored higher. Dohrenwend and Dohrenwend concluded that the higher scores for Puerto Ricans probably reflects a response set or a cultural means of expressing distress rather than actual rates of disturbance.

Although an improvement on point research, linear approaches have a major drawback. Even if multiple comparisons demonstrate that a construct developed from one cultural perspective is applicable in another culture, the question still remains as to whether a construct developed from an alternative perspective can better explain the phenomena under study. In other words, linear studies do not actually balance ethnic perspectives in research. They simply test the adequacy of one perspective in the absence of the other. Almost all linear research has focused on the cross-cultural applicability of constructs derived from an Anglo-Saxon viewpoint. Aside from perpetuating the dominance of the Western emic, such cultural contrasts often mask important individual differences within a cultural group.

A New Emphasis: Parallel Research

To truly represent ethnic minority perspectives, research must develop separate but interrelated ways of conceptualizing the behavioral phenomena of interest, one based on a Western conceptualization, the other reflecting an ethnic minority interpretation. Essentially, parallel designs consist of two linear approaches, each based on an alternative cultural viewpoint. In parallel research, it is incumbent upon the researcher to develop *a priori* two sets of descriptive and explanatory variables. Too often misinterpretations of ethnic minority behavior occur due to the lack of a proper conceptual framework. We simply have failed to develop innovative conceptual "tools" that one can more appropriately apply to ethnic minority groups. By requiring the concurrent examination of different cultural explanations, the parallel approach fosters divergent thinking—the type of reasoning needed to develop solutions to adequately address the paradoxes involved in ethnic minority problems.

We have adopted a parallel strategy for studying the function of assertive behavior in Asian interpersonal relations. Asians frequently have been stereotyped as being nonassertive and passive. Nonassertion is seen as resulting from inhibitory anxiety (Wolpe, 1958) and/or the lack of certain verbal and nonverbal skills associated with an assertive behavioral topography (Rich & Schroeder, 1976). However, what is typically considered to reflect nonassertive behavior as a consequence of anxiety or skill deficits on the part of Asians actually may be the function of *amae*. *Amae* is an interpersonal phenomenon at the core of many Asian relationships. It has no direct counterpart in Western cultures. Kumagai (1981) defines amae as a distinct pattern of social interaction

> comprised of two complementary postures that prescribe, respectively, an individual to indulge himself in love...or to defer in love....Hence, the amae interaction can be seen as comprised of two acts: the taking posture, to indulge oneself in amae (or permissive love) [and] the giving posture, to defer to the other (or to allow the other's self-indulgence) in amae. From this pattern we might also deduce that the "taking" posture allows the actor simultaneously *to be assertive* in ego-affirmation; and the "giving" posture, *to be non-assertive* in ego-suspension. (pp. 249,252)

Rather than in response to inhibitory anxiety or lack of skills, and Asian-American individual may act nonassertive out of deference of "altruistic self-withdrawal," as Kumagai suggests.

Examining Asian relationships in terms of amae radically alters the functional implications for nonassertive behavior among Asians. First, nonassertive behavior may not always be maladaptive. On the contrary, it may involve acts that help develop and maintain a relationship. Second, at times nonassertion is associated with positive affects such as love and caring. Third, in certain contexts nonassertion is an approach behavior rather than an avoidance response. An individual is nonassertive because the person desires to express affection in a nonverbal way. In this case nonassertiveness is not the result of anxiety reduction. By considering the ramifications of an alternative construct, amae, the conceptualization of assertive behavior diverges from an ethnocentric perspective.

The development of competing constructs based on differing cultural vantage points allows one to determine the overlapping and nonoverlapping effects of different cultures. In previous research, when cultural differences did appear, it frequently was not clear if such differences actually existed or if the construct of interest was differentially applied to the two cultural groups. In the parallel approach, the salience of a construct is empirically tested by comparing it with another equally plausible explanatory concept developed from the ethnic group's host culture. In this manner, both sides of the antinomy—cultural differences and commonalities—can be directly evaluated. Commonalities and differences between cultures can occur at both a cognitive and a behavioral level. Parallel designs should address both types of comparisons. For example, in the assertion study it is hypothesized that certain Asian and Caucasion-American individuals will not act assertive with friends but for different reasons; the latter more from social apprehension anxiety whereas the former more from the wish to defer and enhance the friendship. That is, given similar behaviors, cultural differences may exist in the causes for the behaviors. Moreover, given the same situations, culturally dissimilar individuals may exhibit different goals and behaviors. An Asian student who wants a reevaluation of a grade given in a course may define as goals change in the grade as well as maintenance of a respectful and harmonious relationship with the professor. A non-Asian student in the same situation may simply want the grade changed and be more confronting with the professor. By studying different cultural groups, responses across various situations involving assertiveness, and goals for one's response, we hope to test competing positions (e.g., the inhibitory anxiety/lack of skills perspective with the amae perspective). Thus, the research is intended to go beyond a simple contrast of the level of assertiveness between culturally dissimilar groups. Such a contrast is often used to note cultural differences and masks within group variability. Parallel research allows inferences to be drawn not only between groups (using competing cultural theories) but also within groups (individual differences within a culture).

In summary, many ethnic minority investigators have been dissatified with current research on their groups. We propose that much of the dissatisfaction occurs because of the fact that (1) research on ethnic minority groups frequently involves two or more conflicting values, (2) each value is valid or justifiable, (3) one side of the conflict is dominant at the expense of the other, (4) the dominant side is perceived by many as etic when it is actually an emic phenomenon, and (5) the dominant perspective is one that fails to recognize the legitimacy of cultural minority views.

The legitimacy of the less dominant value or perspective can never be fully appreciated through what we call *point* or *linear research*. It is recommended that research on ethnic minority issues follow our notion of a parallel model. This approach develops two or more separate but interrelated construct systems as a means for conceptualizing ethnic minority behaviors from different cultural perspectives. Because at least two valid conceptual systems are concurrently examined, cultural commonalities as well as differences become evident. In addition, the focus on cultures as interacting explanatory constructs enables the study of an ethnic minority group on its own terms, which in turn, highlights important individual differences within the ethnic group. In these ways, use of a parallel strategy helps one attend to both sides of the paradoxes that characterize ethnic minority issues.

REFERENCES

Allport, G. W. (1954). *The nature of prejudice*. Reading, MA: Addison-Wesley.

APA Ad Hoc Committee on Minority Affairs. (1979). *Report to the APA Board of Directors*. Washington, DC: Author.

Baldwin, J. (1957). *Notes of a native son*. Boston: Beacon Press.

Banks, W. C. (1976). White preference in blacks: A paradigm in search of phenomenon. *Psychological Bulletin, 83*, 1179–1186.

Bernal, M. E., & Padilla, A. M. (1982). Status of minority curricula and training in clinical psychology: 1980. *American Psychologist, 37*, 780–787.

Brand, E., Ruiz, R. A., & Padilla, A. M. (1974). Ethnic identification and preference: A review. *Psychological Bulletin, 81*, 860–890.

Brislin, R. W., Lonner, W. J., & Thorndike, R. M. (1973). *Cross-cultural research methods*. New York: Wiley.

Brown, T. F., Stein, K., Huang, K., & Harris, D. (1973). Mental illness and the role of mental health facilities in Chinatown. In S. Sue & N. Wagner (Eds.), *Asian Americans: Psychological perspectives* (pp. 212–231). Ben Lomond, CA: Science and Behavior Books.

Campbell, D. T. (1967). Stereotypes and the perception of group differences. *American Psychologist, 22*, 817–829.

Clark, K. B. (1972). Foreword. In A. Thomas & S. Sillen, *Racism and psychiatry* (pp. xi–xiii). New York: Brunner/Mazel.

Connor, J. W. (1974). Acculturation and changing need patterns in Japanese-American and Caucasian-American college students. *Journal of Social Psychology, 93*, 293–294.

Costello, R. M., Fine, H., & Blau, B. (1973). Racial comparisons on the MMPI. *Journal of Clinical Psychology, 29*, 63–65.

Crosby, F., Bromley, S., & Saxe, L. (1980). Recent unobstrusive studies of black and white discrimination and prejudice: A literature review. *Psychological Bulletin, 87*, 546–563.

Denton, H., & Sussman, B. (1981, March 29). Race relations: Gains seen for blacks, but what lies ahead? *Seattle Times*, p. 47.

Dohrewend, B. P., & Dohrewend, B. S. (1969). *Social status and psychological disorder*. New York: Wiley.

Fischer, J. (1969). Negroes, whites and rates of mental illness: Reconsideration of a myth. *Psychiatry, 32*, 428–446.

Gordon, M. M. (1978). *Human nature, class, and ethnicity*. New York: Oxford University Press.

Gordon, T. (1973). Notes on white and black psychology. *Journal of Social Issues, 29,* 87-96.

Gynther, M. D. (1972). White norms and black MMPI's: A prescription for discrimination? *Psychological Bulletin, 78,* 386-402.

Inkeles, A., & Levinson, D. J. (1969). National character: The study of modal personality and sociocultural systems. In G. Lindzey & E. Aronson (Eds.), *The handbook of social psychology* (Vol. 4, pp. 418-506). Reading MA: Addison-Wesley.

Jorgensen, C. C. (1973). IQ tests and their educational supporters. *Journal of Social Issues, 29,* 33-40.

Kitano, H. H. (1980). *Race relations.* Englewood Cliffs, NJ: Prentice Hall.

Klineberg, O. (1981). International educational exchange: The problem of evaluation. *American Psychologist, 36,* 92-199.

Korchin, S. J. (1980). Clinical psychology and minority problems. *American Psychologist, 35,* 262-269.

Kramer, M., Rosen, B. M., & Willis, E. M. (1973). Definitions and distributions of mental disorders in a racist society. In C. V. Willie, B. M. Kramer, & B. S. Brown (Eds.), *Racism and mental health.* Pittsburgh: University of Pittsburgh Press.

Kumagai, H. A. (1981). A dissection of intimacy: A study of "bipolar posturing" in Japanese social interaction—*Amaeru* and *Amayakasu,* indulgence and deference. *Culture, Medicine, and Psychiatry, 5,* 249-272.

McConahay, J. B., & Hough, J. C. (1976). Symbolic racism. *Journal of Social Issues, 32,* 23-46.

McGrath, J. E. (1980). Social science, social action, and the *Journal of Social Issues. Journal of Social Issues, 36,* 109-124.

Nobles, W. W. (1973). Psychological research and the black self-concept: A critical review. *Journal of Social Issues, 29,* 11-32.

Olmedo, E. L. (1979). Acculturation: A psychometric perspective. *American Psychologist, 34,* 1061-1070.

Olmedo, E. L. (1981). Testing linguistic minorities. *American Psychologist, 36,* 1078-1085.

Padilla, A. M., & Ruiz, R. A. (1973). *Latino mental health: A review of the literature* (DHEW Publication No. 74-113). Washington, DC: U. S. Government Printing Office.

Pasamanick, B., Roberts, D. W., Lemkau, P. W., & Krueger, D. B. (1959). A survey of mental disease in a urban population: Prevalence by race and income. In B. Pasamanick (Ed.), *Epidemiology of mental disorder* (pp. 183-191). Washington, DC: American Association for the Advancement of Science.

Pettigrew, T. F. (1973). Racism and the mental health of white Americans: A social psychological view. In C. V. Willie, B. M. Kramer, & B. S. Brown (Eds.), *Racism and mental health* (pp. 269-298). Pittsburgh: University of Pittsburgh Press.

Powell, G. J. (1973). Self-concept in white and black children. In C. V. Willie, B. M. Kramer, & B. S. Brown (Eds.), *Racism and mental health.* Pittsburg: University of Pittsburg Press.

Rappaport, J. (1981). In praise of paradox: A social policy of empowerment over prevention. *American Journal of Community Psychology, 9,* 1-25.

Rich, A. R., & Schroeder, H. E. (1976). Research issues in assertiveness training. *Psychological Bulletin, 83,* 1081-1096.

Sears, D. O., Speer, L. K., & Hensler, C. P. (1977, August). *Opposition to busing: Self-interest or symbolic racism?* Paper presented at the meeting of the American Psychological Association, San Francisco.

Sue, D. W., & Kirk, B. A. (1973). Differential characteristics of Japanese-American and Chinese-American college students. *Journal of Counseling Psychology, 20,* 142-148.

Sue, S. (1977). Community mental health services to minority groups: Some optimism, some pessimism. *American Psychologist, 32,* 616-624.

Sue, S., Sue, D. W., & Sue D. (1975). Asian Americans as a minority group. *American Psychologist,*
30, 906–910.

Thomas, A., & Sillen, S. (1972). *Racism and psychiatry.* New York: Brunner/Mazel.

Trimble, J. E. (1976). Value differences among American Indians: Concerns for the concerned
couselor. In P. Pedersen, W. J. Lonner, & J. G. Draguns (Eds.), *Counseling across cultures.*
Honolulu: University of Hawaii Press.

Williams, R. L. (1974). Scientific racism and IQ—The silent mugging of the black community.
Psychology Today, pp. 32, 34, 37–38, 41, 101.

Wolpe, J. (1958). *Psychotherapy by reciprocal inhibition* (Vol.7). Stanford: Stanford University
Press.

Yammamoto, J., James, Q. C., & Palley, N. (1968). Cultural problems in psychiatric therapy.
Archives of General Psychiatry, 19, 45–49.

INDEX

Printed in the United States
45381LVS00002B/12